TRIUMPH
OF THE
SOUL

★★★

MICHAEL R. JOENS

Fleming H. Revell
A Division of Baker Book House Co
Grand Rapids, Michigan 49516

© 1999 by Michael R. Joens

Published by Fleming H. Revell
a division of Baker Book House Company
P.O. Box 6287, Grand Rapids, MI 49516-6287

Printed in the United States of America

Library of Congress Cataloging-in-Publication Data

Joens, Michael R.
    Triumph of the soul / Michael R. Joens
        p.   cm.
    ISBN 0-8007-5702-5 (pbk.)
    1. World War, 1939–1945 Fiction. I. Title.
PS3560.0246T74   1999
813' .54—dc21   99-35161

For current information about all releases from Baker Book House, visit our web site:
http://www.bakerbooks.com

TRIUMPH
OF THE
SOUL

Also by Michael Joens

The Crimson Tapestry
The Shadows of Eden
The Dawn of Mercy

To David—*my brother,
my friend, my hero*

PROLOGUE
★★★

October 1943. France. Colette cleared her breakfast dishes from the table: a bowl for her oatmeal, a cup for coffee, and a heavy pewter soup spoon. Her needs were simple, now that the men were gone.

She placed the dishes in the washtub and poured the last of the hot water from the kettle over them, letting them soak for a moment while she looked out the small window of the cabin. The yard was empty except for a few chickens pecking at the ground. Beyond them was the barn; it too was empty.

As usual, at this time of the morning, a fog was rolling down through the trees off the summit to her right, drawing a gray gloom over the mountains. It quickly filled the basin of the meadow on which the cabin and steading were situated, then spilled over the rim and on down the mountainside to the river far below. With the fog there came a desolation into her chest, a feeling of loneliness that drew an involuntary sigh from her throat.

Her eyes, a half-lidded glaze of pensiveness, moved to the place on the slope where she knew the white stone lay beneath the black pines. But she could not see it now; there were only the vague shapes of the trees caught in the fog, their limbs raised, like lost souls pleading for mercy. She knew it was there, of course—the stone—she had helped set it in place.

As she stood looking out the window, her fingers found the silver crucifix at her breast. Vague thoughts sifted through her mind. Then an image of her mother baking sweet cakes came suddenly, brightly and completely, with the hot, luscious smells of the kitchen, with all the noise and chaos and laughter of a family at home. A trickle of tears leaked down her cheek.

She dismissed the scene abruptly. That was before the war, she knew, before the war and the shortages. There was no sugar to bake sweet cakes now; there was only the war.

A movement caught her eye. The rooster was chasing one of the hens across the yard, raising a squall. A smile struggled to her lips and died. Her eyes moved to the right of the yard where the road wound down through the trees and into the town at the base of the mountain. Lines of worry edged into her brow. *Perhaps today,* she thought. *They are overdue.*

She put away her breakfast bowl on the wooden shelf next to the window and hung the cup on a dowel beneath it. The spoon she returned to a drawer of utensils—everything in its place. Then she swept the smooth wood floor, making a small pile of dust near the door; she opened the door and swept it out into the yard.

As Colette stood in the doorway, broom in hand, she could feel the wind shift on her cheeks. And with it came the hollow knocking of her father's ax in the distance, knocking, it seemed, against the vast loneliness of the mountains. A shiver went over her arms. It was autumn, and the cold rains were coming. Rubbing her arms, she leaned against the broom and sighed.

"Maybe today," she said to no one in particular. The sound of her voice sounded strange in the empty quiet, as though it had come from someone other than herself, from a long distance away.

"Maybe today," she repeated in a hushed, almost guilty whisper. A breath of hope stirred in her bosom, like a curl of wind over a placid lake. It caused her to stand up straight, raise her head up, throw her shoulders back. Her eyes gleamed with determination.

"Yes, today!" she said defiantly. "And why not? It is time for them to come home!"

She got out four place settings and set the table. Outside, she collected an assortment of pansies and begonias from the bed she had dug along the south wall of the cabin and placed them in a vase for a centerpiece. She smiled approvingly at the table. She looked up, saw the Christ hanging on the wall, his eyes rolled plaintively to heaven. She crossed herself with a short prayer for mercy, then looked away. "Now I must take a bath," she said. "I must be clean!"

Full of resolve, she went down to the cellar and brought up the large metal washtub and placed it next to the stove. She added several pieces of wood to the fire and closed the grate. *Good,* she thought, hearing the roar of hungry flames in the iron belly. *That will do.* Taking up the kettle, she went outside to the pump next to the barn and began filling it with water.

The fog was thicker now and it clothed everything in a mysterious light. It seemed a living thing, creeping over the ground like the Death Angel of the Exodus—a thing without warmth. *The fog will lift*, she told herself. *The sun will shine.*

She looked up suddenly, slowly lowering the handle of the pump as she peered intently at some indefinite point in the distance. She listened. *No,* she chided herself. *I am imagining things.* Then as she crossed the yard, she stopped and listened, looking once more down the road that led into town. She could not see anything now through the fog. *If anyone were coming,* she thought, *they'd be on top of me before I'd know it.*

Frowning, she thought, *I wish they'd taken me with them. They know that I can take care of myself, that I am not afraid of danger.* She made a face at a recollection. "'Oh, no . . . this is man's work,'" she mimicked her older brother. "Man's work," she laughed. "Why, I can outshoot the both of them."

She made several trips with the kettle until the large pot on the stove was filled with water. She looked into the pot. Nothing yet, not even tiny bubbles on the bottom. Off she went, busying herself with the remainder of the morning chores: feeding the chickens, feeding and milking the cow, mucking out the stalls.

Having finished her chores, she crossed the yard, looking once more down the road. "Maybe today," she whispered hopefully, then entered the cabin. The ceiling of the cabin was slung low and the walls were built of thick logs to contain the heat, and as she closed the door behind her she could already feel the warmth of the stove.

By now the water was boiling. Steam wavered off the surface. Colette lifted the heavy pot off the stove and, taking a towel in her hand to steady the bottom, poured the water into the tub. Then she added several kettles full of cold water to adjust the temperature, testing it each time with her hand until it was perfect.

Wrapping a towel around her shoulders, she lowered onto her knees and dipped her head into the tub. Then with a bar of soap she lathered up the mass of her hair on top of her head, kneading her scalp vigorously with her fingertips until she could feel the surge of blood beneath her skin. She dipped her head into the hot water several times to rinse it, then wrung out the excess water with her hands.

With her hair toweled on top of her head, she quickly undressed in the small bedroom off the kitchen, then came back out and climbed into the hot soapy water, drawing her knees up in order to fit into the tub.

As she luxuriated in the hot water a tune she had once heard on a phonograph in town came to mind. It was a love song about a boy and a girl who, like two desperate seedlings pushing up through the earth, surmounted all difficulties to flourish in the sun. She could not contain the feeling that something good was going to happen—a bit of warming light breaking through the fog. She was singing the love song as she scrubbed herself clean.

Afterward, she dressed in a fresh white blouse and black skirt that fell to her calves. She remained barefooted, preferring the smooth feel of the wood floor against her feet to the confinement of shoes. Then she took out a small round hand mirror from the top drawer of her dresser and adjusted it on its wire stand.

She made a part down the middle of her scalp with the edge of a comb. Then she angled her head to one side and drew the comb down through her long, thick hair. She frowned as the comb caught in a tangle. The pains a woman must suffer to look pretty, she growled.

She looked abruptly at her face in the mirror. Was she pretty? She remembered the way the young men in town once looked at her, how good it made her feel inside. Surely they thought she was pretty. But there were no young men now; the men she had noticed were mostly gone off to war or had been killed by the Germans. The others had collaborated with the enemy, and she would have nothing to do with such men. There was only Major Dubois now.

Major Dubois was kind enough to her, but she had no feelings for him. She had known him since she was a little girl—why, he was like an uncle to her, she had once told Jean-Claude. Jean-Claude had chastised her. "You will not find a better man," he had told her. "He would provide well for you, and he would be an excellent father." She was sure that he would, but she did not love him. She loved him, of course, but not as a woman should love a man she would marry.

"Paagh! These are the words of a silly girl," Jean-Claude had said. "Words you have probably found somewhere in a book."

"When I marry I will marry for love," she had told him firmly. "I will marry for life or I shall not marry."

Of course, Jean-Claude did not understand. He was a man; men did not think of such things. A smile flourished over her face as she thought of her brothers. She loved them dearly. *I do hope they remember to bring some sugar,* she thought. *It would be lovely to have some sugar for the coffee, perhaps even to bake some sweet cakes.*

Feeling clean and pretty, Colette put the hand mirror away; she went to the door of the cabin and waited. She glanced down the road that led into town, but there was no one. The chickens pecked at her feet; it seemed they were clucking mockingly at her. She shooed them away. Once more she looked down the road. Then as she turned to go back into the cabin, she looked up suddenly.

She had heard that sound many times before—her father was a wood-cutter, after all. Yet now the sound of the ax carried with it a sad and lonely feeling; it shook something inside her. And then she heard the distinctive crack, the death cry of a tree as the life was torn from it, and, moments later, the muffled crash as it fell to the ground.

Once again the mountain was quiet. A hush settled over the yard and over the cabin; it came into the cabin and settled over the girl. Her shoulders sagged beneath it; her head bent forward as the tremendous weight of solitude, pushed back for a brief respite, now pressed down upon her soul. And leaning against the doorjamb she sighed.

The fog never lifted that day.

1 ★ ★ ★

October 14, 1943. 0945 hours. *"Black Thursday." The skies over Belgium.* The duel didn't last but a few seconds. The American pilot had made an error, and there wasn't time to correct it. Disbelief sheeted over his mind the instant before a burst of 20mm rounds tore through his P–47 Thunderbolt with a shudder that came up through his teeth. And then it was over.

Thick, oily smoke belched out of the jagged vents and streamed alongside the fuselage. Oil spattered against the cockpit, its thin black rivulets jiggling then flattening and smearing along the glass like streaks of blood. The stricken plane bucked and coughed as if it wanted only to fold its wings and let the earth take it.

The American struggled to hold the plane in a horizontal attitude and fought desperately against a tremendous torque that threatened to flip the plane over into a spin. He looked over at his left wing and saw that the tip had been shorn off and was trailing bits of metallic debris. He cursed. *Sorry, girl,* he thought, for she was a girl to him—his girl. *First time out and I get your tail shot off!* Only then did the realization that she was dying push through his initial shock and anger. He knew that he could not hold her for long. "Got to get out!" he said calmly.

Immediately he reached for the canopy latches and gave them each a quick jerk. But the canopy wouldn't budge. Again he jerked. Nothing. *Runners must be crimped,* he thought. "Come on—give!" he growled. It wouldn't give. "GIVE!" A string of expletives chattered through his teeth. The canopy wouldn't budge. He was stuck.

Then the full weight of it began to spread over him like a film of lubricating oil, smoothing down from his head, along his limbs, to collect in the pit of his stomach. He suddenly saw a very clear picture of it in his mind. He'd seen the footage in training, the look of terror on the faces of men as they struggled to get free of their burning planes. He could hear the screams rising in his throat.

"Got to keep a clear head," he said aloud. "Don't panic. Don't panic. Panic kills." He banged at the base of the runners with a gloved fist, then pulled at the latches. The canopy wouldn't budge. "That's okay, you'll get it. Just don't panic." He banged and pulled. "That's okay. Come on, baby— give!" he said intimately. "Come on, baby!"

Then, like a shark surfacing, the Messerschmitt rose into his field of vision and rolled to show the dead, gray color of its sleek underbelly. The enemy plane leveled smoothly out, straight-backed and blunt-nosed, to appear thirty feet off his shorn wingtip.

The American could clearly see the face of the German pilot. In one swift sweep of his eyes he saw the distinctive Luftwaffe markings on the 109's fuselage, the black cross, the division and wing, the rank of the pilot, the several ranks of "kills" stenciled on the vertical stabilizer and the rudder behind the black swastika. His eyes continued down the body and he saw the word *Katharina* painted in scarlet on the engine cowling over the exhaust ports. Then, sweeping back to the face of the German, he saw the eyes, the cold-as-death predator eyes, studying him with clinical dispassion. The German pilot made a gesture with his gloved hand, as if to say, "Open the canopy, you fool."

Right, Billy grimaced. *What do you think I'm trying to do, you lousy Kraut?*

Thick, black smoke was curling into the cockpit now, making it difficult to see. Tongues of flame licked out of the smoke up the sides of the fire wall and spread over the leg well. Little darts of flame speared up past the picture of his sweetheart that was taped to the instrument panel—a pretty girl who wrote the inscription in a loopy hand: *Always and forever, Laura.* Within seconds Billy was engulfed in smoke and heat, and Laura was gone in a crinkle of fire. It was then he felt the attitude of the plane shift. A violent tremor shuddered through him as something somewhere in the plane's entrails gave loose, and he knew he could no longer hold her.

"Oh, God," he prayed in a quiet horror. "Not this way. Please, not this way, God." He yanked on the latches. Nothing. He banged the runners and yanked. Nothing. He banged and jerked and yanked. Nothing. A rage came over him so swiftly that he struck his fist against the glass, shouting, "Open, open—OPEN!" Still the canopy held fast.

Billy sat back in his seat for a moment, stunned, at a loss as to what to do. He saw their faces again, the desperate look in their eyes as they pounded futilely at the sides of their cockpits. He could feel it rising in his throat. "Oh, God! Please!"

Through the smoke he could just make out the vague outline of the Messerschmitt, the predator waiting, it seemed, for its prey to roll over and die.

Billy cared nothing about the German now, only of getting out of the plane. "Okay, Billy . . . okay, Billy. We'll do this, won't we, baby? Come on now," he said, once again with intimacy. He continued working the latches that wouldn't give. The flames were climbing up his legs now and searing his trousers. "Why won't anything budge? Come on. Give! Give! GIVE!" He felt the heat against his legs and panic came up in a rush. "My legs! Dear God, no!" He banged at the canopy. "Come on—OPEN! OPEN! OPEN!" He cursed.

Frantically he jerked the latches. Nothing. "Mama!" he cried. "I'm sorry, Mama! No, no—Mama!" Again. Jerk. "Anything, God!" he said, his voice developing an airy shallowness as he alternately cursed the plane and vowed his soul to God. Again. Jerk. The canopy moved an inch. "That's it!" he said, a giggle stuttering in his throat. "Anything, God, anything." Again he jerked. The canopy slid back two inches. "That's a baby. Come on— that's it, baby—give! Give! Anything, God, anything! You name it!"

Just then the canopy slid back as though on greased runners, and smoke boiled out into the atmosphere. Billy found a handhold for each hand, steadied himself, then leapt free of the plane; the rudder, screwing toward him, just missed slicing him in two by inches.

Free-falling. For a moment it seemed as though he had died; everything was so cold and disorienting. The patchwork ground twirled silently up at him, the horizon tumbling away, then reappearing, a swirl of dizzying colors—grays and greens and browns, yellows and reds—twirling away to the sky, and then to the ground, closer now, twenty thousand feet away . . . falling at a terminal speed of 120 mph . . . eighteen thousand . . . seventeen . . . now fifteen.

Everything was quiet . . . dreamlike . . . nauseating.

He grabbed hold of the D ring. *Hold it,* he thought. *Wait.* He'd been told to hold off as long as possible. Get as low as you can. German pilots were known to strafe parachutes. *Hold it. Get lower. Wait until you get below ten thousand. Now!*

A bright white spear of silk opened suddenly against the lowering sky, billowing out like the gelatinous mass of a jellyfish pumping gracefully through the ocean. He felt the sure pull of the silk against his shoulders and thighs as the chute snatched hold of the sky and pulled. Then he heard the wind, the keening rush through the shrouds, the distant sound of embattled fighters and machine gun fire below, and the steady drone of aircraft high overhead. He glanced quickly upward and saw the trailing box formation of B–17s, fiery glints of light now, heading east, as well as the white contrails of the higher bombers marking their parallel courses against the slate-gray sky. Here and there he saw aircraft going down, the trailing black curls of smoke from their engines describing their long, slow augers to the earth. It was as terrifying as it was exhilarating.

Just then the Messerschmitt roared past him, sucking the wind out of his chest. "Holy mackerel!" he cried, ducking his head. He looked up in time to see the enemy fighter waving its wings. And then it was gone, climbing back up to the ceiling on a long and beautiful chandelle. Billy shook his head in wonder.

He looked down and saw a column of smoke rising from some trees in the distance. His Thunderbolt, he presumed, now nothing but a bright signal flare to the Wehrmacht. "Sorry, baby, I don't blame you for turning on me," he said, truly feeling sorry. "I let you down."

He drifted over the low country of Belgium, the wind driving him on a general southerly course, everything quiet, save the shrill hum of the wind through the parachute's shrouds. He saw a little town on the horizon, a silver thread of river snaking through it, and a small line of what appeared to be military vehicles, tiny dark specks moving steadily along a thin strip of road in his general direction.

"Swell!" he said. "Out of the frying pan . . ."

ॐ∞ॐ

"*Einen Fallschirm, Herr Hauptmann!*" a German soldier cried, pointing over the horizon.

The captain commanded his driver to halt. The driver handed him a pair of binoculars, and the captain peered through the eyepieces. "It is an American," he said, following the parachute's descent. "I want him!"

ॐ∞ॐ

Second Lieutenant William "Billy" Hochreiter, closer to the earth now and feeling as vulnerable as a Franklin grouse on a dead limb, saw three motorcycles with sidecars and two troop carriers strip away from the column and head cross-country toward his position. A tract of wood stretched away to the south, he noted. The river leading from the town curled through it, some vineyards were just beyond, then a farmer's cottage and outbuildings, and fields of plowed-under earth. He worked the shrouds to put him clear of the trees and behind a low rise.

When he hit the ground, feet together, knees bending as he rolled backward to break the fall, a sharp bit of October wind blew the chute back over him, and he got all tangled in the silk and lines. Everything was a sudden bright, white womb of silk. For a brief, illusory moment he had a feeling of security, like the feeling you got as a child when you pulled the covers over your head to shut out the monsters.

Billy pulled the chute free of his head, shattering the illusion, and, climbing to his feet, stumbling, setting his feet again, found himself caught in the lines. The throaty growl of motorcycles mounted on the wind. He couldn't see them just yet because of the rise of ground, but he knew that they were closing fast. He slipped his hunting knife from its sheath and began furiously hacking at the lines. But his fingers were suddenly arthritic, disconnected from his brain. Anger flared on the fuel of his fear: anger at being shot down, anger at his stupidity, anger at his predicament, anger at the prospects of being captured or killed. Stupid . . . stupid . . . stupid. Then the wind caught a fold in the chute, ballooning the silk like a spinnaker sail, and dragged him several feet over the ground before he again found his footing.

The sound of the motorcycles dipped momentarily, and Billy knew that they had reached the far base of the hill. He cut away the last of the lines, and the silk sheet flattened over the ground, lifted, then curled over on itself. *No point hiding it,* he thought. Hopping free of the harness, he stripped off his Mae West and broke into a dead run.

As he ran he sheathed the knife and removed his father's nickel-plated Colt from its shoulder holster. He shot a look over his shoulder in time to see the motorcycles cresting the rise of the hill about three hundred yards behind him, and immediately the brittle air was shattered with the chatter of machine gun fire. The soldiers in the sidecars fired short then long bursts at him with their submachine guns. Bullets spat over the ground, kicked up little clods of dirt here and there at his feet, and cracked about his head. Billy imagined the impact of a bullet in his back and winced at the thought of the white-hot jolt tearing through his flesh. He raced ahead of the image, zigzagging, dodging, his head bent forward as he pumped toward the distant line of trees. He fired the Colt over his shoulder once and hit nothing.

It was a wide-open foot haul to the trees he knew he must reach if he was to survive. Coming to a low, stone wall that enclosed a grain field, he hopped it in a bound. He then dipped down the riverbank and felt the immediate pull on his legs as he began fording the smooth, heavy-flowing current. The water was cold and swirled about his thighs as he leaned against the weight of the current and threshed forward with his arms. Once he reached the middle of the river the current lifted and carried him a few feet. Billy regained his footing and threshed wildly until he reached the opposite bank.

He scrambled onto the long, narrow stretch of pebbly beach, then darted upriver. His fleece-lined flight boots were saturated with water and felt as though someone had poured cement into them. Several nightmares came to mind as he shogged, heavy-legged, upstream. To his right was the stone wall. On his left was a five-foot bank of rocky, red earth that ran up to a grassy field. Climbing that now, he knew, would offer the Germans a clean shot of his head and back. About two hundred yards ahead the bank lowered to about a foot off the river, and beyond were the dark trees, some of which crowded the lip of the bank and overspread their big limbs from both sides. Once he reached those trees, he ran a little farther, then hurdled over the side and up onto the flat, grassy ground and into the woods. The Germans opened up as Billy dove for cover behind a tree.

Nursing a stitch in his side, he peered around the trunk of the tree and watched intently as the three motorcycles drew up to the stone wall. He could see the small, white faces of the soldiers looking in his direction. *Lousy Krauts*, he thought. Then the motorcycles continued along the wall to the river's edge. The driver of the first motorcycle surveyed the river, shouted something at the others, and immediately all three motorcycles roared away downriver.

As yet there was no sign of the two troop carriers. He had bought some time, he hoped. Without wasting a moment of it he lifted each leg to drain the water from his boots, filled his lungs with air, and struck off through the trees. He was a good long-distance runner. He ran on a northeasterly course, the opposite direction in which he needed to travel if he were going to reach the mountains of Spain and escape back to England. But he could not think of Spain now. Escape the immediate threat first, Spain later.

Penetrating deeper and deeper into the forest, he was struck by the old-world atmosphere of the place. It was cool and damp, primordial, as if the trees had been there since the dawn of time, or even that time was irrelevant here, not at all like the forests he had known back in the Beartooths of southwestern Montana. The trees here were old and dark—big, thick monsters with gnarled root systems and heavy gesturing limbs, thick with autumn foliage. There were wide-open spaces between the trees, yet the floor was dark and damp and mossy from the intricate bower overhead. The ground was soft and springy. Brown leaves sifted down from the dark ceiling like little papery hands, and bore him silently through the forest. There was an eerie quiet pervading the wood, a quiet that had been perhaps undisturbed for centuries, until a bullet tore through the bark of the tree nearest his head, leaving a long white blaze across the trunk.

The motorcycles had somewhere forded the river, he saw, and regained their ground. They were now feeling through the heavy trees, the sidecars bouncing over the sharp obstacles of tree trunks and boulders, then bouncing down hard and settling. When they had a line of sight, the men in the sidecars opened up with their machine guns.

He looked through the trees to his left and saw the two troop carriers pull up along the edge of the woods and halt. Soldiers piled out of the carriers and spread over the ground in a long line that began closing on his position in a kind of pincer movement, ten men going out one way, ten going out the other, and the outer flanks sweeping slowly inward. They walked bent over their rifles with their heads lowered and looking side to side as they hunted him. They looked like toy soldiers, he thought, all sharp-angled and uniform in their movements as they advanced, machinelike, through the trees.

Billy took off through the trees ahead, and when the Germans caught sight of him they fired a volley; then the whole line stepped into a trot. They looked less like machines now and more like men with square heads. Billy was about three hundred yards ahead of them, he guessed. Every now and then he would hear the mean buzz of a bullet homing through the trees, the sharp spat or thud of the impact nearby, and the lag of the report. By these he was able to judge the distance, counting in his mind: one-one thousand, two-one thousand, like you do with lightning. He ran easier now that the stitch was gone. His stride lengthened to a cross-country gait, and with every step he thanked his track coach for riding him hard.

The trees stretched away from him to the right now, and across the river there were more trees. To the left was a length of field, and beyond it a vineyard. The vines were cut back so that every vine looked like a small, gnarled cross, row upon row upon row of them, like a vast cemetery of crosses that spread out before a tiny farmhouse situated on a low hump of ground. His first impulse was to head across the vineyard and hide in one of the outbuildings of the farmstead. Then he realized that he was thinking like a bear. Bears will head for the high ground when they are in trouble, and you can expect the hounds to have him somewhere snagged in a tree when you catch up to them. It was then that he spotted a third troop carrier pulling in front of the house and ten or so soldiers piling out. He veered back toward the river.

Billy felt the trap closing around him. Glancing ahead, he continued running through the trees, hoping to outdistance the pincer movement. He hoped like crazy the trees would hold, for the thought of the motorcycles getting him into open ground worried him greatly. He knew he needed to get back across the river if he were going to evade capture or death, so when he came to a place where a dead tree had fallen across the river and formed a natural bridge, he thought it was as good a place as any to ford. He tested it with his foot. The snag was shucked clean of bark and its surface slick with years of rain and wind, but it was solid, so he carefully sidestepped over the river. Once he cleared the opposite bank, he jumped free of the snag and ran quickly into the wood. He was thankful for the trees, and he was thankful for the luck that had been with him so far, if luck was what it was. He didn't want to think about the luck though, for fear of jinxing it.

Suddenly, the weather shifted, as if he had run from one pressure front into another. As the temperature dropped, Billy noticed a shift in the terrain. Ahead of him the forest rose sharply, the trees thinning with rocks and big boulders jutting along a ridge. Creeping down the face of the slope through the big boulders and trees were diaphanous tendrils of fog. It was difficult going—up two strides, then back one, sliding back as the soft shale earth gave way under his feet. Each time it cost him. His intense feeling of exhaustion reminded him of hunting elk in the Beartooths, only he was the one being hunted now, and he had no idea of what to do except run. *Maybe that's how the elk thinks when he knows he's being hunted,* Billy thought; *he runs until his luck runs out and he's brought down.*

ॐ∽૰ॐ

The German sniper raised his Mauser rifle and peered into the Zeiss scope. The rocks and scrub grass and the trunks of trees showed bright and cleanly focused in the circle of the scope. He found the American scrabbling up through the rocks and judged the distance. Then he took a breath and let half of it ease out through his nose as he steadied the crosshairs between Billy's shoulder blades, just below the white of the wool collar. *The collar makes a good mark,* he thought, as he set his finger on the trigger. He let off on the trigger. *It is a beautiful jacket though,* he observed. *Perhaps they will let me keep it.* He raised the muzzle and found Billy's head, let his breath ease out slowly through his nose, steadied the crosshairs and squeezed.

☜☞

Billy lost his footing and slid down a foot in the soft shale the instant the rifle roared behind him. He was in mid-reach to steady himself against a boulder when the bullet whined off the face of the rock, peppering his cheek and hand with a spray of chips. He whirled around in time to see the German soldier leave his point and run across a narrow corridor of ground, about a hundred yards beyond the foot of the slope. Billy fired his pistol and saw where the bullet landed in a spurt of dirt, far to the right of the soldier's feet. He cursed, wishing he had his Model 70. He was a crack shot with a hunting rifle, better than this fellow, he knew, but he couldn't hit the broad side of a barn with a single-action revolver.

Billy continued to make his way up the slope, traversing back and forth, using the rocks and what trees there were for cover, wondering how the Germans had gotten across the river again so quickly. Then he realized that there was only one man on his heels, a point man with a sniper's rifle. Here and there a bullet spat in the dirt or caromed off a rock, as a part of his body became exposed to the German rifleman. Once over the summit, safe behind the brow of the hill, Billy hid behind a tree to catch his breath. *Got to save my wind,* he thought. *Can't keep up this pace. Can't outrun a rifle.*

He took a quick survey of the terrain. Ahead the hill sloped more gently away from him in either direction; to the left of him the pine trees thinned, and through the trees and the tattery fog he could just catch glimpses of the vineyard across the river; to his right the trees were thicker and of the old-world kind. The fog was heavier to the right, as well, the big trees seeming to gather the fog with their thick limbs and hide themselves in veils of gray. He could see nothing beyond a hundred yards.

Billy heard the German's breath laboring up the slope, heard the rocky soil grating under his boots. He waited for a moment, committing himself to a course of action. Then he raised the pistol at a right angle to the ground. He felt the solid heft of the pistol in his palm, the smooth yellowed bone of the grips against the meaty crook of his thumb and forefinger as he pulled the hammer back quietly with his thumb.

His pulse thickened in his throat. He'd never before killed a man. He'd killed plenty of game but never a man. He wasn't trained to kill men; he was trained to kill airplanes. An airplane was a machine; it mattered little that there was a man inside. You didn't think about the man, you only thought to beat his thinking and to kill his plane; that was why you didn't strafe men with parachutes. He could feel the cool of the fog fingering at the base of his neck and a shiver went down his spine. He noticed the muzzle of his pistol shaking, so he brought his left hand up to support the grips.

He tensed when he heard the German clear his throat then mutter something indistinct. He was near the summit, Billy knew. The sound of his breath heaving and rattling and the tired shovelling of his feet in the loose ground grew nearer and nearer. He waited until he thought the man was right on top of him, and when he could no longer wait he rolled out from behind the tree and leveled the gun with both hands. The top of the man's head was no more than ten feet away, his left hand just extending to steady himself as he stumbled over the last rise of ground. The German stood upright and, when their eyes met, Billy saw his eyes go wide in amazement. For just a moment he marvelled at the face—it was a boy's face, really—and seeing the short-cropped bristle of hair around the pink ears beneath the helmet, the downy flush of his cheeks, and the fear caught in the wide blue eyes, he hesitated pulling the trigger.

The German looked down at his rifle in a panic. A little shriek got caught in his throat as he fumbled with the bolt. He worked it frantically, looking down at the bolt then looking up at Billy as he raised the muzzle with a jerk.

The heavy Colt jumped in Billy's hand. He saw the German buck away from him down the slope in a dreamlike slowness, his eyes clenched, mouth twisting, his body twirling with his hands flung wide like wings. Billy watched him fall onto his back with the rifle twirling away, watched the rifle, then followed the German sliding down the hill amid a small avalanche of shale until he folded limply into the trunk of a tree so that his feet were down one side of the trunk and his head down the other—all of this in the unreal slowness of a dream. A rubble of tiny pebbles trickled after him.

Billy did not hear the crash of his pistol, only the echoing report that came back sounding so far away. Afterward, silence rushed back to fill in the void, and time sped back up in increments. He blinked at the dead soldier for a moment, stared dazedly at the limp body and the spreading mass of blood that he could just see on the chest where the .45 slug from the

Colt had struck him, point blank. A sadness came up inside him. He felt none of the exhilaration or happiness as when he came upon game, only a curious horror at having killed a human being.

But he had no time to think about it or to grieve, for a movement at the base of the slope had caught his eyes. He looked and saw a group of soldiers crowding behind trees and rocks, setting themselves. More soldiers came behind them in the trees, and immediately the sad quiet was shattered by the pop-pop-pop sounds of small arms fire. A bullet smashed through a tree branch near his head and skirled away. He emptied his pistol at several vague man shapes, hit nothing that he could see, cursed the pistol, then took off into the thick woods to his right.

He ran into the thick, white bank of mist, hearing only the sound of his breath and his own footsteps. The fog thickened with every step, forcing him to pull up now and then as the trunk of a tree loomed suddenly out of a wall of wet gray.

The earth was soft beneath his feet and his footsteps a muffled crush of wet autumn leaves. He looked down to see if his feet made depressions in the leaves. He didn't know if the Germans were trackers or not. He hoped not. Then he didn't care. He didn't care about anything at the moment. Shivering with cold and fear, he looked over his shoulder and saw only the dark gray shapes of trees falling back into the gray gloom, and heard nothing, the sounds all crushed out of the forest.

2 ★★★

A silvery blade of sunlight lanced through the single window next to the stove where Colette was bent over, lighting a fire with a taper. The light struck the wood floor and played over the heavy table against the far wall, illuminating the framed picture of a crucified Christ that hung over the table. The Christ looked sad and pitiable. There were four chairs around the handcrafted table and one off to the side, everything worn smooth. There were four place settings around the table, a bottle of wine, glasses, and a half-eaten loaf of bread with a kitchen knife setting next to it. It was early in the afternoon.

Smoke billowed suddenly out of the stove, and the girl frowned and muttered something to herself. She adjusted the kindling delicately with a poker until the fire caught, then she closed the grate and listened as the flue drew the flames upwards in a roar. She hefted a large pot of water onto the stove, wiped a strand of fallen black hair from her eyes, opened the window, and looked out beyond the barn to the trees on the slope. Immediately the smoke swirled and cleared as the crisp autumn air breezed into the cabin. The air smelled of pine and of the high altitude of the mountains, with just a hint of rain. She loved this time of day and, as always, the promise of rain in the mountains stirred a happiness in her. She didn't know why, nor did she think about it. Perhaps it reminded her of years ago when she was a little girl, before the Germans, before the horrible killing, when her family sat around the table together, eating and talking pleasantly, and laughing as Jean-Claude made a joke, and everyone listening to the rain against the window. Thinking about it was too painful.

Looking out that very window she could just see her father through the dark of the trees that wound up the slope past the barn, and she could just make out the flash of white showing at his feet. The woodcutter was standing stump-still with his head bent downward, his thick muscular shoulders sagged and his back bowed. The whole of him looked like a statue of a sad troll or ogre, or of something lost or abandoned in the woods. The happiness went out of the girl, as it always did watching him through the window, every day at this same hour, and wishing that it was her lying beneath that dreadful white scar on the slope.

She breathed a sigh, cleansing her lungs, and then she breathed another deeper one. But the sighs did little to hold back the heaviness in her chest.

Going over to the stove, she added larger pieces of wood to the fire; then she went over to the low wooden sideboard next to the stove and began peeling two large potatoes with a paring knife. She stopped what she was doing and looked out the window, at nothing this time. She stood staring for several moments at the bit of bright sky showing through the trees, whispered something under her breath, then looked down at her hands. She was twirling the paring knife in her fingers.

When she finished paring the potatoes, she cut the carrots and the onions. The onions made her eyes water, and she wiped them with the back of her hand. A movement outside the window caught her attention. She turned her head, warily at first, then, seeing the team of mules pulling the cart up through the trees, their heads hammering against the burden, accompanied by the two men wearing dark pullovers and berets, she smiled and the happiness returned.

"Jean-Claude! François!" she exclaimed. "*Dieu merci!* Thank God!"

Her brothers paused in the clearing at the head of the road that wound up to the cabin. They looked up at the round bulk of the man on the slope. The woodcutter looked down at them, the white of his big face showing, then he looked back at the grave at his feet. The two men waited respectfully, but the mules, smelling the hay in the barn, threw their heads and snorted impatiently.

The girl checked the pot on the stove, wiped her hands on a cloth, and went outside. The air was bright and clear, the ground a reddish color brightened by the sun beating through the clouds. As she walked silently across the yard, feeling the soft bed of pine needles beneath her bare feet, the chickens moved irritatedly out of her path. The two brothers were standing, conferring quietly, and they did not see or hear her approach.

"Jean-Claude! François!" she called out.

They turned from looking up at their father and waved.

"Colette," Jean-Claude greeted her. "*Comment allez-vous?*"

"What has kept you? I have been worried!"

Jean-Claude turned to François. "We are in trouble, I think."

Colette threw her arms around her brothers. "Thank God, you are safe!"

Jean-Claude looked at her. "How is it with Papa?"

She made a so-so gesture with her hand. "Next time you will take me with you, Jean-Claude, and François can stay home and cook and do the chores."

François shook his head. Jean-Claude smiled and said, "Has he been unbearable?"

She looked up the slope and saw their father coming down through the trees. She made another so-so gesture with her hand. Her brothers chuckled.

"How is Uncle Maurice?" she asked.

"He is well. Safely away," Jean-Claude said.

"Good. And Uncle Guillaume?"

The boys turned as their father reached the base of the slope and started across the open, pine-needled yard, coming now with the short-legged stride of an ox.

"I will put the team away," François said quickly.

"No, allow me," the girl said, taking hold of the lead. "Next time I will go with you, Jean-Claude," she said again. "You know that I can handle myself in trouble. I have had a good teacher."

Jean-Claude smiled at her. He pulled a large burlap sack from the rear of the cart as it passed. "Off you go."

Colette led the mules and the empty cart, used for hauling lumber and firewood, over to the barn.

The woodcutter stood looking intently at the two boys, his stout bulk in contrast to their slighter, taller builds. He drew his thick, calloused hand over his stubbled face as Jean-Claude described to him the events during the past three weeks of their absence.

"Maurice is well?"

"Yes, Papa. The aeroplane took off without trouble," Jean-Claude said. "We have since received news that he arrived safely in London."

The woodcutter grunted. "And Guillaume?"

"He would not go."

"Not go?"

"No, Papa."

"This is good," the woodcutter said reflectively. "Guillaume is a good man. He does not run like the rest."

The girl returned from the barn. "Why would he not go?" she asked, her face showing obvious concern.

Her father looked sharply at her, then turned to his eldest son. "What other news?"

"There has been a great air battle to the north," Jean-Claude said. "We have seen many formations of Messerschmitts and Focke-Wulfs, all morning long."

The big hand paused momentarily over the wide, stubbled face. "Ah, yes," the woodcutter said, looking north over the mountains. "This morning I too have seen many planes going across the sky from the west."

"They were probably from Calais," Jean-Claude imagined.

"Yes," his brother agreed. "Where else? I don't know. Perhaps Amiens. Could you tell what kind of planes they were, Papa? Were they single engines, or double?"

Colette stood watching the three men in silence.

"What do I know of engines?" the woodcutter shrugged. "Where was this battle?" he asked Jean-Claude.

"We do not know for certain," he said. "Across Namur, perhaps into Germany."

"Germany?"

"So it seems, Papa. It is early yet," Jean-Claude said. "We have heard only that there is a great battle to the north, and that there are many Allied planes fallen."

"Were they bombers?"

"Yes, they were bombers, I think. The big ones."

"Yes," François concurred. "The American Flying Fortresses. It is not good. There are downed American fliers everywhere across Holland and Belgium."

The father grunted, then resumed pulling at his face. "Bombers," he mused.

"Should we contact Major Dubois?" François suggested.

The girl looked at him. The father, looking at François without turning his head, then looking at his other son, said, "We will do nothing."

"But, Papa—"

"We will do nothing. There is work to be done here. You are back not ten minutes and already you wish to leave? Have you forgotten how to do an honest day's labor?"

"It is good that your mother, God rest her soul," the woodcutter said crossing himself, "it is good that she is not here to see such sloth in her children."

"The work can wait, Papa," Jean-Claude grinned. "Look what François and I have brought!" He pulled a demijohn of wine from the sack.

His father took it and held it up to the light and grunted.

"For tonight, Papa. And here, Colette, is some meat to broil. Some real meat instead of always chicken." He handed her a joint of mutton, a wheel of cheese, and a stringer of smoked fish. "And this," he added, hefting a sack from the cart.

Her eyes widened with delight. "Sugar?"

"Perhaps you can bake us some sweet cakes," her brother suggested.

"I shall bake us a dozen each! Wherever did you get all these, Jean-Claude?"

"If I tell you that I traded honestly for them, I would have to confess my sins to Father Michel. He would tell me to say three Hail Marys and an Act of Contrition." He grinned suddenly at her. "Since I am not very contrite, my sister, I will tell you only that they are a gift from a prominent member of the Vichy."

"You *stole* them?"

"Appropriated is a better word," François said brightly. "Even so, I think that we have done him a great service."

"How so?" the girl wondered.

"Now he will no longer have to lay awake at night wondering if someone might raid his root cellar." The boys laughed.

"We shall be canonized," Jean-Claude grinned.

The girl and her brothers laughed.

"You make jokes," the woodcutter said sullenly. "There is no joking with the Vichy." He spat on the ground. "The traitors!"

"Yes, Papa, you are right," Jean-Claude said. His face cleared of humor. "I am sorry. The Vichy are everywhere helping the Boche to hunt down the Americans, and it is not funny."

"They have drawn a very tight net over the countryside," François interjected. "We were forced to show our papers three times. I do not think that the Americans can escape such a net."

Jean-Claude raised his eyebrows at his father and shook his head.

"There was no trouble with your papers?"

"No, Papa. We were delivering lumber. It is our living."

"It is a long way to deliver lumber."

Jean-Claude shrugged. "There was no trouble. The Boche are looking for downed American flyers." The shadow of a cloud passed over the ground, held, then it was gone, and the sun swept warmly over the reddish earth of the mountains.

The girl glanced quickly at her father, then looked at her brothers. "Will the Boche come here do you think, Jean-Claude?"

"What would they find?"

"They would find the guns."

"They would not find the guns."

"The Germans are very thorough."

"It is an arduous trek into the mountains in pursuit of saws, two old mules, and too many chickens," Jean-Claude assured her. He smiled. "Do not trouble yourself, sister. The Boche will not come."

"What of Major Dubois?" the girl asked. "Is there no word from the FFI?"

"Go and tend to supper," the woodcutter said brusquely.

"Yes, Papa. I just thought that, perhaps—" She caught his eyes. "Yes, Papa. Supper will be ready in one half-hour."

She turned and started back to the cabin. She walked, holding the joint of mutton and the stringer of fish out to her sides for balance, looking down at her feet as they traced an invisible line to the door.

"A supper of broiled meat!" Jean-Claude called after her.

She turned and smiled at him. "I thought we would have chicken," she said.

"No! Heavens, no! Meat! I'm starving for red meat! And besides, we must destroy the evidence!"

Colette laughed. Jean-Claude always made her laugh. She went inside the cabin, enjoying the happiness of having her brothers home. She set the meat and fish and cheese aside, then peeled two more potatoes and placed them into the boiling water, along with the carrots and onions, and covered the heavy pot with the lid. She stood looking out the window at her father still talking with her brothers. Idly, she fondled the silver crucifix at her breast, then she looked up at the awful blaze of white just showing on the slope.

3 ★ ★ ★

They kept coming; one after the other they came. They wouldn't give him a moment's peace. Billy wished he'd kept going through the fog and taken his chances in the open. But there was no use thinking about it now. He'd made his choice. He'd have to tough it out. Sitting high up in the crook of an old sycamore, spent of wind, he slowly ground his teeth as images of the last few hours came at him one after the other. Like waves. He couldn't shake them; they kept coming, especially the one.

He peered through the pointy apertures of the leaves into the fog, seeing nothing of the soldiers but the face of the one he'd killed, a young face, no older than his own, and the astonished—almost obscene—look in the eyes. That was the one. He couldn't shake it. He knew he never would shake it. It kept coming up at him, rising out of his chest, then falling away with the arms spread wide like the wings of a dying plane—like Joe Thompson's plane banking away from him after they'd seen those Messerschmitts and Focke-Wulfs attacking the Fortresses.

"Here we go, Montana!" Thompson's voice crackled over his radio. "Drop your belly tank and stick close to me!"

"Like a tick on a hound, Joe!" Billy grinned cockily.

It seemed a year ago now when he had taken off with his squadron from East Anglia—sixteen P–47 Thunderbolts—rising in pairs off the airstrip into the gray line of dawn like winged champions. He remembered feeling the exhilarating rush of his first mission, the bursting pride as his squadron aligned with the other squadrons of the Group, then the Group rendezvousing with the B–17s 29,000 feet over the coast of Holland.

He had followed Captain Joe Thompson tight as he jumped that Focke-Wulf 190, banking and diving neatly with him to the left. He saw the burst of Thompson's wing guns, the tracers showing that he was behind the German fighter, then Thompson drawing closer, realigning, holding tighter, getting inside the 190's circle and firing another burst of eight .50s. Billy saw the hits all over the German plane, the pieces of metal flying off the wings and tail section, the white puffs of smoke burping out of the engine cowling. And then the explosion, the fiery shards of metallic debris and smoke smashing against the sky, and somewhere in it was a man.

"One dead Hun!" Joe's voice crackled. "Still with me, Montana?"

Billy was speechless as he gaped down at the glittering pieces of metal.

"Wake up, Montana! You watching our tail?"

"Huh? Yes, sir!" he said, jerking a look over his shoulder. The sky was full of planes, scores of them, swooping and diving in a deathly choreography. The Flying Fortresses, like a ghostly herd of humpback whales, moved in slow motion through the sea-green ocean of the sky, with a pack of sharks rising fast and attacking their underbellies, fore and aft, and the P–47s breaking and going after the sharks. Every so often a humpback would fall away from the herd, looking tragic and noble as it trailed a stream of black ooze into the benthic gloom. Billy swore that he could hear the high-pitched screams of the men in his headset, as though he had the ears of God.

"Paydirt, Montana! Pair of 190s at six o'clock low! Here we go! You with me?"

"What?"

"Where are you, Hochreiter?"

"Right here, Joe," Billy cried. However, when he swung his head back his element leader was gone. "Where the—?"

He craned his head back and forth, up and down, looking for Joe's plane and, not seeing it, felt a sick panic crawling in his guts. Then the Messerschmitt jumped out of the sun at 350 mph, and it was a whole new ball game.

Shifting his position in the tree, Billy cursed audibly, thinking of what had followed, wishing he could take it all back and play it differently. But one after the other the images came to him as fresh as when they happened, only they came faster and faster now, like the dizzy images of a carousel going round and round. Then he heard again the stentorian roar of cannon fire flashing over his head the split-second before his plane was shot out from under him. The carousel came screeching to a halt. He winced involuntarily, tasting bile in the back of his mouth, and took hold of a branch to steady himself.

Laying his head against the trunk of the tree, he rolled it slowly back and forth. He didn't *want* to think of anything now. There would be time to think of failure later. Still the images came. One after the other. Billy felt a prickling of warmth wash over his scalp, prickling as though he were watching a horror film and knowing there was a scary part coming. He looked around suddenly, then shrank instinctively into the leaves.

The dark, hazy shapes of German soldiers ranging through the trees looked like dead men. He could only see eleven or twelve of them at a time, going out into the fog until they disappeared. Their eyes were dark, featureless holes beneath their square helmets. The soldiers moved warily through the trees, their heads thrust forward, their eyes working like hunters when tracking a dangerous animal that might, at any moment, leap upon them from the wall of the thicket. Now and then they paused cautiously to look up into the branches of a tree before moving on to the next tree, and then on to the next, everything soundless in the foggy wood except for the muffled clinking of their field gear and the odd curse.

Billy held his breath as they stalked past his tree, about fifty feet away. The soldiers nearest him paused, looked up the trunk into the big limbs, with their dark eyes carefully sweeping the bower around him. One of the soldiers glanced back at him and froze, peering, then trudged away. Billy watched them hunch over their rifles, disappearing into the fog with the other "dead" men.

Everything went quiet. A soft wind soughed through the bower and culled a handful of leaves. A drop of water spattered the back of his neck and startled him. Looking up, he could see nothing but a dim diffusion of light through the canopy, the leaves dark against the watery gloom of fog. Then another drop struck his cheek. It turned into a slow, thick pattering of rain, the heavy drops thudding against the leaves and against the limbs of the trees.

A movement caught the tail of his eye, and he peered through the foliage in time to see a man angling toward his tree. Billy gripped his pistol and, with a jolt of horror, remembered that in the rush of his flight, he had forgotten to reload it.

The man stopped just below him, held out his hand, palm side up, and cursed. He was an officer, Billy observed, a lieutenant.

The lieutenant looked ahead into the forest with his hands on his hips, the Luger in his right hand with the muzzle pointing down at the ground behind him. A crimson glow flushed above his collar. Other soldiers came up behind him, and he directed them forward with several short wags of the pistol. The men hurried off. The lieutenant looked up into a tree, and then up into Billy's tree, staring straight at Billy for a full second. Then he glanced behind him into the thick, fog-batting of the wood. His eyes snapped angrily. He gave a petulant stamp with his boot, then stepped away quickly, holding the Luger behind his back.

Billy felt his blood suddenly thicken, pulsing along his neck.

The rain began to fall in thin sheets, sounding like waves hissing through the leaves; then it came in a sudden continuous downpour that drenched him through to the skin.

He waited for others to show. None did. But they would come back, he knew. They would hunt him. His jaw clamped shut against the images coming back to him, his teeth grinding slowly as his eyes trained on the growing puddle of water at the base of his tree. But they did.

He kept seeing the face of that German soldier, no older than nineteen, his arms thrown out as he fell away. And then the air battle would come to him, and the screams of dying men would come into his head and everything got terribly confused, coming round and round. Billy began to hyperventilate.

He vomited. He vomited again, cursing as he slammed his fist against the tree.

The rain lasted about an hour longer and then trailed off with a thinning train, spattering noisily, sheeting off the leaves then dripping big, thick drops that rolled off branches and down limbs, down into the vent in the nape of Billy's collar. He pulled up the collar over his neck. The thick fog rose from the ground about twenty feet and got caught among the branches, leaving the forest floor clear and brightly wet. A chill went over the surface and up into his tree and he began to shiver.

He rummaged around in his survival kit and found the chocolate. He unwrapped it and took a bite to mask the taste of bile in his mouth, and to ease the aching gnaw in his belly he'd only noticed now. The chocolate was hard and bittersweet to the taste. *Nothing to do but wait for the shelter of night,* he thought. He folded the chocolate wrapper into his survival kit and shivered. He waited, hunkered down in his jacket, while the images all raced out of him, one after the other, the fiery shards twirling brightly out of him before the slow, wet passage of time.

In time the branches let go of the fog and it lifted like a giant down comforter and rolled away. The afternoon sun, slanting now to the west, streamed in through the dark canopy and played its deep golden light over the thick, glistening limbs of the old trees. Gradually the old-world forest gathered in the shadows and drew a cloak of glowing scarlet over its rounded shoulders.

The forest seemed to harbor a sad and ancient gloom, and Billy peered out from the gloom for signs of his enemy. There was no sign of them at the moment. But he knew they would not give up, not until they had captured or killed him.

He thought about his buddies and wondered how many of them had made it back to the base. They were in the canteen by now, he was sure, or at the Golden Guinea, drinking warm, dark beer, throwing darts, and having a good time of it. A smile formed over Billy's face then faded. They were of another world now, another age and time. He felt profoundly lonely. A disconsolate mood hit him suddenly and completely, hollowing him out, and he lay his chin against his chest for a moment's rest.

Billy started awake. Immediately he felt the passage of time. It was pitch black now, with a field of stars twinkling brightly overhead. At first he thought he had been having a really bad dream, but then he saw that he was up in a tree and remembered very clearly how he'd come to be there. He realized he was tense with alarm. Something had awakened him, he knew, still hearing the echo of it in his mind. He looked around him and saw nothing. He felt his pulse thick and heavy along his neck, felt the labored chug of his heart against his rib cage. He had heard something. He waited a few moments. Nothing. *Must have imagined it,* he thought. Chiding himself, he was about to climb down out of the tree when he heard a noise, a soft crush of leaves, footsteps, several of them drawing nearer, and then the muffled sound of voices. Foreign voices.

He peered into the blackness of the forest and saw a flicker of light moving stealthily through the woods, advancing slowly, hunting. The light shone up one tree and then another, moving closer to the one in which he was hiding. A bolt of hot panic shot through him, igniting every nerve ending. Closer and closer they came, the men, several of them, and the oval light guiding them like a bloodhound.

Finally there was a huddle of voices at the base of his tree, and the glare of light probed the limbs until it moved past his chest. The light sharply returned and shone on his face. Shielding his eyes, Billy reached for his Colt and pulled back on the hammer. For just a moment while his hand clenched around the smooth bone grips he wondered if he had remembered to reload his pistol.

Yes, he had, he remembered, taking aim on the nearest face.

4 ★★★★

*O*ctober 14, 2100 hours. "Black Thursday." Albatros Tavern, Wilhelmshaven, Northern Germany. The squadron leader sat at the table off to one side of the large fireplace. The fire in the hearth played off his bent-over form, showing half of him in the warm, yellow glow of the flames, while resigning the other half to the uncertain shadows. A candle in a glass globe wavered in the middle of the table and lit his dark eyes. The little flame darted nervously in the large central room, a room dark-paneled in wood with animal heads covering its walls and crowded with people.

The man stared into his nearly empty beer glass, a sullen frown furrowed across the broad length of his brow, his flat-eyed stare looking through the bottom of the glass into an infinite horizon. His head sloped forward, as though the weight of it was too great for its pedestal, and the neck, thickly corded with the muscle and sinew of youth bent forward from the bow of the collar. The man's arms rested heavily upon the table, his hands folded around the glass as if to keep it from sliding off the small table.

Music hammered in the background—a driving up-down, left-right Wagnerian strump. There were some soldiers in the adjoining room off the bar to the left as you came into the place. The men were singing, some of them with their arms draped around girls, the girls singing, swaying to the music, and laughing. No one was dancing just yet, but everyone in that corner was laughing and smoking and lifting their glasses of beer. Everyone else in the tavern had to strain to hear themselves talking at their tables, but they were enjoying themselves because the food and drink were good, the women respectable and friendly, and it was generally a happy place to come during Oktoberfest and celebrate after a good day of business or war.

The pilots came to Wilhelmshaven on liberty, since there was nothing to do at the air base but write letters or read. They came to this particular tavern because Werner, the proprietor, gave them their first round of drinks free of charge after each mission.

Werner, a stoutly built man with a red face and bright blue eyes, had flown in the First World War. Tonight, he was regaling several young pilots with the story of how he had shot down a Sopwith Camel, showing all the maneuvers with his hands, including how the enemy pilot saluted him as his plane went down in flames.

One of the young pilots glanced over at the solitary man by the fireplace. He had been observing him all evening. Finally, he had worked up his nerve and started toward him, but his friend caught him by the arm and shook his head. "Leave him be," the friend said. The young pilot watched the squadron leader from the corner of his eyes and a great wind of pride blew through his chest. *How can Germany lose with such men,* he wondered.

The squadron leader raked his long fingers through a mess of brown hair and let it fall a careless rake over his eyes. He had a wide, rugged face with a sensual mouth that was clamped shut against the gaiety in the room. A Knight's Cross with Oak Leaves hung at his throat. The man tilted his glass to one side, allowing the foam to collect in a little crescent on the bottom. Then he lifted the glass and drained the contents, set it gently on the table, and folded his hands around it.

Just then the tavern door blew open, and a lean, handsome, Nordic-featured man wearing a leather flight jacket and white scarf stepped into the room. Looking like something out of a Leni Riefenstahl film, he stood just inside the door with his feet widely spread, his body wavering slightly as he took a drink from a silver flask. He slipped the flask back into his jacket, removed his cap, and smoothed his hand over his shining blond hair that was combed straight back and neatly cropped around the ears. His lively blue eyes darted from table to table.

He grinned suddenly, showing the gleam of his teeth beneath a trim, blond moustache. Slamming the door behind him, he threw his hands into the air and strode jauntily through the crowd toward the table nearest the fireplace.

"Da bist du, Rolf!" he growled loud enough for half the crowd to turn and look at him. "There you are!"

The squadron leader glanced up sullenly, then looked back into his empty glass. "Hello, Viktor."

"Hello, Viktor? Is that all you have to say?" the flight lieutenant grinned. "Well? Do you notice anything new about me?" he crowed, running his hand over the fleece collar of his jacket. "It's American. Cost me plenty, you can bet." He hiked the collar up behind his head and affected a rakish look. "Do you think it makes me look like Clark Gable?"

"You look like you could be shot for being out of uniform," Rolf said.

"You are jealous, I see. Maybe if I curled my lip. How's this? 'Frankly, Scarlett, I don't give a—what do you think? No?" Viktor's eyes lost their humor as he took the chair opposite his friend. "Come, Rolf, what's eating you? Ah, I see that you have drained your glass!" He produced the silver flask. "Here, this should take the edge off your troubles."

Rolf shook his head.

Viktor took a drink himself and leaned across the table. "You must shake it off, my friend. Every time it is the same. It is true, we lost many friends today, but we are warriors! Every one of us is dead already, right?"

He chuckled sardonically, took a long pull from the flask, screwed on the little cap, and returned it to his jacket. "I am told we scored a great victory today," he said, wiping his mouth with a deft flip of his moustache. "The men think you are the Second Coming."

The squadron leader looked across the table, an unwavering coldness in his eyes.

Viktor eased back into his chair.

"A great victory, you say?" Rolf grunted. "Then you have heard that they bombed Schweinfurt?"

Viktor's face clouded momentarily. "Yes, Specht told me. He also told me that we'd shot down over sixty Fat Autos."

"The bombers keep coming, Viktor."

"Yes, and we keep shooting them out of the sky, don't we? These Americans are crazy." Viktor brightened. "Come, my friend, have another glass of beer and put thoughts of the war behind you. Soon you will think only of nothing."

"Is that why we fight, Viktor? So we can think of nothing?"

Viktor chuckled. "No, Rolf, we are fighting for God, country, and the Führer, of course!" He leaned forward conspiratorially. "Not in that order, mind you."

"God?"

"Yes, God. And I have it on good authority that he is still on our side."

"Is that why they keep coming with their bombers—the Americans by day, the British by night? We shoot them down and still they darken the skies like a plague of locusts, making rubble of our cities—Regensburg, Schweinfurt, Ploesti, Hamburg." He struggled on Hamburg and gazed into the hearth.

Viktor took out a pack of Chesterfields and offered him a cigarette. Rolf shook his head.

"They're American."

Rolf stared into the fire.

Viktor lit a cigarette and shook out the match. "I had friends in Hamburg too, Rolf. Really, you must—"

The squadron leader looked briefly at him.

"I'm sorry," Viktor apologized, meaning it. "I know it's not the same. It was a foolish thing to say."

Suddenly an accordion blared over the crowd. The soldiers in the adjoining room began to sing enthusiastically. They were standing now with their arms draped around the girls and one another, everyone swaying to the music and singing.

Viktor watched them, tapping his foot to the music. He patted the table with his hand. A smile spread over his face. "I think I am in love," he said, observing a pretty brunette serving the table across the aisle. "What do you think, Rolf? Does she not take your breath away? I think I will marry her."

He glanced over at Rolf to see if he had heard, then back at the brunette who was leaving with a tray of dishes. Viktor frowned briefly, then waved his head with the singers in the other room. He smoked his cigarette and tapped his fingers on the table. He looked over at Rolf. "Specht said you scored four kills today."

Rolf looked at him, distracted. "Pardon?"

"The Group Commander. He said you scored four kills."

"Ah, yes, four kills," the squadron leader repeated without emotion. He grunted. "And tomorrow it will be another four. And the day after, four more."

"I should be so fortunate, my lucky friend," Viktor chuckled. "Today I shot down a third of an airplane. A third. They actually credit me with a third. How can you shoot down only a third of an airplane, I would like to know? Some genius in the High Command, no doubt, who made his living as a butcher before the war has it all figured out. 'I'll take a third of an airplane, if you please, sir. Just the wings—leave the undercarriage, if you don't mind, they've too much gristle. I'll be in tomorrow for the fuselage.' *Paperhangers*," he growled. He tapped his ash into the tray.

Rolf twirled his glass in his hand.

"Still, we should be proud of our boys today," Viktor perked, watching the singers again. He slapped his knee. "It was something, wasn't it? And those 110s from the 26th were something, I tell you."

Rolf set the glass smartly on the table and pushed it away from him. "We need more fighters, Viktor. Fighters! General Galland *must* persuade the Reich Marshal that we need more fighters, or we shall lose the war."

Viktor shook his head. "What am I going to do with you? He tried, remember? Göring laughed at him. He said it was—how did he put it?— 'harebrained, flabby defeatism.' That's it. No, my friend, the Führer wants more bombers, and so the Führer will get more bombers."

"Bombers," the squadron leader spat contemptuously. "We cannot defend our homeland with bombers. The Führer thinks we are still fighting the Czechs."

"All right then, this is what I will do. I will place a call to the Führer tomorrow morning and tell him, 'look, Adolf, Rolf—you remember Rolf, hero of the Reich?—well, Rolf is upset that you do not order more fighters for him.' And then the Führer will say, 'not Captain Rolf Schiller, scorer of one hundred and ninety victories?' And I will say, 'the very same. Only he has shot down four more planes and he is upset about it.' And the Führer will say, 'I will speak to Reich Marshal Göring at once, and tell that fatso to order more fighters so Rolf won't be such a wet blanket when he is out on liberty with his best friend.'"

"You're drunk."

"Almost. Ah, if only the paperhangers in Berlin would let us run the show for a while, we'd have the war shaped up in a couple of weeks, wouldn't we?" He took a drag from his cigarette and blew several rings of smoke over their heads. "Perhaps they should make us generals, Rolf. What do you think? I think it is my most brilliant idea."

The squadron leader allowed a smile. "They may have to," he said. "Lately the generals seem to be dropping like flies."

"*Flies?* Nonsense!" Viktor laughed. "Like bombs, you mean! Churchill is bombing us with generals."

"You're crazy."

"Yes," Viktor agreed. "So let us enjoy the evening, Rolf. Eat, drink, and be merry! Live a little while you may. It is Oktoberfest! Tomorrow they will make us generals and we can shoot ourselves to show our loyalty to more bombers."

Viktor laughed, and Rolf chuckled at him.

Viktor said, "Now I wish to get drunk with no further interruptions from wet blankets." He looked over at Werner and raised two fingers. However, the proprietor did not see him, since he was demonstrating an aerial tactic to two more obliging young pilots.

Viktor waved to one of the waitresses. "Two Atkien, please!" he called across the room. "Hurry, my lovely! We are dying of thirst."

Soon a Rubenesque girl, dressed in a peasant outfit, with a round, red face and two long blond braids that wound around her head, jiggled through the crowd balancing two large frosty steins on a tray.

"Two beers," she smiled as she set the steins down, the thick foam sliding down the barrels onto the table. "Did you win the war today, my heroes?"

"I had a most glorious victory today, Liebchen," Viktor said, stubbing out his cigarette. "I shot down a third of an airplane. It was a fine accomplishment."

The girl wrinkled her nose.

Viktor let out a bark of laughter and pulled her to his lap. "I am going all weak inside, looking at you!" he said melodramatically. "You are so lovely! Isn't she lovely, Rolf? Tell me that you are not married, Liebchen, or I shall kill myself."

"You must wait until you are a general first," Rolf grinned.

"You are right! And I would be loyal to the end." Viktor gazed dreamily at the girl. "How can Germany lose with such beauty to inspire great courage, Rolf? Tomorrow I shall shoot down two-thirds of an airplane for my lovely girl here!"

"I think she is the Führer's secret weapon," Rolf suggested.

Viktor looked at him, puzzled for a moment. He laughed, "Yes, yes! That is it!"

The girl looked at Rolf. "How many planes did you shoot down today, Captain?"

Viktor was aghast. "Him? Pay no attention to this lucky show-off," he scowled, waving off the question. "Anyone can shoot down four planes when they line up in front of you. But to shoot down only a third of a plane—this takes incredible skill."

"I must say," the girl smiled.

Rolf sipped his beer, his eyes now glittering with humor.

"Do not look at this wet blanket anymore, Liebe," Viktor said, tracing his finger around the girl's ear. "Don't you think that I look like Clark Gable in my new jacket?"

"I think you are crazy in the head," the girl said. She pushed away from the flier with a giggle, and flounced across the room.

Viktor patted his heart, looking after her. "That is what we are fighting for, my friend. Never forget it."

Rolf crooked an eyebrow at him. "A moment ago we were fighting for God, country, and the—"

"Yes, but now we are fighting for women. Women first, remember that! First, last, and always!"

"And the Führer?"

"He can find his own women."

Both men roared, drank their beers, and watched the soldiers singing in the other room. The volume of laughter and singing in the place swelled to a mind-numbing pitch. The accordion blared. People danced happily. The diners bent forward and shouted to one another. Viktor danced with several girls while Rolf watched him from the table and laughed. Waitresses hurried back and forth with trays of beer.

Viktor came over to the table with the pretty waitress and a brunette. "Come, Rolf," he implored. "This pretty has no one to celebrate with."

The brunette looked at Rolf.

"No, that is all right," Rolf said. "You dance with her, Viktor. There is enough of you to go around, I see."

"This is true. But come, Rolf. For tonight. Eat, drink, and be merry, for tomorrow we die!" He grinned sloppily.

Rolf danced with the girl. The music was loud, and everyone was up from their tables, moving to the driving cadence. The floor was crowded with people, their faces flushed with celebration.

The brunette looked up at Rolf and said over the noise, "You are a fine dancer, Captain Schiller."

"Rolf. Please call me Rolf. The other is too formal."

"You are a fine dancer, Rolf," she said, smiling at him. "And you are a gentleman."

He was bumped against her. He smiled. "For a sardine, you mean?"

She laughed. She was pretty, he saw. Her blue eyes sparkled up at him from time to time as they danced. The music swelled, reached a feverish pitch, then all at once the tempo slowed and the mood flattened and changed. Several people went back to their tables, feeling it change. The soldiers began to sing "Deutschland über Alles" with much feeling. People's heads moved up and down across the tavern like gentle rollers, everyone sang, and some had tears running down their faces. The gaiety was gone now; only a fierce devotion of patriotism remained.

Rolf, sitting once again by the hearth, began to sing along with everyone under his breath, only mouthing the words of the song to an even slower tempo. His hand tapped the rhythm on the table. He sipped at another beer, and his eyes were dark and wistful, looking faraway and growing misty in thought as he sang the proud anthem of his people.

Viktor, his face flushed from vigorous dancing, returned to the table, sat down with a jolt and lit a cigarette. His tunic was opened at the neck. He fanned himself as he lustily eyed the Rubenesque blond across the room. She was wearing his leather flight jacket and, as she carried a tray of empties into the kitchen, she cast him an alluring glance. Viktor blew a stream of smoke at the ground like a bull about to charge. "It is good to be alive!" he roared, slapping the table. "She cannot keep her eyes off of me!" He grinned at Rolf. "We are heroes of the Reich, you and me, my friend. We are gods! That brunette is something. What was her name?"

Rolf did not hear him.

Just then the door to the tavern opened and five men entered the room. It seemed a bit of night fog fingered in after them. A few heads turned, and then a few more, and finally there was a sweep of heads and the music broke. A hush fell over the tavern. One of the men stepped forward as though the silence had been his cue.

He was a smallish man with sharp aquiline features and neatly combed black hair. He wore the crisp, black uniform of the SS. Looking over the crowd with an arrogant sweep of his eyes, he began to pull off his gray gloves one finger at a time.

"What have we here?" Viktor said.

Rolf grunted.

"Why don't you invite them over to our table, Rolf?" Viktor suggested. "We could ask them how Herr Himmler is getting along. I hear he is just miserable until he's had a dozen Jews for breakfast."

The people continued abruptly with their conversations, everyone behaving as though they weren't aware of the SS men. The music resumed, although it was somewhat dispirited, and the soldiers and girls returned to their seats, the happy abandonment gone from their faces. A tension clung to the air that the music couldn't release.

Werner went over to the SS officer and asked him if he and his men wished to be seated.

Lieutenant Klemmer, wearing his black cap canted rakishly to one side so that the bill shaded his left eye, waved him off with a flick of his gloves. Still looking over the crowd he produced a photograph, which he showed the proprietor.

Werner took the photo and angled it to the light.

Lieutenant Klemmer slapped his boot impatiently with a brass-ended swagger stick as he continued looking over the crowd.

"Very dramatic," Viktor whispered. "The skull insignia on his hat is quite a dramatic touch, don't you think?"

Rolf watched Klemmer intently. An image came into his mind of a small rooster. Then Werner pointed across the room to a shadowy niche where two men in civilian attire, one old and gray-haired, and one younger, were bent over a small corner table. He saw a panic go over their faces.

"Arrest those two!" Klemmer ordered his sergeant. Four soldiers started across the room.

The two men in the corner jumped to their feet with a clatter of chairs, and began running toward the rear door of the tavern. People everywhere at once dropped to the floor, so that only the two men running across the room were exposed. A rifle crashed and the younger man bucked, his arms and head bowed sharply back as he crumpled sideways to the floor.

The older man spun around and threw his hands into the air. "Do not shoot!" he cried, his eyes darting back and forth at the faces of the soldiers as they came at him with their rifles.

Two of the soldiers took him by his arms. Indignant, the man demanded, "What is the meaning of this? I have done nothing wrong."

The soldiers paid him no mind.

Lieutenant Klemmer adjusted the bill of his cap as he made his way through the crowd, nodding his head and excusing himself politely. His spit-shined jackboots drummed over the wooden floor with martial authority. The people rose to their feet and cleared a path for him, then angled their heads to see the dead man on the floor.

"Excuse me, pardon me," Lieutenant Klemmer said, holding his hands up in a conciliatory manner. "Thank you, thank you." Two of the soldiers backed the crowd away from the body with their rifles.

The older man spoke rapidly to the SS lieutenant as he passed in front of him. "There has been some mistake, Lieutenant."

Lieutenant Klemmer stopped beside the dead man, careful not to step in the pool of blood spreading out from the head. He took note of the way the head lay against an out-thrust arm. "He looks asleep," he said to one of his men. He nudged the body with his boot, looked at the wound at the base of the skull, and grunted amusedly. It had been a fine shot. "He's quite dead, I think." He commanded two of his men to carry the body outside, then he pulled the photograph from his coat pocket and went over to the older man.

The older man looked at the photograph, looked back quickly into the pale blue eyes of the SS lieutenant, and began a rapid defense. His lips trembled between the words. Klemmer merely held the photograph beside the man's face, oblivious to his words, looked back and forth from face to photograph, then told the soldiers holding the man to take him outside.

The older man's eyes grew wild. He made an impassioned appeal to various faces in the crowd: He had fought in the first war and been decorated; his loyalties to the Fatherland were unquestionable; he would show them his medals. The people looked away as he passed by. One of the soldiers opened the door. The older man went limp, and the soldiers were forced to carry him.

"That is all, good people," Lieutenant Klemmer said, smiling pleasantly at the crowd as he pulled on his gloves. "Please forgive the intrusion, and do continue on with your celebration." He nodded courteously to the pretty ladies along the way, smiled at one of the younger soldiers, then drew up sharply when a man stepped out of the shadows into his path.

The SS officer started. Then seeing the rank and the flat-eyed stare of the man wearing it, he clicked his heels in the characteristic Nazi salute. "Heil Hitler!"

"Heil Hitler," Captain Rolf Schiller returned vaguely. He was standing with his feet slightly apart, his left foot pushed in front of the other in a boxer's stance.

Viktor gaped incredulously. "What are you doing, Rolf?"

Ignoring him, Rolf demanded, "What is the meaning of this demonstration, Lieutenant? This is a tavern, not a shooting gallery. There are women and civilians here."

The congenial look narrowed from Klemmer's eyes. "This is none of your concern, Captain," he said coolly. "It concerns the SS. I suggest you return to your drink, and there will be no further trouble."

"Trouble? Are you threatening me, Lieutenant?"

The SS man chuckled.

Rolf doubled his fists. "I ought to break you in half."

"No, Rolf," Viktor said, stepping in front of him. He grinned at the SS man. "Pay no attention to this wet blanket. He's had too much to drink.

You know how these heroes are—just blowing off a little steam. Isn't that right, Captain?"

Rolf ignored him.

Lieutenant Klemmer glanced at his name tag. "So you are the Squadron Leader Schiller I've heard so much about. How fortunate for me to make your acquaintance. It is indeed an honor." He smiled and bowed smartly, clicking his heels.

Rolf stared at him coldly.

A change went over Klemmer's face. "Perhaps some afternoon we might have a schnapps together in the officer's club, Captain. You are from Berlin, I believe. You have family there . . . a *sister?*"

Rolf's fingers were suddenly around the man's throat. Lieutenant Klemmer choked in astonishment. He clawed at Rolf's viselike grip on his Adam's apple.

Viktor pulled at his arms. "Rolf! What are you doing?" he yelled. "You're killing him! Rolf!"

Rolf released him suddenly. "You dare threaten my family, you little cockroach!"

Klemmer gaped at him in disbelief. Rubbing his throat, he coughed, "You . . . you meant to *kill* me!"

Rolf grunted.

Klemmer regained his composure, shot a proud look at the roomful of astonished faces. Two SS soldiers appeared behind him. "You should have killed me, Captain."

Viktor stepped in front of Rolf. "No, Rolf. No!"

The corners of Lieutenant Klemmer's mouth curled upward with a trace of a smile. "You have had your little moment, Captain." He clicked his heels and saluted. "Heil Hitler."

Rolf snarled, "Go to—"

"Heil Hitler," Viktor interjected quickly.

"Good evening, Captain, Lieutenant," Klemmer said, nodding to each man respectively. He turned smartly on his heels and strode out of the tavern, slapping his palm with the swagger stick.

Moments later there was a muffled shot.

A jolt went through the room. Everyone watched the door in the awful quiet.

"That is all," Werner said brightly. He ordered a boy to mop up the floor, then he moved quickly from table to table, smiling as though nothing had happened. "Come, come, everyone!" he boomed. "A free round of drinks! It is Oktoberfest! It is a time for celebration!"

A tentative buzz crackled over the tavern.

"Ja, ja, that is it," the proprietor thundered. "Laugh! Dance!"

A pilot stood with a raised stein of beer and toasted the day's air victory by Jagdgeschwader 11. People raised their glasses and toasted the brilliance of the Luftwaffe. Praised the Fatherland. Hailed the Führer. A shout went up. The music blared and the dead were forgotten.

"You say that God is on our side, Viktor?" Rolf grunted, still looking at the door. "I wonder whose side we are on."

After leaving the tavern, Captain Rolf Schiller turned on the switch in his room at Jever Aerodrome, the light suddenly harsh and glaring off the gray-painted brick walls. He stood for a moment leaning against the doorjamb and staring at the Spartan furnishings of his quarters.

There was a single bed against the right wall with a wall clock over the bed reading 0230. A photograph of Reich Marshal Göring, presenting him with the Knight's Cross with Oak Leaves after scoring his 100th air victory, hung next to the clock. A window on the left wall opened to the airstrip. The room was cold and smelled of autumn.

He closed the door behind him and his eyes went automatically to the framed photograph that sat atop the table beside the bed. He walked over to the window and looked outside at the dark shapes of the hangars lined across the strip. The trees beyond were sharp against the moon, and everything for miles was blacked out against enemy bombers, but all was quiet and peaceful now. He stared at the hangars for a long while, allowing his head to clear. Then he took a deep breath, closed the window and pulled the blackout shade over it.

Rolf walked over to his bed, sat down, and began to take off his shoes. He sat up quickly to slow down the spinning in his head. *Too much to drink,* he chided himself and shook his head ruefully. That Viktor. He'll be wrecked tomorrow.

He glanced over at the framed photograph on the table, picked it up, and stared at it for a long while. Darkness seemed to creep from the corners of the room and close around him. He lay back on his bed and held the picture face down on his chest, his hands folded over the frame as though it kept the room from spinning off its axis, while he gazed at the gray isolation of the ceiling.

5 ★★★★

The moon broke through the clouds and shone into the cabin. Colette suddenly looked out through the window at the dark shape of the barn across the yard. But she did not see the barn. For just a moment she saw a bright green meadow of flowers running down to a river, and there was a tree with large branches hanging over the river, shading it. Beneath the tree a blanket was spread out with food. Her mother was preparing a meal of bread and cheese and wine, and her father was sitting next to her laughing, drinking the wine. Her mother slapped his hand away as though the two of them were lovers in a public place. Jean-Claude and François had tied a knot at the end of a rope hanging off a tree branch and were taking turns swinging, yodeling boyishly. She saw the fierceness of their faces as they thumped their chests while they swung out over the river.

In that moment she could feel the cool of the river on her feet, hitting the back of her calves, the mud oozing between her toes as she waded along the bank hunting crawfish in the reeds. She could even smell the fragrance of the grass and flowers breezing down over the river, and the thought of that day blossomed a sweet nostalgia in her and raised a wistful smile to her face. She held onto it as long as she could, but the weight of it was too great, and the dream grew sadder and sadder as she came back to her hands in the pail of soapy dishwater.

Someone touched her shoulder and she jumped. "Oh!"

Jean-Claude chuckled. "I've startled you!"

"You should not do that when I have a plate in my hand," she scolded.

"Didn't mean to spoil your thoughts," he grinned, and handed her his dishes. "That meal was sinful," he said. "I shall have to say three Hail Marys and an Act of Contrition for that meal."

"So much for your sainthood."

He folded his hands in prayer and made a pious face toward the ceiling. "Bless me, Father, for I have sinned. I did not know that my sister was some she-devil and would tempt me to such gluttony." He kissed his fingers. "But—ahh!—such sweet gluttony!"

She slapped his hand. "You are terrible."

"Did you miss me?"

"Terribly."

"That's my girl. Now, a penny for your thoughts."

"What thoughts?"

"I was watching you. Your face is quite expressive."

She looked down at her hand holding the plate half-immersed in the soapy water. She chuckled as she ran a dishcloth over the plate. "I was just thinking of the river," she said.

"Ahh!" he said.

"Mama fixing our lunch and Papa laughing. You and François swinging on the rope and your silly yodeling."

"Yodeling? What yodeling? We were never yodeling. We were practicing our Tarzan yells, like Johnny Weismuller." He grunted. "What do girls know of yodeling!"

"I miss her, Jean-Claude."

He allowed her words to settle. "Yes. We all do." Then he looked at her. "You're crying."

She wiped her eyes with the back of her hand. "It's silly of me. This war. I hate it. All the killing."

"The killing is necessary. You know that."

"And Mama?"

"Because of Mama and all the other wickedness."

She said nothing.

He patted her back. "Colette. Dear Colette. The war will not go on forever, now that the Americans are in it. It will be over soon, you'll see." He grinned at her. "Enough of this sadness and gloom! Soon you will be singing and dancing and enjoying life!"

"Do you promise?"

"Would I lie to you?" he asked. "Do not answer that question." He looked at her. "Is that a smile I see?"

"You and your faces."

"Yes! You see? Already you are smiling. I saw it clearly with my magic eyes and already it has come to be."

"You are silly."

"The silliest."

"And love," she said. "What do your magic eyes see of love?"

"They see that love is blind."

"Do not be silly, Jean-Claude. Tell me truly."

"Love is the easiest to see, if one has eyes to see," he said. "And there is no silliness in it. Some day you will meet a lucky man and make him a fine wife."

She shook her head and smiled. "Resistance fighter, you mean."

"Correction: You will make some lucky man a fine wife and Maquisard. You shall have many young Maquisards to take care of, and diapers to clean, and floors to scrub, and he is a crazy man if he does not worship your cooking."

"This man sounds like much work."

Jean-Claude shrugged. "You take the good with the bad. One must be practical. You cannot live on love alone."

"I would like to try it."

"You are a dreamer."

"And you are a silly," she smiled, happy that her brothers were home and the family together again. "Where shall I find such a man that I must cook and clean for, Jean-Claude? You forget that we do not live in Paris, and I do not often get out of the mountains for the dances."

"Major Dubois is fond of you."

"And I am fond of him too," she said. "He is like a brother to me."

"I don't think he sees you as a sister. He is a good man, Colette. A bit formal perhaps."

"But I do not love him," she said. "When I marry it must be for love and not for expedience."

"There is no love in wartime," he said very practically. "There is only a hedge against loneliness. There are distractions but never love." He looked at her suddenly. "Listen to me. I'm sorry, Colette. I'm tired. When I get tired I say stupid things." Jean-Claude went back to the table.

කං

Colette wrapped a knitted shawl around her shoulders, cracked the door of the cabin, and looked back into the room. Her father and brothers were talking heatedly about Uncle Guillaume and matters of the war. She was very tired of the war. She slipped outside into the chilly autumn night. She walked across the yard, heard the livestock moving inside the barn and the chickens in their coop, and, going beyond the barn a few yards, she cut up sharply along the narrow path that wound up through the pines. She found the flat white stone that marked her mother's grave, the stone reflecting a ghostly luminance in the moonlight. There were no flowers on the grave since the summer flowers were all gone now, but it was smooth and great care had gone into its maintenance. She crossed herself, whispered a few prayers, then crossed herself again.

"Hello, Mama," she said after a time of looking down at the grave. "It is me, Colette. Jean-Claude and François have come home safely, isn't that wonderful?" She smiled. "That Jean-Claude never ceases to make me laugh. He can be such a silly. Do you remember the faces he makes, Mama? Sometimes I think he will never grow up. He tells me that Major Dubois is fond of me. You remember Major Dubois—Jean-Claude says that I would make a fine wife for him. Isn't that just like men? What do men know of what is good for women?

"You will be happy to know that Uncle Maurice has gone safely to England. I too am happy for him. Perhaps he will cook for General De-Gaulle. Uncle Guillaume has decided to stay, however. But do not worry about him, Mama, he is a smart man, as you know. He will be fine, I am sure. Still, I will pray for him."

She stood for a long time talking to the grave of her mother. She recounted many times they had shared together, the good times and the bad times, and told her mother how much she missed her, and how she looked forward to seeing her in heaven. She was not afraid of dying, she said. Sometimes she even looked forward to it. Is that wrong? she asked. She took a deep breath and stood for a long time saying nothing. Looking down through the trees, she could see the yellow light flickering through the window of the cabin. Finally she said, "Mama, did you marry Papa for love or for expedience? I think love. Jean-Claude says there is no love in war. If this is true I would rather die and come home to see you and Jesus." She sighed deeply. "I'm so lonely, Mama. Did you ever know such loneliness?"

6 ★★★

"No, no, monsieur, do not shoot. We are not the Boche!" one of the men said in heavily accented English. "We are Maquis."

"Maquis?"

"*Oui.* The Underground . . . *l'resistance.*"

"You're French?"

"No! No! Belgique—Maquis."

Billy lowered his pistol. "You sound French."

"I assure you, *mon ami,* we are not."

Billy shouldered his pistol and began to climb out of the big sycamore. "Thank God."

"*Oui.*"

"Are they gone?" Billy asked, after dropping the last length to the ground.

"*Oui.* They search the hills—*Comment dit-on?*" The Belgian made a gesture indicating the northeast.

Billy followed his point and nodded his understanding. "How did you know I was in the tree?"

"The Boche are not the only ones to see your parachute."

There were five of them. Each of them wore a dark pullover and trousers and a dark shapeless cap of some kind, and each carried a British Sten gun. Billy couldn't make out their faces in the light, just their shapes; all five of them were shorter and stockier than himself. *Like five large trolls,* he thought. The men, or trolls, stood as still as five black boulders, only the whites of their eyes catching the moon now and then betrayed any sign of life. They stared silently at him.

The one who spoke English smelled of old, rank wine and perspiration—close to the smell of old whiskey and sweat on the ranchers back home.

The man who had addressed him was the leader, Billy assumed, and he stretched out his hand to him like he would back home in Montana.

"Second Lieutenant Billy Hochreiter," he said. "I guess you know I'm an American?"

The stocky Belgian paid no attention to his hand, nor to his question. "We must hurry," he said curtly. "The Boche will not be fooled long." The man started away at a trot and the others followed, leaving Billy standing alone in the clearing.

"Hey! Wait up!" He caught up to the leader. "Where are you taking me?" he asked. The Belgian appeared not to have heard him. Billy repeated his question.

The Belgian grunted. "You come."

The men swept Billy along at a fast clip; the dark, faceless men on all sides of him trotted short-stridedly, like a small herd of wild boars. The trees fell behind him in a flickering procession. The moon jumped in and out of the canopy of leaves and flashed on the men's faces, showing their dark eyes ranging over the path. Billy's mind struggled to claim some order, some perspective from which to view himself, but things were moving too fast. He got the feeling he was in a dream, with everything moving just beyond his consciousness, so strangely unreal.

Meadows opened before them and the men slowed warily, scenting for danger as an animal might when approaching a water hole. One of the men would run ahead on silent cue, only to return minutes later with a grunt or a hand gesture that everyone but Billy seemed immediately to understand. And then they would be off again, moving quickly.

Rain had brushed over the fields and low hills, muddying the ground, but now the moon shone glistening on the grassy slopes. They headed southeast for about two hours, stopping every so often for a brief rest before moving on.

During one of the stops the men gave Billy some goat cheese and bread, and a swallow of bitter-tasting wine from a leather bota. The men were very businesslike in their demeanor, Billy thought. They did not speak to him. They did not look at him, but he felt their eyes. He felt remote from them and yet connected, as though he was a valuable commodity. Smiling awkwardly, he offered the men chocolate from his survival kit, but they refused.

"American cigarette?" one of the men asked abruptly.

The question startled Billy, since no one but the leader had thus far spoken to him. He shook his head. "I've got some snuff though," he said. "Want some?" He pulled out a tin of Copenhagen and offered it to the man.

The man looked at it. "American cigarette?" he asked again.

Billy shook his head and put the tin away.

Again they were off. For hours, it seemed, the five trolls kept up the incredible pace, skirting small farms and towns, cutting across plowed fields and vineyards, fording streams, crossing narrow country roads, and ducking every hint of danger. So far they had not seen a single German. But there were plenty of Germans out scouring the countryside for him, Billy knew; he could see it in the faces of the men.

When at last they came to a broad, smooth-flowing river the leader signalled the men to stop in the shadow of a drainage ditch.

"*La Meuse*," the Belgian whispered to Billy.

"Oh," Billy said. He glanced over at the river and watched the moon reflected peacefully on its surface.

There was a rickety wooden bridge above them, shining from the rain, that went across the river. The road leading to it wound away into some trees on the other side.

Upon the Belgian's signal, one of the men climbed the incline of the ditch and, stooping to his knees, peered down the road both ways, north and south. Then he aimed a flashlight to the south and clicked it once long, and then three short clicks. A moment later, a pair of headlights winked twice quickly from the umbrage of the tree line across the bridge. The man hurried down the ditch and said something to the leader.

The Belgian touched Billy's arm. "*Vien*. Come with me."

Billy followed him up the slope, glancing back at the rest of the group. "Aren't they coming with us?"

"Do you see men by truck?" the Belgian asked, pointing across the bridge.

"What truck?"

"By trees," the Belgian indicated.

Billy looked at the long, dark line of trees and saw the tiny silhouettes of two men standing beside a truck. "Yes."

"You must go," the man said. "The French will take you now."

"The French?"

"*Oui*." He indicated the trees. "France. *Dieu vous protètge*."

Billy glanced at the two men by the truck. Then he turned back to the Belgian to thank him, but the squat leader and the four other trolls were gone into the night like they were never there. He blinked into the darkness, wondering if indeed it had all been a dream. The headlights winked at him from the tree line.

Billy climbed onto the road and looked in both directions. The road was clear, darkly bright, and lonesome-looking as the moon peered through a break in the clouds. He ran to the bridge and, as his feet pounded over the old, wet wooden planks, he could feel the cool air rising off the river, smelling like a river in autumn should smell, all bright and sweetly pungent. It reminded him of home and of crossing the Yellowstone into town on a Saturday night.

"Come quickly, monsieur," one of the two men said as he reached the trees. "The Boche, they are everywhere looking for you."

In the moonlight Billy could see that one of the two silhouettes was a man of medium height in his early forties, and the other one a boy, maybe fourteen or fifteen years old, and half a head shorter. Billy saw the likeness of the older man in the face of the younger. They were dressed like farmers, both wearing dark coats and berets. Neither of them carried weapons that he could see.

"This way, monsieur," the older one said, indicating the rear of the truck.

Billy thought to introduce himself but checked the impulse and quickly climbed over the wooden rails and down into the truck bed. There were two black and white Holsteins feeding at a trough behind the cab. The cows looked up at him, each with a mouthful of hay, then went back to their feeding.

"I am sorry, monsieur," the man said through the slats. "But it is all that could be arranged on such short notice."

"That's all right," Billy said with a grin. "They look better than some of the girls I've dated."

The humor didn't translate to the man. He and the boy climbed into the truck without making comment.

Billy shrugged his shoulders then found a seat in the rear corner of the bed, away from the cows. The engine turned, caught, and the truck lurched forward out of the trees and swung, rattling, up onto the road. He put his hand down to steady himself, grimaced when he felt a warm, wet clump ooze between his fingers. He frowned at the Holsteins. The Holsteins paid him no mind. He shook his hand then wiped the residue on the wooden rail.

The truck rumbled down the road, following the course of the Meuse, fields opening now and then between the banks and the road. The cows continued to eat, stomping their hooves and swishing their tails contentedly. Billy watched the stars through holes in the clouds, thinking of the nights he had lain awake, staring at those same stars from his bedroom window in Columbus, Montana, and hearing the cattle lowing in the fields.

A stream of thoughts began to trickle through his mind. He tried to ignore them, but the one of his mother sitting on their front porch was strong in him—she would rock slowly back and forth before the steady descent of the sun, snapping beans and praying for each of her children, smiling her Irish blessings upon her brood. The heaviness of the image pushed him so far down into the abyss of loneliness that the darkness covered him with sleep.

He started awake when the truck ground suddenly into a lower gear.

"Mon Dieu!" the Frenchman cried. "Monsieur, hide yourself quickly," he called back to Billy. "The Boche are just ahead."

Billy peered down the road through the rails and saw an SS unit arriving at an intersection, about a quarter-mile ahead. There were several troop carriers, and soldiers were piling out of one of them. "Can we turn around?"

"No, no, monsieur, it is certain they have seen us." The man looked gravely ahead.

The boy looked over at his father's taut face. The father glanced at him and patted his knee.

The SS captain, a stoutly built man wearing wire-rimmed spectacles, held up his hand. Soldiers carrying rifles stood next to him. The truck slowed, then ground to a halt. The soldiers quickly surrounded it on all sides. The officer stepped forward and shined a flashlight on the driver's face.

"Bonsoir," the Frenchman said. His eyes twitched in the glare of the light and he shielded them with his hand. "What is the trouble?"

"Kindly turn off your engine," the officer demanded in French.

"Yes, sir."

"Your papers, please."

"Yes." The Frenchman produced identification papers from his coat pocket and handed them to the German officer. "Is there some trouble?"

The boy stared intently at his father's face.

The captain took the papers, read them carefully in the light, checking the signatures and the photograph, noticed the star-shaped birthmark beneath the left eye in the photograph, then shined the light on the man's face and studied it. "What are you doing on the road at this hour?"

The Frenchman, forcing a smile, jerked his thumb toward the rear of the truck. "We are taking these to Vouziers to sell at the market. It is in the papers."

The German watched him closely, glanced at the papers, then he shined the light on the boy. "Who is this?"

The Frenchman smiled. "Henri. This is my son Henri. It is in the papers."

"Step outside," the captain ordered.

"We have done nothing," the Frenchman objected. "We must hurry to the market before dawn."

"The sooner you step outside, the sooner you will be on your way." The officer addressed three of his men in German.

Each of the men took a different part of the truck. One opened the hood and inspected it for hidden contraband; another poked around inside the cab then peered under the vehicle; the third climbed the wooden rails and shined a flashlight over the floorboards that were splattered with manure. The light swept over the cows and fixed on the feeding trough.

"Nothing here but cows," he called to the officer.

The boy glanced quickly at his father.

"You see?" the Frenchman chuckled nervously. "We are hiding nothing."

"You did not search inside the bed," the captain growled.

Grumbling, the soldier climbed down into the bed and pushed the cows away with his rifle. He was mindful of his feet. He began prodding the trough with his bayonet, lifting the hay like a fork and stabbing through to the wood. He went along the entire length of the trough, cursing at the floorboards. One of the Holsteins bawled plaintively and stamped her feet.

The Frenchman glared anxiously at the rear of his truck. His fingers folded and unfolded slowly. "If you told me what you were looking for, Captain, perhaps I could be of some help."

The SS captain ignored him.

The soldier climbed out of the bed and shook his head. "Nothing, Captain. Just cows."

The captain shined his light on the man's papers and then on his face, studying him once more carefully. "You are free to go," he said at last.

The Frenchman smiled, then he and his son climbed into the cab. "My papers," he nodded.

The captain handed the man his papers and waved him through. "*Guten Abend*," the Frenchman said to the officer, and he put the truck in gear. The truck rattled forward. The Frenchman nodded to the various groups of soldiers, then, passing through the intersection, he glanced over into the side mirror. He looked ahead on the road as the truck picked up speed.

"Where is he, Papa?" the boy whispered.

"I do not know."

"Do you think he believed the papers?"

"I think so."

A hundred yards or so beyond the intersection the road curved sharply around to the left. The truck followed the curve, slowing because of the wet surface, when the headlamps lighted a man springing up from the ditch onto the right-hand edge of the road, waving his arms. He looked ghoulish in the sudden glare of light.

"Papa!" the boy gasped.

The Frenchman slammed his foot on the brake and cranked the wheel to avoid hitting him. The truck shuddered and skidded sideways, and the two Holsteins slammed against the rails in the back. The man ran alongside the truck and swung up onto the running board.

"Don't slow down!" Billy said, crouching and looking back at the intersection.

The Frenchman steered the truck forward, upshifting, then accelerated smoothly. His lips were clamped shut, his eyes glaring straight ahead. He looked quickly into his side mirror then looked ahead on the road. "*Mon Dieu!* How did you get across the road?" he asked.

"Slicker'n a greased pig," Billy grinned, wiping the mud off his jacket.

"*Que dites-vous?*"

Billy said, "Let's just say I'm glad you didn't turn left back there or I'd be walking now."

The boy watched him climb back into the truck bed, then smiled at his father.

"*Mon Dieu! Mon Dieu!*" the Frenchman kept saying, wagging his head incredulously.

"*Oui,*" the boy said, and crossed himself.

⁂∞⁖

After the truck passed, the SS captain ordered a few of his men into positions at each of the four corners of the intersection. He had them set up a big MP 34 machine gun facing north and a troop carrier on the east and west corners to secure the roadblock.

He paused, took off his spectacles, and wiped them carefully with his handkerchief. He put them back on and began pacing around the circumference of the intersection. He paused at one point and looked down at the ground in thought. Something was troubling him.

The purr of a motorcycle climbed on the wind. He turned, and for a moment watched a single, jiggling slit of light coming toward the intersection.

The motorcycle with sidecar throttled down, the two riders leaning into the turn as it swung around the intersection. The headlamp glared off the faces of men and vehicles. The officer was standing by the edge of the road near the west corner of the junction, and as the light swung past him, something below him in the shadows alongside the road caught his eyes. He bent over to inspect it.

"Give me a flashlight," he ordered his sergeant.

He directed the light along the drainage ditch to where it dead-ended at a right angle to the ditch following the crossroad. Running north and south under the road was a cement culvert, about two feet in diameter, connecting to the ditch on the other side of the road. A trickle of muddy water ran through and spilled into the ditch.

The captain peered down the road the Frenchman had taken, the moon showing it a bright thread of silver winding away into the darkness. Once again he looked down at the culvert.

The motorcycle driver swung off the seat while the soldier seated in the sidecar waited, holding an MP 28 submachine gun. The driver raised his goggles, removed his gloves, and folded them neatly on the seat, then strode over to the captain and saluted. "Dispatches from headquarters, Captain," he said, handing him a canvas pouch.

The officer took the pouch and waved him off. The driver saluted and turned to leave.

"Corporal?"

"Yes, Captain."

"A moment, please."

"Yes, Captain."

The German officer peered down the road. "A truck carrying livestock passed through here a few minutes ago, Corporal. On the south road. I want you to catch up to it and make certain that there are only two people in it—a farmer and his son. If there is by chance a third man I want you to arrest the three of them."

The corporal glanced at his watch. "I have other dispatches to deliver, sir. I am on a tight schedule."

The captain's eyes flared. "You will obey my orders, Corporal."

The corporal saluted once again, clicking his heels. "Yes, Captain." Climbing onto the motorcycle, he pulled on his gloves and fixed his goggles over his eyes. The man in the sidecar looked up at him. The corporal shook his head, and gave the starter pedal a kick.

The SS captain folded his hands behind his back, and watched the motorcycle fishtail off the shoulder and onto the road, then disappear.

ॐॐ

Billy felt the road through the bed of the truck. The jarring motion and the smell of manure reminded him of home, and of hauling livestock to Billings. He readjusted his seat in the corner, settled back, and drew his knees up to his chest. The Holsteins were dark silhouettes and he could see their tails moving as they fed.

He turned suddenly, angling his head away from the wind, thinking he had heard something. There was nothing. He lowered his head onto his crossed arms and closed his eyes. He looked up. It was faint, but he definitely heard it this time, dipping in and out of the wind. He peered through the slats in the rail and saw nothing. Then he saw the slit of light rounding a bend, slicing through the darkness, and jiggling up the road at a high speed. The sound of the motorcycle ascended rapidly. He hurried up to the cab, squeezing past the cow on the left, and banged on the roof.

"Krauts!"

The boy looked back, then said something to his father. The Frenchman glanced into his door mirror and saw the motorcycle coming up fast and straight, closing, then swinging wide to pass on the left. The motorcycle pulled alongside the driver's side window, and the man in the sidecar signalled for him to pull over.

"We have been cleared," the Frenchman shouted out the window, jerking his thumb behind him.

The man in the sidecar gestured with his submachine gun.

The Frenchman nodded his head and downshifted. The motorcycle slowed alongside the truck. The two German soldiers climbed off the motorcycle. Both of them eyed the truck cab suspiciously. The soldier holding the submachine gun retrieved a flashlight from inside the sidecar, and they approached the truck.

"You will both step out of the cab," the corporal ordered.

"Pardon me?"

"I said, step out of the truck."

"I don't understand," the Frenchman protested. "We have already been cleared."

The German leveled the gun at him. "Now! *Schnell!*"

The Frenchman and his son obeyed.

The soldier with the flashlight said in German, "I will check the back." The corporal nodded. "Papers," he demanded of the Frenchman.

The man produced his papers and the corporal stepped in front of the motorcycle headlamp to read them.

The other soldier climbed up onto the bed of the truck. He swept the light over the two cows, into each of the far corners, then, sweeping it to the rear, caught the face of a man and a flash of metal. The German's eyes went wide. *"Mein Gott . . ."* But the protest was caught in his throat as the blade severed up through his vocal cords and into the cerebral cortex of his brain. Reeling off the truck, the dead soldier sprayed the air with a burst from his submachine gun.

The corporal at the front of the truck swung around, reaching for his pistol. *"Was ist los, Karl?"*

In one swift movement the Frenchman stepped forward behind the corporal, took hold of his forehead and chin, then gave the head a sharp upward twist to the right—his neck snapped with a sickening pop. The corporal clattered lifeless to the ground where the slit of the headlamp played across his eyes.

కూచి

While examining a set of footprints in the soft mud of the drainage ditch, the SS captain jerked his head toward the echoing report of the submachine gun. His pale blue eyes and Aryan brow narrowed into a scowl. *"Maquis!"*

కూచి

The Frenchman handed the submachine gun to his son. He went through the pockets of each of the Germans for papers and currency, then stripped them of their ammunition clips. "Help me, monsieur," he said to Billy, dragging one of the bodies to the edge of the road. Billy took the ankles of the other one and they rolled the bodies over into the ditch.

The boy gripped the submachine gun and clips and looked anxiously at his father.

The father went over to him. "You must take the American pilot to the place of rendezvous," he said in French. "Take the motorcycle!"

"No, Papa!"

The Frenchman took his son by the shoulders. "You must hurry, Henri. I will lead them away in the truck."

"No, Papa!"

"Henri!"

"No!"

"Henri!"

The boy looked at his father, tears spurting from his eyes. He threw his arms around his father's chest. "Oh, Papa, they will kill you."

Billy looked down at the ground.

"No, Henri," the father said softly, patting his son's back. "The Boche will not kill me. Now do as I say, and I will meet you at the rendezvous as planned."

"But, Papa . . . "

"Go quickly, son."

The boy looked up at his father, reeled away, and swung onto the motorcycle. He wiped his eyes and glared at the road ahead of him. Billy took the submachine gun from him and stepped down into the sidecar. He felt awful. He looked over at the boy's father. "Listen, I can make it on my own."

The Frenchman ignored him and climbed into the truck. "Tomorrow, Henri," he said. "Go with God." He engaged and disengaged the clutch. The cows shifted their weight as the truck lurched forward and rattled away down the road.

The boy started the motorcycle and followed his father for about two miles, where a small dirt road opened into some trees on the left and he took it.

Billy bounced in his seat, holding the German submachine gun in his hands. He looked over his shoulder until the trees and the night covered the road in darkness, then glanced up at the boy's face and saw in the moonlight that it was wet with tears.

7 ★★★

Dawn spread a gray line to the east. The gray grew over the fields and trees, wrapped over the low, bosomy hills dotted with grazing cattle and sheep, and continued west. A yoke of oxen trudged heavily along the river, towing a barge through the tattery mist. A small, sleepy boy slapped a willow switch against their rumps, and an oarsman on the barge leaned against the tiller. A tint of gold infused the gray and flourished over the countryside, and a cock crowed in each of a thousand different coops.

Billy opened his eyes and there was a girl staring at him. He sat up with a start and pointed his silver-plated Colt at her chest.

The girl lowered down the ladder a step. *"Je suis venue vous apportur de la nuriture,"* she said, indicating a basket of food.

Billy eyed her curiously as the sleep cleared from his mind. "Do you live here?" he asked. He realized he was still pointing his pistol at her and lowered it quickly. "Come back. I won't hurt you."

A moment later the girl peeked over the edge of the loft.

"I won't hurt you, see?" Billy shouldered his pistol. "Who are you?" he asked. "This ain't workin'," he said, then he asked, "What's—your—name?" very slowly and well pronounced.

The girl frowned at him. *"C'est pour vous,"* she said, pushing the basket and a bottle of wine toward him. She made a gesture with her fingers toward her mouth.

"For me?"

She was nineteen or twenty, Billy thought, looking at her. Maybe older. He could never judge the age of women. She was pretty, he saw clearly, with long, black hair that fell well below her shoulders and down her back, cheek bones that were high and beautifully mounded, and full and pouty-looking lips. Then there were the eyes. They were wideset and beautifully shaped and of the palest turquoise blue, reminding him of the color of a robin's eggs.

She stared at him a moment then lowered from his view. It seemed for just a moment after she had gone that the two almond-shaped orbs of turquoise light remained suspended in the air, still gazing at him.

"Wait a minute!" he called down after her. "Aren't you going to have some?" He heard the quiet patter of her feet, a door open and close, and she was gone.

A thick silence spread through the air and settled. Somewhere below him a mule brayed.

He glanced up at the roof as a spill of gray light poured in and shone down on his surroundings. A barn, he thought, and it came back to him how he and the boy had gotten here sometime during the night. He remembered three men, one older and two younger, but no girl. The rest of it was a blur, like when you were awakened by your father as a child and carried to bed. Everything felt disorienting and eerie.

Billy looked down at the basket, thinking of the girl, thinking of her watching him while he slept and wondering how long she had been watching him. He saw the unearthly blue of her eyes, that were even now burning their imprint on the retina of his mind.

He raised the red-and-white checkered cloth from the basket. Inside there was some bread, a spoon, and a little covered pot. He raised the lid of the pot and smelled the contents. It was a bouillabaisse stew; fish and potatoes and carrots and onions steamed up into his face. Suddenly he realized how hungry he was and quickly dispatched the meal. It was good. He could not believe how good it was as he soaked up the last of the stew with the bread. He drank the wine slowly, feeling it spread warmly through him as he glanced around the loft, following the slits of light knifing through the roof to the floor. I wonder if she'll come back, he thought, as he palmed the cork into place. He lay the bottle in the basket to one side of the little pot and folded the cloth over them.

He climbed down the ladder with the basket. Reaching the floor he brushed the bits of straw from his clothes, then went over to an open window. Trees stood all around the barn, he saw, tall blue-green pines, mostly, and some second-growth timber. The trees were shrouded in mist, and down below, a half-mile or so, he could just see a river threading southeast, running gray as gun metal as it snaked away into the mountains. He did not know if it was the Meuse or some other river, since the boy and he had crossed many rivers or streams during the night. The trip seemed like a dreamy blur.

He tried to imagine where he was. He was high, he knew, just by the smell of the air. Also, he could see the pointy tops of trees through the trunks of the nearby pines; some of the trees were cut and cleared farther down the slope to open corridors of view of the forest across the river. *Must be a mountain farm or something,* he thought, remembering climbing up the grade in the sidecar of the motorcycle last night.

There were two mules in the stalls at the rear of the barn, he saw, and there were saws of all kinds hanging from the walls, and a table and band saw against one, with a small gasoline-powered motor below to drive them. Next to the motor a red petrol can was set against the wall with an old red rag stuffed in the spout. Against the other walls were stacks of lumber, some planed, some barked logs, and the floor was strewn with sawdust. Everything smelled of pine and mountains and cut wood.

A chicken pecked the sawdust near his feet.

Billy looked up when he heard the approach of men's voices. One of the doors opened, allowing a wedge of gray light over the sawdust floor, and showing for a moment a small wooden cabin across the yard. Four men entered the barn. It was the older man and the two men with him that he had met the night before. The fourth one was Henri. The men looked over at him.

"Oui, oui," said the woodcutter, not taking his eyes off Billy. He was a burly man perhaps in his mid-fifties, Billy noted, wearing dark woolen trousers and a dirty white shirt. Thick, hairy forearms and hands showed beneath the rolled-up sleeves, and his fingers, short and as thick as cigar stubs, were calloused and looked like they could crush walnuts. His head was bare and balding, with wiry curls of black and gray over his ears, and two curly thumbs of hair over dark, wide-set eyes in a face that seemed as wide as a frying pan.

The woodcutter said something in French to the two men with him: his sons, Billy reckoned. The sons looked at Billy. They were in their early twenties, Billy guessed. Men's ages were easy to guess. Both were taller and leaner than their father by half a foot and fifty pounds, and one of them— the older one—had those unearthly turquoise-colored eyes. The other son was dark-eyed like his father, and held a bundle under his arm. They talked some more—rather, the father talked and the sons listened—and Billy began to feel like a commodity again.

The boy leaned back against the right door of the bay, and every so often he looked out into the yard.

"Come," the woodcutter said in English to Billy. He made a thick, shouldery gesture with his arm. "We talk." The man saw the basket in Billy's hands and frowned. *"Colette!"* he called bruskly over his shoulder. *"Viens ici, va faire ton menage et presses-toi!"*

Billy got the feeling he'd made some breach of etiquette.

The girl came into the barn. Her eyes went first to her father, then slanted quickly at Billy. Billy watched her with interest. She was wearing a white blouse and a long, black woolen skirt that hit her calves. She was barefooted. A crudely wrought crucifix clapped against her breast. The woodcutter took the basket from Billy and thrust it at her. She took it, looked at Billy with a blush of crimson on her cheeks, then left without a word. She moved quickly across the floor, looking down, with the awkward self-conscious gait of someone knowing there were eyes upon her.

Billy was embarrassed for her.

The woodcutter pinched his thick lips as he looked over the American flier from head to toe. He dragged a hand over his dark face, and Billy could hear the black stubble bristling beneath the thick cigar stubs. "You have eat well?" he said in halting English.

"Yes, thank you—er, *merci*," Billy smiled. "It was delicious."

The woodcutter turned to the elder son. *"Qu'est-ce que c'est,* delicious?" *"Délicieux."*

The woodcutter turned to Billy. *"Bon!* You stay here. No Boche." He made a sweep of his hand past the window. "Many kilometers. Some Boche in village but they are old men. Some Vichy too." He spat on the ground. "We kill them later," he said. "Is bad luck to hunt in one's own field."

Billy smiled, marvelling at the universality of the proverb.

The two sons looked at each other and shrugged.

The woodcutter crooked an eyebrow at Billy. "You fly the bomber planes?"

"No, the Jug."

Billy watched the man's face translate his words, then settle into a frown. "Jug? What is Jug?"

"Thunderbolts, you know—P-47s."

"Ah . . . Jug." Billy watched the shrewdly dark eyes record the information. "You shoot down many Boche in this Jug?"

"No. It was my first flight."

The man grunted. Billy felt whatever esteem the man may have had for him plummet. Henri said something to the woodcutter in French. The man looked sharply at Billy. "You kill Boche with knife?"

"Yes," Billy admitted.

"*Bon, bon.* Is good to kill Boche, no? Knife is best."

Billy weighed his words carefully.

The woodcutter read his hesitation. "Americans have soft heart," he said. "Can no win war against Boche with soft heart." He took the bundle from his son and handed it to Billy. "*C'est pour vous.* These are for you. Then come. We will talk more about this soft heart. Maybe you will next time kill plenty Boche in this Jug."

The man turned and walked away from him, heavy-legged and sullen. He reminded Billy of an old bull that was tired but still plenty dangerous. His feet seemed to strike against the earth as if they were exacting some unatoneable vengeance. His sons fell in behind him, and the three of them exited the workshop into the now yellow sunlight.

Henri nodded at Billy, then left him alone with the chicken.

Billy looked at the bundle in his hands—clothes. *Next time,* he thought. *Sure, next time I kill plenty Boche.*

He shrugged off his flight jacket. The trousers scratched his legs, and were too wide in the waist and too short. He put on the shirt, holding the trousers up first with his left hand and then with his right. The shirt was too big, of course, but at least it was clean. He buttoned the lower buttons and tucked in the tails, and while he buttoned the rest of his shirt, spreading out his knees to keep the trousers from falling, he glanced out the window and was surprised to see the girl by the water pump.

She was bending against a backdrop of smoky timber as she worked the handle, the water gulping out of the spigot into the bucket that was sitting on a block of wood beneath it. She looked up, flipping her long, black hair away from her face and letting it fall to the other side of her head, to catch the morning light in those brightly foreign eyes.

Holding up his trousers, he smiled and, waving at her, nearly lost them.

The girl looked quickly down and continued working the handle. She shot a glance at him as she walked away with the bucket, and Billy saw something go over her stride, an uncoupling stiffness in her gait as though she had led off on the wrong foot.

"She's a beauty all right, Billy boy!" He strapped on his shoulder holster, felt the solid heft of the pistol against his rib cage, then he put on the dark woolen jacket. It fit fairly well and hid the fact that nothing else did. Then he rolled up his flight clothes in his leather jacket and crossed the sawdusty floor of the workshop, still holding up his trousers with his left hand.

He started out the doors but pulled back sharply when he saw a line of men's heads and torsos climbing the curving dirt road that led steeply up through the trees to the cabin. The men were dressed in dark woolen pullovers and berets, each shouldering automatic weapons and wearing a bandolier of cartridges across his chest, a pistol at his side.

He glanced over at the cabin. The woodcutter and his sons were standing in the yard amid a squall of chickens, watching the men, and everything seemed all right. Henri came out of the cabin and stood to one side of the others. The German submachine gun was slung over his shoulder on a long canvas strap, and he lay his right forearm on the gun barrel like a sling.

Billy watched the men approaching from the shadow of the barn.

The six men trudged silently up the last length of the road. All but their feet showed now against the dark backdrop of trees, their eyes ranging over the grounds. One of them called out and waved as the group walked up to the woodcutter and his sons. The one who had called out, a tall, dark-haired man with a strong military bearing, stepped forward. He went over to the boy and lay a hand on his shoulder; he said something to him that Billy could not understand.

The boy's head went down.

Billy cursed. He remembered the face of the man as he waved good-bye from the truck.

"We are all proud of him," the tall man said in French.

Henri looked up at him then looked back at the ground.

The tall man addressed the woodcutter. "You are finished here, Arnaud."

"What do you mean?"

"Guillaume . . . he will—"

"He will not talk!" the boy said sharply. "The Boche cannot make him talk! He would die first."

"I believe you, Henri," the tall man said. "No one can make him talk. Still we must go." He looked at the woodcutter. "We are no longer safe here, Arnaud. The Gestapo will check everything, even if Guillaume does not talk."

"He will not talk!" the boy insisted angrily. He turned away from the man and kicked at the ground.

The woodcutter looked at the tall man. "This is my home, Antoine. I will not leave. If the Boche come they will die."

"So will you, Arnaud."

"Yes. Like my Christina died." The woodcutter looked at the ground and crossed himself. His sons did likewise. "I will not leave her. No, this is where I will die."

"All this talk of death," Jean-Claude said. "You must listen to Antoine, Papa."

The woodcutter looked at him with half-lidded eyes. "What is this chirping I hear? I have cowards for sons? Is that what you are telling me now? That your mama bore only women? It is good she is not here to see the three women she bore."

Jean-Claude shook his head. "Papa, you know that I am not afraid to die. But this is foolishness."

A flash of red went over the woodcutter's face. "Is it foolishness to fight for your home? For your country? No, it is not foolishness. I tell you it is foolishness to let the Boche chase you from your home and your country." He struck his fist against his palm. "No. We will not run away. We will fight the Boche here, in the mountains."

"It is no disgrace to leave, Arnaud," the tall man said. "You will fight them with the Free French in London. Here they will hunt you. They will line you against a wall and shoot you like dogs."

Henri rubbed his eyes and looked away.

The man glanced at the boy, then peered intently at the woodcutter. "If you do not care what they do to you, Arnaud, think of what they did to Christina—what they will do to Colette!"

The woodcutter said nothing.

"There will be a plane in one week, Arnaud. It will take your family to London."

The woodcutter looked at him suddenly. "A plane?"

"Yes."

"What plane? How can there be another plane?"

"Believe me," Antoine said. "It is all arranged."

"This plane is for the American?"

"No. It comes for some of our people who must get to London. There may not be room for the American." He smiled at the woodcutter. "That is all I can say for now, Arnaud. You are finished here. You must gather your things that we may go quickly."

The woodcutter stiffened. "No! I am not finished here. Here I am Free French. Here I will die Free French! Here I will live free and not run!"

Antoine narrowed his eyes. "This is not a request."

Billy watched them intently. It occurred to him that there were four distinct groups in the yard: the six men were one group; the woodcutter and his sons were another; the boy was a group by himself; and then there was the girl who had just appeared in the doorway with a dish and towel, her hand wiping the dish pensively as she watched the groups of men.

Billy looked back at Antoine. He was building a case, he could tell. The woodcutter argued with him passionately, sometimes raising his voice to a roar and throwing his hands into the air, then pointing at the cabin, then stabbing at the ground, then gesturing at each of his sons.

Antoine looked down at the ground suddenly, and there was a long silence. Each of the four groups looked off in a different direction. Then Antoine straightened his back, looking more military than ever, and said something to the woodcutter. His voice was low and without emotion.

The woodcutter looked up at him sharply. His head and shoulders hunched menacingly like a bull's, and Billy thought sure it would go to blows. The five men behind Antoine came to life. Glaring at the men, and then at Antoine, shoulders slumped forward as though they could no longer support the enormous weight of the sky. He shook his head resignedly.

As Billy walked across the yard, the men turned and looked at him. Billy felt the girl watching him.

"L'américain?" the tall man asked the woodcutter.

"Oui."

Antoine stepped forward. "You are the American pilot?" he asked Billy in perfect English.

"Yes."

"I am Major Antoine Dubois of the FFI."

"The FFI?"

"Yes. The Free French Intelligence."

"Second Lieutenant William Hochreiter, sir." He remembered to salute.

The major returned his salute. "I know who you are," he said, then glanced back at one of his men who had a little notebook. The man handed it to him. "You seem to be in good health," the major said, looking Billy over. "That is good, you will need it. Tell me now, Lieutenant, what is your unit?"

"My unit?" Billy glanced at the woodcutter. The woodcutter looked away sullenly. "I'm with the 52nd Fighter Group, sir."

"Your squadron?"

"The 61st."

The major looked at the notebook. "What is your mother's surname?"

"Say, what is this?"

The major pulled out a pistol and leveled it at Billy's chest. He said in a low voice, "I do not have time to play games with you, Lieutenant. If you do not answer correctly, then I will assume that you are not who you say you are, and I will shoot you."

Billy stared at the pistol, stunned at first, then angry. "McInnis . . . Beulah May McInnis. You want my shoe size too?"

"No," the major chuckled as he returned the pistol to its holster. "No, I do not want your shoe size. *Mais, je pense que nous pourrions trouver un pantalon que vous ailles mieux,*" he said over his shoulder. The men with him laughed.

"What's so funny?" Billy looked down at his trousers and saw that the right side was drooping down off his waist. He hiked them up.

The woodcutter glanced at the trousers and shrugged. He said something to his sons and they went into the cabin. The girl followed them.

"I am sorry to seem untoward with you, Lieutenant," Major Dubois said, folding the notebook and handing it back to his man, "but the Gestapo try to infiltrate our ranks with so-called downed fliers. We cannot be too careful."

The heavy drone of aircraft grew steadily louder on the wind, so that you could not help but look and expect to see some spectacle. The men looked north and saw the sky darkening with scores of airplanes. Billy knew them at once to be a B–17 group with fighter escort.

"They are yours?" the major asked him, raising his voice to be heard over the planes.

"Sure."

"They will bomb Germany perhaps?"

"You bet. Bomb it to kingdom come."

The men watched the bomber group slide across the sky until they were tiny black specks in the east. The two sons came out of the cabin, wearing rucksacks and carrying four British Sten guns. Jean-Claude handed a rucksack and a gun to his father, a gun and rucksack to Billy, then he went to the barn and turned the livestock loose. Billy got down on one knee, rolled up his clothes and stuffed them into the rucksack. François quickly showed him how to feed the clip, work the bolt, and hold the gun. Billy assured him that he knew about guns.

Just then the girl came outside wearing a dark wool sweater and black pants that showed her figure. The trousers were tucked into a pair of leather boots. Her hair was tied back in a ponytail, showing the shape of her head and jaw line, and she wore a black beret pulled to one side. The men looked over at her.

Billy got slowly to his feet, his mouth opened a little bit in awe.

She came over to him and handed him another pair of trousers. She looked up at him with those inscrutable robin's-egg eyes. "Jean-Claude's," she said, indicating one of her brothers.

They looked at one another for a moment. Billy remembered to say, "*merci*," but the word came out "mercy," and he thought he caught a ghost of a smile flit across her full, pouty lips.

The girl walked a few paces away and turned her back to give Billy privacy. He changed quickly into the trousers, which fit him much better, and when he looked over at the girl he saw Major Dubois walking over to her.

"*Bonjour, Colette,*" he said to her. The major was smiling at her, and Billy noticed for the first time that he was handsome.

"*Bonjour, Antoine,*" she smiled.

"*Comment allez-vous?*"

"*Bien, merci, et vous?*"

"*Bien, merci.*"

Billy watched them intently. He had no idea what they were saying, only that the major was smiling at her in a way that disturbed him. He had disliked the major since the business about his mother's surname, and now he found he was disliking him very much more. He watched the girl to gauge her reaction to the major, and he found that, as it was with judging women's ages, he could not read her face one way or the other.

Then it was time to leave. The major, seeing that everyone had their rucksacks on and their weapons ready, called out in French, "*Vien!* We must hurry!" He patted the girl's arm, then strode away from the cabin down the road. Billy hiked up his rucksack, looked quickly at the girl, then fell in behind the major's men. He was glad to be going.

The two sons and the girl fell in behind him. Colette glanced up at her mother's grave, crossed herself and said a prayer, then crossed herself again. She felt numb and empty and sad and angry, and a host of other emotions that accompany the loss of everything you have known and held dear for all of your life. Tears trickled down her cheeks. She thought she might cry, but steeled herself against it and adjusted the canvas strap on her Sten gun. She knew she must not think about it. Not now. Later, but not now. So, looking straight ahead, she stared very intently at the road winding down through the trees, the sun showing a golden rosiness in the dust kicked up by the men. Her eyes were drawn to Billy's broad back and shoulders, and yet another emotion was added to the host of others that she must steel herself against.

Meanwhile, as the woodcutter started away from the cabin, he walked as though a great weight were pulling him down into the earth. He paused, looked once at the white scar on the slope, and then back at the cabin. "*Henri*. Come."

The boy was standing in the middle of the yard, stiff-shouldered and tight-lipped. Chickens stabbed the ground at his feet. "No," the boy said, his voice growing thick. "I told Papa I would wait for him."

The woodcutter walked back to the boy and shook his head sadly. "He will not come."

The boy looked at him fiercely. Tears streamed from his eyes. "He did not talk!" he cried. "Papa did not talk. He could not . . ."

"No. Guillaume was a brave man. I have always said this to be true." The woodcutter put out his thick arm. "Come, Henri, we will together avenge the soul of a brave man. We are finished here."

The boy wiped his eyes with his sleeve. The woodcutter put his arm around his shoulder and they walked heavily down the road. The mules, standing in the barn, watched the men disappear behind the trees. One of them brayed. The woodcutter did not look back.

Scarcely an hour had passed when a Waffen-SS armored unit rumbled into the yard. Soldiers scrambled from the vehicles and spread out in all directions, ransacking the cabin and workshop, and combing the trees. The SS captain with the wire-rimmed spectacles stepped out of his Volkswagen staff car and placed his hands on the open window of the door.

A sergeant came out of the cabin. "There is no one, Captain. No one."

"Nothing in the barn, Captain," said a soldier coming from the workshop.

The captain looked at the man, at the stock ranging freely about the yard, and banged his fist on the window and cursed. "Bring me the radio!" he barked.

8 ★★★★

0730 hours, Friday. Jever Airdrome, near Wilhelmshaven, Northern Germany. Home of Jagdgeschwader 11. The film showed a P–47 Thunderbolt evading the tracking camera in a series of aerial maneuvers. Streamers of tracers hurled suddenly at the plane, showing the bullet trails behind it, missing. Then the plane closed to within four hundred yards, the P–47 rolled, the camera sticking with it, another stream of bullets missing just off the tail.

"It is poetry, I tell you. Sheer poetry!" Viktor's voice called out from the rear of the darkened room. "Have you ever seen such flying?"

"I see that you have hit the sky very well and solidly!" someone hollered from the front.

"Just watch, funny man!"

The screen showed the camera closing, another burst of machine gun fire, the bullet trajectories bending toward the P–47, climbing toward it, then striking along the engine cowling. A thin trail of smoke streamed from the plane.

"See there?" Viktor growled exultantly. "This is what some paperhanger calls only a third of a kill! Look at this third of a kill. I suppose that smoking engine is a bad carburetor. He is done for, I tell you."

The plane continued to turn with the P–47, pursuing it, closing to three hundred yards, tracers hurling again out of the screen, hitting nothing, another burst, nothing, and then the P–47 rolled off the screen into a dive. The camera suddenly swept away and showed sky. White screen.

"Why didn't you finish him off?" a voice called out.

"With a squadron of P–47s chewing on my tail? Ha! would like to see you finish him off."

"Next time open your eyes when you shoot," someone laughed.

The lights came on, showing a room full of sixty or more pilots, most of them in their early twenties, leaning back in their chairs, laughing and smoking. An aisle divided the room in two, and toward the rear of the aisle a technical sergeant was taking the reel of film from Viktor's nose camera off the 16mm projector. Streams of cigarette smoke rose from both halves of the room and swirled against the ceiling. The men talked as they awaited the next camera footage. There was another outburst of laughter. Viktor waved it off.

Rolf sat beside Viktor in the second row from the rear. "Do not let them get your goat," he said.

"They are jealous of my third of a plane," Viktor grumbled.

Someone nearby was demonstrating with his hands how he came at a B–17 and gained his third victory. A confident air blew through the place, for it was clear after most of the debriefing that the Luftwaffe had chewed the Schweinfurt raid to pieces.

Group Commander Specht was seated at a desk off to one side of the room in the front. He was a lean, rugged-faced, no-nonsense man, who, though wearing a patch over his left eye, was still an able flier and leader with twenty-eight victories to his credit. "Whose film is next?" he asked.

"Squadron leader Schiller's," the tech sergeant running the projector said. "It is the last one."

The man sitting behind Viktor gave him a nudge. "Ah, finally we shall see a fighter pilot at work."

"They were suicides," Viktor grunted. "They threw themselves in front of his guns."

"Do not listen to this sour grape!" the man in front of him gibed.

There was a ripple of laughter.

"Roll the projector, Schmitt," the group commander said.

The tech sergeant finished threading the projector, then signalled to a soldier sitting next to the light switch. The room went black. Moments later a flash of rectangular light glared against the screen, showing briefly a silhouetted pall of smoke floating across it.

The screen showed a boil of leader, a flash of numbers spilling atop one another, followed by the head slate showing Captain Schiller's name, Schweinfurt Raid, and the date of October 14.

White screen.

Suddenly they saw a rocket spiral out in an erratic twirl of vapor at a formation of B–17s. A moment later the rocket struck the midsection of the lead Fortress, and the bomber disintegrated in a mushroom of fire and smoke. Victory number one. Ten men dead. White screen.

Voices murmured approval in the darkened room.

The shadowy bulk of another B–17 edged onto the screen. Its ball turret gunner and tail gunner were firing at the camera, their faces clear and intent, their twin .50s spitting tongues of fire amid little puffs of smoke and a sparkling stream of ejected casings. The camera pushed closer as Schiller's plane banked toward the Fortress. Four hundred yards. And closer. Now two hundred and fifty. There was a collective intake of air in the room. Suddenly white hot tracers snapped out of the camera at the lumbering behemoth and struck along the right wing. Pieces of metal skin chipped off the wing and peppered the sky. The bomber lowered out of screen and then there was only sky. White screen.

Immediately the screen showed the same B–17 from a lower angle, the bomber in a desperate flight with its number four engine trailing a thin line of black smoke. Again the fast-moving bullets, like streamers of sparks arcing away from the camera, struck the plane along its flank and number three engine. White screen.

The B–17 yawed to the right, a boil of smoke pouring from its engines and gaping holes along its flank, a cripple now, dying, falling through the sky. Inside the hull, several dark man shapes ran past the holes, one trying to climb out of the fiery cockpit. Another burst of Schiller's 20mm cannons and the right wing snapped like a piece of balsa wood. The bomber convulsed then plummeted to the earth in a twisting spiral of flame and smoke and twinkling shards of metal. No chutes. Number two. White screen.

Another exhale of applause.

A formation of P–47 Thunderbolts showed rising into the screen, breaking formation; then a confusion of Me–109s, FW–190s, and P–47s, with bullets spitting out of the camera at a pair of P–47s, missing the lead plane. A P–38 Lightning suddenly roared through the screen. They saw white screen as Schiller's plane pulled up to avoid collision. More confusion. 109s going down, FW–190s going down, too many of them crisscrossing the screen, slicing the air into burning fragments, a P–47 rising, an Me–109 descending, the camera tracking with another pair of P–47s. White screen.

A hush over the crowd.

Schiller's plane descended on the second plane—the lead plane gone. They saw the pilot's head wagging, looking for Schiller, not seeing him—the shark—rising. Then he looked back and saw the camera. They watched him panic, pulling up on the joystick—an error. Then a burst of 20mm cannon fire and the left wingtip of the American fighter was shorn away, and streams of black smoke belched from the engine cowling. White screen. Victory number three.

Now they watched a sky full of B–17s regrouping, low in the field, tiny, herding together in tight boxes for protection, each formation a cubic mile of killing air space. No escort fighters could be seen. They were on their own. The sky suddenly filled with Me–109s, 110s, and FW–190s like a frenzy of sharks, the sharks attacking, hitting, stabbing in quick forays against the unprotected herd. In fast, out fast. The Fortresses began to fall rhythmically from their boxes, everything moving in slow motion—one going down without a tail section, one a blazing inferno, another seemingly untouched, just falling gracefully through the sky as though it had simply given up its will to live. A man fell through the screen with his chute in flames, his mouth agape. White screen.

Next on the screen was a B–17 fleeing overhead, the great dark belly exposed, Schiller's plane lining up on it, sweeping up, closer, then rolling, like a shark rolls before it strikes. The ball turret and tail gunner fired in the other direction, then they saw several lines of tracers stutter from behind the camera, reaching like fiery tentacles for the midsection of the B–17, reaching then crawling over the wings, the thin metal skin wincing under the strikes, pieces flying. Then the wings folded and the plane collapsed in on itself, hurtling through the heavens like a fallen angel in a fireball of spent grace. Victory number four. White screen.

The room was silent. The pilots were in awe over the beauty and the horror of battle. The flapping of the film against the projector punctuated the silence. There was a collective exhale. The lights glared on.

"That's the last of it, Group Commander," the technical sergeant said, his voice breaking the strange quiet.

Someone blew out a long low whistle.

Captain Specht stood up and walked to the center of the room. "Three fat autos and a P–47. Nice shooting, Rolf. That makes one hundred and ninety-four, doesn't it?"

Rolf shrugged.

"He thinks he will catch Eric Hartmann," someone said.

"The Americans are not Russians," someone else countered.

"Make this man a general," Viktor's voice rang out. "Never have I heard such a profound statement."

The men laughed, needing to laugh. And then it was back to normal.

"Any chutes?" Captain Specht asked Rolf.

"Just the P–47," he replied. "The Wehrmacht will pick him up. He is a young one, I think."

"Let us hope they are all young ones," Captain Specht said. "That is all then." He nodded to the group adjutant.

The adjutant stood up and faced the men. The men rose from their chairs, clicked their heels, and saluted, shouting, "Heil Hitler!"

The men were dismissed, and they began filing out of the room into the adjoining hallway amid a boil of conversation. A soldier went along the far wall raising the drawn shades over the windows. Morning light streamed into the briefing room.

"Rolf, Viktor, may I see you a moment," Captain Specht called out over the din of voices.

Rolf and Viktor turned back at the doorway. "We're in for it now," Viktor winced.

The group commander waited to speak until the room cleared. "Sit down, men," he said, smiling. "Sit down."

The two pilots took seats in the front row.

Captain Specht leaned against his desk and continued to smile at them. Viktor eyed him suspiciously.

"What's up, Günther?" Rolf asked.

The group commander picked up an official-looking envelope from the desk. "I'll get straight to it, Rolf. There's been more talk at Headquarters about giving you your own group."

"Not again."

"I told them that you were considering it seriously."

Rolf rose to his feet. "And I've already told you that I didn't want it."

"I know, I know," Captain Specht laughed. "Still, you deserve it, and High Command is not used to hearing no from its pilots. Frankly, Rolf, this is merely a courtesy of protocol. You know the brass doesn't much care what you want; it's what the Reich needs that matters to them. Try telling Göring otherwise."

Rolf looked down at the cement floor. "What would I do with a group, Günther? I'm a pilot. My job is to shoot down enemy aircraft. Give me a group and I'd spend half my time shuffling papers, or writing letters home to parents of dead pilots, or requisitioning this thing or other from the paperhangers back in Berlin. You know I don't do well with politics."

The group commander chuckled. "That is true." He angled his head to favor his good eye. "I just want you to consider it. Say you'll consider it."

"What's really on your mind, Günther?"

The group commander continued to look at him. He stood up and leaned against his desk.

"Here it comes," Viktor said under his breath.

"This morning I got wakened by a call from a Lieutenant Klemmer of the SS," Captain Specht said. "Ever heard of him?"

Rolf nodded his head.

"Want to tell me your side of it?"

"He killed a man in Werner's last night," Rolf said. "There were women in there—civilians. I merely told this Klemmer fellow to take his fun and games elsewhere. That's all."

"Did you assault him?"

"I wanted to kill him."

Captain Specht looked at him.

"The little weasel threatened my family!" Rolf said. "I won't tolerate that from anyone, least of all from the SS."

Captain Specht turned to Viktor. "What's your side of it?"

"It's just as Rolf says, Captain," he said. "We were enjoying a quiet drink at Werner's and this little martinet and his squad goose-step into the place and shoot a man. Rolf was the ranking officer. He was merely doing his duty."

"By going for the man's throat?"

Viktor shrugged.

The group commander looked down, pinched the bridge of his nose, and massaged it several times. His thumb hooked under the eye patch a bit, then he pulled it back down over his eye. "I've got enough on my mind without having to worry about mixing with the SS." He looked wearily at Rolf.

"What is this, anyway?" Rolf demanded. "We had a minor altercation, that's all. It's over."

"No, it isn't over, Rolf. Not by a long shot. And until I get things settled here I want you to stay away from this Lieutenant Klemmer."

Rolf grunted. "I'd like to get him in my sights."

"I didn't hear that." Captain Specht felt behind him on the desk for a pack of cigarettes. He fished one out of the pack and tapped it into his mouth. "I have put you in for a furlough," he said. He shook out the match and blew out a big cloud of smoke. "It should clear in a week or so."

"Furlough?"

The captain offered the pack to the men. "Cigarette?"

"No. What do you mean furlough?"

"Yes, thanks," Viktor said. He took a cigarette and lit it.

"I don't have time for furloughs," Rolf protested.

"I want you to go to Berlin," Captain Specht said. "I want you to see your family, hobnob with the brass, flash your medals around. You know, let the rear echelon commandos show you off a little—give them a little boost of ego. You're a hero, in case you didn't know it. It will be good for morale."

Rolf started to object.

"I am also recommending you for the Schwertern."

"No."

"It is already in channels," the group commander said. "Might help to smooth over any feathers that this Klemmer may ruffle."

Rolf glared at him. "You act as though this SS goon is related to Himmler or something."

"This 'SS goon,' as you put it, wants your head on a platter. I just don't want you to hand it to him. You assaulted an officer of the Shutzstaffel. He smells blood, Rolf. You know how they are once they smell blood."

Rolf went over to one of the windows and glared out over the tarmac. "I'm supposed to turn and run with my tail between my legs? So help me, Günther, if this fellow has any charges to file, I'll slap him with an insubordination to a superior officer charge he can stick up High Command's rear echelon."

The group commander smiled. "You may file it when you are enjoying your furlough in Berlin."

"I'm not going."

Viktor stared at Rolf.

"It's out of your hands," Captain Specht said, his voice rising. "You are going."

Rolf stared out the window. "You can't force me to take a furlough."

"No, but I can ground you until you do!"

Rolf looked back at him sharply.

The group commander ran his fingers over his scalp. It was a childish thing to say, he knew. He looked over at his friend. "Rolf, we have been through a lot together, you and me," he said. "Good times and bad times. We've buried many friends—too many friends. We stare death in the face every day, then go to the tavern at night, have a few drinks, and kick it in the teeth."

He blew two thick streams of smoke through his nostrils as he tapped an ash to the floor. "You are a brilliant pilot, Rolf. You've got instincts like I've never seen." He laughed. "Sometimes I think you are not a man at all but a machine." He looked down at the floor as the humor cleared from his eyes. "Lately, though, I've seen a change come over you," he said soberly. "Like a sickness. Each time you go up into combat you become more and more daring, going in closer and closer to the enemy guns before pulling out."

Rolf said nothing.

The group commander looked seriously at him. "Rolf, killing off the entire Eighth Army won't bring Katharina back."

Rolf glared at him. He felt a sickness crawling up into his throat, choking him. He coughed, then looked quickly out the window at the line of gray hangars. The bays were open and several of the ground crews were tending the Messerschmitts.

The group commander ground out his cigarette, walked over and lay his hand on Rolf's shoulder. "You need a rest, my stubborn friend. I want you to go and visit your family—forget this war for a while. Laugh. Get drunk. Take your beautiful sister out on the town. It will do you good. When you come back perhaps you'll think differently about having your own command."

Rolf stood gazing out at the tarmac, watching the cloud patterns moving over the surface.

"What about me?" Viktor asked. "I was at Werner's last night too. Do I get a furlough?"

Captain Specht laughed. "You'll be lucky if you don't get a court-martial for wasting so much of the Luftwaffe's ammunition."

Viktor grunted. He turned to Rolf. "Perhaps you will visit my parents when you are back home," he said.

Rolf looked over at him. "Your parents live in Dresden!"

Viktor grinned. "It is only a few centimeters on the map."

"A few centimeters. You're crazy."

"Of course. To keep friends such as you who refuse to go home on furlough, one has to be a little crazy."

Just then the wail of an air raid siren screamed over the air base. The three men looked out the window instinctively, saw men running from every direction across the airstrip. There was organized confusion in the hallway as they exited the briefing room. Men were streaming from adjoining rooms and halls, shouting over the scream of the siren, grabbing their chutes and flight gear, and pouring out onto the field.

Dozens of men were running toward the long line of Me–109s that were waiting in front of the hangars, their yellow-painted noses aimed at the sky. Ground crews tended to their planes and pilots with practiced efficiency. Pilots scrambled up into cockpits and went through a series of checklists. Ailerons . . . check. Rudder . . . check. Fuel gauge . . . check. Oil pressure . . . check. A myriad others. Check. A dread of something connected the pilots. Some prayed. Some cursed. A garble of chatter percolated through the radios as the pilots talked it out. Someone cracked a joke and laughed. Others joined him.

"Shut up, Viktor!" Captain Specht's voice interrupts.

"Yes, Group Commander!"

The crews cranked the engines. The engines turned, caught. The air resonated with the throaty roar of fifty aircraft. Barracks windows shimmered against the morning sun. Pilots gave the thumbs up. Ground crews pulled out the wheel blocks. Line crews waved the planes forward in their turn. Planes lined up on the tarmac in twos and taxied into the wind, engines revving. A flare skyrocketed against the sky, and two by two the Messerschmitts ascended into heaven, the crews standing, watching until they disappeared into the clouds.

Heading west, the Jagdgeschwader 11 Fighter Group climbed quickly out of Jever to 35,000 feet. They were hidden behind a thin veil of cirrus clouds, cruising at 250 mph, hunting with the sun at their backs—an advantage—shining like a silvery host of Valkyries.

Sadness stirred in Captain Rolf Schiller's heart, like a breeze moving over a bed of coals. It always happened this way at first. He did not enjoy the killing; he would be a monster if he did. And then a little yellow flame kindled from the coals, warming his heart, a love flame darting up for everything he held dear and believed in: a flame for his Katharina, his beautiful bride who was forever gone; a flame for his beloved homeland, for Germany; a flame for his unassailable sense of duty. It always happened this way. In this order.

Over Holland now he saw the *Valhalla*, the large box formations of B–17 Fortresses and B–24 Liberators far below them, seeming like tiny toy planes— deadly toy planes that would soon rain fire and destruction upon his beloved Germany—and a coldness filled up his chest and smothered the flames. Something cold and dead went over his eyes and they played over the bombers with clinical dispassion. He was a predator now. A killing machine.

He heard the voice of the group commander in his headset giving the signal to attack. "*Horrido! Horrido!* St. Horridus, go with us!"

Rolf signalled his squadron to follow and banked sharply to the left, the men of his squadron sliding one after the other through the air after him. Diving, he chose a mark—his one hundred and ninety-fifth.

9 ★★★★

Her thick blond hair was an insouciant glory on the wind as she walked along the foam-flecked banks of the Stillwater in her bare feet. Her blue jeans were rolled up past her ankles, her red-and-white-checked shirt was tied up off her waist, and he couldn't take his eyes off her. She was the prettiest girl in Stillwater County—rodeo queen two years in a row kind of pretty. Every few steps she would look back at him and smile, and strip the petal off a daisy—her smile always caused him to go weak inside. "He loves me . . . he loves me not . . ." she would say, smiling and frowning alternately with the count, and her pouty look would drive him nuts.

One of the herds was grazing in the pasture that went along the river, and somewhere a calf was bawling for its mother. "I love you, Laura," he said, watching her ahead of him counting off the petals. "He loves me . . . he loves me not." She looked back at him and frowned. "Do you love me, Billy?"

"You know I do."

She smiled that wonderful smile of hers that broke a thousand cowboy hearts, and said, "Yes, darling. And I love you too. Isn't it wonderful?"

"I'm the luckiest guy on earth!" he said. "Ain't nobody luckier." And then he took her and held her beneath the cottonwoods. "I love you, Laura," he said, kissing her and kissing her again. Again the calf bawled. "I won't be gone long," Billy said. "Will you wait for me?"

"You know I will, darling. Always and forever."

"The war will be over, lickety-split," he said, "and when I come home we will build the house over there."

"Over there? By the calf bawling for its mother?"

"Yes. And we will have a herd of our own."

"Of calves?"

"No, of children." Kissing her, he said, "We'll have three boys."

"And three girls," she added.

"And two labs."

"And a calf bawling for its mother? Best see what's ailing that calf. . . . It is time to be moving, monsieur!"

"I've got to go," Billy said, sitting up out of a dead sleep.

"It is time to be moving." Pierre, one of Major Dubois's men, smiled pleasantly at him.

The moon had risen during his sleep, and there was a fleeting moment when he was back on the ranch. "Right," Billy said and jumped to his feet. "I'll just see what's ailing that calf."

Pierre smiled at him queerly and walked away.

Billy turned his head when a calf bawled in the distance, and he knew suddenly and very clearly where he was. The moon was low on the hills and it flickered through the black lattice of leaves, giving everything an almost surreal appearance. In the strange light of the moon the dark shapes of the other men began to rise, like shades from the black-mounded earth on All Hallows' Eve. And Laura Miller was a million miles away. *Yeah, right,* he thought. *I'm the luckiest guy on earth.*

He looked for Colette. She was already on her feet with her rucksack in place, adjusting it as she leaned forward against the weight. He stared at her for a moment, saw her shape outlined in the moonlight.

She looked over at him abruptly. Her eyes sparkled for just a moment in their dark hollows before she looked away.

Billy felt something rise in his throat. He shook his head. *This is crazy,* he thought. He picked up his rucksack and shrugged it over his shoulders, adjusting the straps so that the weight would ride high on his back. He checked the safety on his Sten gun and shouldered it, watching as the other men adjusted their gear.

Major Dubois was talking to someone on the radio. Then he handed the receiver back to the radioman and signalled with his hand. The small troupe of Maquis exited their covering of trees and climbed a low hill into the bright moonlight. They showed as black silhouettes against the skyline—eleven men and the girl—advancing in single file, with the low-slung moon casting their long shadows over the countryside. They were well rested and moving quickly and with purpose, heading, as always, in a southerly direction. Everyone leaned forward against the weight of their pack and watched the heels of the person in front of them as they fell quickly into their hiking intervals.

On the evening of the fourth night the black outline of the Vosges mountains rose sharply against the eastern sky, cutting the sky in two, before dipping down on the other side into the valley of the Rhine and Germany. The major led them through the river valley of the Meuse, over a rugged hilly region, and then along the Moselle, always travelling at night. They camped in out-of-the-way places during the day, farms mostly, in bombed-out villages when they came upon them, oftentimes assisted by the local Resistance with food and drink. They didn't see a single German.

Billy marvelled at how tirelessly the girl kept pace. Never once did she complain; never once did she lag behind; never did the inscrutable cast of her eyes betray what she might be thinking or feeling. He often wondered what she might be thinking or feeling. When such a thought surfaced, he would glance behind him, and sometimes he caught her gazing at him before she could look away. Then the robin's egg blue eyes would seem to stay with him a few moments, haunting the air, and it would set him on a whole new course of wondering what she might be thinking or feeling.

Her father, on the other hand, looked as grim as ever as he trudged heavily along at the rear of the line, complaining of his feet. His big shoulders rocked back and forth, broken-gaitedly like a lame bull, as though each step took a supreme effort. His eyes, small and black amid the wide, flat face, stared sullenly ahead at the rolling terrain. The boy walked alongside him, looking up at him every so often; then his dark eyes would again range over the countryside, staring intently at nothing. Every so often the woodcutter would lay a big hand on Henri's shoulder.

A truck met the troupe west of Épinal and drove them about a hundred and fifty miles along the foothills of the Jura Mountains. They travelled over a narrow, winding dirt road with many switchbacks before word reached them by radio of several German roadblocks in Saône-et-Loire. Even the rivers there were being watched, they were told. Something was up. The truck was sent back, and the troupe of Maquis again struck out across the fields and hills, again heading south; and again the woodcutter grumbled about his feet.

On the sixth night it rained heavily for several hours, then abruptly stopped. The wet fields and trees glistened in the moonlight and filled the air with a clean, musky autumn scent. When they arrived in Saône-et-Loire, the troupe kept to the hedgerows and shrubbery, fearful they might come upon a German encampment or roadblock. Once they saw a line of

German trucks going along in the distance. They moved more and more tentatively. A tenseness thread through the troupe like a wire, the wire growing increasingly taut the more they saw signs of the Wehrmacht.

By dawn of the ninth day they arrived at a small farm nestled in the foothills of the Juras. As the troupe waited in a stand of naked beech trees on a little knoll overlooking the farm, Major Dubois went down to the house. A dog ran barking up the knoll to challenge him. The farmer came out of the house, and the two of them talked, tracing the flow of conversation with their hands. The farmer nodded his head, then went back into the house. Major Dubois walked back up to the trees with the dog nosing at his side. "It is all right," he said.

"Good," Pierre said.

The farmer was a short, jovial man with lively blue eyes and gray hair that stood up in a great thatch of curls on his head. He put the visitors up in the loft of his barn, a structure built on a high foundation of river rock dredged up from the Saône River. A flight of wooden stairs led up to the loft.

The farmer's wife, a big, smiling woman in her early forties, appeared with some food: bread, goat cheese, salami, and three bottles of wine. An old woman helped her—the farmer's mother, Billy assumed, by her bright blue eyes that were identical to his. She offered him an apple. *"Merci,"* he said. *"Je vous en prie,"* she smiled. There were no children that he could see or hear, only a few milk cows, a sow and a couple of shoats, some chickens, and an old, Belgian draft horse that was whickering in the barn.

After the meal a packet of cigarettes went around, and everyone smoked and talked quietly. The wine made its rounds, and a heavy wreath of smoke ascended and got caught up in the rafters. A barn owl dropped from the cupola and beat heavily out through the bay.

Billy tamped a lipful of Copenhagen into place with his tongue and watched the men, not understanding a word they said but wishing he did. He felt alone and a million miles from home as he sat scratching the ears of the dog that nuzzled beside him. Billy's eyes strayed from time to time to the girl, who was sleeping next to her brothers. He watched her sleep for a while, then he got up to get rid of his chew. The dog followed him.

The girl opened her eyes and watched Billy descend the wooden stairs. Once he disappeared she lowered her eyes and stared at the pieces of straw by her face. She was thinking of how the American made her feel, and she was afraid to think of him. She closed her eyes, but closing them she saw his face in her mind; she saw his eyes and the way he smiled, the way he had waved to her through the window of the barn, the way he was forced to hold up the trousers to keep them from falling. It was silly, she knew. All of it was silly, but she could not stop thinking about him and the way he made her feel inside.

Billy hooked the chew from his lip with his index finger and saw that the sky was beginning to gray in the east. An early morning mist crept over the ground. Then as he turned to head back into the barn a movement near the stand of beech trees caught his eye—the shadow of a man darting furtively, he thought. It was just an impression. Looking, he saw nothing—nothing but the vague outlines of the beech trees and the mist rolling down over the knoll. The dog lowered his head and growled.

A rooster crowed against the morning quiet. He heard the big Belgian snorting in the barn and the cows bawling to be milked.

When he climbed back up into the loft the men were settling down, making pillows of their rucksacks, adjusting the hay beneath them, and soon everyone was sleeping soundly. The woodcutter lay on his back and snored loudly.

Billy lay down and closed his eyes, listening as the farmer came into the barn to tend the animals. He thought of his family's ranch and wondered what his parents were doing at that very moment—eating supper, he imagined, calculating the time difference. He opened his eyes and looked over at the girl. He thought he caught a glimmer of light in her eyes, as though they were open and looking at him, but then it was gone. He shook his head. *This is crazy.* Closing his eyes he tried to conjure up Laura Miller's face—prettiest girl in Stillwater County's face—but somehow he couldn't raise her image. She was gone in a crinkle of fire. Montana was gone, and then Billy was asleep, chasing elk over the Beartooths.

Everyone was awake by mid-afternoon.

The farmer's wife and mother brought out more food and drink, and after the meal the troupe made ready to depart. Night came quickly and was clouded over, making it darker still. A wind had picked up during the day, and the air was thick and smelled of rain.

Major Dubois thanked the farmer and tried to give him a little money, but the farmer refused him. The farmer, his wife, and the old woman waved them off, all three of them smiling, and every one of the Maquisards waved back at them as they headed west away from the farmhouse toward the mountains. The clouds were darkening and they heard thunder in the distance. They could feel the threatening rain and electricity in the air.

It wasn't fifteen minutes after they had left the farm when they heard the shot. The report echoed over their heads, then rippled away into the hills, and everyone stopped and looked back, thinking it was thunder. There was a long pause and then another shot rolled against the clouds, and everyone's head adjusted to the place behind them, triangulating the direction. Another pause. A third shot. With it something went out of everyone's chest. Everyone stood looking numbly at the hills and at the narrow pass they had just come through.

"Did you tell him where we were headed?" Jean-Claude asked Major Dubois.

"No," the major said grimly. "But of course he knew of the American."

"How did they know about the farm?"

"I do not know," the major said. Then he walked quickly away and took up the southerly course of the Saône.

There was a crash of lightning, showing the terrain in a ghostly, flickering luminance, and then it began to rain. Everyone followed after the major, trudging heavily, no one talking. The ground was springy at first and then muddy, and everyone walked looking down at the heels of the person in front of them. A gloom clung to the line of the Maquis like a sodden blanket. It was a dismal, dour trek over the wet countryside, punctuated every so often with flashes of lightning and the thunder beating along the face of the mountains. The rain hissed in the interludes between the thunder.

Billy tried to remember their faces but caught only glimpses of the old woman as she handed him an apple. He tried not to think of them, but the old woman's bright blue eyes—or were they those of the farmer—peered at him through the gloom and condemned him. Three dead because of me. How many more? It was a lousy deal. He glanced over his shoulder. The woodcutter was bent forward, his bull-browed head lowered as though in a charge. His small, black, animal eyes seemed to burn over some red and festering vengeance as he moved sullenly at the rear of the line, no longer grumbling over his feet. The machine gun looked small in his big hands.

Henri was glaring at the horizon. His hair was plastered over his forehead, and big drops of rain dripped off his nose.

On the eleventh night the rain quit, the clouds broke apart, and they saw the wreckage of a British Lancaster off to their left—black against the skyline with the moon glinting dully on it. The tail section was shot away, the fuselage was riddled with bullet holes, and the nose dug into the earth. It looked as though it had pretty well been cleaned out.

Billy wondered what had become of the men. Had they gotten out safely? Were they picked up by the Maquis? Or had the Germans gotten them? Then, looking out into the blackness of the night, he remembered his vow to God. *Anything, God. Anything.* He glanced heavenward, but the sadness was too heavy on him, and he was forced to look back at the ground.

Major Dubois now shifted to an easterly direction, and the terrain leveled out. Ahead of them, across a mile or so of fields, was a town of some size. Billy saw the dark roofs of the houses spreading away from the bell tower of the church. They were moving down a tract of hilly ground toward a road that cut across their path. There was a vineyard on the other side, but, coming to the road, they took it heading south again, and the going was easier.

They walked along the edge of the road in the gravel to avoid leaving footprints in the mud. Suddenly the major raised his hand, cupped a hand behind his ear, then waved everyone down into the ditch alongside the road. Immediately the rumbling sound of several trucks charged into the silence, and they saw the light slits of the headlamps cutting through the dark around a bend in the road. Everyone got into the ditch in time, but there was little cover.

Billy flattened himself as best he could. The left side of his face was pressed against the wet incline, and he could feel the ground shaking because of the trucks. He glanced over at the person next to him and saw that it was the girl. Her body was flattened against the grass, and he could see the profile of her face, of her long, shapely-bowed neck as she looked up at the trucks going by. When the last of the trucks had passed, the major gave the signal and everyone began to climb out of the ditch. The girl slipped on the slick surface, and Billy caught her arm and helped her out of the ditch. He felt her muscles tense under his grip.

"*Merci,*" she said, looking quickly at him. She fell in with the company of her father, the boy, and her two brothers, and, once again, she seemed to walk in that awkward, coltish gait. Billy passed her and moved on to the head of the line with the major. They hiked for several more miles, past two more villages and several farms. The strain of travel showed on everyone's face.

"How much farther?" Billy asked the major.

"Only a little bit."

Billy wondered what "only a little bit" translated to in miles. He was beginning to feel as though they were taking him to Spain after all. He was about to slip back in the line when the major said, "There is an old barn about two kilometers ahead. We will wait there for the others."

"Others?"

The major said nothing more.

They swung wide of another town and then, in the distance, silhouetted upon a low rise of ground, Billy saw the barn. A stone wall went around the rise of ground, the barn on the rise, and beyond the barn was a dark line of trees that stretched over the horizon. The moon was bright on the fields.

The major waved everyone to wait. He climbed the stone wall and slipped into the darkness. Several minutes later he returned and waved the group forward.

The barn seemed about ready to collapse. There were slats missing from the walls, the roof sagged like a swayback horse, and a large section of it had fallen in. The woodcutter sat down against the barn, took off his rucksack and boots, and gave his feet a good rubbing. The boy sat down next to him, glared briefly at the horizon, then lay his head down on his folded arms. The other men quickly settled along the wall of the barn.

The girl eased the rucksack from her shoulders and stretched, took a drink of water from her canteen, then poured a little into her hand and wiped the back of her neck and face. She stood talking with her brothers. The boy looked up at them, then lay his head back down.

Billy removed his rucksack. His legs felt suddenly tired and rubbery, and his shoulders and back ached from the strain and weight of the pack. He wanted only to lie down and sleep, but he remained standing because the girl remained standing. He looked over at Major Dubois and saw he was talking on the radio again. He was looking at his wristwatch and nodding as he talked quickly in French, glanced once up at the sky, then shoved the receiver back into the box. The radioman laid the box next to the barn, in the place where the others had set their rucksacks.

They hadn't been there but a half hour when a group of men came over a low hill from the northeast, the moonlight showing clearly that there were at least eighteen of them. Everyone took hold of their rifle or gun and watched intently as the men approached Major Dubois. The woodcutter looked up and continued rubbing his feet. "Maquis," Jean-Claude said to Billy.

"Right," Billy said.

The second group came over to the barn. Most of them took off their packs and set down their rifles and stretched out in the grass or against the barn. No one talked or went inside. Four of them were older men and did not look like fighters, Billy thought after giving them the once-over, but he could tell they were important by the way Major Dubois was talking with them. Then he saw that two others were dressed in civilian clothes, and he guessed they were Americans.

These two looked over at Billy. They were Americans, all right, he thought. Everything about them screamed it: the way they stood lighting their cigarettes, blowing smoke and spitting bits of tobacco off their tongues, and the way they just ranged over to him, grinning, like they owned the place.

"American?" one of them said.

"Yeah," Billy said, wondering what it was about himself that had given him away.

"What outfit you with?"

"The 52nd."

"No kiddin'? I'm with the 4th."

"Is that right?" The 4th and the 52nd were rivals. Both fighter groups were in a race to see which one would break a hundred victories by the end of the year.

The pilot from the 4th stretched out his hand. "Lieutenant Harding," he said. "My friends call me Butch."

Billy shook his hand. "Glad to know you," he nodded. "Billy Hochreiter." He looked at the other American and noticed that his arm was in a sling.

"Caught a chunk of flak," the man said. "Thought I'd bought the farm."

"When'd you go down?" Billy asked him.

"The Schweinfurt run."

"Same here. You with the 390th?"

"No, sir—the 93rd."

"Liberators, right?"

"Yes, sir. I was right waist gunner."

"How about the rest of your crew? And knock it off with the 'sir' business."

"We lost the skipper and the navigator," the waist gunner said. "Sammy on the belly gun bought it too. Rocket took him out—left a big hole in the floor. The rest of the guys got out, but I don't know where they got to. Krauts got 'em, I guess."

"Swell," Billy said.

"The place was lousy with them," the waist gunner said. "I thought I was cooked. I laid low in some bushes until these fellows picked me up a week ago. Nice fellows. Don't talk much though." He shook his head. "We got chewed to pieces. I doubt if any of our group got through."

"That's tough."

"Sure is."

Butch Harding whistled. "Say, what's with the dame? She's some dish."

Billy felt a jolt go through him. He looked over at the girl, who was still standing and talking with her brothers. "She's a tough gal," he said and left it at that.

Butch made a crack as he undressed her with his eyes. Billy felt a rush of fury in his throat that took him by surprise. "Lay off her," he growled. "She ain't none of your business."

"Hey, take it easy," Butch grinned. "You got her staked out or something?"

"Just lay off her." Billy was about to leave when Major Dubois walked over and told the three of them that the field was just over the next hill. He said to hold tight until further word.

"We're here?" Butch asked.

"Yes. However, the plane has been delayed several hours across the channel because of fog."

"You can't land a plane here."

"It will land over there, across the trees," the major said, pointing at the long dark rise of trees.

"Where are we anyway?" Butch asked him. "Our boys were pretty tight-lipped."

"They are good men," the major said as he walked away.

"All this cloak-and-dagger stuff," Butch said.

"Pretty lucky us gettin' a plane, though," the waist gunner said. "Didn't fancy hoofin' it all the way to Spain with a busted wing."

"Don't kid yourself, pal," Butch said. He pointed at the four older men. "It's those fellas the plane's for. French brass or something. We're just piggy-backs."

"Where'd you hear that?"

"I heard it." He grunted. "If there ain't enough room on the plane you can bet who'll be hoofin' it still."

Billy heard something in his voice. "Where you from?" he asked.

Butch looked at him, hesitated. "Billings, Montana—why?"

"We got a spread just south of Columbus," Billy said.

Butch just looked at him.

"We're practically neighbors," Billy said. "Shoot, I go to Billings all the time—to the auction."

"I haven't lived there long," Butch said. "I grew up mostly in Ohio." He looked over at one of the Maquisards he had come with. "Say, pal, you got anything to eat? I'm starving."

Billy and the waist gunner watched him take off. "What's with him?" the waist gunner said.

"Beats me," Billy said. "You figure it out. I'm bushed." He went inside the barn to get some rest, feeling suddenly spent of social graces. If the girl wanted to stand around all night that was her business.

The moon shone in through the hole in the roof and spread over the floor. A cool breeze blew over the ground, and there was a smell of old, wet wood and hay—the smell of something that has long been abandoned to decay. It was a good smell. The rafters groaned against a light wind. Billy lay his head back on his rucksack and shut his eyes. He opened his eyes suddenly and saw the girl standing in the open bay. She was looking down at him. She did not look away.

Billy felt his throat thickening. "Well, shoot!" he said, sitting up. "Come on in—Colette, isn't it? That's your name, right? Come on in." He indicated a place on the ground. "We can talk, or—shoot—we can just sit here and look at each other."

The girl stared at him a moment longer, her eyes sparkling in the moonlight, then she disappeared. He looked after her. *This is crazy,* he chided himself. *Nothing but pure crazy.* He rolled over onto his side, away from the moon. He blinked at the ground, thinking how crazy it was, when he felt someone behind him. He looked, and there was the girl standing in the bay, looking at him.

As Billy sat up he felt everything moving inside him, like an enormous ice shelf giving way over a precipice. There was a moment of exhilarating abandon and terror.

She started toward him slowly, hesitated, then came forward quickly and sat down beside him. The two of them looked at each other in the brightness of the moon. Neither said a word. Billy could not speak for fear that his voice might crack. The girl continued to stare at him, with her hands folded on her lap. An embarrassed smile spread slowly over her pouty lips. The message of her eyes was a mystery to him.

"You're so beautiful," he said at last, feeling the words grating in his throat. "I've never seen anyone so beautiful." He reached forward to touch her hand, and she let him take it.

"I think I'm nuts about you," he said, smoothing his fingers over her hand. "Crazy, isn't it?"

She smiled at him.

"You don't understand a word I'm saying, do you?"

She started to speak, but a voice outside called her name. "Colette?"

The girl rose quickly to her feet. *"Oui?"*

Jean-Claude was in the bay looking at them. The brother looked over at Billy and then at his sister. *"Viens, Papa vent te voir."*

"What is it?" Billy called after her. "What'd he say?"

The girl glanced back at him before disappearing. Billy gazed intently at the open bay; then he heard the curt tone of the woodcutter through the walls of the barn.

10 ★★★

The motorcycle pulled alongside the Volkswagen utility vehicle and signalled to the SS captain. "Radio," he shouted over the engines.

The armored trucks and motorcycles of the Waffen-SS unit pulled off to the shoulder of the road. Waiting for the radioman, the captain removed his spectacles and breathed over each lens, wiping them off with a handkerchief. He placed the spectacles on his head as the radioman came up to his window.

"It is Kessler, Captain."

"Finally." The captain took the headset and spoke into the receiver. "Yes, yes, Kessler."

"We are near Mâcon," the voice came through in flawless German. "We are waiting in an old barn on the north side of the village. There is a large field two kilometers from the barn where the plane will arrive in three hours. You must hurry."

"How far north of the village?"

"About four or five kilometers. I must go, or they will miss the radio." The receiver went dead.

The captain handed the headset to the radioman and told him the information. The motorcyclist told each of the drivers, and the vehicles roared away.

৯৯৩

The man sitting hidden behind the low encircling wall watched the barn. There were a few men still gathered at one end of it, smoking and talking quietly. Their hands were cupped over their cigarettes, and he could see the glow on their faces when they smoked. Their backs were to him. He looked at the other end of the barn and saw no one. He started to exit his covering, then drew up quickly when he saw one of the Americans exiting a clump of bushes, about fifty yards from his position. He waited until the American had gone around to the other side of the barn, then moved quickly across the open ground and slipped into the shadows of the barn. He put the radio next to the rucksacks where he had found it and looked quickly in either direction. No one saw him.

ॐॐॐ

Billy woke up when someone tripped over his feet.

"Sorry, pal, didn't see you there," Butch Harding said. "Didn't wake you, did I?"

"No," Billy lied. "I was just resting my eyes. You been out?"

Butch grinned. "Had to see a man about a horse."

"Haven't heard that expression in a while."

"Is that so?" Butch said, stretching out on the floor.

Billy glanced across the barn at the people sleeping. He could just make out the recumbent form of the girl between her brothers against the wall. Thinking about her—he could not stop thinking about her—he could feel her coming to him, the turquoise eyes slipping around the barriers that he did not even know were there. But they were there all right; he'd put them there against the loneliness. Still, he let her come.

A cool breeze fingered through the barn, and the rafters groaned beneath its touch. The moon finally slid off his face. Crickets ground their legs furiously, and frogs hammered against the stars. Everyone was sleeping now except the few men outside, and Billy listened to their soft voices sounding distant and more distant. And then he didn't hear a thing.

He woke up amid a clatter of metal. Looking across the barn he saw two of the men waking everyone up.

"It is time," Pierre said to him in English.

"Right," Billy said.

"Soon you will be safe." Pierre smiled pleasantly.

"What I'd give for a soft feather bed," Butch Harding said as he dragged to his feet. "I'm gonna sleep for a week."

Billy was adjusting the straps of his rucksack so that they might not cut into his shoulders when he felt someone's eyes on him. He looked across the barn, and the girl was looking at him. He could see in her eyes, even in the darkness, an ache, or a hunger, or a loneliness that sounded deeply in him and made him want to rush over to her and pull her into his arms. But the other men were going by in the waking confusion of making ready their gear, and her brothers were there beside her, not to mention her father and the boy, so they could only look at each other from across the barn.

Major Dubois walked over to the girl, and the moment was broken. Billy picked up his Sten gun, leaned against the weight of his pack, and stared at the gun in his hand. *This is crazy. Nothing but pure crazy.*

It was time now to depart, and everyone moved outside in the ornery grogginess of sleep. The air was sharp with cold, and it woke everyone up to the fact that they were outside at this miserable hour of the night instead of at home in bed. Their breath made clouds in the air.

Huddling in their coats, the two groups of Maquisards followed Major Dubois across the field toward the dark line of trees. The moon was bright behind the trees, showing them a jagged black rift in the sky. The air was clear and sparkly, and the stars hanging low over the trees twinkled like little diamonds against the jet-black sky that showed through the clouds. The night noises were gone; there was only the eerie quiet of pre-dawn.

No one said a word as they crossed the field. Everyone knew the end of it was just ahead and took comfort in it. Billy was thinking that it was the end of it, too, but somehow it made him feel hollow and lonely. He thought of the girl; he thought of his wrecked plane; then he thought of God. *Anything, God. Get me out of this mess and I'll do anything.* He pulled his collar up over his neck and sank down into the protective fleece.

They were about fifty yards from the edge of the tree line, coming over the last, low elevation of ground, when they heard the rumbling of armored vehicles. There was no mistaking the diesel engines and the heavy-machined clanking of treads. Everyone turned at once and saw the dark, bulking shapes moving along the edge of the trees, black against the black background, moving on an interception course. Just then a spotlight hit the group, and the glare of the light showed everyone's face frozen in various grimaces. The Germans opened fire and three Maquisards went down.

"*Cachez-vous! Protègez-vous!*" Major Dubois shouted. "Take cover!" He trained his Sten gun on the spotlight, loosed several short bursts, and it shattered with a crash.

Everyone ran scattering toward the tree line, turning their automatic weapons on the yellow flashes of fire. A German on a motorcycle careened over, and the engine revved abruptly as it crashed end-over-end.

"There is a traitor among us," Major Dubois shouted to the leader of the second band of Maquis.

"Yes," the second man agreed. "Or the Boche."

Colette was running with her father and brothers; Henri was behind them. The other two Americans were running alongside the boy, both of them firing wildly into the air. Maquisards ran past Billy into the trees, some pausing to train their guns on the dark armored shapes of the vehicles. All around him were the starburst flashes of light and frenetic chatter of small-arms fire. He squeezed off a burst of his machine gun, then followed the girl into the woods.

The woods were not thick. There were patches of open ground where the moon splashed brightly. The ground was broken, though, and they fell headlong over stones and snags as they ran for cover up the slope. Here and there a bullet homing through the trees found its mark, and a man would go down.

The Germans were forced by the trees and broken ground to halt their vehicles at the edge of the woods. Soldiers piled out of the vehicles, firing as they ran for cover.

The Maquisards, ahead of them on the slope, had the advantage of higher elevation. The forest rose steadily behind them and continued on to the summit, and the open patches of moonlit ground below gave them clear fields of fire. Each one found cover behind a rock or tree, hunkered down, and trained his fire down at the advancing Germans who had the clear advantage of numbers and firepower.

As he knelt behind a boulder, the SS captain directed his men into positions up the hill with his pistol. A squad of men toting a big MG 34 settled quickly behind a fallen log and set up the gun on its tripod. One fed the belt into the magazine, and the other turned the gun at the main body of Maquis. Suddenly the throaty *bawp, bawp, bawp, bawp* of the big machine gun cut through the small-arms chatter.

The man crouching next to Billy stood up holding his face, then he fell back to the ground. Billy ducked as the big gun swept over his position. Shards of bark jumped into the air, and he watched in astonishment as the big machine gun cut along the log like an invisible meat cleaver, hammering, chopping, probing for flesh and bone.

Everything was moving so fast. Everywhere tongue-flashes of light from the muzzles threw random shadows across faces and limbs; the ear-splitting noise and the screams of men being hit were impossible to comprehend. They were all swept along with it like a leaf in a strong gale.

Billy came up with his submachine gun and loosed a covering burst into the trees. He squeezed off another burst, firing low, then, feeling the torque of the muzzle climb, let off on the trigger. He ducked, waited, and came up again, this time training his sights on a muzzle flash across the clearing. He loosed a short burst, saw the man reel into the darkness, then crouched back behind the log.

Coming up again, he saw a man running cleanly silhouetted in the moon, saw where he was headed. He took aim, leading him, and squeezed the trigger. *Click.* Again. *Click.* Empty. He cursed. He yanked the spent clip from the breech, fished a fresh one from his bandolier, and, as he fed it into the breech, the magazine clicking home, he could see Colette out of the corner of his eyes, kneeling behind a stump and firing her Sten gun. Her brothers were just beyond her up the slope, and beyond them were several more men, with Pierre directing them with his hands. His face shone with a benign pleasantness, and Billy thought he'd never seen anything so angelic or brave.

A spray of bullets forced the girl down. Moments later she came up and loosed off several short bursts, her face glaring in the light of her muzzle flashes. She was a tough girl, all right, he thought. Still, he was afraid for her and wanted only to get her safely to the summit, where he hoped the plane would come and take them away. But he had no confidence in that now. He had no confidence of life beyond the next few yards of the slope.

Major Dubois moved behind them, calling out and waving everyone toward the summit. The Maquisards advanced up the hill from tree to tree, rock to rock, laying down a heavy field of fire, then moving upward in leapfrog patterns—four men covering while four ran ahead, then these covering while the others came forward, with the wounded and dying bodies of their comrades marking their steady ascent.

The Germans advanced in quick forays. They would dart ahead, ducking as bullets kicked up little sprays of dirt and pieces of bark and stone around their feet and heads, then move forward. The MG 34 was moved forward, and the four-man squad set it up quickly and efficiently. Immediately the long, perforated barrel of the gun swung upward and *bawp, bawp, bawp, bawp,* the tracer rounds described the incredible rate of fire tearing into the upward-moving positions of the Maquis.

A German soldier stood up and threw a stick grenade, but it fell short and only tore up the ground and through the overhead branches. Billy was hunkered down about ten yards from where it struck, and he felt the sudden sharp concussion of air, the ground rising with a big *ka-whump* of noise. Bits of shot dirt and rubble rained back down through the leaves.

A Maquisard responded by throwing a fragmentation grenade down the slope, the grenade smoking and hitting then rolling into a nest of men.

An instant later there was a tremendous flash of light, and the earth threw up a fountain of dirt and two man-shapes lifted back with the explosion. A third man clutched his face and stumbled down through the trees; his helmet, secured by the chin strap, was blown back off his head. The Maquis threw several more grenades, forcing the Germans to lizard-crawl back out of range.

They were at the final leg of the climb now. The elevation was steeper here, and the trees thinned considerably until they reached the summit. It was dangerous ground, Billy thought. Up ahead the night sky showed beyond the trees, and from somewhere above, a cool, wet, grass-smelling air streamed down over the ground like a flow of water.

The four older Frenchmen spoke to Major Dubois briefly. *Here it comes,* Billy thought. Then the major shouted to the woodcutter, "Take everyone to the field, Arnaud! Hurry! The Americans and your family! We will hold the Boche as long as possible!"

But if the woodcutter had heard the major he ignored him and continued to fire down at the Germans. Billy caught the gist of what the major had said and had to resist clubbing the woodcutter over the head with the butt of his gun.

"I will take them," Pierre said.

"Go, Pierre! Go!" the major yelled. "Take two others with you for cover. Here is a flashlight to signal the plane. Three dots, two dashes."

"Three dots, two dashes," Pierre repeated, taking the flashlight. He gestured at two of the men. "You two, come with me!"

Major Dubois looked at the girl. "You must go, Colette," he said. "Go with God! And with my love," he added.

"Good-bye, Antoine," she said. "May God protect you!"

Billy rushed forward and took hold of her arm. "Let's go!" he shouted.

"No, no—wait! Papa!" she cried. She rushed to her father's side. "Papa, you must come!" she cried. "Jean-Claude, François, you must come!"

Jean-Claude looked earnestly at his father. "It is time, Papa!"

"There's no time for this!" Billy growled. He pulled the girl away from her father and headed up the slope after Pierre and the others. Just ahead of them one of the older men sat down abruptly and fell back against a tree trunk. A trickle of blood leaked from the side of his head. Billy hurried past him with the girl. "It's not much farther," he said. "We're almost there."

The girl looked down the slope and cried, *"Papa, tu dois venir! Jean-Claude! François!"*

Jean-Claude and François crouched beside their father. "Papa, you must come!" Jean-Claude pleaded.

The woodcutter waved them away. "You go! You fight the Boche in London with your Uncle Maurice. Henri and I will fight them here. He raised his gun over his head and shouted, "Long live Free France!"

Henri looked proudly at him. He fed a new clip into his gun, sent the bolt home, and squeezed off several short bursts.

Jean-Claude shook his head. "Papa . . ."

"Go!"

The two sons hesitated, looked at one another, then started up the slope.

The woodcutter, Henri, and the other Maquisards trained their fire down through the trees on the advancing dark shapes of the enemy. Then Major Dubois saw several German soldiers spreading up the hill to flank them, and he waved two of his men ahead to cut them off. The remainder of the group scrabbled upward a few yards, loosed off several short bursts from their British-supplied Sten guns, moved up another few yards. They worked steadily up through the dangerous ground of the thinning trees while firing down at the advancing Germans and throwing more fragmentation grenades, all the while the battle drawing closer to the field at the summit.

જન્

Billy guessed the field at about twelve hundred yards in length and maybe half that in width, the lay of land gently sloping away from both sides of the crest to afford a decent landing strip. The moon was bright on the grass and lit the trees on the far side of the field. Billy still held the girl's hand, thinking only about the plane now and getting her on board. *Where is it?*

The group spread out along the edge of the field—Pierre and the two Maquisards in the center, the three older men to their left, and Billy, the girl, and the two Americans to their right. Billy made a mental tally and wondered how everyone would fit on the plane. Everyone was thinking the same thing, he knew. *The girl will fit on the plane, that is for certain. The rest of them can go hang themselves. Come on, plane. The plane, God,* he prayed. *Anything you want.*

The chatter of small-arms fire grew steadily louder and louder behind them. The sound of it sheeted over their heads, and, cutting through the echoing report, came the throatiness of the big machine gun. Everyone looked down through the trees, knowing that soon it wouldn't matter about the plane. *Get us out of here, God. Anything.*

Colette squeezed Billy's hand.

He looked at her, and she smiled at him fully now. Then the wind shifted, and with it he heard the far-off drone of a plane, a single engine by the sound of it. He studied the sky and saw nothing but the moon. Could he have imagined it? As the wind shifted again, he heard only the sound of the battle behind him drawing closer and closer, the ugly sputter of the big machine gun chopping through it like a meat cleaver.

"Regardez!" the girl cried, pointing at the sky. *"L'avion!"*

Billy followed her point in time to see a tiny, dark speck glide silently across the moon. The drone of the engine grew louder and more steady with each second, and he felt the first jolt of real hope go through him. His mind began to weigh the approach of the battle against the arrival of the plane. There was hope, just a glimmer of hope. A footrace for hope.

A bullet ricocheted off a nearby stone and whined off into the night. Billy looked quickly down through the trees. The battle was clawing up to them, he saw, the pitch of battle ascending and growing fiercer, with more and more starburst muzzle flashes winking up through the dark tunnels of the forest. Explosions shook the ground. The cries of men punctuated the hellish din. He searched the sky for the plane. *God. God. Anything, God.*

Suddenly a loud burst of machine gun fire roared just behind him, and, whirling, he saw two Maquisards lying dead at his feet, their bodies riddled with dark bullet holes.

"You will drop your weapons," a man said in English.

Billy looked up and found himself staring down the muzzle of a Sten gun. Pierre was holding it.

"What's going on?"

"I said drop your weapons, or I shall be forced to kill you." Pierre gestured to the three older men with his gun. *"Allez par là."*

The three Frenchmen moved over next to the Americans and the girl. The Americans looked at one another.

"Say, what is this?" Billy laughed.

"He is Vichy," the girl spat. "A traitor."

Billy looked at her. She had spoken in English.

Pierre chuckled at the girl. *"Vous et les reste des français libres sont fous.* You are fools."

She glared at him.

Billy looked from the girl to Pierre. The thought of him being a traitor had still not registered in his mind. And then it was clear. "You let the Krauts know where we were, didn't you? The farm. Now this."

"Clever boy."

"You were shooting at the Krauts."

"They were shooting at me," Pierre said, smiling in that benignly pleasant way of his. "Now drop your weapons." He pointed the muzzle at Billy's chest.

"We'd better do as he says," Butch Harding said. "Better to be a live POW than a dead hero." He dropped his gun to the ground. The waist gunner from the 93rd did likewise. The three older men produced three small pistols, then stood gazing impassively at the man.

Billy and Colette lowered their machine guns.

"The shoulder gun as well," Pierre gestured to Billy. "Thumb and forefinger."

Billy eased the Colt from its holster and dangled it before him. The moonlight caught the nickel plating and it shone brilliantly along the barrel and engraved relief.

"It is a beautiful weapon," Pierre said. "Drop it—gently."

Just then Jean-Claude and François came crashing up through the trees to join them.

Pierre jerked his head at them and swung the muzzle of his gun. In that instant Billy flipped the Colt back into his palm, cocked the hammer, and fired. A tongue of flame tore through the air, and Pierre went down in a violent twirl. He lay flat on his back, his arms straight out to his sides, and blinked wonderingly at the stars. A pulse of blood spread out from the dark hole in his chest.

Jean-Claude and François looked down at the two dead Maquisards, then over at Pierre. The disbelief registered on their faces.

"Nice bit of work," Butch said.

Billy bent over and took the machine gun from Pierre's searching fingers. Pierre stared up at him, his eyes losing their focus. *"Herr, Erbarme Dich mir!"* he coughed. "Lord, have mercy on me." He blinked thickly. The lids folded halfway down over the staring eyes and settled.

"He spoke in German," Billy said.

Jean-Claude bent over the dead man and rifled through his pockets.

"Is he not Vichy?" Colette asked him.

"No, he is not Vichy," Jean-Claude said, reading his papers. "His name was Eugen Kessler. Boche."

"Boche?" Butch Harding asked, picking out the word. "You mean he's a Kraut?" He looked down at the half-lidded eyes. "You could've fooled me."

"*Oui*, monsieur."

The roar of the plane drew their eyes to the far tree line.

The girl glanced anxiously down through the trees. "Is Papa not coming?" she asked her brother. "No Henri?"

"No, Colette," Jean-Claude said.

"We've got to signal the plane," Billy said. He picked up his Sten gun and the discarded flashlight lying in the grass. "Anyone know the code?"

"Three dots, two dashes," the girl said in English.

Butch Harding took the flashlight, and he and the waist gunner ran out onto the field and began to signal the plane.

The plane, a big Lysander, came in low over the treetops, nearly clipping them, then put down in the middle of the field about a hundred yards from the edge of the trees.

"Let's go," Billy said. He took the girl's hand and bolted toward the plane. The three older men followed after them. Jean-Claude and François hesitated, looked back toward the fighting, then took off across the field.

Bouncing along on big balloon tires, the plane rolled over the field, its single engine popping throatily. The pilot slowed the plane enough to turn it, then, revving its engine and cutting its rudder, swung the tail neatly around. The airplane straightened, taxied forward, and the pilot made ready to take off.

Everyone was running toward the plane: the two other American airmen, Billy, Colette, and her two brothers. The three older Frenchmen were trailing and huffing wind. A door swung open in the fuselage of the Lysander. An Englishman leaned out and helped the two American fliers on board.

Billy and Colette arrived at the plane, with Jean-Claude and François close behind.

The Englishman counted the remaining heads. "Awfully sorry. Can't take all of you, chaps," he said. "Won't clear the trees."

The three older Frenchmen arrived and crowded past everyone into the plane.

"We can take two more, is all," the Englishman said.

Billy looked at the girl. The girl looked at her brothers.

Suddenly there was a tremendous crash of sound, as though someone had yanked open a door in the wall of trees behind them and out spilled the battle. Everyone turned and saw that the fighting had broken through the edge of the field. They could just see the dark shapes of the Maquisards working their way back slowly along the trees. The men were crouching and firing into the woods at the unseen Germans, then backing up along the tree line and firing.

Jean-Claude looked earnestly at his sister. *"Dieu vous protège, ma sœur!"* He looked at Billy. "Take care of her, *mon ami.* You are a good man, I know." Smiling, he added, "I think that she is in love with you. She is a good cook too."

"What?"

"Au revoir, Colette!" Jean-Claude kissed his sister, then he turned and ran back across the field.

François was right behind him. *"Au revoir, Colette!"*

"Jean-Claude! François!" the girl cried. She pulled away from Billy and started after them.

Billy caught her arm. "What are you doing!"

She looked up at him, her face torn in anguish. "Do you not see, my love?" she said, searching his eyes.

Yes, he did see. In the brightness of the moon everything of the mystery became suddenly clear in the turquoise light of those beautiful robin's eggs eyes that he knew now and understood very well and wanted. Yes, wanted. He wanted to kiss her. For he knew in that moment that he loved her, truly and completely loved her, and he wanted very badly to hold her in his arms and kiss her. "Colette?"

"Oui?"

"Come with me," he said. "Please come."

Then it all changed. The struggle was gone from her eyes. All that remained was a look of resignation that drew the brightness from her eyes, and it made him feel sick and hollow inside. "No, please, Colette . . ." And then he saw it was no good.

She pulled the silver crucifix from around her neck and thrust it into his hands. "I will pray for you," she said. "May God go with you and my love!" She turned to leave.

"No!"

She stopped him with her hand. "This will be for nothing if you do not live," she cried. She stepped up onto her toes and kissed him tenderly on his lips. "I love you, William," she smiled. She whirled away and ran after her brothers.

"Colette—no! Colette!" He started after her.

"Where're you going, you crazy fool!" the Englishman called from the plane. "We can't wait!"

Billy ran, calling after the girl, pleading with her to stop running. Then he saw as she glanced over her shoulder a turquoise flash of loving sadness in her eyes. "NO!" he shouted. "NO!"

It was a footrace against time and hope—the plane behind, freedom behind, but the girl ahead, running. He was consumed by the conflicting emotions clawing in his chest: hoping and loving, the girl running, the tenderness of touching, of longing and desiring, love and anger and fear, and loving and reaching for and wanting and not having, the girl running, when his toe caught a root and he sprawled headlong to the ground. He jumped up with a curse. Tears streamed down his cheeks as he stumbled forward into a run, the girl farther away now, still running, when a rake of bullets tore up the ground around his feet and forced him to pull up. Looking up-field, he saw that the Germans had broken out of the tree line.

The Lysander revved its engine and began to roll forward. The Englishman in the door waved furiously at him. "Come on, you crazy Yank!"

Billy leveled his Sten gun at the Germans and loosed off a burst. The plane was rolling faster and away from him. The girl was still running in the opposite direction. Billy cursed, shouted after her, feeling the helpless drain of hope and will, and another spray of enemy bullets drove him after the plane.

The Lysander accelerated, bullets peppering the fuselage and rudder, as Billy ran after the plane. Everything was gone inside him now—the girl and everything gone—and he thought only of getting on the plane. Angry tears spurted from his eyes.

The Englishman reached out his hand. "Come on, Yank! You can do it!"

Billy tossed the Sten gun and leaped into the hatch, just managing to hook his elbows inside the door panel. His legs dragged over the ground as he struggled to kick himself up into the cabin.

The Englishman took hold of the seat of his trousers and he was inside. "There's a lad!"

The plane was up and climbing slowly, heavily, just brushing the treetops, with the field steadily falling away in the spill of moonlight, as the plane wheeled in a slow banking turn.

Billy looked quickly out the window, ducking instinctively as a bullet tore through the cabin and out through the ceiling. Peering out the window, he saw the little troupe of Maquis, tiny and dark against the field, moving back along the edge of the trees. He saw little spits of fire from their guns and those of the Germans as the battle spilled out into the field. And then he saw Colette, knowing it was her, fighting valiantly, and he prayed feverishly that God would protect her, that his angels would keep watch over her. That somehow he might see her again, hold her in his arms, look into her beautiful eyes. But when he saw her fall to the ground, the prayers died in his throat. He stared dumbfounded for several terrible moments, then slammed his fist against the bulkhead.

The field fell out of his vision, sweeping away from him in a cloud. Everything went suddenly cold and dark in his chest. He stared numbly out the window.

The men in the plane said nothing. There was nothing to say. The relief of having escaped the battle was spent in the knowledge of what their sitting in the plane had cost. They looked at one another sheepishly at first. It was the right thing to do, of course, every man told himself, but still there was shame in it and they each looked quietly at the floor. The roar of the big engine filled the cabin.

Billy sat bent forward with his elbows dug into his knees, the crucifix dangling through his fingers. It glinted dully in the ambient light of the cabin, twinkling now and then when some lancing shaft of the moon caught it. He gazed at it feeling nothing but a big hole in his chest—a hole so black and numb and full of nothingness that he thought he might fall forever in it.

The fields of France and the sounds of war fell quickly away as the Lysander planed over the village of Mâcon, then, flying at an altitude below the German radar, droned silently toward the coast. And somewhere during the crossing of the channel he forgot his vow to God.

11 ★★★

Octber 31, 1943. 1600 hours. Halesbury Airdrome, East Anglia, England. Home of the 52nd Fighter Group. First Lieutenant Joe Thompson looked at his cards speculatively. He had just drawn a ten of clubs. He slid it in next to the jack of diamonds, the king of diamonds, and the ace of spades. He folded the cards then spaced them out evenly so he could just see the corners. He frowned. He either had a straight going, or nothing—nothing, no doubt, the way his luck had been going all afternoon. Need a queen. A nice-looking kid of twenty-four, he was of medium height, muscular build, with dark brown hair and the penetrating green eyes of a fighter pilot.

"Whaddya bet Zeb's raking him over the coals?" the man on his left said.

"Sucker bet," Joe Thompson said, thinking about his next card.

"Shoot, Zeb'll probably have him pickin' up butts—remind him to keep his head down." Pete Skagway chuckled. "Say, that reminds me . . . you got a butt? My spares are in my footlocker."

Joe gave him a cigarette.

Skagway took it and fumbled around his pockets for his lighter.

Joe eyed him. He knew what was coming.

Skagway found his lighter and snapped his thumb over the wheel. It wouldn't light. He closed the lid and banged it against his palm. He tried again. No flame, just sparks. He looked up at Joe.

Joe shook his head. "I swear, Skagway. If you ain't the biggest mooch." He flipped open his lighter and touched the flame under the cigarette.

Skagway took a big drag and blew out a cloud of smoke. "Yeah, there's a guy with some kind of luck," he said. "Steps in it but good and comes out smellin' like a rose."

The fifth card came around and Joe picked it up and looked at it. Three of hearts. He cursed silently.

Skagway picked up his card and chuckled. He chuckled after every card he drew, and Joe regretted having given him a cigarette. Skagway was a smallish fellow with an acne-scarred face, and one of those hairlines that receded high off the temples, then came around into a narrow, sand-colored peninsula that appeared to be waging a losing battle on the forehead.

The dealer was a handsome kid by the name of Wilfred Suggs, but everyone called him "Sugar" because of his pretty boy face, and because of his gentle Baton Rouge accent. He looked at the man on his left and drawled, "Any cawds?"

"I'll take three, Sugar," Captain Warren "Turtle" Turlock said with a worried look in his eyes. He watched anxiously as Sugar Suggs dealt three cards.

Skagway started chuckling, pulling on a mustache that he was trying too hard to grow. "What you bet he's prayin' for a pair?"

"Shut up, Skagway."

"I swear, Turtle, you college boys come up with the cleverest rejoinders."

Everyone called him Turtle because of his slow Yankee drawl, and because it always seemed to take him an hour to walk across the street. He looked at his new hand, and his expression widened into a picture of doom.

Skagway chuckled with delight.

☜☞

Billy Hochreiter slung his duffel bag over his shoulder and walked away from the administrative building. His ears were still burning from the blistering the group commander had given him over the fundamentals of aerial tactics and common sense. He was glad that was over.

It felt good to be outside. Everything was so big and open and clean. Feeling the saline tartness of the air against his face, it suddenly felt good to be alive and standing on ground where people weren't trying to kill him. It was like being told by the doctor that he'd made a mistake on his first diagnosis—you were going to live after all. And not just live, but "What do you know, son, you're as healthy as an ox."

In the glaring brightness of the mid-afternoon, France seemed to recede into his subconscious—like the shades of a bad dream upon the first waking light. All of them—the Maquis; Henri and his father; the woodcutter and his sons; the vision of Colette gazing up at him as she fell against that bright and terrible field—gone, receded into a dark haze. Then something else rose from the haze, suddenly and unexpectedly. He stopped in his tracks and looked behind him. There was no one behind him. Still he felt it rising in him like an inchoate mist, a vague swirl of brain synapses and emotions that ossified slowly into a stony knot of remorse—or guilt. He had no idea of its source, only that it produced in him a sense of dread.

A faint saline scent crept in off the North Sea coast, a few miles to the east, and fingered down into his jacket. A shiver went through him. He reached into his jacket pockets to warm his hands and felt the little silver crucifix. Without thinking of what it was or what it meant, he ran his thumb over the blunt edges. Then he remembered and immediately felt loneliness edging up through his arm. He removed his hand from his pocket, shrugged up his fleece collar against the wet, autumn chill, and headed toward the row of Nissen huts next to the big T2 hangar, where the 61st Squadron was billeted.

The autumn-stripped trees of Tealbrook Wood were dark against the sky. Exiting the trees, the rows of drab green Nissen huts were on his right. Off to his left were the large A-shaped runways, and the brick and glass control tower, with its bright orange wind sock fingering the wind. Beyond were miles and miles of farmland, the multicolored fields stitched together over the low country like an enormous patchwork quilt.

Somewhere the big Pratt and Whitney engine of a Thunderbolt coughed, sputtered, then roared to life. Another throttled to life, and then another. Billy paused and watched as a flight of Thunderbolts rumbled in pairs down the main runway, heading northeast into the wind. He watched as they climbed against the gray, clouded English sky. It felt good to be home. Good to be alive.

Billy stood for a long moment looking into the Nissen hut. A row of bunks lined the walls on either side, ten bunks to a side, with four windows on each wall. The men were huddled over a game of five-card draw in the center aisle, next to the stove. The stove squatting in the center of the hut, with the pipe running up and out through the ceiling, threw off a terrific heat. The men were sitting on a grouping of footlockers. Some were playing cards, others were watching, but everyone's attention was on the game. A blanket was spread over the floor, and there was a pile of British pound notes heaped in the middle of it. Cigarette smoke rose from the huddle and swirled against the curved ceiling that was plastered with pinup girls: Betty Grable, Rita Hayworth, Greta Garbo, Ginger Rogers. Billy felt the heat from the stove working toward him.

"Hey, Thompson, gimme another butt."

Billy felt the sure pull of the ground under his feet. It had all come home to him. The stony thing was gone.

"Get your own, mooch," Joe Thompson growled. "I'll take two. Make 'em winners, Sugar."

Wilfred Suggs dealt him two cards.

Joe picked them up, looked at them, and frowned. He threw his hand down. "I'm out. Lousy game."

"Come on, Thomps, gimme a butt," Skagway begged. "Mine are in my footlocker."

Joe relented, fished a cigarette from his pack, and looked over at the door to see who had come in. His eyes went wide. "As I live and breathe!" He stood to his feet, his forgotten pack of cigarettes suspended before Skagway's face. "Look what the cat drug in."

Someone wolf-whistled as everyone turned to face Billy. Skagway grabbed a cigarette, then, seeing his chance, quickly snatched two more and stuck one behind each ear.

Joe absently stuffed the pack of cigarettes in his pocket. "If it ain't Hotshot Montana," he laughed. "Back from the dead."

"Hey, fellas," Billy grinned. He walked down the aisle and came to his old bed, directly across from where the men were playing cards. A mattress was rolled up against the headrail.

Some of the men came over to him. "Hey, Hochreiter!" "Whaddya know!" "Say, Billy Boy!"

"Sure swell of you fellas to throw a party like this for me," Billy said.

"Shoot, we'll throw you a party."

"Where you been?" Joe asked him, grinning big. "Lose your Red Ryder compass or something?"

"He's been sightseeing all over France, I hear," someone answered for him.

Billy grunted. "Sightseeing." He unrolled the mattress and straightened it to fit over the springs.

"Sure, strolling down the Champs-Élysées," Wilfred Suggs grinned. "All that French cooking . . . the wine . . . the bread . . ."

"The French dames," someone interjected.

Billy chuckled uneasily. "You guys've been watching too many movies." He spread the sheets and blankets over the mattress.

"Zeb give you a pasting?"

"Pinned my ears but good," Billy admitted.

"I'll bet he did."

"Gave me the 'bandits out of the sun' drill."

"They going to send you to the Pacific?" Turtle asked, his big, brown eyes wide with gloom. "They send all escaped pilots to the Pacific, don't they?"

"Nobody said anything to me," Billy said. "Shoot, everything was a blur. I couldn't tell one French town from the next."

Skagway saw something in his eyes. "Tell me you didn't meet any French dames," he hooted.

Billy ignored him.

Skagway seized his advantage. "Ooh, la, la!" he jeered lewdly. "I guess his plane wasn't the only thing that got shot out from under him."

Billy walked over to him and yanked him to his feet by his collar. "Shut your mouth, Skagway, or so help me—"

"Hey! What're you so sore at?" Skagway laughed. "Come on, Hochreiter, I didn't mean nothin'."

The party atmosphere in the place was suddenly dead. Everyone looked at the two of them. The card game was forgotten.

"Leave him alone, Montana," Joe said. "He didn't mean nothing. Take it easy."

Billy dropped him hard against a bed, so that the bed scraped against the cement floor. "Just shut your big mouth," he said. He went across the aisle and began to unpack his duffel bag.

Skagway climbed to his feet and glared at him, his fists doubling. The other men looked at him and then at Billy.

Billy rolled some socks and dropped them into his footlocker. It was so quiet in the room that all one could hear was the roar of the stove. Billy turned and faced Skagway. "Hey look, Skag, I'm a little on edge, okay? Call me a jerk."

Relief spread over Skagway's face. His fists relaxed. "Ain't nothin'," he said. He pulled a cigarette off his ear and grabbed it with his teeth. He kicked a footlocker between his legs and sat down on it hard. "Let's play cards. Anybody gotta light?"

"Whose deal is it?" Sugar asked, snapping the cards.

"Mine, I believe," Turtle replied. "It is mine, isn't it?" The game resumed, and the gambling atmosphere came back in stages.

Billy wrapped the shoulder straps around his Colt, then laid it in the corner of the footlocker on top of some dungarees. *Where did that come from?* he wondered. *Skagway is a Class A jerk, but where did that come from?*

Joe was watching him. He stepped across the aisle. "You all right, Montana?"

"Sure. Never better."

"You sure?"

"Sure I'm sure. Just a little edgy, like I said. I'm okay."

"What happened in France?"

"Nothing," Billy snapped.

"Nothing?"

Billy tossed another pair of socks into the footlocker.

"All right," Joe said. "Let the dead bury the dead. It's over. Tell me then, hotshot, what happened on the Schweinfurt Ramrod? I lost my wing man somewhere over Belgium."

Billy looked at him. "You can knock it off with the third degree, okay? I already got both barrels from Zeb." He threw a pair of trousers, unfolded, into the footlocker. "I just want to get back in the air and do my job, all right?"

Joe's green eyes were so intense they seemed never to blink. He continued to stare at Billy with a look that could cut through metal. "Sure," he said.

Billy looked at him hard. "You want somebody else as your wing man? Fine by me. You got every right. Take it up with the colonel. Just get off my back."

"Settle down, Lieutenant."

"Sure thing, Captain. Whatever you say, Captain." He threw his shaving kit into the footlocker.

Everyone from the card game was looking over at them.

"Carumba, amigos, what is this? A lovers' spat so soon?" Happy Molina, a wiry Puerto Rican with a mess of black hair and dark brown eyes, came over to them flashing his beautifully white teeth. "What say we go over to the Guinea and have a few warm beers? You two can kiss and make up while I make time with what's-her-name. Everything will be hunky-dory again." He grinned broadly. "Whaddya say?"

Joe continued staring at Billy.

Billy stood looking down at the pair of shorts in his hands.

"Well?" Happy grinned. "We gonna stand around here all day and grow moss on our teeth?"

"You fellas go ahead," Billy said. "I'll catch up to you later. I got some letters to write."

"The letters can wait," Joe said. "Come on, Montana, you can thrill us all with lies of your daring escape. These losers around here are depressing."

"You said it," Happy agreed. "Cleaned you out but good, didn't they, Thomps?"

"Speak for yourself. Montana, here, has some back pay coming, don't you, hotshot?"

Billy saw that the blowtorch eyes had cooled. It was Joe again. A smile spread over his face. "I guess I'm buying."

"Now you're talking, amigo!"

Joe clapped his hand on Billy's shoulder. "This time, you stick close to me, hear?" he grinned. "I don't want you getting your tail flamed by any of the locals."

"Get outta here."

Happy howled, "Carumba! Are we gonna have a hot time tonight!"

12 ★★★★

Jane Worthing looked into the mirror over the bathroom sink and added the finishing touches to her makeup, carefully tracing her lips with a bright cherry gloss. She pressed her lips together, pursed them, then studied her face. One of her eyebrows arched.

"I look like a trollop," she frowned.

She picked up a hand towel, wet it with her tongue, and wiped off the lipstick. She looked at the rest of her face, opened a jar of cold cream and, in an almost guilty panic, worked a dollop over her eyes and cheeks until everything was scrubbed clean and glowed with an oily shine.

She rinsed the oily residue of the cold cream off her face and looked back into the mirror. Big drops of water sheeted off her brow and nose and gathered her eyelashes into little spears. She studied herself for several moments. She wiped her face with a towel, padded back to her bedroom, and stood in the doorway looking in. It seemed she couldn't make up her mind whether or not to enter the room.

The bedroom was a small room where the furnishings—typically pubescent female—were somewhat incongruous for a twenty-two-year-old married woman. The bed was set against the right wall—a single four-poster with a white, lacy bedcover and overhead canopy. A shelf beetling out from the wall was lined with several dolls, little books, knickknacks, and tiny clay pots with dried flowers spouting from them.

To the left of the bed was a mahogany wardrobe, opened to reveal an assortment of tweed skirts and jackets, hanging neatly. Beside these were several cotton blouses, a space of empty hangers, then several younger-style dresses and a neat array of schoolgirl uniforms. An assortment of shoes were lined across the wardrobe floor, ranging from low-heeled pumps and flat-soled everyday wear to tennis shoes and brown Mary Janes with the toes and heels scuffed. A watercolor print of a peasant girl leading a gaggle of geese hung on the wall between the bed and wardrobe.

She walked into the room, sat down at the small desk, and looked out the window over acres and acres of fields and hedgerows of the flat, English countryside to the gentle foothills of the Chiltern Hills. The trees and shrubbery of every sort were in autumn colors against a gloomy slate gray sky.

She picked up a magazine off the desk and flipped through it in a desultory manner, pausing briefly to study this new fashion or that. Hems were up, hair down, simple, elegant lines—the Coco Chanel look. But her mind was clearly a thousand miles from Paris.

Pausing to rub a sudden chill off her arms, she glanced out the window as a flight of Thunderbolts slid slowly across the late afternoon sky in the distance, the drone of their engines just reaching her. Her eyes grew pensive, softening as her mind flew off to another place. Then she saw her father and brother walking across the field toward the house, both of them holding shotguns, with their two Irish setters prancing alongside. She smiled and flipped through a couple more pages without looking at them; then, laying the magazine down on the desk, she stood up and went over to the dresser that stood against the left wall of the room.

Picking up her brush, she began to work it through her heavy brown curls, angling her head first to one side, then the other, her hair spilling down well past her shoulders in long waves. Looking into the mirror she saw her mother's reflection appear in the doorway behind her.

"It's nearly tea," Mrs. Bellamy said.

"I'll be along in a moment, Mum," Jane said, still brushing her hair.

Her mother looked at her from the doorway. "I think it splendid you getting out and enjoying yourself, dear," she smiled. "You've been working so hard."

Jane said nothing. Her strokes suddenly became choppier, and her thick hair crackled with electricity.

Mrs. Bellamy walked into the room. She was a tall, silver-haired woman with an angular face that was softened by the clean, elegant lines of good breeding. Her skin was without blemish, of a milky, almost translucent, color that was bereft of age spots. Looking at her, one thought of a porcelain vase made of bone china, with a single, long-stemmed white rose spouting from its slender neck.

She put a hand on her daughter's shoulder. "It's been forever now, it seems, since you've gotten out and had a little fun," she said, her gray-blue eyes twinkling intelligently. "You'll have a wonderful evening, you'll see."

Jane grunted ironically. "Oh, yes, I'm sure."

"Of course you will. I'm certain of it." Mrs. Bellamy looked at her daughter's face and her features sharpened. She brushed her fingertips over Jane's cheekbones. "A little rouge wouldn't hurt, would it?" she thought out loud. "Bring out the color a bit. You've such lovely bone structure, Jane . . . maybe a little something around the eyes. Set them off, you know?"

"We're just going to the cinema, Mother."

"Yes, of course. But I'm sure you'll want to pop in at the Golden Guinea for a bite afterward, won't you?"

"I've no intention of popping anywhere. Julie and I just thought to catch a film, actually. We'll be home directly."

"We'll have done with supper by then."

"Then I shall just have to have a second bag of popcorn, won't I?"

Her mother smiled politely at her. "They've such lovely cakes and sweets and things at the Guinea," she said. "It's such a splendid place for people your age to get out and socialize."

"Mother, really," Jane frowned. "What you mean to say is that the Guinea is a favorite haunt of all the soldiers in town. Most of them eligible bachelors."

"It's been a respectable time, dear, since . . . ," she patted Jane's hand. "It's just that I don't like to see you knocking about the house like a . . . like a . . ."

"Like a *what*, Mum?"

Her mother stiffened slightly. "It's been nearly a year. It's time we face facts. It's time we get on in life." Again she broke off. "Yes. Well, I've said enough, haven't I?" She glanced over Jane's face once more, cupped a hand to her cheek, and said, "You're still young. You've plenty of opportunities yet."

"Can we just drop it, Mother?"

Mrs. Bellamy retrieved her hand as though it had been wounded, fidgeting with a pleat in her blouse. She cleared her throat. "Right, then. I'll just see to tea." She touched her daughter on the shoulder, then turning to leave, added, "A little gloss on the lips wouldn't hurt either, dear."

Jane's look drove her across the room. Mrs. Bellamy glanced once more at her daughter before closing the door behind her.

A gloom settled in the void her mother left. She could hear her mother calling to Anna as she went down the stairs. Then everything became very still and quiet and heavy in the gloom.

Jane looked at herself in the mirror, studied her dark blue eyes, followed the line of her jaw, the length of her nose. A complete stranger was looking back at her, someone who seemed suddenly ugly to her, suddenly dowdy. A shade of despair went over her face. *Whatever am I to do?*

She looked down at the picture on the dresser. A man in an RAF uniform smiled up at her. *Has it been a year, Edmund? Has it really?* Then the gloom became too heavy for her to fight against, and everything seemed to go out of her in a rush of tears. "Oh, dear God," she cried.

࿇

Mr. Bellamy threw open the door and he and his son, Robert, and the setters burst into the foyer. He was a stout, barrel-chested man in his early fifties, with bright blue eyes and a snarl of sandy gray hair curling over his ears. The autumn chill shone on his ruddy cheeks. "We're home, Mum!" he roared as he shut the door behind them. "I trust we're not late for tea."

"Two minutes!" Mrs. Bellamy's voice sang from some hinder part of the house.

"Ah! How's that for timing, then, Bobby?" Mr. Bellamy said. He set his double-barreled shotgun in the corner behind the door and hung the brace of ptarmigans on a coat peg by their tied feet.

"I do hope Anna has baked raspberry tarts like I asked her to," Bobby said, glancing down the hall toward the dining room.

"If she hasn't we shall boil her in oil!" Mr. Bellamy said, pulling off his rubber Wellingtons. "Be a good lad, Bobby, and take the birds into the kitchen. Give 'em a good cleaning now."

Robert was a large-boned lad of fourteen with a mop of brown hair tossed over his forehead and bright red cheeks. He put his single-barreled twenty-gauge next to his father's, then kicked off his Wellingtons. "Why do *I* always have to give them a good cleaning?" he whined.

"I shot 'em, you clean 'em, that's the rule. Had you shot them I'd be cleaning them now, wouldn't I?"

"Seems to me the last time I shot a bird I had to clean it too."

"And a good job you did of it, didn't you?" his father grinned. He tousled the boy's hair.

Robert took the birds off the peg and went straight down the hallway toward the kitchen, grumbling as he passed the flight of stairs on his right. The setters pranced at his heels and sniffed at the birds.

Mr. Bellamy looked up as Jane came down the staircase. His eyes went wide.

She was dressed in a light blue, woolen skirt that hit her just below the knees, a white cotton blouse with lace around the collar and cuffs, and she carried a short, gray tweed coat folded over her left arm. Her rich brown hair was parted on one side and held in place with a red barrette to show off her high, intelligent brow and temples. The rest of it fell down over her shoulders in a thick, springy mass that bounced heavily against her back as she took each stair. She had redone her makeup, not so ostentatiously as before, but her face and eyes and figure shone with a beauty that traced its graceful lines back through generations of landed gentry.

Her father blew a long whistle. "There's my girl!" he boomed. "Let's have a look at you then!"

"Oh, Dad."

Her father looked at her proudly. "Go on, give us a turn."

Jane made a quick half-turn and waved a deprecating hand. "You're being silly."

"Silly, is it? Silly, is it?" Mr. Bellamy beamed with delight. "Give us a kiss then for silliness."

Jane broke into a smile. She kissed her father's cold and stubbly cheek, then lay her head against his chest. She felt the taut bulk of her father's strength beneath her fingers and drank in the cool, rich autumn smells of the countryside that had collected in the tweed of his coat. When he moved to let her free she held onto him.

"Don't let me go, Daddy."

Mr. Bellamy pulled her close to him. "Let you go? Not likely, princess." He kissed the top of her head.

She looked up at him and smiled.

"What's this, then?" he said, lifting a tear off her cheek with a big forefinger. "Seems a bit of rain has leaked onto your face." He frowned up at the ceiling. "Have to rethatch the roof, won't I?"

Jane giggled. "I love you, Daddy."

"There's a girl," he said, patting her back. Then he pushed away abruptly, put his nose into the air, and sniffed. "What's this then? Could it be steak and kidney pie?"

Jane sniffed the air. "Oh, definitely!"

"What are we waiting for?" He took off his coat and hat, hung them on the peg on which the birds had just hung, then put his arm around Jane's waist and walked her toward the dining room.

Anna, a plumpish, open-faced woman in her early forties, was approaching them from the kitchen, carrying a plate of cucumber and butter sandwiches. Mr. Bellamy and Jane drew up to let her pass into the room before them.

Mrs. Bellamy was sitting at one end of the dining table reading a little book of verse. She did not look up as they entered the room. Anna set the plate of sandwiches down, pausing to make sure that everything was properly set on the table. The kettle whistled from the kitchen.

"I'll just get it, Mum," she said.

Jane took the seat next to her mother. Mrs. Bellamy looked up from her book, glanced appraisingly over her daughter's appearance, and smiled. "You look lovely, dear."

"Thank you."

The cold afternoon light streamed into the room through the bay window on the left side of the room, throwing a vague trapezoid of diamond-shaped shadows over the floor and wall. Mr. Bellamy went over to the fireplace and jabbed a poker into the coals. He picked up the scuttle and poured a layer of coal over the bright orange and yellow bed of coals, spacing them with a pair of brass tongs. The fire threw off a wonderful heat that spread to every corner of the room.

Robert galloped into the room, his eyes wide, smacking his lips as he leered over the sandwiches and pastries. The setters raised their noses to the varied scents.

"Did you wash your hands?" Mrs. Bellamy asked the boy.

He groaned.

"About-face, young man," she ordered. "I'll not suffer the stench of bird entrails at my table."

The setters sneaked around the opposite end of the table and curled up before the fire.

It was a wonderful tea, considering the war shortages. Anna came into the room and poured a final round of tea, then began to clear away the dishes. Mr. Bellamy lit his pipe, drawing with several quick puffs, then drawing long and smooth as the bowl glowed warmly. He blew out a big wreath of smoke, shaking out the match, then tossed it into the fire. Then he cleared his throat, angled his feet toward the fire, and closed his eyes in thought.

Outside, the gray light had darkened to a reddish glow, though it was still not dark enough yet to turn on the lights. It was the time between the worlds of light and darkness, when everything seems tinged with a passing air of melancholy.

The faint chime of a bicycle bell tinkled outside.

"That'll be Julie," Jane said.

Everyone turned toward the bay window as the top half of Julie Ellerby floated by over the low hedge that went across the front of the house. She pulled up abruptly, leaned her bicycle against the hedge, and entered the yard through the white picket gate. The sun glowed brightly through her hair as she walked briskly up the walkway toward the front door. Nearing the stoop, she looked over, saw Mr. Bellamy and waved at him, before she disappeared behind the window.

Mrs. Bellamy turned to her son. "Do be a sweet, Robert, and let her in, won't you?"

Robert grabbed the last raspberry tart as Anna was clearing the plate, and swung out of his chair.

A moment later the boy returned, followed by a thin, pleasant-looking girl about the same age as Jane, with bright blue eyes, fiery red cheeks, and a face full of freckles. "Hello, all," she smiled, showing a slight overbite in her front teeth.

"Hello, Julie," Mrs. Bellamy said. "Don't you look lovely."

"I'll say," Mr. Bellamy concurred.

Julie giggled as she quickly kneaded her fingers through an incorrigible mass of frizzy red hair.

Jane got up from the table and put on her jacket.

"It's dreadfully cold out," Julie said. "You'll want your muffler as well."

"Rubbish," Mr. Bellamy said. "It's good for your constitution."

Mrs. Bellamy smiled beatifically at her daughter. "Wear your muffler, dear. I'll not have you catching your death of cold."

Mr. Bellamy grunted as he fumbled through his pockets. "Here, princess. Take the Talbot," he smiled, holding out the keys to her.

"Thank you, Dad."

"Don't use up all the petrol now. We've only a few gallons left us for the month."

"Shouldn't use too much," she smiled. "We're just going to the cinema and back, right, Julie?"

"Oh. Why, yes, of course," Julie agreed, then winked conspiratorially at Mrs. Bellamy.

"We shan't wait up," Mrs. Bellamy said. "Have a splendid time, girls."

Jane bent over and kissed her on the cheek.

13 ★★★★

The Golden Guinea was a pub that sat on a well-worn corner in the center of town, about four miles from the air base. The street lamps stood black against the overcast of the night, like blindfolded sentinels. The little shops and pubs that crowded around the market square had their blackout shades drawn against the threat of enemy bombers—in the street you could hardly see your hand in front of your face.

A shiny, black taxi pulled up in front of the Golden Guinea. Billy, Joe Thompson, and Happy Molina got out of the cab and paid the driver. They gave him a handsome tip.

"Ta, Yanks!" the driver said, then drove off.

The Guinea was their second stop. They had gone to a little pub in Holton, the tiny farming town that abutted the air base, and had eaten supper there, for the food was better by far than anything in Halesbury. Halesbury, on the other hand, was where the action was—at least the kind of action to be found in a quiet English town near the North Sea coast, twenty-five miles from the nearest big city.

The Americans entered the pub and paused just inside the doors, allowing their eyes to adjust to the sudden brightness of the room. A pall of smoke eddied across the room, just above head height, and a happy din pressed against the three pilots. They were quite conspicuous in their American uniforms and leather jackets, with their hats canted rakishly off their foreheads and their hands shoved down into their pockets as though they were reaching for their garters. Some heads turned and looked their way, while others ignored them.

A cigarette dangled carelessly from the corner of Joe Thompson's mouth as his green eyes swept over the room, ignoring the pan of faces just below his eye level. "Something will open," he said.

Billy, feeling himself a bit of a spectacle, nodded at a group of old men huddled at the table nearest him.

"Oy, Yank," one of the old men greeted him with a toothless smile. He raised his glass of dark beer. "'Ere's to ye."

The others looked at Billy and nodded, raising their glasses off the table. "Here! Here!"

Billy allowed a smile. Then a loud bark of laughter drew his eyes to the rear of the pub, where Pete Skagway and the others were throwing darts. He shook his head. "I thought they were going to the Knight's Arms."

Joe shrugged.

Billy noted a group of RAF pilots sitting at a couple of tables to the left, near the bar, who were staring at Pete and the other Americans in the back. A booth opened about halfway down the wall that separated the pub into two rooms.

"Here we go," Joe said.

Billy followed Joe and Happy into the pub. The RAF pilots turned and watched them as they passed by.

"Chihuahua," Happy groaned.

"Ignore 'em," Joe Thompson said. "We just came for a quiet drink, right?"

"Roger that," Billy said. One of the RAF pilots, a dark-haired man, watched Billy intently. He had him pegged, Billy could tell, just by the look in his eyes, and he felt his insides constrict around a hard little knot of bile.

Happy Molina nodded to the RAF pilots and flashed his pearly whites at them, tipping his hat, but the Brits only stared at him.

The waitress was wiping off the table. "Be with you luvs in a moment."

"Take your time," Joe said. He slid into the booth, his back to the RAF pilots; Happy slid in next to Joe, and Billy sat facing them.

Happy lightly patted the table with his small brown hands, smiling and nodding at passersby.

Billy looked over the dividing wall into the dining room through the row of windows. It was crowded with people: huddles of men and women with hard, ruddy, weathered faces that were bright with cheer. He glanced back at the RAF pilots; the dark-haired Brit was still staring at him. Billy started to rise out of his seat.

"Sit down, Montana," Joe said.

Billy sat down. "Friendly chaps, these limeys," he said.

"It's their country."

"No call to be jerks about it though." Someone howled at the rear of the pub. It was Skagway. "Nuts."

The waitress, a tall, bosomy woman on the backside of her prime, came over to their table.

"Hello, Frieda," Happy said, smiling up at her.

"Hello, Luv," she said. "What'll you Yanks have?"

After all three ordered, Happy watched the waitress leave. "Carumba!"

"She's old enough to be your mother," Joe said.

"You leave my mother out of this."

When the drinks came Billy and Joe sipped theirs slowly. Happy looked at the dark—almost black—ale, the foam brimming a light brown creaminess over the lip. He raised the glass and finished it in a couple of long pulls.

"Take it easy, Haps," Joe said. "You in a race or something?"

"I don't like the taste," Happy said. "I want it to get where it's going without tasting it."

The Americans playing darts let out another string of hoots. Everyone in the pub looked back at them.

Billy glanced over his shoulder and shook his head. "Maybe we ought to head down to the Knight's Arms."

"Aw, they're okay," Joe said.

"I like it here," Happy said, drumming his palms on the table, building rapidly into a flourish. His dark eyes suddenly fixed on something across the room. "I'll be right back," he said, and excused himself.

Joe watched him leave. He pulled out a cigarette, tamped the end against the table, and lit it. "Come on, Montana, spill it," he said. He blew a big cloud of smoke in the air. "What's up?"

"Up?"

"What happened over there in France? Something's eating you."

"Nothing's eating me," Billy said. "Skagway gets on my nerves is all."

"I'm not talking about Skagway."

"I'm all right."

Joe stared at him, the blowtorch fierceness back in his green eyes.

Billy took a sip of beer and glanced over at the RAF pilots. They were keeping to themselves now. *That's good,* he thought. *Just came in here for a quiet drink.*

"I got to know that everything's right in your head," Joe said. "We've got another Ramrod in a couple of days."

Billy looked at him. "That soon, huh? Well that's somethin'!"

Joe watched him closely.

"I'm fine, Joe," Billy growled. "You can lay off the mother hen routine."

"You're okay, then?"

"I told you I'm all right, so you can just drop it. I just saw another side of it is all. I'm fine. My head's fine, my feet are fine, everything in between is fine, all right?"

"Okay. I'll drop it."

A howl went up on the other side of the dividing wall. The Brits this time. A red-faced woman threw her head back and laughed, then, cackling, wagged a finger at someone. Billy smiled at her then hunched forward. "Any idea where the Ramrod's going to be?"

"Not a clue. Something big though," Joe said. "The whole wing is going up. Assuming the weather holds."

"That's good, that's good." Billy leaned back into his seat. He felt the warmth of the ale smoothing out into his limbs, felt the hard knot in his stomach loosening, smoothing out in the spreading warmth that moved slowly up into his head. He chuckled and looked up at Joe. "You sure you want me up there with you?"

"Look who's not dropping it now."

"Tell me straight."

"Sure, I want you," Joe said. "You're a good pilot. You'd be a great pilot if you didn't get so spooky in the head."

"Okay, I'll drop it."

"I wish you would."

"Zeb told me the 4th was getting the new P–51s," Billy said. "Whaddya think?"

"We're still gonna beat 'em to a hundred." A big grin spread across Joe's face. "And to top it off, we're gonna throw a big bash to rub their noses in it."

"No kiddin'?"

"Would I kid you? Best line up a date, sport. It's gonna be a hoot."

"A date?"

"Yeah, you know—boy meets girl, boy takes girl out on the town, boy kisses her, girl slaps him. A date. Love 'em and leave 'em. It's an American tradition."

Billy's face changed. As he looked into his glass he was in the five-and-dime back in Columbus, "Moonlight Serenade" was playing on the Wurlitzer, Laura Miller was gliding over the linoleum tiles, and he was right there with her. She was looking up at him, and he could smell her perfume. He could feel the soft, talcumy creaminess of her skin beneath his fingers, and it brought an ache to his heart. She was crying because he was going away the next day, and because she did not know how long it would be until she saw him again, or if she would see him again.

"Oh, Billy, I couldn't take it."

"I'll be careful," he had said.

"I just couldn't take it, Billy."

"There now," he said, smiling confidently. "You're a brave girl. Would I let any lousy Kraut get near me?"

"I think I would just die, Billy. Please promise me you'll be careful."

"You know I will."

He kissed her, and she said, "Promise me you'll write every day."

"Every day I am able."

"Promise, Billy."

"Cross my heart and hope to die."

"Don't say it. Not even kidding." They had danced for a while, her head resting against his shoulder as they moved in slow, dreamy circles, then she said, "Dumb old war. It just ruins everything."

Ever since their engagement they had planned their lives tighter than a banker's investment portfolio, so that there would be no surprises: the house, the kids, the cattle, the dogs. And then came the war—the first surprise—although it wasn't a surprise, really. Everyone knew it was coming; they had read about it, had talked about it, but with Pearl Harbor it sank in, and there it was. And then there was the dogfight over Belgium—the second surprise. That was a surprise you train for and think about and pray against, and hope to God he hears you; thank God it was behind him. And then came the third. There was no planning for the third, and there was certainly no praying for it. He was thinking about the third now, and it was eating away at him.

"What's the matter?" Joe asked him.

"What's that?"

Joe laughed. "If you don't beat all. You got somebody waiting for you back home or something?"

"Or something."

"And you think she's reserved a seat under the apple tree for you? You're gonna go back home after the war and pick up where you left off, is that it—live happily ever after?"

Billy looked at him.

"I see." Joe finished off the last of his drink. "A wise prophet once said 'there's a sucker born every minute.'"

"P. T. Barnum."

"A sucker if ever I knew one," Joe laughed. He raised his empty glass. "Well, here's to the suckers. And to living happily ever after back home on the range, where the deer and the antelope play."

"Stuff a sock in it."

"You bet."

Billy sipped his drink. He was thinking about Colette now—the third surprise—her brightly haunting eyes lifting off the back of his mind and moving toward him to softly kiss him on the lips. In that moment the three boys and three girls, the labs and the cattle were suddenly irrelevant.

"You still with me, Montana?"

"Sure. What's up?"

Joe grunted. A dark look gathered under his brow and two green rods of fire bore out across the table. "You're here now, pal, and she's there. You're worlds apart. You're dead, she's dead. The sooner you get that through your thick skull, the sooner you'll be worth a lick as a fighter pilot."

"You're really quite inspirational, Joe," Billy said evenly. "You know that? Ever think of going into politics, Joe?"

"Finish your drink."

"Yes, sir, Joe. Eat, drink, and be merry, for tomorrow we die?"

"Day after tomorrow."

"That's right," Billy grinned. "Ramrod in two days."

Happy came back to the table and bounced into the booth. "You two having another lovers' spat? I can't even go to the can two minutes without you lovebirds getting into it. Now, come on, you love doves—let's kiss and make up."

"Shut up," Joe said.

"That's better."

The waitress was over talking to the RAF pilots now, and at one point she glanced back at the Americans. "Look, Haps," Joe said. "She can hardly keep her eyes off you. Why don't you ask her to the dance?"

"The dance? You mean the Sadie Hawkins thing?"

"None other."

Happy looked confused. "But aren't the girls supposed to ask the guys?"

"That's it. But what do English girls know about Sadie Hawkins?" Joe winked at Billy. "Look at her over there with her back to you, taking money from those RAF boys. She don't give a hoot about them fellas. Look at her laughin'.'"

Billy shook his head. "Haps, don't mind this dope. You want to ask that girl to the dance, you ask that girl to the dance."

Happy looked at her. "You think so?"

"Sure."

"I don't know; she's pretty tall," he lamented.

Joe laughed.

"Aw, go on."

Skagway came over to their table. His face was flushed. He stood wavering over them, a tuft of hair standing up on top of his head, and his eyes were a dull glaze of watery blue. "Any of you boys up for gettin' beat at darts?"

"Count me out," Joe said.

"How 'bout you, Hochreiter?"

"Not me," Billy said. He could see the RAF pilots looking at them.

Skagway stood erect, wavered slightly, and grinned. "'Fraid I might take your money?"

Billy looked over at Joe.

Skagway, eyeing Billy, took a big swallow of beer, dragged his sleeve over his mouth, then pulled a cigarette from behind his ear and grabbed hold of it with his teeth. "Could be a yellow streak I see crawling up your back?"

Billy stared into his glass. He hated messing with drunks. There was no good way of dealing with them other than to take them outside. He was about ready to do just that when the front door opened, and two girls entered the pub.

The girls paused for a moment, looked into the bar area, then went over to the dining section.

Skagway blew a sloppy wolf whistle. "Say! Will you get a load of the dame! Now there's a swell-looking dish." He took another pull of beer.

Happy followed his eyes. "Where?"

"She's mine," Skagway said. "I saw her first."

Billy watched him career away, his movements sloppy and overcompensating. The RAF pilots were watching him too, he saw.

Julie Ellerby looked up as Skagway rounded the dividing wall and drove toward them. "Don't look now, Jane, but there's a Yank heading this way. He looks positively blind."

Jane glanced up quickly, then looked woefully at Julie. "Oh, Julie . . . no."

"Don't worry, I'll get rid of him."

Pete swaggered up to their table, holding a drink in one hand, with the cigarette still clamped between his teeth. "Say, dolls! Ain't seen you in here before. I must'a died and . . ."

Julie gave him an icy glare. "I beg your pardon?"

Pete took a drag from his cigarette, then, bending closer, more intimately, he put his hand on the backrest of the booth, behind Julie's head. An ash fell onto her shoulder. "I'm with the 52nd Fighter Group," he said, leering sloppily at Jane. "I'm . . . fighter pilot."

"Isn't that nice," Julie said, brushing her shoulder and scooting away toward the wall.

Jane looked helplessly at her.

"I'm an American," Pete said. "With the 52nd . . . you know . . ."

"Really?" Julie said.

Billy looked at them through the glass partition. The brunette—an auburn brunette, really—was looking down at the table. The redhead was shaking her finger at Skagway. When he saw the RAF pilots getting up and going over to the dining area, his stomach constricted into a hard, acidy knot. "Wait a second," he said, sliding out of the booth.

"What's the hurry?" Joe asked. "Where you goin'?"

"Gonna throw some darts?" Happy asked.

Joe looked back through the window at the group of RAF pilots gathering around Skagway. "Swell."

By the time Billy got into the dining room, the RAF pilots had Pete's arms pulled up behind him and had backed him into a corner. Pete's glassy eyes ranged from face-to-face. "Say, what happened to the dames? I got dibs on the brunette. I . . . saw her first."

Billy walked up to the Brit who was thrusting his finger at Pete's chest, grabbed his arm, and spun him around. "That's enough, fellas," he said. "Party's over."

The dark-haired Brit glared at him. "Stay out of it, Yank."

Billy looked at him for a moment. Then he looked down at Jane. She was staring at the tabletop, her hands clutched together tightly on her lap. "Let's go, Skag," he said. "You've overstayed your welcome."

"Shove off, Hochreiter!"

Billy took him by the arm and pulled him free of the Brits.

"Hey, leggo my arm. Who'd you think—" Pete swung wild and missed, spilling the remaining contents of his glass onto the table. Julie reeled in horror.

Pete steadied himself against one of the Brits. "Think you're so tough?" He threw his arm around the Brit's neck. "He's with the Gold . . . Gloves, you know," he said intimately. "Thinks he's real tough. Ain't so *tough*," he bawled suddenly.

Joe Thompson and the other Americans had gathered in a group now. Everyone in the pub was watching the proceedings.

Warren Turlock stepped forward and took Skagway by the arm. Pete fought with him. "Leave me alone," he growled. He flailed his arms.

"Take it easy, Skag. It's me, Turtle."

Pete swung his head around. "That you, Turtle? Say, whaddya know, it's Turtle. Le's you'n'me go down th' Knight's Arms. Ain't no fun here."

"That's right, Yank," the dark-haired Brit said to Billy. "Why don't you just clear out of here—you and the rest of your flamin' heroes."

"No need for your lip, pal," Billy said evenly.

"Let him have it, Montana," someone nudged from behind.

"That's right, Billy, let this jerk have it."

The Brit started working his finger toward Billy's chest. "You chaps think you can just come over here, flash your money about, and expect everyone to dance 'round your feet like little piggies."

"You said it, pal. I didn't," Billy said. He turned to leave.

The Brit put out his arm to stop him. "I'm not finished, Yank."

Everyone cleared back a step to give them room.

Billy pushed past him. "Yes, you are." He gestured to the others. "Let's go, fellas." He saw the punch coming before the man ever threw it.

The Brit wasn't a fighter, it was clear. His feet were all wrong, and there was too little shoulder behind it. It was all arms and lower torso, wide-open and undisciplined.

Billy reeled to his right, set his shoulders compactly, then stepped forward with a left hook into the man's solar plexus. As the man doubled over Billy drove a right down across his mouth, and the Brit went down hard into a couple of chairs. He lay in a tangle with his head thrown back against the leg of a table, a trickle of blood beading up at the corner of his mouth.

Some of the other RAF boys stepped forward.

"You want some of this?" Billy gestured with his hands. "Come on then."

"Way to go, Billy!" someone gloated. "Give 'em another one!"

"Stop this!" Jane shrieked. "Won't you just stop this!"

The two girls gathered their belongings and scooted out of the booth. The men standing in their way opened up to let them pass.

Jane glowered at Billy as she brushed past him. "You conceited Yank. Why don't you just—" She caught herself. "Why don't you just go home!"

Billy stood looking after her as the girls disappeared out the front door. He raised his hand to her. "Hey!"

"Just leave her alone, mate," one of the RAF pilots said.

"You her brother or something?"

The man shook his head, then helped the Brit into the booth. "Somebody get a towel. Got a nasty split on his mouth."

Billy watched them curiously. "Is there a law against being friendly with the womenfolk around here? Maybe you just don't like the competition?"

"You got it all wrong, mate," the man going for a towel said. "Nobody here is after Jane. Not with her husband unaccounted for."

"Her husband?"

"That's right," the dark-haired Brit said, nursing his lip.

"His Lancaster went down over North Africa," said the man helping him. "Not a word of him for a year now. He's done for, poor blighter."

Billy looked at the door of the pub.

Joe took his arm. "Let's go, Montana."

Billy looked at him. "Yeah, sure, Joe. Let's get out of here." They walked away. "Just wanted a quiet drink to forget about the war."

ೋഷ

Billy walked into the Nissen hut and shut the door quietly behind him. Hours had passed since he'd left the others at the Knight's Arms and gone off on his own. He spent most of the night riding his bicycle through the countryside, pausing now and then to look up at the stars, listening to the quiet voices on the wind, feeling the rhythms of the night like he would do back home on the ranch when he had thoughts or feelings that needed sorting. Tonight, however, they weren't sorting so well.

He heard Pete Skagway down at the far end of the hut, snoring loudly, and a couple of the others were accompanying him. The sky had cleared and the moon shone in through the windows of the hut, one of the bars of light spreading over his bed. He saw that someone had put mail on his pillow. There was a package, about the size of a shoe box, and a bundle of letters.

He sat down on the bed and looked at the return addresses. Most of the letters were from Laura, and were scented with her perfume. The box was from home. He opened the box and smiled. Inside the box, setting on top of a sheet of wax paper that covered the chocolate chip cookies, was a letter. He opened the letter, then, biting into a cookie, angled the letter into the moonlight. It read:

Dear William,
I had a free moment and thought I would write. All is well here on the ranch. The stock is fine, the beef prices are up, and your father

got a good price at the auction. Tyler and Kate are doing well in Chicago. Trout is growing an inch every day it seems. Can't keep him in shoes. He's taking good care of your rifle . . . oils it once a week. You boys and your guns! He brags about you all the time at school and at church. I don't mind the school part, but at church I feel I must pull him aside and tell him it's not polite to boast. I must confess, though, I've bragged about you a little myself.

I pray for you whenever I think of you, William, which is just about every waking moment. Your father prays for you too. I can hear him when he walks along the river at night. You know how it is when everything is quiet at night on the ranch, and you can hear the calves bawling on the wind, way off in the distance? Isn't it interesting how difficult times bring the prayers out in people?

Speaking of that, Jenny spends so much time now talking about spiritual things with Sammy Two Feathers. He comes over just about every night, after she has put little Grace down for the night, and I can hear them talking on the porch, sometimes into the wee hours. Your father thinks Sammy is more interested in Jenny than he is in the Bible, but God works in mysterious ways, doesn't he? He is good.

I must go now, son. We haven't heard from you in a while. Hope all is well. We hear such terrible things about the war. Be careful. We miss you so much. I love you.

Mother

P.S. Hope you like the cookies.

Billy finished the cookie as he reread the letter, picturing everyone's face in his mind. He remembered a typical morning in the kitchen with everyone blowing in and out at breakfast time, the strong smells of flour and pancake batter, of bacon frying and coffee combining with the heady scent of fresh-cut alfalfa breezing in through the screen door. Yes, and he could hear the calves bawling on the wind.

A wave of loneliness spread over him. It was a good, aching feeling, and with the moon shining in on him the same silvery way it did through his bedroom window at home, nostalgia built up in him so powerfully he thought he might bust.

He folded the letter and set it on his nightstand. He picked up the most recent letter from Laura, smelled it, and wondered what had become of the perfume scent. The others were scented but not this one. He opened the letter and stopped reading after the third line. "Perfect," he said under his breath. He let his hand holding the letter fall between his legs. "Good old 4F Tom Baxter. Just perfect."

No point in reading the other letters, unless maybe to get a chronicle of it. He stared out the window for a long while, thinking about Laura and trying to picture her face. But that well was dry now. Perhaps it had always been dry, empty of surprises, and it took that business in France to show it to him. Still, he felt hollow inside.

He folded the letter, set the bundle on his nightstand, and looked over at Joe Thompson sleeping in his bed. Good old blowtorch-eyes Joe. Joe the cynic. Joe the element leader. Joe the never-take-your-eyes-off-my-tail-again. Don't worry, Joe.

Billy lay back on his pillow, pulled up the box of cookies under his right arm, and gazed up at the ceiling. He remembered his mother's words and tried to recapture the warm feelings he had felt in her kitchen. But that was all wrecked now. Even the secure touch of the shoe box didn't help. He lay there and tried to pray. "Isn't it interesting how difficult times bring the prayers out in people?" But he had no prayers in him.

The moon slid quietly off his face, darkness drawing over him. *Wish I'd handled that business in the pub better,* he thought. *Shoot, there's always a better way to handle it.* Then, closing his eyes and thinking of the English girl, he heard a voice echoing in the melancholy stillness between the worlds of waking and sleep: "I love you, William," she said, kissing him. "This will be for nothing if you do not live." He sat up, staring into the darkness. The robin's egg blue eyes seemed to lag behind a few moments, haunting the air, and it set him on a whole new course of thinking.

14 ★★★★

November 1, 1943. 0530 hours. Monday. Outside Berlin. Captain Rolf Schiller stared impassively out the window of the train as the first gray light of dawn gave monochromatic definition to the low, flat, almost featureless German countryside that was his homeland. He loved this part of the country the same way a Jew loves the barren deserts of the Negev, or a Sioux Indian the prairies of Montana: It is in his blood. It is home. There are more beautiful places, like the Bavarian Alps in the south and those along the borders of Switzerland and France, but they are not home. The mountains are for skiing, for taking hikes, and for enjoying the edelweiss that grows in the highest reaches, as he had done with his family when he was a boy. But home is where the soul takes winged refuge, and home is where the bombs were now falling.

Observing the progression of the countryside, Rolf knew exactly what was coming next, only there were no feelings of excitement. Seeing it now evoked loneliness in him, and brought forth feelings of dread that moved just beneath the strong current of his thoughts—a dangerous thing stalking him silently beneath the waters.

He forced his thoughts through different channels: his father, his mother, his sister Gretchen, his brother Ernst—little Ernst. He thought of each one, remembered their faces. Still, every one of the channels seemed to spill out into the same pool of dread. He closed his eyes, opened them, and it seemed for a moment that the huge shadowy thing had moved away; or perhaps it was beneath him, just out of his sight, waiting for the right moment to breach.

The soldier sitting next to him groaned as the soldier sleeping on the floor of their compartment rolled over and disturbed his sleep. Rolf adjusted his seat, then looked across at the seat facing him. Three dark shapes huddled against one another. There were soldiers sleeping out in the aisle, their rifles and field gear rattling with the train's movement. He wondered if most of them were going home on furlough, like himself, or if they were en route to new duty stations, changing trains in Berlin. Again he looked out the window, and, seeing again the shattered countryside, he felt as though he were being lifted on a swell that would surely swamp him.

The scream of the train whistle jolted him out of his sleep. The head of the man on his left bobbed on Rolf's shoulder, his lips agape with a thin line of spittle connecting them. Rolf jostled him in the ribs and the man startled awake, wiping his chin apologetically. He was a sergeant, a cherub-faced man, with liquid blue eyes rimmed red with fatigue. The eyes seemed too old and veteran for his face.

A conductor, picking his way through the recumbent clutter of soldiers, called out that they were arriving at Zoo Station.

The whistle screamed again, and Rolf looked out the window to see the familiar skyline of Berlin rising in the distance. It looked the same as he remembered it three years before, its stark, triumphant silhouette gleaming proudly in the Teutonic sun. However, the closer the train drew to the city, the more he saw the unfamiliar, sundry evidences of war. Here and there the dark, bomb-smashed buildings rose sadly through the diaphanous shrouds of early-morning mist that otherwise veiled the stippled terrain. There were many buildings not yet touched, he saw, more in fact than had been; still the hollowed-out shells of buildings were the objects that drew his eyes. Rolf's mind superimposed the skyline he had once known over the one before him now.

He took a deep breath to vent the anger and the sadness in him.

The train shuddered to a halt and the whistle screamed. The soldiers and civilians rose to their feet and collected their things. No one looked at anyone else; no one spoke except to excuse the jab of his elbow or rifle. Every man alone in his thoughts, waiting in the press that wasn't moving, back to front, shoulder to shoulder; every man looking at the back of the head in front of him or off to the side at nothing with a patience born of five long, war-weary years. Each face had the same drawn, gray look. All eyes bore the same red-rimmed fatigue as that of the cherub-faced sergeant. The smell of stale body odor sullied the air.

Rolf remained seated and stared numbly out the window, knowing that there was no point in standing yet. There was a throng of people on the platform; some were waiting impatiently to board, to secure decent seating, while others were waiting expectantly to greet passengers. His eyes probed the crowd for a familiar face. He didn't see one. Just a pan of white moons. A thought jumped into his head that there would be no one to greet him, that he had somehow forgotten to wire ahead that he would be coming.

The press of soldiers began to move, somberly trickling out of the compartment into the aisle. The disposition of the crowd on the platform was stirred by the emergence of the soldiers. Rolf stood up, grabbed his bags from the overhead rack, passed into the steadily moving stream in the aisle, then stepped off the train into the oil-streaked chill of the early morning.

A dark-haired boy of fifteen made his way through the press on the platform, jumping up and wagging his head back and forth to see over the crowd, his blue eyes scanning the stream of soldiers off the train, dismissing them. Then, seeing Rolf, he ran ahead, snapped his heels together smartly, and thrust out his right arm in a Nazi salute.

"Heil Hitler!" he shouted.

Rolf set his bags down on the platform and looked him over. "What have we here?" he smiled. "This cannot be little Ernst, can it?"

The boy was tall, slender, and well built. His brown hair was cut neatly on top, and shorn clean around the ears and back of the neck. He was wearing the uniform of the Hitler Youth: a light brown military shirt and cap, black knee shorts and tie, white kneesocks, Sam Browne belt, and, on his left sleeve, a black armband with a black swastika stitched against a white circle.

"Heil Hitler, Captain!" the boy repeated with greater fervor.

Rolf threw his hand up deprecatingly. "Oh, heil Hitler," he said.

Ernst stared at Rolf as though he were a god suddenly incarnate. His mouth parted in awe as his eyes moved worshipfully to the black metal cross dangling at his brother's throat, a cluster of oak leaves gleaming in the colorful ribbon. "The *Eichenlaub*," he said. A shudder seemed to go through him. "It is true then that you wear the Oak Leaves."

"What's that? Oh, yes," Rolf answered. "What is this Captain business?"

"I'm with the Hitler Youth now, sir," the boy said. He clicked his heels. "You are my superior officer."

"I am your older brother."

"Rolf?" a woman's voice called out over the clamor.

Rolf looked up as a slender, blond girl of twenty made her way through the crowd, holding her hands up to guide passersby from her path and then waving at Rolf. The smile on her face grew broader with every step. "Oh, Rolf," she squealed, waving wildly as she cleared the press and broke into a run.

"Gretchen?"

Ernst stepped mechanically to one side as Gretchen threw her arms around her brother and squeezed him. Tears squirted from her eyes. "Oh, Rolf! It is so good to see you!"

Rolf held her out before him. "Let me look at you." Her very blond, almost platinum hair was fine and straight, so fine that a comb could move through it as though it were a loom of silken threads. She wore it parted down the middle, with neatly trimmed bangs, and, falling straight along the line of her jaw, the ends were cut straight above the shoulders with a slightly inward, forward-pointing curl that swayed or bounced as a unit as she moved her head. She looked beautiful, radiant, in fact. "You're all grown up," he said, marvelling at her.

"Yes, all grown up," she said with a giggle. Her eyes darted quickly about his features as though they were a pair of hummingbirds. However, she avoided lighting on his eyes as she smoothed her hand over the flat, firm breadth of his lapel. "And don't you look handsome in your uniform?"

Rolf smiled at her. "Does it show that much?"

She looked into his eyes, steadier now, put a hand on his cheek as though to heal a wound. "You look tired, Rolf. It has been awful, hasn't it—the war?"

"War? Has there been a war?"

"There you are, you silly," she giggled. She squeezed him again. "You'll be fine now that you're home and can get some rest, won't you?"

"Yes, unless you squeeze me to death. How are Papa and Mama?"

"Wait 'til you see!" she said, breaking away from him. "Mama's making a big supper . . . roast duck, and dumplings, and potatoes—the little red ones that you like—and sauerkraut! Apple pie and cheese for dessert. Oh, I could go on and on! It will be such a wonderful supper!"

"Roast duck? How on earth can she manage roast duck with the shortages?"

"You know Mother," Gretchen laughed. "She could manage a block of ice in the desert."

"She certainly could. And Papa?"

She feigned a scowl. "He's been an absolute tyrant all week," she growled. "He wants everything to be perfect for your arrival. Hasn't given Mother nor I a moment's peace with his inspections. Has he, Ernst?"

The boy just looked at her.

"Mother finally sent him off to the doctor's this morning—his leg, you know?"

"Papa still loves his ailments."

"He's refined his ailments to an art form," she smiled, averting her eyes from his intense stare. "Hasn't he, Ernst?"

The boy looked away from her and grunted. "Papa thinks the Hitler Youth is foolishness," he said sourly. "What do you think of the Hitler Youth, Captain?"

"I think this Hitler Youth should take my bags to the taxi."

Ernst looked down at them.

"That's an order." Rolf winked at his sister. She giggled. Rolf put out his arms. "Come." He pulled her to his side and the two of them began walking, arm in arm, down the platform. Ernst, struggling with the bulkiness of the bags, hurried as best he could after them.

"It is good to be home," Rolf said, breathing in the familiar air of the station town.

Gretchen noticed his drawn features more clearly now, the radial lines etched at the corner of his eyes. "You will eat well and rest," she said with authority, taking his arm with both her hands and leaning against his shoulder. "We shall go to the cinema, and to the opera, and we shall have wonderful walks through the Tiergarten, and—"

"Slow down a minute!" Rolf laughed. "You are getting me tired just thinking of all the rest I'm going to have."

"Don't be silly," Gretchen laughed. "Yes, yes, be silly! Oh, Rolf, just think... three glorious weeks!" She squeezed him and her eyes brimmed with tears.

Ernst caught up to them, panting, with the bags rubbing against his legs. His left kneesock was shucked down to his ankles. "Have you... have you shot down any more planes, Captain?"

"A few, little brother. A few." Rolf relieved him of the heavier bag, and all three walked through the station.

"What, what kind were they? Thunderbolts? Spitfires? Maybe you've shot down ... more Fat Autos."

"Too many Fat Autos."

"Really?" He hurried to keep abreast. "How many?"

"I don't know."

The boy changed hands with the bag, leaning against the weight. "You don't know? Don't you keep score?"

"There are too many to keep score."

&0◦6

The shining black taxi turned right off Friedrich Street onto Unter den Linden, a broad, multilaned boulevard lined with beautiful linden trees that cut away from the heart of the city on an east-west axis, through the Brandenburg Gates, and on through the Tiergarten on the Charlotten-burger Chaussee. Through the trees, Rolf saw the smashed buildings with their ruined hulls, like shattered teeth, jagging up against the skyline in a cruel, sardonic grin. Structures that once formed the building blocks of his memory were now gone. Great piles of rubble were heaped in the newly vacant lots between the untouched buildings and along the streets and alleyways. Dogs sniffed among the rubble for rats.

Rolf swore silently against the world. Seeing it now—not just reading about it in the newspapers with the carefully selected photographs and the words depicting the effect of the bombing—convinced him that the propaganda minister, Joseph Goebbels, knew his business well. Gretchen, sitting on his left, laid her hand on his and gave it a gentle squeeze. He looked at her and smiled a quick, almost guilty smile, before turning to gaze back out the window.

The Reichstag building passed by on his right. Then, as the car approached the Brandenburg Gate—a huge, twelve-columned structure built in the architectural style of the Athenian Acropolis—Rolf glanced up in time to see the Goddess of Victory, the very symbol of the indomitable Teutonic spirit of Berlin, as she tirelessly drove her chariot ever westward across its lintel. A note of pride sounded in his breast.

He saw the other things now, the familiar and good things that were, as yet, untouched by the war. He saw people bustling along the wide boulevard, their collars turned up against the chill German wind: old men in porkpie hats and dark coats, walking slowly, talking and nodding, smoking cigars; rosy-cheeked nannies in their Victorian whites, pushing their wicker perambulators and chatting happily; soldiers sitting on the benches with their girls, watching, or not watching, the people stroll past them. Everyone was carrying on with business as usual, as though the war were but a minor nuisance, a clever fabrication of newspaper men that made for interesting reading. Maybe Goebbels was right.

We are a strong people, Rolf thought. *A good, strong, hearty people that are resilient. Perhaps we will do all right,* he thought, the Goddess of Victory stirring his soul onward, westward, to victory, to a triumph of the will. He clapped Gretchen on the hand. "Truly, it is good to be home!" he said abruptly.

She smiled at him. "Yes, Rolf. Yes." As the taxi sped along its route, she watched him out of the corner of her eye.

Everywhere, the trees lining the boulevard and sidewalks, as well as those spreading over the wide, well-maintained grounds of the park, were in their late autumn colors; what remained of their leaves clung tentatively against the advance of winter. The overcast spread a cool gray light over the park and statuary and reflected a spectrum of grays in the many small ponds.

The taxi turned down Potsdamer Strasse through the park, heading south, and then right onto Tiergarten Strasse, the park passing by on their right now. As they turned down their street, tall mature elms spread their naked, rattling limbs to the chilling autumn breeze. Leaves scattered over the street in capricious swirls.

The taxi slowed as a ball rolled into the street, followed a moment later by a small tousle-headed boy. The driver beeped his horn and said something under his breath. The boy picked up his ball and frowned as the car sped past him.

Rolf allowed a smile. *Yes, we are a strong people,* he thought, looking at the boy. He did not see the man wearing a black leather coat and sitting in the black Mercedes across the street, smoking a cigarette and reading a newspaper. But, as the taxi passed the parked Mercedes, the man in the black leather coat glanced out his window and saw Rolf. His eyes narrowed briefly, imperceptibly. He watched the taxi grow smaller in his rearview mirror, until it pulled over to the curb in front of the large Victorian on the right, before returning to the carefully scripted news of the war.

15 ★★★

The taxi pulled up in front of a large two-story, red brick house. Rolf paid the driver then stood looking at the house. It was solidly built, as solid as the name Schiller in the community, and dated to pre-Victorian times. An intricate network of ivy went up the face, showing patches of brick and the windows through the burnt red of the tiny star-shaped leaves. There was a little yard in front, the dead, brown grass neatly edged along the walk, and a narrow yard going along either side of the house. The rose bushes were cut back for the winter, pushing up against the walls with their bony fingers. A wrought iron fence ran along the front, and hedges ran back along each of the side yards. A curl of blue smoke rose from the chimney and flattened against the slate gray sky of boldly moving clouds.

Rolf held the gate open for his sister and brother to pass through, then, glancing up at the house, grinned as a round face appeared briefly in the downstairs window. Moments later the front door flew open with a squeal of laughter.

"Rolfie!" his mother cried, throwing her hands to her face. "My dear, dear Rolfie!"

Margaret Schiller stood on the landing, tears streaming down her cheeks. She was a tall woman and built solid like her house; it was from her that both Rolf and Ernst received their strong square shoulders, height, and brown hair. She bounded down the steps like a schoolgirl, her arms reaching out to him, and wept happily in his arms.

Rolf patted her back. "It's all right, Mama. We're all home now, aren't we?"

She looked up at him and searched his eyes. "It is really you, isn't it, Rolfie?"

"Yes, Mama."

Ernst pulled his socks into place. He looked at his brother. "Will you speak at one of our rallies while you're home, Captain?" he interrupted. "They do not believe me about the Oak Leaves."

A shade went quickly over Rolf's face. "Ernst," he snapped.

The boy looked at him.

"Do not call me by my rank when we are at home," Rolf said, tempering his look.

"But we are always soldiers," the boy insisted.

"Yes. But we were brothers before we were soldiers. Being brothers is a higher calling."

Ernst looked at him queerly.

"When we are in public you may call me Captain," Rolf conceded. "But here at home you will call me Rolf. This is my second order to you."

"Yes, sir," the boy said, clicking his heels.

"You may leave the 'sir' at the front gate, as well as the clicking of the heels."

"But—"

"It is my third order."

"Yes, si—er . . . Rolf."

His mother smiled, her dark, soulful eyes twinkling maternally. She stepped over and touched the boy's shoulder. "Ernst, would you carry your brother's bags to his room, please? He has had a long ride on the train."

Ernst shrugged his shoulder away from her with a dark look.

"The calling of a mother is higher than even that of a brother," Rolf said, grinning. "I have seen generals tremble at the sound of their mother's voice."

Ernst picked up the bags grudgingly. "It is a sign of weakness," he muttered under his breath. He trudged heavily up the stairs, his head down, showing the white of his neck through the short-cropped bristles of his brown hair.

Rolf watched him disappear into the house.

"He is proud of you, Rolf," Mrs. Schiller smiled.

"Worships the ground he walks on, you mean?" Gretchen corrected.

Mrs. Schiller chuckled. "Yes, I'm afraid you are right. He has talked of nothing else since he has joined the Youth movement." She glanced pensively at the stairs of the house. "How quickly they are no longer children."

Rolf stepped forward, smiling broadly, and lifted her up in his arms. "Then let us talk no more of the war. This is my fourth and final order of the day."

His mother laughed and squeezed his neck. "Oh, Rolfie!"

They climbed the steps and Rolf opened the door for the two women. The drone of aircraft overhead drew him to pause before entering. The sky was still gray and bright in the morning overcast and, looking up, he saw four tight formations of tiny dark specks that he knew were FW–190s out of Staaken airfield. He went into the house.

Inside, everyone stood for a moment in the long, high-ceilinged entryway that was covered with an old, thick-piled carpet.

Mrs. Schiller patted her son on the hand. "Welcome home, Rolfie. I keep saying it," she said, holding back a rush of tears. "Welcome home, son."

The smell of cooking filled the house. "Hmmm. Smells delicious," Rolf said, lifting his nose. "I'm starving."

His mother shooed him away. "We shall have an early supper. You two go into the library now. I don't want you tasting anything until it is time to eat."

"All right, Mama," Rolf smiled. He watched his mother disappear down the hall into the kitchen. Then he followed his sister through the double doors on the right into the library.

It was as though he had never left; everything was exactly how he remembered it. The library was decorated in the style and furnishings of late Victorian times: high-backed reading chairs; mahogany end tables and Tiffany lamps; a grand piano in the bay that opened onto the street; a mahogany desk that commanded a view of the library doors; a wooden bar against one wall stocked with crystal decanters and glasses; and large rectangular Persian rugs that covered the varnished hardwood floor. Everything had worn well, he saw, and was holding up beautifully and sturdily against time, because of the fastidious care that was everywhere apparent.

Rolf and Gretchen sat down on one of the two matching settees of crushed, crimson velvet that faced each other in front of the already coal-banked fire that was waiting to be lit. Gretchen drew her legs up onto the seat, crossing them, and looked at her brother.

Rolf unbuttoned his military blouse and settled comfortably in the settee, then lay his arm over the backrest. The Eichenlaub dangled at his throat. "How are you, Gretch?" he smiled.

"Fine. And you?"

"Fine. It is good to be home. I keep saying it."

"Just like Mama." She smiled at him and patted his hand. "You can't imagine how we have looked forward to this day."

"I *can* imagine." He glanced at the library doors. "Mama looks good."

"Yes."

"You look good too."

"You have told me already. Do not tell me anymore or I will get a big head."

"I'm sure all the good-looking men in town are beating a path to your door." She smiled. "No, not really."

"I don't believe it."

"It's true," she said. "All the decent ones have gone off to war. There is no one."

"I see." Then with a short laugh, he said, "What of Georg Bundt? Now there's a name. I remember when all we heard around here was Georg this, and Georg that. Remember? Blond hair, blue eyes—the cream of Aryan stock." He poked her shoulder. "He was a god, as I recall."

"I was younger then," she said. She looked over at the grandfather clock that stood in the far corner of the room. "I don't know what became of Georg. He went one way, and I went another. Everything changed so quickly."

Rolf clucked his tongue. "Poor Gretchen."

"'Poor Gretchen,'" she frowned playfully. "I've gotten calls from other men, I'll have you know. But I was not interested in them. They stopped calling eventually."

"The poor fellows."

"Poor fellows indeed. Poor Gretchen, you mean." She affected a sad face. "Perhaps I should consider a convent."

Rolf laughed. "A fine calling for a Lutheran." His laughter trailed off.

"This war," she sighed. "I do wish it would end soon."

Rolf looked at her soberly. "You look so grown up."

"You've already told me that too."

"I have? Have we already run out of things to say?"

"I can't believe it. It has been three years," she said. "There is so much I want to talk about."

"Well?"

Gretchen's smile thinned away, leaving only the awkward fumbling expression of someone who has run out of conversation. Rolf saw it in her face and knew very well what she was thinking, or at least part of it. There was so much to talk about, and yet nothing to say. Three years is a long time in war. A lifetime. So much passes under the bridge in three years, and so quickly, that time itself seems compressed, and feelings are repressed or ripped apart or killed, and everything else is aged unnaturally and strangely, like bad wine.

She adjusted her seat, smiled at him, then looked down at her hands folded in her lap. There was a pendant silence between them, a dangling void that was as awkward as it was unnatural. "It's been frightfully cold," she said, rubbing her shoulders. "I think we will have an early winter."

"Shall I light the fire?" he said.

"Not just yet. We must save it for the evening."

"All right. But if you're cold—"

"I'm fine. Really." She smiled at him. "Wait till you see what Mama has cooked for supper, Rolf."

"I can smell it—roast duck, dumplings, the little potatoes I love."

"Oh, that's right. I told you, didn't I?"

"Now who's repeating?"

She smiled at him, then looked out the bay window as a swift wind knifed through the air.

What is the rest of what you are thinking, Gretch? he wondered. *That you no longer know me? That I am not the man you knew three years ago, the man to whom you wrote letters, and no doubt prayed for? That man is dead, Gretchen. He died in Hamburg. I do not know him anymore either.*

She looked at him and said, "I am so sorry about Katharina."

He looked at her quickly, an incongruous smile flashing on and then off his stricken face. "Yes," he said. "Thank you."

"I have been praying for you, Rolf. You must have loved her deeply."

He smiled at her politely.

"I'm sorry, Rolf. If you don't wish to speak of it . . ."

"Perhaps later. I'm a little tired from the trip."

"Of course. It was stupid of me."

"You're not stupid."

"Yes, I am," she said. "I wasn't going to mention it, and here I go mentioning it."

"We can talk about it later," he said.

"We don't have to talk about it at all if you don't want, Rolf."

"All right. Let's just drop it then. She's dead."

Gretchen looked at him.

Rolf stood up and walked over to the hearth and put both hands on the mantel and stared at the clock. "What is there to talk about?" He dropped his head. *Is this how it's going to be, Rolf?* he wondered. *Are you going to destroy this too?* "I got your letters," he said. "They helped very much. You have a strong faith. I admire it."

Gretchen looked down at her hands. The fingers of her right hand were now balled around her left thumb. She was crying.

He looked at her from the hearth. "I'm sorry, Gretch."

"No, Rolf, it isn't you. I just wanted everything to be perfect for your homecoming."

"It couldn't be more perfect."

"You're just saying that." She took out a handkerchief and dabbed her eyes. She chuckled throatily. "Look at me."

"I am. And I can't believe the boys are not knocking the door down."

She laughed. "Oh, yes, I'm sure they would think I was beautiful with my black eyes."

"They're not so black," he smiled. "For a raccoon."

She laughed. "Thank you very much."

"My pleasure."

They looked at each other. "I think—" "I wish—" they both said at the same time.

"You first," he said.

"No, you first . . . really."

"All right. I just wish you could have met her," he said. "She really wanted to meet you."

"Katharina?"

"Yes. You would have been friends. Good friends."

"Oh, Rolf, I'm sure of it. All the lovely things you wrote about her," Gretchen said, smiling easily now. "She sounds like such a wonderful person."

"She was."

"Would you like your photograph back?"

Rolf looked puzzled.

"You know . . . the one of you in Hamburg, in front of her parents' house."

"I'd forgotten I'd sent it to you. I'm holding her up in my arms, right?"

Gretchen stood up. "I'll get it for you."

"You don't have to now."

"I won't be a minute." She skipped out of the room. Rolf listened as she pattered up the flight of stairs.

He was alone. He went over to the curio cabinet in the corner and looked at himself in the mirror. "Have I changed that much?" he said, studying his features.

The grandfather clock chimed the half hour, the gong sounding deep and rich and confident. The mantel clock tolled a second later with a distant-sounding echo. And then he heard the cuckoo chirp from the kitchen, and the one in the hall. The house shuddered in the clangor of time. He took a deep, cleansing breath.

He walked in the heavy quiet of the room, his hands folded behind his back as he glanced over the wall of books and the knickknacks of his past. The rich, comfortable smells and textures and voices of the house plumbed the dark and forgotten reservoirs that flowed deep and still within him.

It was good to be home.

He looked at the framed photographs sitting on the piano before the bay window, each chronicling some chapter of his family's history: the wedding of his young parents, the two of them passing beneath the raised swords with full military pomp; his mother laughing; his father looking proud in his lieutenant's uniform; each of the three children at their christenings; the awkward progression of each one through childhood and adolescence. He picked up the one of him wearing lederhosen and holding a toy wooden airplane. He smiled. Deep calling unto deep. Yes. Yes. Then he looked at the one of his father in his Army uniform, older now, a colonel, the cuff of his right trouser leg pinned to his waist, when Field Marshal von Hindenburg was awarding him the *Ritterkreuz* for bravery under fire against the Russians. Again he smiled.

He turned as he heard the harsh metallic clatter at the front door.

The front door swung open, and a gray-haired man in his late fifties, aided by a pair of crutches, stepped woodenly and with much difficulty into the house. He worked around the door, using the right crutch to shut it. Then he swung forward with his left leg, hefting the hollow weight of the prosthetic leg around until it fell with a muffled clomp in the thick pile of the carpet. "Is he here, Margaret?"

Rolf winced, seeing him. It seemed his father had aged into an old man since he had seen him last. "There you are, Papa!" he said, walking to the library doors.

Karl Schiller stopped, looked to his right, saw his son, and swore. "I am late." He shook his head and swore again. "These idiot doctors. I tell you, Rolf, there is no pride in their work. I was forced to wait twenty minutes like a common laborer."

"There goes the Reich," Rolf grinned.

"Yes," the elder Schiller agreed. "There is no respect for veterans. It is disgraceful. They just don't know—"

"It is good to see you, Papa."

Mr. Schiller blinked at him. "Yes."

They stared at each other for a moment: father looking at son, his eyes appraising, searching; son looking at father, noticing the work of time around the eyes and shoulders, the added gray in the once-blond hair. Rolf stepped forward and threw his arms around his father and held him in a long embrace.

"Welcome home, son," the elder Schiller said.

Rolf looked into his father's eyes and they were wet. "Yes, well—" Mr. Schiller said, recovering. "You're here."

"In the flesh."

Then with a burst of laughter the two men shook hands and slapped each other on the shoulders, as men do when they are uncomfortable with their emotions. Observing his father's ruddy face up close, the hardset military jaw and neck that would bend for no nonsense, the impeccably trimmed mustache that showed his grooming, Rolf saw the old robustness in his father come through at last to strip away the effects of time.

"You look good, Papa."

"Nonsense. Tell me, Rolf, have you made your father proud?"

"Not too proud, Papa."

"Oh, you are the kidder," the father laughed. "I have heard such things! Such things!" He felt the muscles in his son's arms.

৯৽৽৻

After supper the men of the family gathered in the library before the fire that was throwing off a wonderful heat. Rolf, wearing civilian clothes now, and Ernst, still in his Hitler Youth uniform, sat on one of the two settees that bracketed the hearth. The senior Schiller was ensconced comfortably in his brown leather reading chair that was situated between the settees and faced the fire. His artificial leg was propped up on the matching ottoman.

"Ah, the men!" he said proudly. "Together at last without the women." He sipped brandy from a crystal snifter, then, lighting a match, held it over his pipe. "Quickly, Rolf," he said, pulling on the flame until the smoke streamed freely from the sides of his mouth and nostrils. He waved out the match and dropped it in a glass ashtray. "Tell us of the war in the west, before your mother comes in. I do not believe the papers."

"I will tell you what I am able," Rolf said, which he proceeded to do. He described the Luftwaffe's aerial strategy and tactics, the plusses and minuses of German, American, and British fighters, the skill of the enemy pilots, the incredible firepower of the B-17 Flying Fortress and the box formation.

Ernst leaned forward in rapt devotion to catch his brother's every word.

Mr. Schiller nodded curtly during the course of the debriefing, drawing smoothly on his pipe and adding grunts of punctuation.

Rolf stood up as his mother entered the room carrying a silver tea service. "Let me help you, Mama."

"You sit down," she ordered, shooting a scowl at Mr. Schiller. "Your father thinks I do not know what you are talking about. He thinks everyone is as deaf as he is."

Mr. Schiller grunted. "I sacrificed my ears to the artillery, and she mocks me."

"How would you know who mocks you?" Mrs. Schiller left the room.

Mr. Schiller grunted again. "Now what of these bombings, Rolf?" he continued. "Will they continue? That business in August. Did you see it on your way from the station?"

"I saw it," Rolf said.

"How is it that they are getting through the Luftwaffe? As bombs are falling on our heads our beloved Hermann tells us that the air war is going splendidly. Where are all the fighters?"

"They are spread out in the south and east," Rolf said. "With three fronts it is difficult to maintain a concentrated defensive."

Ernst perked. "Defensive?"

"That's right. We cannot fight bombers with bombers."

Ernst sat back in his seat and blinked at him.

"If we had more fighters," Rolf explained, "we could clear the skies of enemy bombers. We would give our munitions factories time to retool and produce, so that we could take the initiative again. We *must* have more fighters!"

"Then why don't we manufacture more of them?" the senior Schiller demanded.

"That is classified information."

Mr. Schiller grunted with contempt. "Classified. Then I will declassify it for you. It is because that fat fool Göring doesn't know his head from a knot of wood."

Ernst glared at him. "It is treason to speak so against the High Command!"

"Who are you to speak of treason?" his father roared. "This is my house. I was decorated during the Great War for service to my country, and I don't need my fifteen-year-old son or any paperhangers in High Command telling me of treason!"

Ernst eyed him sullenly. He looked at his brother. "You aren't saying the Führer is wrong about the bombers, are you, Rolf?"

"If we manufactured more fighters, we could stop these air raids," Rolf said. "As it stands, we will lose the air war by attrition."

Ernst stared at him in disbelief.

Mr. Schiller drew on his pipe and saw that it had gone out. "Treason," he snorted. "You can speak to me of treason? Where was treason at Tannenberg, my right leg asks you? Where was treason at Verdun? I'll tell you where there was treason . . . signing the Versailles Treaty, that's where there was treason."

He shook his pipe at the boy. "You think wearing uniforms and marching in a straight line gives you the inside story? Who are these schoolboys who teach you of treason? I will tell you who they are. They are brainless idiots, and it is my house to say it." He fumbled with a match, lit his pipe, then raised his snifter at Gretchen as she entered the room. "Be a dear," he said to her.

She brought the decanter and poured more brandy into his snifter. Mr. Schiller continued to stare at his youngest son.

"He meant nothing, Papa," Gretchen said, placing the decanter in its carriage. "Did you, Ernst?"

Ernst turned to his father. "If the Führer thinks we need more bombers, then we need more bombers."

Rolf looked at him.

"Let us not argue on Rolf's first night home," Gretchen said. She sat down opposite Rolf and Ernst.

Mr. Schiller fiddled with a match. "If the Führer told you the world was flat, would you believe him, smart boy?" he growled. "Is that what they teach you at these rallies? I'll tell you where there are some flat heads."

Ernst looked away bitterly.

Mrs. Schiller entered the room with a silver platter of finger cakes, and said, "Enough of this war talk." She set the tray on the table between the two settees and put her hands on her ample hips. "All this killing. We will have no more talk of the war and of killing. It was your very order, Rolf, and I must see that you enforce it."

Rolf smiled as he reached for a cake. "You are correct, Madam Field Marshal."

There was a knock at the front door.

"That'll be Martin," Ernst said, leaping out of his chair and running to the front door. A moment later he returned with a carbon copy of himself, only slightly shorter and with very blond hair. The carbon copy glanced quickly over the room and then stared at Rolf.

"Will you come to our meeting with us, Rolf?" Ernst asked proudly. "It would be a great inspiration!"

"There will be no inspiration tonight," his mother answered for him. "Your brother is tired."

"I asked Rolf, Mother," the boy said coldly.

"She outranks me by age and gender," Rolf smiled. "I will go with you another time."

"When?"

"When is your next rally?"

"Next week."

"I will be most inspirational next week."

"May I bring the Eichenlaub to show them?" the boy asked. He frowned smugly at the carbon copy. "No one believes me about the Oak Leaves."

The carbon copy glanced at Ernst for a moment, not changing his expression, then continued to stare at Rolf. He seemed to have only one expression.

Rolf grinned. "You may take the Oak Leaves and plant a tree, if you like."

"Pardon?"

"Wait—you would need acorns for that, wouldn't you? Why don't they award us the Knight's Cross with Acorns?" He laughed. "We could multiply ourselves then, couldn't we?"

Ernst missed the humor, and he and the carbon copy left the room.

The four adults listened as the two boys ascended the staircase, then looked at each other in the silence that followed.

"Treason, indeed," Mr. Schiller grunted. Moments later the boys thundered down the stairs, the front door opened, and Mr. Schiller winced as the door banged shut. "All this soldiering for boys. It is foolishness, I tell you."

Mrs. Schiller frowned at him. "You should not let Ernst hear you say such things, Karl. He is at an impressionable age."

"Is he here? Do you see Ernst?"

"He knows how you feel."

"And is that a crime? Should I be afraid of what my son knows in my own house?" He grunted. "Impressionable age. I will make an impression on him."

Mrs. Schiller waved him off. "Oh, isn't there a paper you can read?"

He ignored her and looked at his son. "You did not tell him of the Schwertern?"

"After he gets used to the Oak Leaves, I will tell him of the crossed swords," Rolf smiled.

"I am so proud of you, son. Two hundred enemy planes. It is something for a father to be proud of."

Rolf smiled at him.

"Enough of this talk of war and medals and shooting down airplanes," his mother exclaimed. She sat down next to Rolf and took his hand in hers. "It is so good to have you home, Rolfie."

"It is good to be home, Mama."

"I have prayed every night for this moment. That God would keep you safe in your airplane."

Rolf smiled at her but said nothing. He looked at the fire, the dark penetrating eyes withdrawing gradually to the shadows beneath his brow.

Mrs. Schiller looked at her son a long while. "I am so sorry about Katharina," she said. "I can't imagine the pain you must feel."

Rolf stared into the flames. "I'm fine, Mama. Really."

Looking at him, Mrs. Schiller compressed her lips then scowled at her hands.

There was another knock on the door.

"Who is that now?" Mr. Schiller growled. "It is like Berlin Station around here."

"I'll get it," Gretchen said, rising.

Rolf waved her down as he stood to his feet. "No, I will."

A Waffen-SS dispatcher was at the door. "Captain Schiller?" he asked, eyeing Rolf's civilian clothes skeptically.

Rolf stepped out onto the landing and closed the door behind him. He glanced beyond the dispatcher at the motorcycle parked at the curb, and at the moonlit silhouette of the soldier sitting in the sidecar. "Yes, I am Captain Schiller."

As the dispatcher opened his satchel, Rolf caught the vague sneer of contempt flirting at the corners of his mouth. Anger jumped into his throat. "Did they not teach you in the SS to salute Luftwaffe officers, Corporal?"

The corporal looked at him abruptly then snapped his heels. "Heil Hitler!" he saluted.

Rolf glowered at him a moment, then returned his salute. "State your business, Corporal, and be quick about it."

The dispatcher proffered an envelope to him. "A message from High Command," he said. He produced a pen and clipboard from his satchel, and added, "Sign here, please, Captain."

Rolf signed it, returned the dispatcher's salute, walked into the house, and shut the door. He entered the library and paused to read the dispatch.

"Who was at the door, Rolfie?" Mrs. Schiller asked. She saw his face change. "Rolfie?"

Rolf folded the letter and put it in his breast coat pocket. "It's nothing, Mama. An invitation to Reich Marshal Göring's hunting lodge."

"Karinhall?"

"Yes."

"How lovely."

"Invitation?" Mr. Schiller grunted. He folded his hands on his stomach and closed his eyes. "Orders, you mean."

A thought entered Rolf's mind and his face dropped.

"Is something the matter?" Mrs. Schiller asked him.

Rolf looked at her. "No, Mama. I am just tired. When I am tired I begin to imagine things under my bed. Do you remember when I was a little boy?" He smiled at her. "There are no monsters under my bed now, are there?"

"I should say not," his mother said. Then, smiling, she raised the silver teapot. "Won't you have some more tea?"

Rolf leaned over and kissed her cheek. "No thank you, Mama. I think I will go to bed now. The trip has caught up with me I think." He looked over at his father, whose chin was resting peacefully on his chest. He was snoring softly. He leaned over and kissed his sister. "Good night, Gretch."

"Tomorrow we shall have a wonderful day," she said.

"I'm looking forward to it," he said, and walked across the room.

"Do not forget to say your prayers," his mother smiled. "Remember how I used to tell you every night?"

Rolf paused in the doorway and looked back at her. "Prayers, Mama? I think maybe God has forgotten his German." He turned and went upstairs.

Mother and daughter looked at one another.

16 ★★★

The Tiergarten was once a royal hunting preserve where kings and generals hunted red stag, wild boar, and game birds; it was now a park where families came to picnic or to visit the Zoological Garden with its monkeys, zebras, cheetahs, elephants, and other exotic animals. It was a place where people came to stretch their legs after an evening meal, to walk with their dogs. Lovers came here as well, strolling arm in arm on the way to their secret places.

It had rained during the night, and the sky was now a deep azure blue, with clouds scudding smoothly over it that were so fluffy and white they seemed surreal. There was a briskness in the air, cold and bright after the rain, with the damp autumn smell of it still lingering. Everyone in the park was dressed warmly and seemed pleased that the park was still intact for them to enjoy.

Rolf, in his winter gray uniform, and Gretchen, wearing a dark blue overcoat over a light woolen dress, walked along one of the pathways that wound through the park, neither of them talking as their eyes wandered freely over the beautifully tended grounds. They came to the Landwehr canal and crossed over the Charlottenburg Bridge, pausing at the crown of the bridge and looking over the wall as a barge, loaded heavily with coal, pushed a wave of dark water slowly toward them.

The bargeman waved up at them from the cockpit, and they waved back, watching the dark puffs of smoke going up from the stack and trailing in the wind, until the barge was under the bridge. They could hear the rumble of the engines echoing and the propellors churning the water heavily under their feet, and feel the pavement shuddering from the engines. Then, turning, they saw first the sudden puffs of smoke going up from the other side of the bridge, and then the barge chugging out and moving slowly away. A wake of dark, silky water spread out behind it and splashed against the banks of the canal.

Rolf and Gretchen started off the bridge. They strolled on the footpaths that went through the trees, kicking through the fallen leaves that had not yet been raked, until they came to the Neuer See.

The lake was as blue as the sky and sparkled in the sun that shone brightly on its surface. The white fluffy clouds reflected in the lake like a mirror. Every now and then, the wind, like a child suddenly scribbling over its drawing, would sweep over the surface and turn everything dark. There were men fishing along the opposite shore and people in boats rowing back and forth across the lake for pleasure. A little boy ran with a kite.

"I wonder if they are happy," Gretchen said.

"They seem to be."

"They do, don't they?" Smiling, she took a deep breath, and the autumn chill shone on her cheeks. "This was a wonderful idea, coming to the park, don't you think?"

"It was your idea," Rolf said. "You shouldn't congratulate yourself on your own good ideas."

"It was still a wonderful idea, and I'll say so if I want," she smiled. "This afternoon, after we have a lovely meal in town, we'll go to one of the art museums. And tomorrow evening we'll go to the opera. What do you think of those ideas?"

"Wonderful! But the Reich Marshal is expecting me tomorrow evening."

Disappointment showed on her face. "I'd forgotten that," she frowned. "Why can't they leave you alone on your furlough? They've had you for three years. It isn't fair."

"I'll be sure to mention it to the Reich Marshal."

"You wouldn't."

"You're right. We can go to the opera the following evening."

"And you'll leave the Reich Marshal at Karinhall?"

"Yes, with his toys."

"Wonderful idea!" She put her arm through his. "See, Rolf, how much fun we are going to have?"

"It pains me to think about it. I can't keep up with how much fun we are having."

"You silly."

As they walked over a blunt knoll overlooking the lake, Rolf pointed to a group of children at the water's edge who were coaxing the geese and wild ducks with offerings of bread crumbs. "Do you remember when that goose chased you halfway around the lake until you dropped your crust?"

"*Do* I? Do not remind me," she said. "Silly goose."

"It was very funny."

"You weren't any help with all your laughing. I was terrified of that goose."

"You certainly were. But we soon cooked his goose at Christmas, didn't we? Or maybe it was his gander."

She laughed. "Do you see, Rolf? Already the park is doing you wonders."

They passed an old man just as he was launching a sailboat from the shore. "Why don't we hire a boat, Rolf?" Gretchen suggested. "It would be fun."

"I am a pilot, not a sailor," he said. "I'm likely to scuttle us."

Gretchen laughed with sudden ebullience, throwing her head back so that her silky blond hair shook behind her like a gossamer veil. She skipped ahead of Rolf. "Remember how we used to come here and ice-skate?" she laughed. "Oh, weren't those fun times?"

"Yes. Yes, they were. They were good times."

"Remember how we would warm ourselves over the braziers, eating hot pretzels and drinking the spicy apple cider the vendors would bring?"

"Yes."

"And how you and your friends used to make little jumps in the hill, and how you would take Ernst tobogganing?"

"How I was *forced,* you mean?" he said. "Mama never understood that I was ten years older than him. Everywhere I went Ernst had to go. Rain or shine."

"The lot of an older brother."

Rolf grunted. "I did not like my lot very much in those days."

"You could be so mean to Ernst."

He got an innocent look. "Me? Mean? Never."

"Fibber. The way you used to laugh when he rolled off your back into the snow. Heaven help him if there were a ditch or snowdrift in your path."

Rolf affected his saddest basset hound look. "Could I help it if he couldn't hold on?"

"Who could hold on with you bouncing down the hill like you were crazed, zigzagging through those trees!"

Rolf clucked his tongue remorsefully. "Poor Ernst."

"Yes, poor Ernst." They walked along the footpath. "Will you really go to one of his rallies with him?"

"I said I would."

"It will be good," she said. "You spending time with him, I mean. He's been difficult. Papa and he quarrel so. Papa does not try to understand, and Ernst can think of one thing only. They are both so pigheaded."

Rolf looked at her.

"He needs you, Rolf. He needs the strong hand of a big brother to guide him."

"My lot again?"

"Your lot."

Rolf cast an ironic glance at the sky. "Too bad there's no forecast of snow," he said. "I could guide him on my toboggan."

Gretchen made a face at him. "See how mean you are? You are the meanest."

"It is true, I confess. I am a brute."

She slapped his arm lightly. She looked down at the ground and said, "I wish we could have those days again. Don't you?"

Rolf said nothing.

"We were so happy as a family. It makes me cry when I think of all the lovely times we had." She looked at him, tears pooling in her big brown eyes. "I am so happy you're home, Rolf."

He smiled at her.

She hugged him. "I don't ever want to lose you."

"Here I am."

They came to the Avenue of Victory where there were marble and bronze effigies of past German heroes along the path. Painters were positioned before each one with their easels, and their boxes of oils or watercolors on the ground next to them as they painted: art imitating art imitating a certain general, or king, or emperor carved in stone or bronze. Some people gathered in little huddles admiring their work, others looked on, admiring, then walking away, still others just rested on the marble benches, enjoying the crisp morning air.

Rolf and Gretchen stood behind a red-haired painter with smudges of paint on his smock and in his hair and Vandyke beard. He was painting the Column of Victory, which stood at the very hub of the park. The painter was very enthusiastic, humming Wagner's "Götterdämmerung" movement from *Der Ring*, as he jabbed liberal amounts of oil onto the canvas with the violent flair of a symphony conductor.

"He thinks he is van Gogh," Rolf said in a whisper.

"He's an Impressionist," Gretchen whispered back. "They paint with feeling and boldness. They capture the ceaseless mutability of life with short, dramatic strokes of light and color."

"I am impressed."

"Shall we ask Vincent if he will paint our portrait?"

"Are you sure he'll be able to keep up with us? We are like the wind."

"Look how dramatically he uses the reds and yellows!"

"Very dramatic," Rolf declared. "We shall commission him then." He looked up at the winged Goddess of Victory atop the pinnacle of the fluted column. Then he looked at the painting and scrunched his nose. "On second thought, I don't think you would like his impression of you."

"I think he is doing a lovely job," Gretchen said. "You're not looking at it correctly."

"I get dizzy looking at those swirls."

"Those are clouds."

Rolf grunted. "No clouds I've ever seen did that, and I know clouds."

"They are passionate clouds. You must not analyze them; you must feel them. You must look at them with your soul."

"My soul is getting air sickness."

"Rolf the art critic."

"Rolf the realist," he corrected. "Which is more than I can say for Vincent here. He and his impressions are fired. Shall we go?"

As they started toward the Victory Column, Rolf looked up and saw the brilliance of the sun against its gilded surface, giving it the appearance of a gigantic torch. Rolf and Gretchen crossed the street to the entrance.

There were a few people on the observatory platform at the top of the column: a soldier and a young woman admiring the panorama and some children poking their heads through the iron bars and watching the wind carry their spittle.

After climbing the last step, Gretchen put her hand on her bosom to catch her breath. She was slightly bent over. "Whew! That's quite a climb, isn't it?"

"Are you speaking to me?" Rolf grinned, making a supreme effort to control his breathing.

For a while they said nothing as they looked out over the treetops, each of them enjoying the elevated change of perspective.

"Oh, it is simply marvelous!" Gretchen looked down on the boulevard that led away from the base of the column in a straight line east and west. She observed people walking along the long, wide boulevard, some of them taking the roads and footpaths that radiated out from the hub of the Victory circle into the park. "There is our Vincent," she said, pointing. "He doesn't look very dramatic from here, does he?"

Gretchen watched as a young man and woman on horseback trotted gaily along one of the bridle paths. "When I was little I used to come here when I wanted to get away from the world," she said. "Up here no one could touch me. I know it sounds silly, but it made me feel so close to God."

Rolf smiled, admiring the vista.

"I used to imagine that I was sitting on a cloud and watching the world go by," she said. "Like an angel. I would wonder about each of the people . . . who they were . . . where they lived . . . and where they were going . . . wondering if they were happy or not. I would make up happy stories for them."

They walked around the platform slowly, moving counterclockwise, taking in the changing perspective. The colors were mostly in the browns now, but there were still some reds and yellows left of the autumn. From their vantage point, high up over the trees, they could see clearly down the Charlottenburger Chaussee to the Brandenburg Gate in the east, and beyond it the medieval spire of the Marienkirche, with the Müggelberge hills in the distance. They took it all in for a long time.

"Rolf?"

"Yes?"

Gretchen looked at Rolf. "What did you mean last night about God not speaking German?" she asked him.

Rolf continued looking at the hills in the distance. "I do not believe in prayer anymore," he said. "That's all."

"You can't mean that."

"You asked me." As he continued around the platform, he could see the dome of the Charlottenburg Palace glinting in the sun and the industrial bulk of Spandau beyond, with its smokestacks painting a dark smear against the horizon.

She caught up to him. "But you've been baptized," she said. "You've taken the sacraments; you're one of his children."

Rolf's expression changed. "One of God's children?" As he gazed over the trees to the north, the lines of his face drew suddenly taut. "Were the fifty thousand who perished in the firestorm of Hamburg not his children?"

She looked at him.

"Why did he not hear their cries?" he asked. "The men, the women . . . the children. Did their prayers not matter to him?"

Gretchen's brows knit together in thought. "I do not have an answer, Rolf," she said. "None that fits neatly into any catechism."

"An honest answer," Rolf replied. He grunted sardonically as a passage of Scripture came to mind. "'God's judgments are unsearchable . . . his ways are past finding out,'" he quoted. "Any other answer would be a ruse."

"You are bitter, Rolf."

"I have reason to be," he said. He paused a moment, looking up at the sky. "Where is God?" he said reflectively. "I do not see God at all. I see only chaos . . . like those impressionistic clouds of Vincent. But there are no dramatic strokes of light and color in them, no reds and yellows; there is only darkness."

A panic went over Gretchen's face. "Rolf, think of what you are saying!"

"Think? You want me to think now? Not *feel?*"

"Yes, I want you to think," she said. "I want you to think of your immortal soul. I want you to think of what you know to be true."

"I think only of you and Mama and Papa and Ernst," he said. "You are the only truth I think about. Everything else is wind, and I don't care a whit about everything else." They came around toward the south now, and Rolf could see the Kaiser Wilhelm Memorial Church poking through the autumn-browned trees.

"We do not always understand what God is doing," she said quietly. "He does not tell us everything."

"What is there to tell? God has put away his easel. He has left us in a swirl of vagueness."

Gretchen looked suddenly desperate. "You must ask him for understanding, Rolf. Please, you must ask him. You must pray—"

"Pray?" He smiled politely, patting her hand. "I see we have come full circle," he said. He looked below and there was the impressionistic painter once again. "Ah, there is our Vincent."

Gretchen looked down at the iron rail between her hands as tears trickled over her cheeks.

"Let's have none of that," Rolf said. "We came here to have fun, remember? Enough of this talk of theology."

"I am so stupid," she chided herself. "If only I knew my catechism better—"

"It would make no difference," Rolf said. "If there were a God he would not be contained by a proper catechism. Proper catechism went out with Hamburg."

She pulled out a handkerchief and dabbed her eyes and nose. "If only Pastor Bonhoeffer were free to answer your questions. He would know about such things."

"He would tell me to have faith. He would say that God took Katharina for a reason. Then he would say that the just shall live by faith. It's no good, Gretchen; I have no faith. Not anymore. Faith died with proper catechism."

Then Rolf looked at her strangely. "What did you mean if he were free?"

Gretchen was puzzled. "Pastor Bonhoeffer?"

"Yes."

"I don't understand. You know he's in Tegel prison of course."

Rolf stared at her. "He's been arrested?"

"This past April," she said. "I wrote you."

"You wrote me about this?"

"Yes. Three times, I think. Yes, three."

"When did you write?"

"I told you. This past April—Rolf?"

Rolf felt an airy buoyancy rising in him, as though someone had let go a tether that held him to the ground.

Gretchen frowned at him. "You didn't get my letters?"

Rolf was staring past her now, his mind adrift over a current of thoughts. He had received many letters from Gretchen over the past three years, one a week usually, but none of them ever mentioned Pastor Bonhoeffer being arrested. Not that he remembered. But he wouldn't forget that, would he?

His mind drifted back to the month of April. Seven months is a long way to drift, but there had been a mix-up in the mail, as he recalled, which made it easier. He saw the month clearly now, saw the neat stack of letters tied with a piece of twine as the clerk handed it to him, saw the strangely contrite look in his eyes. Did certain of her letters get lost in the mail, rerouted to another division during the mix-up? Perhaps. It was a common occurrence in the military. He searched the month of April again, and he searched the clerk's eyes. What was it about the clerk's eyes? And then another thought occurred to him. It came subtly, worming out from some dark fold in his brain, and turned his head in wonder. He felt a sudden prickling go over his scalp.

"Rolf? Didn't you get my letters?"

"What?" Rolf's face contracted. "What else did you say in the letters?"

"What else? I don't know," she said, thinking back. "Nothing else, I suppose. Only that the Gestapo had arrested Pastor Bonhoeffer. Nothing else. The rest was family business."

"You said nothing else about the Gestapo?"

"Nothing."

"You're sure?"

"Yes. Why?"

"Why was he arrested?"

"Papa said it was political. He said the charges were trumped up. It was because he stood against the National Reich Church, of course." She grunted contemptuously. "National Church. You cannot call it a church. A church does not arrest pastors and priests for preaching the gospel."

"You didn't put that in the letters, did you?"

"Why?"

"Did you?"

"No—not that I can remember," Gretchen said. A shiver went over her arms. "Rolf, you're frightening me."

"It's important that you remember clearly, Gretchen."

"Do you think they have been reading my letters? What on earth for?"

Rolf didn't answer. Instead, he watched as a cloud passed over the sun, drawing a veil of shadow over the ground. For just a little while a gloom passed with it and then the sun returned. "Just watch what you write in your letters, all right?" he said. "I don't want anything to happen to you."

"Nothing to happen to me?" She laughed bitterly. "Rolf, everything in the world has been turned upside down! My country is being bombed. My city is being bombed. I can't go to sleep at night without wondering if a bomb is going to fall on my head. And now you suggest that the Gestapo has nothing better to do with their time than to read my letters?"

Rolf pounded the iron rail with his fist. "We will stop the bombers," he said.

"Will you, Rolf? Will you stop the bombs? When will you do this? After you have killed more of the English and the Americans? After they have bombed our home into rubble? When, Rolf? When are you going to stop the bombs?"

Rolf said nothing.

"Why do we not make peace?" she cried. "Don't you see that we are fighting an immoral war we cannot possibly win?"

Rolf said nothing.

"Don't you see, Rolf? God will not allow it."

He looked at her and grunted bitterly. "God has told you this of course?"

"Think of it, Rolf. Martin Bormann said that National Socialism and Christianity are irreconcilable, didn't he? That is why Pastor Bonhoeffer was arrested. That is why they read my letters. That is why the Nazis will

not rest until every last member of the Confessing Church is behind bars."
She grunted. "They're such silly, little, stupid men."

Rolf looked away from her.

"They've replaced the Bible with *Mein Kampf*," she went on. "Imagine that! The struggles of Adolf Hitler instead of the passion of Christ. How can we expect God's protection when our soldiers fight for a man who hates his Son? For men who hate his very Word!"

"I fight for Germany," Rolf said quietly. "Not for Adolf Hitler."

"But it is because of Hitler that Germany fights. It is foolishness." She took his hands and looked at him. "How many more Hamburgs must burn, Rolf? How many more souls must be lost to the flames before we realize that we are being judged?"

"That's enough!" he said, yanking away from her. "Just shut up, won't you! I do not want to hear of your God, or your Christ, or any more talk of religion!"

She stepped back, caught herself against the railing, and steadied herself. She blinked numbly at his back for several terrible seconds. Rolf shook his head and she watched his hand go up to his face. She went over to him and wrapped her arms around him and lay her head against his back. She held him tightly.

"I'm sorry, Gretchen," he said. "I am a fool."

"Let's not quarrel, Rolf," she said. "Not you and me . . . especially not you and me. If we fight then all Germany is lost."

"You keep talking like that and you'll end up with Bonhoeffer."

"I don't care."

"I do." He turned around, looked down at her wet face, then pulled her close to him. "Nothing is going to come between us."

"I will pray for you, Rolf. I will have faith for both of us. I will have faith for our home and for Germany."

"Does that fit into your catechism?"

"I don't care."

He stroked the back of her head. "I tell you what let's do," he said. "Let's go over to that little café on the corner of the park where we used to go and have some coffee and apple strudel. There's something to take your breath away."

She looked up into his eyes. He was smiling. "Oh, Rolf, things will get better, won't they? The war won't go on much longer, will it?"

"Not if I can help it," he said, wiping her tears with his thumbs.

"Oh, Rolf. I do love you so."

"Me too," he grinned.

"You're impossible."

They headed down the stairs of the column.

Moments later a man wearing a black leather overcoat and holding a camera with a telephoto lens stepped out of the shadows on the lee of the column. He looked below and saw the enthusiastic red-haired painter with a little group of people gathered around him. And then he saw a man and woman coming out from the base of the column, the man's arm around the woman's waist as they headed west along the Charlottenburger Chaussee. The man was wearing the uniform of a Luftwaffe officer, he saw, and the young blond woman was wearing a dark blue, woolen overcoat. He raised the camera, rotated the lens, everything becoming suddenly bright and crisp through the viewfinder. As the couple paused to look at the painting, the woman pointing at it and smiling, showing her face clearly with the sun on it, he pressed the shutter release.

17 ★★★★

November 3, 1943. 0700. Halesbury, Suffolk, East Anglia. Billy watched the messman behind the counter spoon the poached eggs onto his plate. They were real poached eggs. He spooned them carefully, as though he didn't want to bruise them, and he did it under the watchful eyes of a little dark-haired man with a thin mustache, who hovered behind him like a hawk.

Billy had not seen the little man before. He was a Frenchman, he could tell. When the little man said something to the messman, he heard the wonderfully foreign accent that always made the English language sound beautiful. The Frenchman looked at him and smiled, then followed him as he stepped to the right and nodded at the potatoes. The messman monitoring this station scooped the potatoes politely onto his plate, smiling like a spaniel that had just brought in the paper.

"Thanks," Billy said. It was all very intimate and nonmilitary, and he wondered what was going on.

He stepped over to the strips of bacon that were neither undercooked nor too crispy. They were lined carefully on a linen towel in a polished metal tray next to the thick slices of English bacon that were arrayed neatly like fallen dominoes, one atop the other. He took two of each kind and then signalled to the messman minding the toasts as they were coming off the coils a golden brown. The little Frenchman glanced at his plate and made no indication about anything, except to twirl his thin mustache as he went back to the head of the line to pick up the next airman. He glanced back at Billy. His eyes narrowed almost imperceptibly, it seemed, as though he were censuring a bit of misplaced garnish, and Billy thought everything very odd.

He went over to the coffee station, looking down at his food, really looking at it now and seeing the diced onions and the red and green peppery bits of seasoning over the potatoes, and thinking of the little dark-haired man. He set his tray down, took a white, thick-lipped cup, and turned the black wooden handle of the large stainless steel percolator. The black coffee poured into the cup, hissing and splashing up the sides, and making big hot bubbles that roiled about in the cup as it rose, steaming and smelling wonderful.

Billy raised his tray and scanned the mess hall until he saw Joe Thompson at a table in the corner hunched over his breakfast. As Billy walked over the hard linoleum tiles of the Officer's Mess, he smelled the warm vapors of everything all mixing together and rising from his plate, and he felt his mouth watering, like it did on really cold mornings when he'd come in from the stock all cold and numb and ravenous and his mother had a good, hot breakfast going.

Joe Thompson was spreading a big dollop of orange marmalade over his buttered toast, like he was afraid it would get away from him. "The new cook is something, isn't he?" he said as Billy sat across from him.

"Who is he?"

"Beats me. Some Free French fellow, I think," Joe mumbled, taking a bite so big that some of the marmalade stuck to the sides of his mouth and cheeks. "Fighting the Krauts with a stove now, I guess."

"Free French, huh? How'd we rate him? This smells delicious."

"Wait'll you taste," Joe said. "Those potatoes! He did something indecent to them I know." He took another bite of the toast, paused a moment, tasting it, then added, "I tell you, they feed us like this, and it makes me think it's our last meal or something."

"Hey, knock it off."

"You superstitious or something?"

"Or something."

"You getting spooky again?"

"Shut up." Billy tined the two poached eggs onto the potatoes with his fork, then cut them into little cubes. He sprinkled some fresh ground pepper onto them, cut a wedge of English bacon, stacked it all on his fork, and put it into his mouth. He looked down at the table as he chewed thoughtfully.

Joe Thompson leaned forward onto his elbows. "Well?"

"We must have done something very bad, or very good," Billy admitted. Joe chuckled throatily.

"This Free French fellow should be given the *Croix de Guerre*," Billy added. He took a too-big sip of coffee and fanned his hand over his mouth. "Oh, this is good! This is good! I think you're right about the last meal business." He chuckled and hunched over his plate, the elbows crowding it on either side, his left arm draped protectively in front.

When he had finished his meal and wiped the plate with the last of his toast, getting up the last of the yolk and the juices from the potatoes and bacon, the two of them sat back in their chairs, sipping coffee as they glanced over the mess hall from a lofty satedness. For several minutes neither of them had much to say as they sat listening to the happy clatter in the room.

Billy was thinking about Colette, though the guilt and the hunger pangs of loneliness it brought to the surface could not be satisfied by any French chef. He tried to force his mind on other things, like thinking about the English girl in the Guinea three nights ago, or about the next Ramrod, or about his folks back home, but, as always, the French girl was waiting in ambush for him.

"Where'd you go off to?" Joe asked him.

Billy looked at him. "What'd you say?"

Joe chuckled. "Bet you were thinking about that dame at the Guinea."

"Not a chance."

"That was some dame—class down to the bone," Joe said. "Crosshairs for eyes though."

"Skagway has a way of drawing fire."

"I'm talking about you. You were the one in the line of fire, in case you didn't realize it."

"That couldn't be helped."

"If you say so," Joe said, grinning. "I didn't go charging over there like Sir Lancelot. Neither did Happy."

"Skagway was a jerk, and he needed some cooling off."

"Seems to me you cooled the RAF boy pretty good," Joe said. "Did I miss it when you cooled Skagway?"

Billy shook his head. "I've got nothing for that girl, so you can lay off it, Joe."

"I never said you did, hotshot. I just said that she was a classy dame."

"For a married woman, you mean."

"For a widow, I mean."

"She's a widow theoretically. She's married technically."

"Okay," Joe said. "It seems a crime to waste all that theoretical talent on technicalities."

"You're the talent scout, not me," Billy said. "Leave me out of it. I'm through with it and all the other dames."

"What's eating you?"

"Nothing."

"Something's eating you." Joe Thompson looked at him. "The Ramrod?"

"Lay off it, Joe. I told you I'm through with it." The drone of airplanes drew his eyes to the window. He looked out over the plowed fields that stretched away from the mess hall and were broken by hawthorn hedges and by Tealbrook Wood. A flight of P–47s was coming in low over the woods, one after the other, the morning sun glinting off their flanks like splinters of lightning, then slanting behind the leafless trees onto what he knew to be the main runway. "Those our Jugs?"

Joe glanced out the window. "They're with the 4th."

"The 4th?" Butch Harding came to Billy's mind. "What are they doing here?"

"Refueling. Got a deep one today, I hear."

Billy grunted. "Think maybe they've got a chance to beat us to a hundred?"

"A snowball's chance in South Texas," Joe Thompson grinned, then looked at his wristwatch. "Time to saddle up. We got a briefing in fifteen."

"Roger that." Standing up, Billy felt a flutter of butterflies in his stomach.

As they carried their trays to the scullery, Billy caught the Frenchman staring at him with an uncertain expression. Billy nodded at him. The little man looked away quickly, but Billy saw something in his eyes that brought a prickling of danger over his scalp. Joe must have seen it too, for he said, "What's with him?"

"Beats me," Billy said. He and Joe went outside and mounted their bicycles and peddled west toward the briefing hut.

༈

Colonel Zeb Pilke briefed the three squadrons of the 52nd Fighter Group. It was to be Wilhelmshaven this time. Another Ramrod into Germany.

A buzz of Hey, whaddya know's and How about that's perked through the room. The men adjusted their seats, flicked their cigarettes, and looked at one another with winks and nods. Something whined tautly over the room. A few lighthearted remarks sailed up and shattered against it. Colonel Pilke told a joke and the men laughed quickly and easily, although everyone knew that Wilhelmshaven was no milk run.

Using a pointer, the colonel indicated the route on the large wall map of England and Europe, showing how the B–17 "Big Friends" would come in high over the North Sea, heading east as they skirted the radar and, hopefully, the flak batteries along the Frisian Islands. Then he showed the area of Jade Bay and told them how they would come in and drop their payloads on the U-boat pens along the Schilling Roads, and on any other ship in the harbor. Then he indicated where they would rendezvous with the bombers, going and coming, and which squadrons would escort them in and out.

"Leewarden and Enschede will throw up some tough kites, but we'll probably get the most heat from the 11th Fighter Group at Jever," the colonel said, tapping the base on the map.

Billy again felt a stirring of butterflies. They were up on a light breeze that went through him, and their little, light wings of dust struck against the sides of his stomach. He tamped a lipful of Copenhagen into place and set an old coffee can between his knees.

"You've tangled with them before, men," the colonel went on, "so there's no need for me to tell you that they have some pretty top rate pilots in Jever. Hochreiter can vouch for that, can't you, Hochreiter?"

"What's that?" Billy said. "Oh, right, sir. Top rate."

"Glad to see I'm not keeping you awake, Lieutenant."

Several of the men chuckled. Billy felt a rush of blood to his throat.

"Now, if any of you hotshots happen to see an Me–109 with a checkered nose and the name 'Katharina' written on its fuselage, you'd best bounce him before he bounces you. You won't get a second shot at him. The dope on this guy is that he's flamed two hundred aircraft."

Someone blew a long low whistle.

Billy perked up.

"That's right," the colonel said, "Two hundred. Most of them were Russians, but there are plenty of our boys stencilled on his rudder as well. No more, do you hear me? I want to see all your ugly mugs back here for the Sadie Hawkins dance."

A light buzz went through the place.

Colonel Pilke smiled. "We gonna break a hundred today?"

There were a few you bet's and piece a cake's tossed back. They'd stick it to the lousy Krauts this time.

"Right-o, men," Colonel Pilke said as he stepped aside. "Major Conners has some important words for you now."

The intelligence officer walked to the front of the large Nissen hut and explained more about the antiaircraft batteries that were positioned along the Frisians Islands and mainland coast. He showed them the range of the German radar and then explained the various escape routes in the event anyone was shot down, reminding the men to pick up their survival kits, maps, and currency after the briefing. There would likely be casualties. "Any questions?"

The men stirred in their seats. Billy spat into his coffee can.

The weather officer came up next and briefed the men on the weather conditions, using a lot of meteorological jargon but essentially saying that there would be some good cloud cover before the target. It would be a good day for a hunt. "Any questions?" There were none.

Colonel Pilke stepped to the front again and looked over the men. He was wearing his war face now. "Right then," he said, smacking the palm of his hand with the pointer. "You've got the dope now. Bounce 'em high, men. Don't let some slippery Hun lure you down to the floor. There's no beating a 109 or 190 in a climb. Watch for bogies in the clouds. Watch for bogies in the sun. Wingmen, stick to your flight leaders like white on rice. Any questions?"

"Who'd you have to kill to get that new cook?" someone asked.

The men laughed.

"I'll see you afterward, Skagway."

Skagway sank sheepishly into his collar.

The colonel looked over the Group. There were no more questions. They'd heard the drill before. They could recite it verbatim. It had kept most of them alive.

Billy looked over at Joe Thompson and grinned, then, feeling he'd overplayed the grin, gave him the thumbs up.

"Very good," the colonel said. "Good luck, and good shooting. Squadron leaders, stick around, please."

The colonel dismissed the men. There was an immediate clatter of wooden chairs scraping over the cement floor as the men stood up and began filing out of the room.

&

There were four flights of four planes each that comprised the three squadrons of the 52nd Fighter Group. The flights were designated by color codes: White, Red, Yellow, and Blue. The 61st and the 62nd Squadrons were to escort the Big Friends to their target, and the 63rd would bring them home.

Billy was assigned to the 61st Squadron, Blue Flight. A half hour after the briefing he was taxiing his new Republic P–47D Thunderbolt behind Joe Thompson. The air was morning crisp, with a breeze coming from the northeast and smelling of autumn and grain fields with a saline hint of the sea; the sky was blue with high, fluffy white clouds sailing steadily against the horizon. A beautiful day for a pheasant hunt or a sailboat race.

He pulled out the tin of Copenhagen and tamped another lipful into place with his tongue, then placed the coffee can between his legs and looked down from the height of the cockpit at the ground sweeping beneath the blade of his wings. He guided the plane, sighting along the weedy edge of the tarmac on either side of him, bouncing along on the tires with the tail wheel dragging and making the steering awkward, then revving his engine and using the rudder to steer around the strip that led to the main runway. The throaty popping of the eighteen-cylinder Pratt and Whitney radial engine was deafening.

Looking around the big, blocky, red-painted nose of his plane that obscured everything directly ahead of him, he could see most of his squadron bending away from him in single file as they ventured around the curving strip. He thought how much bigger and how ungainly the Jugs seemed on the ground than they did in the air; it was like looking at bison close-up, without any of the dignity of distance as they thundered over the prairie.

The 62nd was already in the air, and the 61st was set to go now. He glanced across the field of grass on his right as Lieutenant Colonel "Bug" Mallory of White Flight and his wingman rumbled down the main runway and took off into the wind, followed by another two planes. Red Flight took off next, two by two, and then Yellow Flight lined up to go.

Ahead, off his right beam, Billy could see the big, blocky pair of Thunderbolts in front of Joe Thompson's plane going along the taxi strip, following them as they turned toward the runway to await their turn behind Yellow flight. They belonged to Turtle, who was Blue Flight leader, and Skagway, his wingman.

Billy felt the sudden rise of butterflies in his belly, only now they were more like locusts, with the little breeze in him stiffening and going round in a whirl. He felt his mouth go dry, and he knew that the locusts and the nerves would be with him until he was up.

He was glad that he had the big Pratt and Whitney to concentrate on, listening to the engine purr and how it responded to his touch; he was glad that he had the controls to concentrate on, and the oil pressure and the instruments and gauges, tapping the little round glasses with his finger to keep his mind focused. He checked and rechecked the instruments. And then he noticed that something was wrong. He checked each of the instruments again. Panic snapped through him. What was it? He was forgetting something. But there was nothing amiss. And then he knew—the picture of Laura Miller was missing. It struck him with the same dull, emotionless impact as when he first read her letter. He loosed a lipful into the coffee can. She was gone now and there was no going back to her.

Then he remembered everything about Colette in a dreamy pulse of time: her brightly colored eyes, the long, black mane of hair, the creamy, mountain-fresh skin smoothed over the high cheek bones, and the full, rich poutiness of her smile. And he remembered the coltish awkwardness in her stride, the shapely figure moving dangerously beneath the Freedom Fighter clothes. But she was gone too, and there was no going back to her either.

He felt a gentle clap against his breastbone and realized it was the crucifix that he wore now inside his shirt. The crude, twisting form of the Christ beat against his breast like a *mea culpa*, reminding him of his vow to God. *Anything, God. You name it.* And then he knew that he was going to die. Joe was right about the last meal, he thought. It was like a revelation, all of it coming to a fiery head—he had broken his vow to God.

Everything went cold inside him, the coldness of death, and he felt nothing of remorse or fear or anything. He only felt dead, and the dead don't feel anything. The wages of sin is death. There was no *mea culpa*, no *mea maxima culpa;* there was only the knowledge that he was going to die, that God was going to collect his pound of flesh.

He was at the end of the taxi strip now, where it joined the main runway. He looked out his cockpit and saw the signalman waving. Warren Turlock and Pete Skagway were racing away down the runway now, the two big Thunderbolts in tandem, rolling slowly at first, then both accelerating evenly, their engines roaring, then the tails lifting and the great bulk of the planes lifting off and banking heavily into the wind that was coming from the northeast.

The signalman waved Joe and Billy to their marks.

Joe revved his engine and his plane rolled over to the left-hand side of the runway. Billy guided his plane beside him. He was glad to be finally going. He looked down at the signalman, and suddenly the exhilaration that is derived from height, speed, power, and purpose went through him like a narcotic jolt. Peering down the runway, everything blurring but the long, gray barrel of pavement, he could feel in his mind the plane lifting to his will, climbing against the pull of gravity, knifing through the great, blue, swollen expanse. He was in the hands of Fate, or God, now—a hapless chip of wood on a strong current—and he didn't give a hoot.

He looked over at Joe and gave him the thumbs up. Then he let out a howl and pulled his canopy forward. Seeing the flags go down, he pulled back on the throttle, felt the pull of two thousand horses against his back, and with it the pure rush of adrenaline.

18 ★★★

Viktor twisted the cap off the bottle of hair tonic, sprinkled a liberal amount onto his head, and massaged his scalp with his fingertips. He combed his hair forward, ran the end tooth of the comb down the left side of his head, drawing a neat part, then combed the hair back and away from the part, smoothing his hand after the comb to slick it down. He looked at himself in the mirror of his wall locker, turned his face to the right, and then to the left, allowing the morning light to illumine every line.

"This is your lucky day, you handsome devil," he grinned affectionately at his image. "She will not be able to tear herself away from you."

He was wearing a sleeveless undershirt and freshly laundered uniform trousers, with suspenders hanging down in long, gray loops across his thighs. He grabbed the starched white shirt off the back of a chair, carefully fed his arms into the sleeves, then, walking over to the window that looked out onto the hills, opened it, and began to button his shirt up from the bottom.

He took a deep breath of the frigid air, glancing over the gray-green hills in the distance that floated in the morning mist. "Yes sir, this is your lucky day."

Whistling, he tucked the tails of his shirt into his trousers as he walked back to his wall locker and selected a tie hanging neatly from a tie rack.

A long-faced man with a sharp, hawkish nose came into the room wearing rubber shower sandals and holding a white towel around his waist. His hair stood out in dripping loops. "There was no more hot water," he growled, as he made his way to the wall locker between two of the beds in the room. He shoved his leather toilet kit onto the top shelf of the locker. "I will probably catch pneumonia."

Viktor chuckled. "I had plenty of hot water." He raised his chin, pried the neck button away from the starched collar, then pinched it through the buttonhole. "It was a lovely shower. Very steamy."

"Steamy." The other man grunted, spat an epithet, then shivered. "Say, who opened the window?"

"I did."

"Well, shut it, it's freezing."

"The fresh air is good for your constitution, Hans," Viktor said, working his tie into a tight knot, "which from the sound of it appears to have backed up. You really must eat more cereal grains."

"Then you are not going to shut the window?"

Viktor took in a deep gulp of air and whistled cheerfully.

Hans swore as he went over and shut the window. "I will be glad when this blasted war is over," he groused. He walked back to his wall locker, doffed his towel, then shrugged on his clothes with disgruntled thrusts. "Maybe I'll be able to live like a human being again."

"And when were you ever a human being, Hans?"

Hans trained an eye on him. "I'll not dignify that remark with a comment."

"You just did."

Hans told him where he could go.

Viktor chuckled triumphantly. "You are jealous because I have a twenty-four-hour pass."

Hans barked a laugh. "Yes! Because you have been bootlicking."

"That's right, I have been," Viktor confessed cheerily. "I pride myself on my bootlicking. And while you are breaking your tail on duty, I will be enjoying the day with the most beautiful girl in Wilhelmshaven."

"And who is the most beautiful girl in Wilhelmshaven this time?"

Viktor kissed his fingertips. "She is a vision of beauty and charm," he said. "Blond hair . . . cute little dimples on her cheeks . . ."

"Not that pig down at Werner's?" Hans snorted. "The one with the legs of a piano?"

Viktor grunted. "One who has been seen in the company of cows has no ground for criticism."

A shoe slammed against his wall locker. Viktor chuckled as he bent to pick it up. He eyed the shoe. "With a fleet of these battleships we could rule the world," he said. He tossed the shoe into a trash can.

Just then the air raid siren blared over the air base. Both of the men looked out the window.

"There goes your precious liberty," Hans gloated.

Viktor waved him off. "It is probably another drill," he said confidently. He tucked in the tail of his shirt and smoothed out the pleats. "Those with twenty-four-hour passes are exempt from practice drills."

There was a sudden clatter of men and voices outside their room, men yelling and calling to one another. A major put his head into their room. "Viktor, Hans, suit up quickly! Be on the flight line in five minutes!"

"What is it?" Viktor asked. "Another drill?"

"Fat Autos," the major said. "Hundreds of them!"

Viktor stared at him.

"Get your tails moving," the major screamed.

"Yes, sir," Hans said. The major closed the door.

Hans looked at Viktor. "Let's go, Mr. Twenty-four-hour pass," he smiled. "Maybe you will be able to shoot down another third of an airplane."

Viktor cursed, looked at himself in the mirror, and tore off his tie.

19 ★★★

Billy glanced out his cockpit at Joe Thompson off his right wingtip, and, beyond him, going straight out in a slightly forward angle, were Pete Skagway and Warren Turlock, holding the line pretty tight. The other two flights in the squadron were ahead of them, flying parallel courses to theirs in tight, finger-four formations—a tactic borrowed from the Luftwaffe—ranging thirty-three thousand feet above the earth at a cruising speed of 240 mph. The Thunderbolts looked graceful now, looking like skeins of Canada geese as they planed cleanly over a smooth-flowing chinook.

Billy allowed a smile. He loved to fly. Flying cleared the clutter in his head. When he was flying he was loosed in a world between worlds, a lofty perch from which a man could think without distraction. There was no earth to pull him down. No obstacles to obstruct his vision. There was only the vast expanse of glittering blue sky ascending to the throne of God, and the clouds beneath him cushioned his thoughts in radiant white light.

He glanced down as the gray-brown point of land pushed through a hole in the cottony batting of clouds. He could just see the white of the surf curling along the shore. It seemed the land mass was floating. He knew the boxes of Big Friends were flying below and just ahead of them, cruising at 24,000 feet and 160 mph, flying in zigzag patterns to confuse the 88mm flak batteries and the 37mm antiaircraft guns. He wondered if the radar had picked them up yet; he wondered when the peaceful, soul-balming sky would suddenly erupt with hundreds of dark puffs of smoke-enshrouded shrapnel, against which there was only luck and fate—or God, if you believed in him.

He could see the streaming white contrails of the Fortresses now, marking their course for all the world to see. He knew the 62nd Squadron was patrolling somewhere ahead of them, the two squadrons providing a cover guard both fore and aft. They knew the tactics of the Luftwaffe, how they hunted in packs like carnivores—one group hitting high and the other coming up from below to attack the soft underbelly of the unsuspecting herd. He scanned the clouds below him for bogies. But there were only sky and clouds, with the sun in his eyes that made for dangerous hunting.

Then he saw the flak bursts peppering the sky ahead of him and heard the muffled pops that he knew were razing the box formations of Big Friends with deadly shrapnel. *Poor devils,* he thought. *They're taking it now. Nothing to do but ride it out. Some ride.*

∾

Viktor scanned the skies for signs of the Fat Autos. Intelligence had reported at least four hundred of them, flying due east and following a course that could only mean Wilhelmshaven. The RAF had hit it back in February and made a mess of things, but with fewer bombers. *Is there no end to them,* he wondered, recalling Rolf's words. There would be escorts now, he knew, making it tougher. Who knows how many escorts, though? Plenty of them, no doubt. Thunderbolts. Lightnings. Maybe even those new Mustangs they'd been briefed about. He didn't want to think about them.

He scanned the skies for the bomber formations, watched for the contrails that would lead him to them like a road map. Nothing. Just clouds and sky, and twenty-nine thousand feet below him the dark blue of the North Sea, with the gray-brown color of the Frisian Islands gliding beneath the clouds. It sure would be nice to shoot down one of those Fat Autos, he thought. Today was the day, he was certain. Plenty of targets to choose from. He could see himself at Werner's, gloating to Rolf how he had lined up on one and sent a rocket into its midsection. Rolf would be proud of him. He might even put him in for a promotion. Viktor laughed at the thought of a promotion. It had been three years.

He wondered if Rolf was enjoying himself with his family. That lucky devil, he thought. Three glorious weeks away from the war. He thought of Rolf's sister, Gretchen. He'd seen pictures of her. A pretty girl. A little on the thin side, perhaps, but those eyes. Ahh! Those beautiful brown eyes. But she was not his type; she was too classy for him, too refined. Too religious.

Then he thought of the blond-haired waitress at Werner's. What was her name? Heidi? Helga? That girl wasn't at all thin. She looked more like a

Rubens painting. He chuckled throatily. His kind of girl. Lusty, full of life. No religion to speak of. I will tell her what a hero I am when I return, he thought; she, of course, will believe every word and give me a hero's reward.

A grin spread over his mouth as he looked over at the rest of his squadron, forty-eight Messerschmitts gleaming with the sun on their backs, their yellow noses bulleting through the air at 300 mph. He wondered if the Focke-Wulf 190s of Jagdgeschwader 26 out of Calais were on schedule. It was to be a coordinated counterattack; the 11th was to barrel out of the sun and hit them high, while the 26th was to hit the bombers low and from the flanks. They were most vulnerable there—only the turret and tail guns to worry about. He scanned the skies for enemy aircraft. Nothing. Only the sky and the clouds, the easy glide of the islands, and his thoughts turned again to What's-her-name's dimples.

෨෨෨

The sky was crowding with planes. A strong wind drove them from the four corners of the earth to a bright blue firmament of violence high above the earth. The pilots were boys, really, both Americans and Germans alike, most of them not long from the coddle of their mothers' smooth hands, now come to do battle, to prove themselves against their equals. On their rudders and under their cockpits were proudly displayed the victories of battle, making them strong medicine in the eyes of their enemies. And in every beating heart there burned a dream of glory. Silence whined dreadfully over the airy theater—a swollen, electrical synapse before the crash of lightning.

෨෨෨

"This is Tango Blue Leader. Bandits at two o'clock low," Colonel Pilke's voice blared through the radio. "FW–190s! Dozens of them!"

Although Pilke's squadron and the German fighters were at least ten miles ahead of his position, Billy looked instinctively out his cockpit at the two o'clock position below. He listened in his headset as the 62nd began to mix it up with the 190s, hearing the pilots calling out to one another and hearing the muffled clatter of machine gun fire against the throaty purr of his own engine. He shifted his visor against the bright glare of the sun and strained his eyes for a telling glint of metal.

Nothing.

Nothing yet. Only the contrails of the Big Friends.

Then a movement caught his eye and, looking down, he saw the B–17s spread out over miles of clouded sky, with the coasts of the Frisian Islands showing hazily far below. They seemed to be moving at a crawl, plodding heavily forward like a herd of fattened cattle being goaded to the slaughter. They seemed such easy marks, lumbering dumb brutes, that Billy wondered how any of them ever made it to their targets.

"This is Foxworth Red Leader," Lieutenant Colonel Bug Mallory's voice crackled through the radio. "Bogies at four o'clock low! Moving up on the Tail-end Charlies!"

Looking out the right side of his cockpit, Billy saw a dozen Me–109s through the clouds, climbing fast toward the Fortresses at an acute angle, looking as though they were coming straight up the side of a mountain on invisible rails.

"Red Flight and White Flight, drop your tanks and line up on me," Mallory commanded. "I don't think they've spotted us. Blue and Yellow Flights, watch the ceiling!"

"Roger," Captain Turlock, Blue Flight leader, responded.

"Roger," Captain Milton, Yellow Flight leader, responded.

Billy watched Red and White Flights tip away, one plane after the other, toward the climbing Messerschmitts, watched as they fell angling down through a cloud corridor in the sky, then banking wide to line up behind the unsuspecting Germans.

Bug Mallory bounced the lead Me–109, dropping on him like a hawk on a ground squirrel, then firing a long burst of his eight .50 caliber wing guns at its left flank. The enemy aircraft disintegrated in a brilliant fireball. The other Messerschmitts immediately broke off their attack, splitting off the invisible rail in 180 degree turns, and made for the deck. The Thunderbolts chased after them hungrily, each pair cutting away a mark and roaring after it.

Billy shouted. "That's showing 'em! Lousy Krauts."

Suddenly Captain Turlock's voice crackled through his headset. "This is Foxworth Blue Leader. Bandits at six o'clock high! A whole shootin' match of them!"

Billy shot a look over his shoulders and his eyes went wide. It seemed the skies above and behind him were swarming with the speeding sleek shapes of Me–109s. They'd come spiralling down out of a towering cumulonimbus cloud like a host of fallen angels, and the sun lancing through the clouds struck their wings and flashed exultantly, giving them the appearance of burnished metal. It occurred to Billy that those other Messerschmitts had merely been a diversion to cut as many Thunderbolts away from the Big Friends as possible, that they'd fallen into a trap. He felt suddenly cold in his belly.

"It's a whole new ball game, boys!" someone shouted.

Captain Turlock ordered Yellow and Blue Flights to drop their tanks. Then Blue Flight split in two: Captain Turlock and Skagway tipping one way, with Joe Thompson and Billy tipping the other. Yellow Flight swung around and headed toward the downward attacking 109s.

The Messerschmitts broke formation, careering away in every direction like sparks from a Roman candle; some of them mixed it up with the Thunderbolts, while others slid around and got into the B–17s along their flanks.

The chatter of battle in Billy's headset was mind-numbing. The sky was suddenly roiling with the fast-moving shapes of fighter planes. It was like quail hunting down in east Texas, where he'd done his flight training. He'd never hunted quail in Montana, since there weren't any to speak of there, so when he'd busted his first covey—the mass of birds jumping suddenly out of the brush with their wings beating furiously, going every which way in seeming hilarious abandon—he stood, gun in hand, gaping a little stupidly at them. By the time he remembered he was supposed to shoot, the birds were long gone.

Suddenly a flight of Messerschmitts roared over his cockpit at 400 mph, passing within two hundred yards of his head. Billy ducked instinctively, squeezed off a burst of his guns at nothing, then, looking at the planes speeding off in the distance, blew a curse.

"Who're you shooting at, Montana?" Joe growled.

"Uh . . . just checking my guns," Billy winced.

"Yeah, well, watch it! You missed my wingtip by five feet!"

"It won't happen again," Billy apologized.

"You see them 109s?"

"Sure did."

"Why didn't you call out?"

"Uh . . ."

"Keep your eyes peeled, Montana! You want to get our tails shot off!?"

"I'm on it. I'm on it," Billy growled, wagging his head to spot bogies.

Several more planes shot underneath them and disappeared into the clouds. Messerschmitts were everywhere, it seemed, a riot of birds zooming every which way and everyone of them making beelines for the Fortresses. Just then Billy saw four Messerschmitts cutting a sharp angle across the sky toward the rear of the box formation.

"Joe!"

"Me–109s at two o'clock low, Montana!" Joe said at the same instant. "They're lining up on the Big Friends."

"Let's get after 'em."

"You just stick close to my tail," Joe snarled. "And don't shoot it off!"

"Roger that," Billy acknowledged. He felt the glands in his throat constricting. He lifted his mike and spat a stream of tobacco into the coffee can between his legs.

Joe banked to his right and slid off the airstream in a rolling dive, so that he was bearing down on the enemy fighters from high on their left flanks at over 400 mph.

Billy, trailing off his right quarter, watched intently as Joe pulled out of the dive, levelled his ship to line his nose on the lead plane. A jolt of adrenaline shot through his system, clearing his mind, tapering his focus to the silvery blade of Joe's right wing that was cradling the Messerschmitt showing just over it. Everything was moving in unreal, dreamlike slow motion.

Joe squeezed a burst of his guns. But he was behind, Billy saw, seeing the tracers snapping away and jiggling harmlessly through empty space. The pilot in the 109 jerked a look at them. Billy could see the details of his face in pristine clarity.

Joe fired another burst, and Billy saw the strikes along the 109's fuselage and rudder. The German pilot abruptly raced toward the ceiling in a fast climb. The others broke off and made for parts south.

As Joe nosed up after the lead 109, Billy pulled back on his stick, firewalled the throttle, and roared after him. He felt the G forces of the big Pratt and Whitney supercharger, turning at 2,500 rpms, push him hard against the seat. But there was no catching the 109; it pulled away from the heavy Thunderbolts like they were stuck in mud.

At about 33,000 feet Joe gave up the chase and rolled his plane into a level attitude, knowing that the supercharger didn't help much past that altitude. He tipped his wings and began to head back toward the box formations.

Billy heard him cussing a blue streak in his headset.

Meanwhile, another swarm of Me–109s had gotten into the Fortresses. They attacked, slicing through the formation from every direction like hornets diving after a piece of raw meat, coming in fast, striking, tearing off chunks of flesh, then droning off wildly to bank around and come in again. The men inside the bombers swung their .50s on them in fast passing shots, leading them like clay birds in a skeet shoot.

One of the bombers already riddled by 20mm cannon and bullets took a rocket hit to its number one engine. The plane yawed violently to the right, and fire belched from the engine cowling, trailing a stream of oily black smoke behind it. The copilot doused the blazing engine with the wing extinguisher, but the Messerschmitt, coming in low and fast off the nose for the kill, strafed the right flank of the bomber with its nose cannon, killing the nose and belly gunners, before the tail gunner swung his twin .50s on the fighter and, striking it cleanly, sent it twirling to the earth.

Limping tragically along, the stricken bomber tried to maintain its speed with the others and remain in the protection of the box, but it fell steadily behind, black smoke pouring from its engine. Soon it was in the open, a vulnerable cripple. The Fortress looked small and lonely against the broad expanse of clouded sky.

కడుడుడు

A single Me–109 patrolling along the periphery of the battle saw the dissipating smoke in the distance, a long thin train of gray that could only mean one thing: a cripple! The pilot angled his plane toward it greedily. He kept to the cloud cover, warily eyeing the sky above him and below as he followed the dark spoor of smoke that grew thicker every mile. When he caught sight of the wounded bomber limping haplessly along at 23,000 feet and no sign of enemy fighters, he moved stealthily toward it like a shark to the chum, using the contrails from the B–17 boxes ahead of him as a screen.

కడుడుడు

"109 at six o'clock low!" Joe yelled, seeing the lone Messerschmitt cruising beneath the white vapor streams. "Moving in on a cripple."

"I see him!" Billy acknowledged.

"You with me?"

Billy grinned. "Like water on a trout!"

Joe's left wing tipped up smartly and his plane fell into a steep dive. Billy kicked hard rudder and chased after him.

Viktor drew to within three hundred yards of the crippled B–17. It was better than nothing, he thought, as he moved in closer, rising steadily and eyeing the vulnerable underbelly of the wounded beast. He knew well that a wounded animal can still kill. He approached it warily; his mind defining for him the best line of attack. The nose, he thought. Looks like the nose is gone.

Then the tail gunner spotted him and swung his twin fifties on him.

Seeing the little puffs of smoke and the twinkling streams of spent casings pouring from the breeches, Viktor deftly flipped his plane out of the line of fire and rolled up onto the right flank of the Fat Auto, smoothing it out expertly then, throttling forward, and closed to within two hundred yards.

A confident grin spread over his handsome face. He could see the waist gunner turning in his direction now, could see the look of panic contorting his features as he jerked his machine gun in his direction. But Viktor had the bomber centered in his gunsights and, thumbing the ignition switch, fired a rocket and watched it rifle away from his plane in an erratic twirl of white smoke. The rocket struck the bomber mid-flanks with a terrific explosion that catapulted metallic debris and men across the sky, and together they fell—a chuteless burning wreckage toward the earth.

Viktor laughed exultantly. "That's one the paperhangers can't deny me!"

Just then a glint of light caught the tail of his eye. He looked out his cockpit in time to see two Thunderbolts bearing down fast on him. A gasp rushed his throat. Instinctively he slammed the column stick forward and his Messerschmitt bucked into a steep dive. Dive, dive, he thought, then, working his rudder pedals, he banked toward a cumulonimbus column about a mile away.

"He's made us," Joe said.

"Looks like he's high-tailin' it for those clouds," Billy said.

"We'll get him," Joe swore, looking fruitlessly for any chutes. "I swear we'll get him."

The two Thunderbolts drove after the German fighter, following him into the mass of clouds. For several deadly moments Billy could see nothing but bright white. Visibility was down to about twenty feet. Everything was disorienting. He hoped Joe was maintaining his course and speed, else he might end up with a tail section of Thunderbolt in his lap. Watch the gauges, he chanted. Trust them. When they punched through the other side of the gleaming cloud column, Joe was right where he was supposed to be, two points ahead of his left wing. However, there was no sign of the Messerschmitt.

"Where'd he go?" Joe shouted.

"I don't know!" Billy craned his head in every direction.

"Do you see him?" Joe shouted.

"Negative!"

"You sure?"

"I'm sure!"

"Look behind you!"

"I am!" Billy shouted, now looking behind him. He cursed through his breath. "It don't make sense. He couldn't have just disappeared into thin air!"

"Well he has!"

Billy loosed a string of expletives. He looked out his cockpit and saw fluffy tatters of clouds beneath him at 25,000 feet, veiling the coastline, everything looking remote and peaceful, and everywhere else millions of cubic feet of empty sky. The Messerschmitt had disappeared into thin air. "He must've pulled up or something," Billy said, craning his head every which way. "Swung back in the clouds!"

Viktor pulled out of the wide roll, dipping several hundred feet, then, as he stabilized his plane, he saw the two Thunderbolts slightly above him, about five hundred yards off the point of his nose, all three of them on the same line of flight. He chuckled. He was in their blind spot, he knew, just beneath their plane of sight.

He thought about taking on the two of them, reckoning that he could sneak up on the rear plane, take it out with his second rocket, and be on the front one before he knew what had happened. That would be something, he mused, a B–17 and a pair of Thunderbolts. There would definitely be a promotion in it for him. He pushed forward on the throttle lever, and the 12 cylinder Daimler Benz engine drove the Messerschmitt forward like a rocket. He closed to within four hundred yards of Billy's tail, rising slowly, invisibly below his line of sight . . . two seventy five . . . two hundred. At one hundred fifty yards he armed his rocket.

Billy's ears were buzzing with alarm. He looked over his shoulder. Nothing. Looked overhead. Nothing. Where was he? Lousy Kraut. Panic gnawed his gut. Then suddenly his skin crawled along the back of his skull as it struck him. Immediately he barrel-rolled his plane to get a look beneath him, and, rolling to his left, saw behind him the menacing nose of the Messerschmitt lined up on him like a grinning devil, and the fired rocket homing in on his tail.

"Break, Joe! Break!" he screamed, kicking hard left rudder. His plane made a quick snap-roll, and the rocket screwed along the underside of his belly, like the graceful but deadly veronica of a matador and bull. The Jug fell two thousand feet and, leveling out after the roll, his wings seesawing briefly, Billy looked around for the German. He couldn't see him. Then he glanced around for Joe. Couldn't see him either. "Where are you, Joe?" he cried.

"Right here!"

"Where's here?"

"Down here!" Joe shouted.

"Thank God," Billy breathed, seeing him at the five o'clock low position. "Where's that lousy Kraut?" he said, looking behind him.

"Beats me."

Billy felt the hairs prickling along the back of his neck again.

"Behind you, Montana!" Joe screamed. "Roll out!"

Billy didn't look; he didn't roll; instead he hit hard on his flaps to brake his speed. His plane waffled up as though it had hit a cushion of air, and the Messerschmitt roared three feet over his canopy and streamed away from him in a beeline to the horizon.

Billy's plane got caught in the Messerschmitt's prop wash and flipped over onto its back like a turtle and nearly stalled. Righting himself, he coaxed his heart back down into his chest and growled, "Lousy stinkin' Kraut." He watched him growing small against a horizon of billowy clouds. "I see him now, Joe."

"Get after him!" Joe ordered. "I'm coming up after you."

"Roger that," Billy said, as he throttled his plane forward. At 25,000 feet there is no eluding the supercharged radial engine of a Thunderbolt, and Billy roared after the enemy plane.

For Billy, at least, the air war over the Frisian Islands was reduced to a single Messerschmitt and Thunderbolt, a battle between two pilots, each testing the sum of his skills against the other. When the Messerschmitt rolled, the Thunderbolt rolled after it; when it banked, the Thunderbolt banked; when Viktor took his plane through a series of aerial maneuvers, crisscrossing the skies, rolling, banking, climbing, Billy followed after him like a shadow, drawing ever closer to within killing range.

When Billy closed to within two hundred yards, he got the Messerschmitt in his sights and squeezed off a burst of his guns. However, the German had turned the moment he fired, and Billy saw the tracers stream harmlessly through space. He cursed. Can't afford to waste ammunition, he chided himself. Got to get closer.

Viktor shot a look over his shoulder. He could not shake the American. The sky was clear of clouds, so there was no place for him to hide. Sweat beaded on his brow and collected in the thin, blond, Clark Gable mustache. He called into his radio for help, heard some garbled chatter; but there was no response. He was alone. He tried to remember a prayer he had learned in his youth, but the words wouldn't come. He cursed.

Billy closed to one hundred fifty yards and fired; this time the fiery streamers from his wing guns bracketed the enemy's cockpit.

Viktor saw the tracers rifle past his cockpit, and in a panic maneuvered his plane into a dive.

"Gotcha!" Billy grinned, and he followed the German down into a Lufbery circle. He fired a burst of his guns, three armor-piercing rounds followed by two incendiaries, and saw that he was behind. He tightened his circle.

The two planes fell faster and faster, the heavier Thunderbolt gaining on the Messerschmitt, the two of them spiralling in a long, tight auger toward the spinning earth; their vapor screws wound around each other like two serpents in a slow mating dance. Billy feathered his throttle to keep his plane from stalling. The G forces were working against him in the turns, making it difficult for him to move, and wracking his body with fatigue. Then, as the Messerschmitt crossed his path, he squeezed off another burst and saw the tracers bending toward the plane.

Viktor winced as the rounds struck along his left wing and tore up the metal skin in a dozen places. He jerked a look over his shoulder, his face wrenched now by terror, and saw that the American had closed to within a hundred yards. Sweat trickled into his eyes and tickled along the creases of his nose. He cursed again, and began chattering to some god in the universe to save him.

He pulled the stick with all his might, desperately trying to tighten his circle, to gain some speed. His limbs burned with fatigue. Anxious tension chuckled in his throat. Got to get clear of him, he thought. The Thunderbolt was gaining on him, he saw, getting inside his circle. There was no way to outdive him. Not a Thunderbolt. He'd have to get him into a climb if he were going to survive. Have to pull out. Got to. He summoned the last of his resolve and strength.

Billy read his mind and pulled back on his stick an instant before the German. Then, as the Messerschmitt's wingtips closed within the outer circle of his crosshairs, he fired a long burst of his guns. The Messerschmitt's engine exploded with a loud *pop*. Shards of burning metal flew off the plane in every direction. Thick, black plumes of smoke poured from the engine cowling.

Billy followed the plane, firing short bursts at it, seeing the well-aimed hits along the wings and fuselage. It did not seem to him that he was shooting at a man, but that he was shooting at a machine. There was no intimacy like there had been when he killed the German sniper in France. He was killing a machine.

But when he saw the canopy jettison away and the struggling shape of a man rise against the empty sky he let up firing. He watched curiously as the German pilot climbed out of the billowing plane, fumbling for hand-holds, his body all spattered with oil and gasoline and burning like a torch, looking tragic as he held his face against the great tongues of flame that licked up around him.

A pang of remorse shot through him. It was no longer a machine. It was a living thing. It was how he felt when he dropped the big bull elk a year before: the rush of excitement as he came upon the great antlers showing still and magnificent through the autumn brush, which ebbed on seeing the big, sad, open eyes that could no longer see. He watched pensively as the German tumbled from his plane, burning, still holding his face as he narrowly missed the rudder. He watched as his tragic body grew small against the earth. He waited for a chute but never saw one.

20 ★★★

The 52nd was still one victory shy of a hundred. They'd knocked down three FW–190s, two Me–109s, and a single Me–210 on the Wilhelmshaven Ramrod. It had been a good run, none were lost of the fighter group, and word reached them that the Big Friends had done a terrific job over the target. A windy ebullience blew through the briefing hut.

It seemed unreal to Billy, watching the footage of his aerial battle with the Messerschmitt, as though he were viewing the abstract clips of a dream edited into chronological sequence. Leaning back in his chair, he viewed the film with a feeling of remoteness, studying the way the bullets struck along the wings and fuselage of the Messerschmitt the way a medical student might study an anatomy chart.

Everything looked farther away than he remembered; he remembered feeling closer to the action. But when he saw the German pilot climbing out of the burning cockpit holding his face against the flames, everything rushed back so that he could smell, taste, touch the death of the pilot. He sat up in his chair and the screen went white.

The pilots in Blue Flight slapped him on the back, affectionately gave him Dutch rubs and shoulder jabs, made lewd comments. His kill had kept their flight from being skunked. Billy took it in good stride. He felt a part of the team now, a solid contributor, no longer watching the game from the bench. That business in France was gone, the pent-up ghosts released from the crypt in his subconsciousness. It was tough luck about the German pilot, though, he thought. But—shoot—it was the luck of the game. He gave no thought to Divine Providence.

After the debriefing the pilots ate a lunch of smothered pork chops, buttered lima beans, and au gratin potatoes—it took the starch out of anyone's homesickness for his mama's home cooking. The men were in awe of the little Frenchman who paced behind the counter, twirling his mustache with tyrannical conviction as he eyed everyone's plate.

Slumped in his chair in sated indolence, the top button of his trousers uncinched, his legs splayed out beneath the table, Billy stared numbly at his empty plate, wondering if he were going to be able to move.

"This guy's gonna kill me," Joe moaned, looking a mirror image of Billy. "He must be working for the enemy."

"You didn't have to go back for seconds," Billy said.

"Neither did you."

Billy glanced over at the counter and just caught the Frenchman's eyes averting away from the path of his own, as though he had been staring at him. He considered the little man for a moment, grunted, and shrugged it off.

Feeling a need to work off the meal and give their legs a stretch, Joe, Happy, and Billy went outside and mounted their bicycles, then headed toward Halesbury with a stack of mimeographed flyers announcing the Sadie Hawkins dance.

It was a beautiful afternoon. Fat, woolly sheep dotted the low-lying hills, and cattle grazed happily in the fields between the hedgerows and stone walls and along the streams that meandered gently through the countryside. The farmhouses and thatched cottages and medieval stone churches poked through trees that were bright with oranges and reds and yellows, looking like a painting of rural England after the first rush of autumn.

Pedaling lazily along in the rut of a narrow country road, in no hurry to get anywhere, Billy glanced up at the sky and took a deep breath of clean air. Small, fluffy white clouds floated airily across the blue, the sun shining around them and playing warmly over the gently rolling fields.

As they pedaled their way into town, people burning piles of leaves and debris in their backyards paused briefly to wave and shout greetings of "Oy, Yanks!" and "Good show!" Townspeople on bicycles, out to enjoy the uncharacteristic weather, exchanged greetings as they passed.

಄಄

Once in town, the men pinned the flyers up on the kiosk in the market square, handed them to store owners and pub owners to place in their windows or to distribute to their patrons, and offered them to various passersby of the feminine persuasion. They even handed a few to a group of teenage girls leaving school, each of them wearing brown uniforms, kneesocks, and beanies, since two of them looked borderline eligible.

The Americans turned down one of the narrow market streets leading off the square where there was a noisy bustle of shoppers—middle-aged women mostly—perusing, poking, and weighing the hanging joints of mutton and poultry. Thick beef tongues were laid out side-by-side, and assortments of fresh farm vegetables were set out in wooden crates along the cobbled street. The air was warm and close, and flies circled happily around the staring eyes of fish; however, there were no likely looking young women to hand out the flyers to.

Returning to the main street, Billy saw the girl he'd seen in the Guinea, pedaling her bicycle toward the red postbox that stood on one of the corners.

"Where're you going?" Joe asked.

"You fellas go on ahead," Billy said.

Joe saw the girl and shook his head. "She's gonna bite your head off."

"I'll catch up to you later," Billy said, riding away.

"We'll be at the Guinea, amigo," Happy shouted.

"Roger that!"

What was her name, Billy asked himself as he angled his bicycle in her direction. *Jean? Joan? Jane, that was it. Jane Something-or-other.*

Jane Worthing was wearing a lightweight, blue woolen pullover, a pale blue tartan skirt, a pair of brown, low-heeled shoes with straps, and her hair was pinned back on either side with barrettes. She leaned her bicycle against the postbox, then retrieved a stack of letters from the small leather satchel affixed to the back of her seat. Walking around the bike, she bumped against the rear wheel and the bike lurched forward, unsettling its balance. She put out her hand to steady the seat, but in doing so, spilled her letters beside the curb.

"Oh, bother," she frowned. As she stooped to collect them the wheels of a bicycle rolled into her field of vision and stopped, and she saw the legs of a man dismount. She paid the legs no mind.

"Beautiful day, isn't it?" Billy said, looking down at the top of her head.

"Yes, isn't it?" Jane said distractedly. She reached for a letter.

"Need some help?"

"No, thank you," she answered without looking up. As she retrieved the last letter she noticed a dark grease stripe across Billy's right trouser leg where the chain had rubbed. "If you wore a clip you wouldn't collect grease on your trousers," she smiled, standing.

Billy looked down at his leg and grunted. "A bicycle clip, huh?"

It was then that Jane saw his face, and her expression seemed to pass through a revolution—from courteous smile to panic to a flattening out of her features—as she recognized who it was. She stepped quickly back onto the curb.

Billy countered with as affable a smile as he could muster. "Hello, it's me again."

She turned her shoulder to him with a grunt, leaving Billy's smile twisting in the breeze. She began leafing through the letters, to ensure they were all present and accounted for, then swung open the iron door over the mail slot and dropped them into the slot one at a time, very precisely. She made no attempt at conversation.

Cool as a cucumber, Billy thought. He wasn't quite sure what to do: Make some attempt at reparations or hightail it out of there as fast as he could? Then with a quick sweep of his eyes he noticed she was quite pretty—good figure, nice profile, beautiful, thick brown hair.

"I saw you over here," he said, stepping into the awkward silence.

She glanced at him as though it was the silliest statement she'd ever heard.

"Well, of course I saw you over here," Billy smiled, suddenly realizing it too. "That's why I came over."

Jane closed the mail slot, guiding the iron door home so that it wouldn't clank, then, turning her back to him fully, began to fasten the straps on her satchel. She handled the first one with poise. But she struggled with the second strap. The prong on the tiny buckle would simply not fit through the hole in the strap. It was as though her fingers suddenly forgot what to do.

"I wanted to apologize for the other night," Billy said.

Jane bit her lower lip. "Why won't this go into the hole?" she muttered to herself.

Watching her intently, Billy cleared his throat. "Er . . . about the other night?"

Jane became visibly flustered.

"Need help?" Billy offered.

She gave up on the strap with a disgruntled snort, abruptly took hold of her bicycle and began to pedal quickly away without so much as a "by your leave."

Billy stood gaping at her. He'd never been so completely ignored by a woman in all his life. The offense caused his brain to skip a synapse, and for a moment he forgot he was holding his bike. It fell away from him with a clatter and lay in a heap of scrap metal at his feet with the handlebars pointing away from him. He wrestled to get the wheel pointing in the right direction and, mounting, looked up the street at the retreating form of the girl. Let it go, his mind warned him in no uncertain terms. Let it go.

Moments later he was pedaling alongside the girl. "My name is Billy Hochreiter," he said.

She glanced at him coolly, caught a dangerous flash of blue in his eyes, and looked quickly away.

"I said my name is Billy," he repeated.

"That's nice," she said. "We have a goat named Billy."

"That's pretty funny," he said. "I expect a lot of folks do. Your name is Jane, I believe."

She looked at him sharply. "I don't see that as any of your business. And I would appreciate it if you'd not follow me."

"Follow you? I'm not following you. I just wanted to apologize about what happened that night."

"That night?"

"At the Golden Guinea."

"Were you there? Fancy that."

"Well, yes, I was there. Don't you remember? I came over to your table..."

"There was a drunk who came over to my table," she said. "And then there was some fool who beat up a nice RAF pilot who was only trying to protect me." She glanced at him ironically. "Which one were you, the drunk or the fool?"

Billy looked at her. "Nice RAF pilot? That nice RAF pilot swung at me first," he protested. "What was I supposed to do—let him deck me?"

"That's not how I saw it," Jane said matter-of-factly.

"Well, I had a pretty good view of that fist," Billy said. "You got my word on it."

"Yes, well, 'the way of the fool is right in his own eyes,' isn't it?" she said. She turned abruptly down a street and left Billy blinking stupidly at her back.

He swung his bike around. "Hey! Wait a minute!" he shouted. "That's what I wanted to talk to you about!"

The street Jane had taken wound narrowly through a variety of ancient shops and pubs, then led on to where a common abutted the edge of town. There were houses nestled in the trees and shrubs that bordered the periphery of the broad, manicured grounds, everything smoothly rolling and neatly hedged, with the road leading through the middle of it. On the far side of the common the road eased away into the distance through some gently undulating hills and trees, then ran on into the flatness of the east country. Everything looked lovely in the warming sun.

Billy caught up to the girl and held his front wheel just behind hers so that he could keep a watchful eye on her. "I wanted you to know that not all Americans are a bunch of gangsters."

Jane abruptly stopped her bike at the edge of the common and glowered at him. "Are you going to persist in following me?"

"I'm not following you."

"I suppose we just happen to be going the same way?"

"I'm just trying to clear the air," he said. "I'm trying to be friendly is all."

"You've been the perfect gentleman."

Billy eyed her skeptically. "Then we can start over?"

"No."

"Back home when somebody says he's sorry it's usually grounds for a truce."

"You're not back home."

That's the truth, he did not say. "Listen," he said. "I just wanted to apologize. Skagway—that was the drunk—was out of line."

"Do you always apologize for the actions of others?"

"I'm not apologizing for him or anybody else."

"But you just said—"

"I was apologizing," he said quickly. "For me, I guess."

"A moment ago you claimed innocence. Now you admit that you were in the wrong?"

"Just for the way I handled things," he said. "None of us knew—I didn't know," he corrected, "anything about your—well, what happened to your husband. I'm truly sorry about it, that's all. All I'm saying is that I would've handled things differently if I had known."

She looked at him.

"Shoot, I don't know," Billy said. "I'd've just handled it differently. That's all. It must be tough on you."

"Tough?"

"Losing your husband. It must hurt something fierce."

Jane studied his face for a moment, chanced a look into the dangerous blue eyes. "It does," she said, struggling to hold his gaze. "Thank you. Now are you going to leave me be, or do I have to call the constable?"

Billy just looked at her. "You're a hard one to figure."

She looked up and down the street. "There's never a bobby when you need one," she muttered indignantly.

"I'm leaving," he said. "Before I go, though, here." He pulled out a flyer from inside his jacket and handed it to her. "We're having a little dance at the base. Big T–2 hangar, near the Admin buildings, easy-as-pie to find. Can't miss it."

She looked at the flyer, then started to hand it back to him. "Thank you, no."

"No one should be alone on Sadie Hawkins," he said, as though it was the most attested fact in the universe. "Thought you might like to come."

"You thought wrong."

"You'd have a great time," he smiled.

Jane's face went suddenly rigid. "Isn't it just like you Yanks?"

He blinked at her.

"It's our cities and homes that have been bombed, isn't it? Perhaps some of us don't feel quite up to having a great time just yet." She crumpled up the flyer and threw it at his feet. "Everything's just a clever romp to you Yanks, isn't it?"

Billy had had enough. "A clever romp? Is that what you think we 'Yanks' are having? A clever romp? Tell that to the ten boys I saw going down in a burning Fortress this morning. I'm sure they were having a clever romp as tons of explosives blew up in their faces."

Jane said nothing.

"You've been dealt a lousy hand," Billy said. "You want to come to the dance—terrific. If you don't, it don't make no difference to me one way or the other. Not everybody who's friendly to you is trying to seduce you."

Jane's shoulders shuddered menacingly. "Why, you conceited—!" she cried, then slapped his face.

Billy stared at her calmly. "I just came over here to apologize," he said. "I've apologized. Have a great life." He pushed off and began to pedal back into town, and he didn't look back.

Jane stood glaring after him. She thought she might burst into tears she was so angry. She watched the American grow smaller on the road until he disappeared around a corner. There was a moment when she felt her insides filling out like a balloon, rising, the string holding herself to the earth slipping through her fingers; then all at once everything went out of her and the balloon came floating down.

The tension in her shoulders eased, then her hand rose slowly to her face. A few tears leaked down her cheeks. "Oh, Jane, what's come over you?" she said, shaking her head dolefully. "You were a perfect wretch."

The crumpled flyer rolled back and forth in a little breeze as though laughing at her. She dismissed it, then reconsidered it. She stooped to pick the wad up, unfolded it, and, dabbing the corners of her eyes with a handkerchief, read the particulars.

"Who on earth is Sadie Hawkins?" she wondered aloud.

She started at the sound of a bicycle bell and thrust the flyer behind her back.

"Yoo hoo! There you are, Jane!" Julie Ellerby cried out, her bright red hair glowing in a lance of sunlight.

Jane quickly folded the flyer and slipped it into her bike satchel. She fastened both straps without a hitch.

Julie rode up to her, the beam of sun glowing on her freckled face. "I've been looking all over town for you," she said, hopping off her bike while it was still rolling. "I've wonderful news!"

Jane glanced back at the road Billy had taken through town, then looked at her friend. "They discover a cure for men?"

"Silly goose." She laughed. "Why, Jane, you've been crying."

"No, I haven't."

"Don't tell me you haven't, girl, I can see it plain in your eyes. Is there something the matter?"

"Not a thing," Jane lied unconvincingly.

Julie snorted. "Nonsense. In all the years I've known you, you've never been a very good fibber."

Jane looked away from her, gazing intently at the spot on the pavement where the crumpled flyer had rolled chuckling in the breeze. "Oh, I've just had a dreadful row with that American," she groaned. "It's finished now, thank heaven."

"American? What American?" Julie looked around hopefully.

"The one in the Guinea the other night."

"You'll have to be more specific, Jane. There were Yanks crawling out of the woodwork."

Jane's eyebrows knit together. "It was that conceited one who hit the RAF flier."

"He was just here?" Julie looked around again, but of course there was no one. "You mean the strawberry blond, good-looking one with the blue eyes?"

"Good-looking? I didn't notice that he was so good-looking."

Julie laughed. "Jane, dear, you really have been out of circulation, haven't you?"

"Yes, well, out of circulation or no, I slapped him."

"Oh, dear. Slapped him?"

"What was I supposed to do?"

Julie shook her head. "My dear, sweet, sad Jane. Whatever am I to do with you? You can't go around clocking everyone who pays you a bit of attention."

"He was rude."

Julie threw her hand to her mouth with a gasp. "There goes the monarchy!"

Jane looked at her contritely. "Is it me, Julie?"

Julie's face flattened into a deadpan.

"That awful, really?"

"Dreadful," Julie said, then brightened. "Ah, but do not despair, my dear. I have just the cure for it!" She pulled out a flyer from her shoulder purse. "Look! There're some Yanks in town passing these round. There's going to be a dance of some sort. Isn't it marvelous?"

Jane groaned.

Julie scrunched her nose. "Something to do with a girl named Sadie Hawkins or other," she said, reading the flyer. "Must be one of their colonial lovelies. The Yanks are always celebrating people who've thumbed their noses at us." She giggled. "Don't you just love the Americans? They've holidays for everything. Should be a smashing good time, I should think."

"I have no intention of going."

"Well, of course you're going. I can't very well go by myself, can I? Think how that would look. Really."

"I told you I'm not going," Jane insisted. "You'll have to find someone else to go with."

Julie frowned at her. "Jane, sometimes you can be such a prig."

21 ⋆⋆⋆

The brace of pheasants flushed suddenly against the autumn shrubbery, their wings beating furiously as they flattened out over the furrowed field of harvested grain that shone golden in the afternoon reach of sun. Reich Marshal Hermann Göring raised his gun smoothly, sweeping the twin muzzles over and along the accelerating trajectory of the birds, and emptied both barrels in quick succession. The patterns smacked each of the birds with a copper-colored burst of feathers, and then the birds folded from the sky.

"Ah, wonderful!" he boomed.

"A good double, Reich Marshal," the dog trainer on his left said.

The dozen or so generals and colonels of the Luftwaffe standing behind him applauded his good shooting. Göring nodded his head in agreement, chuckling. Of course it was fine shooting.

The dog trainer released the two German Shorthairs standing on point with a verbal command, and the dogs rushed long-stridedly to retrieve the fallen birds.

The Reich Marshal broke the breech of his shotgun, extracted the shells, and tossed them to the ground. A big man, wide-girthed and white-faced, he had pale blue eyes that seemed either to be laughing or on the verge of treachery. He was wearing a dark brown tweed hunting jacket, light brown trousers that were bloused just beneath the knees, kneesocks, hunting boots, and a green felt Tyroler hat with a long cock's feather angling back from the band. He looked like a giant gnome.

The officers behind him were all in their dress uniforms with their medals and brass shining, standing stiffly and maintaining their military bearing and protocol as they watched their host hunting with the dogs.

They seemed as much out of place in the field of cut grain as if they were standing on a beach in tuxedos.

"Would you like to try it, Captain Schiller?" the Reich Marshal asked, offering his gun to the man on his right.

Captain Rolf Schiller had been admiring the dogs, watching them retrieve the two birds, then watching them turn and trot high-headed as they mounted through the grain stubble with the limp birds in their mouths. Rolf waved a deprecating hand. "I am not much good with the field sports, I'm afraid, Reich Marshal," he said. "It has been years. Perhaps one of your other guests?"

A sudden tint of scarlet suffused the bloated whiteness above the Reich Marshal's collar. "Nonsense! You are too modest," he laughed. He turned to the group of officers behind him. "Our hero is too modest, eh?"

To a man they agreed with him.

"Come, my proud squadron leader," the giant gnome smiled. Then laughing he added, "You are my guest of honor."

Rolf detected something precarious behind the pale blue eyes and affable smile. "If you insist."

"But of course, of course," the Reich Marshal laughed. He snapped his fingers and an orderly stepped forward from the group. "Take Captain Schiller's coat."

Rolf removed his military blouse and hat and handed them to the orderly, then rolled up his shirtsleeves. He took the shotgun from the Reich Marshal, a Merkel side-by-side that was beautifully engraved along the barrels, lock plate, and trigger guard with scenes of upland hunters and dogs amid decorative whorls, and fleur-de-lis checkering on the stocks. Then he took two shells loaded with number six shot, fed them into the empty chambers, and closed the breech.

"I assure you, Reich Marshal," he said, hefting the gun in his hands, "I am not being modest." He leaned forward, his weight on the lead foot as he swung the gun over the dogs to get a feel for the fit and the sighting. "It has a lovely balance," he admitted, suddenly remembering the weight and feel of one of his father's fine shotguns. It was a good feel. He lay the gun in the crook of his left arm.

"He says he is not being modest," the Reich Marshal chuckled.

The group of officers likewise chuckled.

The dog trainer gave a verbal command, and the two Shorthairs, sitting at attention and looking up at him, bolted ahead and began working the field back and forth, going up and across the long, even furrows, then working the uncut grain that went along the hedge.

Rolf looked at the men positioned along the edge of the field, waiting with shotguns to stop the birds. Then he looked over at the dogs who were busy in some shocks of grain, working efficiently.

"Stay along the edge here," the Reich Marshal said. "We'll get into some birds in just a minute, you'll see."

The two of them hunted after the dogs, with the trainer walking off to one side directing the dogs with short whistles and waves of his hands. The group of officers followed behind, mindful of their polished boots as they stepped woodenly from row to row.

Very quickly Rolf caught sight of a cock running along one of the furrows.

"Do not worry about that one now," the Reich Marshal said. "He'll hold up when he sees the gunners. We will get him later."

Suddenly the dogs froze on point.

Göring waved everyone to stop.

Rolf readied himself, leaning forward slightly into his shooting stance, and raised the gun to his shoulder. A rush of adrenaline made him feel suddenly cold and alert, so that his vision was narrowed to the acute angle of the dogs' backs and their noses showing the vicinity of the birds.

The pheasants tore out of the shocks with a violent battering of wings. Two cocks and a hen suddenly rose, going straight out over the stubbles, with the *Cak! Cak! Cak!* chucking in the cocks' white-ringed throats as they beat away.

Rolf swung on the lead cock, a flashing blur of garish color, remembering from his childhood to pick out a single bird, remembering to lead the head and not the long tail that made the target seem deceptively three feet in length and impossible to miss. It all came back to him in a smooth-swinging sweep of the gun, the lively feel of it in his hands. He traced the fast rise of the bird, fired, and, seeing the tight pattern of number sixes striking its flank in a metallic trail of feathers, swung on the second cock and dropped him at forty yards.

"Hah, hah!" Göring boomed, clapping his hands. "Marvellous! Marvellous!" He turned floridly, exultantly, to the group behind him. "With such men we shall win glory!"

The generals and colonels applauded and agreed to a man.

"A good double, Captain," the dog trainer said, before releasing the dogs.

Rolf laughed himself, feeling the sudden exhilaration that washes cleanly and thoroughly over everything in the aftermath of the kill. He watched the dogs retrieve the birds, admiring their work, looking expectantly over the field. He broke the breech of the shotgun and pulled out the spent shells, releasing two tubes of white smoke.

The Reich Marshal took hold of Rolf's shoulder. "We are kindred spirits, you and I," he chortled. "Give me a squadron of fighter pilots like you and I would soon put an end to this war, wouldn't I?" He laughed again, clapping his hands.

Rolf smiled.

"Ask!" Göring thundered, sweeping his arms heavenward with the flourish of a Caesar. "Ask what you will of me. I will give you up to half of my kingdom!"

The officers behind him laughed.

Rolf waited until the laughter settled. The giant gnome was beaming at him expectantly, his pale blue eyes twinkling impishly.

"Give us more fighters," Rolf said. "With more fighters we can stop the bombers."

A hint of color rose into the Reich Marshal's throat.

"We can regain control of the skies," Rolf insisted. "Without fighters we cannot hope to win the war."

The Reich Marshal's eyes turned cold and dangerous. A crimson wrath rushed his face. There was a stunned silence that crashed onto the field as the generals gaped at Rolf.

Rolf thought for a moment that the Reich Marshal was going to command his head to be brought in on a platter.

The giant gnome stood, hands on hips, glaring at him. Just then a chuckle bubbled out of his fat face. A sparkle rekindled in his eyes as the crimson hues rushed from his brow and collected in the fleshy rolls of his cheeks and throat. Then he laughed thunderously. "He is brash, is he not?" he said, turning to the generals behind him.

The tension over the field shattered into a million nervous pieces.

"Yes he is . . . brash indeed," Göring chortled. "Ah! The innocence of youth." He put his hand lightly, affectionately, it seemed, on Rolf's shoulder. "We do not wish to end the war too soon, do we?" he said with his affable yet precarious smile. "What would the little Jew haters in Berlin have for their fun?"

The generals thought this splendid, and nodded magnanimously to one another.

Göring chortled throatily, and the ruddy hues leaped about his corpulent face.

Rolf looked down at the beautifully engraved relief on the side plate and trigger guard. He handed the gun back to the Reich Marshal.

෬෧

Karinhall, Reich Marshal Hermann Göring's sporting lodge, was named in honor of his late wife, Karin von Kantzow, and shone in the splendor of a Prussian emperor. The decor was opulent, ornate, with beautiful wood furnishings tastefully arranged throughout the spacious rooms. Crowding the wood panelling were dozens of mounted heads and antlers, tapestries and oil paintings. Mahogany tables, marble shelves, and niches were crammed with crystal and porcelain knickknacks and *pièces d'art,* polished suits of armor, racks of rifles and guns, and medieval weaponry— swords, axes, maces, and piked standards. The lodge was a blend of old-world solidity and new-world fineness, combining in such a way as to reflect Hermann Göring's great but fragile ego.

Men in white waistcoats, black ties, and black trousers, and women in black dresses with white collars and aprons, attended the guests' every need, serving hors d'oeuvres and before-dinner drinks. A string quartet provided Mozart, Bach, and Beethoven.

Present were several high-ranking officers of the Luftwaffe (most of whom had arrived fashionably late after the pheasant hunt) and a few officers of the SS. The officers, carrying steins of beer and glasses of schnapps and pulling on fine Cuban cigars, listened attentively as the Reich Marshal regaled them with his various hunting exploits, moving from head trophy to head trophy and describing proudly how he had severed the life from it. Then he took them through each of the rooms of the lodge, showing off his collections of model boats and trains, much the same as an only child might boast of his collections of marbles or stamps to his neighborhood friends.

The wives and mistresses, on the other hand, were entertained by Emmy Sonnemann, Göring's second wife of eight years. She, with practiced flourish, pointed out the statuary and oil paintings of Great Masters that her husband had "liberated" from several museums and villas in Paris. The women thought this wonderful as they sipped rare French white wine from crystal flutes.

Rolf stood in the doorway of one of the hobby rooms, forcing himself to be attentive to the garrulous antics of the Reich Marshal as he described in great detail the finer points of narrow-gauge rails. He looked down at the ash of his cigar, and glanced about for an ashtray.

"You poor soul," a woman's voice purred behind him.

Rolf started. "Pardon me?" he said. Turning, he saw an attractive red-head in a white, strapless evening gown.

"You look as though you might expire any moment," the woman said in a stage whisper.

Rolf smiled at her. "Does it show that obviously?"

"I'm afraid so," she said. "I have come to rescue you. Emmy sent me."

"How thoughtful of Emmy," Rolf said.

"She is a wonderful hostess," the woman smiled. "I believe you and I are partners tonight, Captain."

Rolf looked at her.

The woman smiled. "You are Captain Rolf Schiller, are you not?"

"Yes, I am."

"At the table . . . my name card is next to yours. Emmy is so thoughtful that way," she said. "You know . . . boy, girl; boy, girl. Keeps the conversation at the table from becoming the men roaring about the war at one end, and the women giggling about babies at the other."

"And what is the name on the card next to mine?" Rolf asked her.

"Olga . . . Olga Strump."

"You do not look like an Olga Strump," Rolf said.

A blush rose to her cheeks. "I don't?" She smiled. "Then tell me, Captain, what do I look like?"

Rolf appraised her features: big green eyes that sparkled like emerald cubes of ice, glossy red lips, and hair that was a blazing wildness of fiery hues that seemed charged with mischief. A quick sweep of his eyes revealed that she was wonderfully curved all the way down to her red-painted toenails. She looked like a movie star.

"I don't know," he mused, her scent reaching him on a subtle finger of air. "A Marlene, perhaps . . . or a Margarete. Something beginning with an M."

"And should I take this as a compliment?"

"Most definitely," he smiled. "Olgas are big-boned sopranos with helmets and shining breastplates."

"I do not look like a Teutonic battle maiden that sings opera?"

"Not in the least."

"Then I shall be Margarete tonight," she said. "Or perhaps I shall just be M. Madame M—that's it! Sounds mysterious, like a spy in a novel, doesn't it?"

"There's certainly enough treachery about."

"What shall I call you?" she asked playfully. "You must have a mysterious name as well."

"Call me Rolf," he said.

She grunted. "You're no fun at all. What kind of name is that for a spy?"

"I do not play games well," he said.

"No? Then I shall play for both of us." The woman took a cigarette from one of the several silver boxes that were strategically placed about the room. "Do you have a light?" she asked, poising the cigarette dramatically. "That is my code phrase. Spies must have code phrases."

"A light?" Rolf patted his breast pockets. "I'm sorry," he said. "I do not smoke."

She looked at his cigar.

"Oh, this," Rolf said. "This is ornamental. Goes with the uniform. It has gone out . . . see?"

"You've just lost your ash."

Rolf looked down at the hardwood floor between his feet. "So I have." He glanced across the room at the Reich Marshal.

Margarete rose quickly onto her toes, catlike, and touched her slender fingers behind Rolf's ear. He felt a tingling sensation go through him, as though her fingertips were charged with electricity.

"I won't tell if you won't," she whispered conspiratorially, her lips almost touching his earlobe. "We spies must stick together."

With the close proximity of her cheek next to his, and the heady weight of her perfume, Rolf became acutely aware of his own presence. He stepped on the ash and smiled. "There. I have just gotten rid of the evidence." He signaled to one of the several attendants in white waistcoats.

The attendant came over and handed Rolf a lighter. Rolf kept it and sent the attendant away with a handsome tip.

Margarete touched his hand lightly while he lit her cigarette. She looked up at him over the tiny coal of fire, her green eyes twinkling with what seemed to be hidden knowledge.

"Thank you," she said, blowing a cloud of smoke at the ceiling. "Come," she smiled. "Enough of these boys' toys. 'The game's afoot,' as Sherlock Holmes would say." She took his arm, and her high heels made a soft clicking sound over the hardwood floor as she guided him away from the group of officers.

Rolf looked behind him. Reich Marshal Göring was holding up a pullman car and showing the generals the tiny spring suspension in its wheels. The generals thought this amazing. "I'll be court-martialed," he groaned.

"Silly. Spies aren't court-martialed . . . they are always shot at dawn."

Rolf made a face. "But I'm not a morning person," he protested.

"Pity," she smiled. "Now, you must tell me everything about yourself."

"I can think of nothing more unentertaining."

"Nonsense," Margarete laughed gaily, shaking her thick mass of red hair. "You are the most entertaining man in the house . . . and handsome. Ask any of the generals' fat wives over there. They haven't been able to take their eyes off you all evening, you know? Are you married?"

"No."

"Wonderful! Wives can be such dreadful nuisances. Any girlfriends?"

Rolf hesitated. He felt a sudden numbness creeping along the edges of his chest like a living deadness. He could not hold it at bay. "No," he said. "No girlfriends . . . no wife . . . no concubines. See how boring I am?"

"I think you are fascinating," the woman said.

He looked at her coolly. "I think you are paid well to say whatever it is you think pleases me."

The woman pulled up abruptly and looked at him, her eyes suddenly flat and expressionless.

Rolf peered at her with a cold, predator stare. "If I am wrong, you have my most sincere apology. And you may slap my face," he added. "If I am correct, then why do you pretend to be offended?"

She looked at him for a moment longer, then, glancing away, took a drag from her cigarette. She chortled sardonically, flicking the ash. "You are a cruel one, aren't you?"

"I told you I was not good at playing games," he said without emotion. "You are a prostitute, and I am a trinket for the Reich Marshal to add to one of his collections. Both of us are—what—clowns in a charade, I think."

"Charade?"

"You, my dear Margarete, or Madame M, or Name-of-the-night, are not what you appear to be. Neither am I. You are here for monetary reasons. I am here for duty. They are both cruel masters."

Blowing another puff of smoke into the air, she looked at him out of the corner of her eyes. Then, looking straight at him, she matched him gaze for gaze, flicking her nail. She studied his steel blue eyes, the flat, masculine planes of his features, the uncompromising line of his jaw.

She chuckled, breaking the tension. She was a different woman now; the first one had walked off the stage. "You are very perceptive," she said.

He said nothing.

"Tell me," she asked. "Are you a sad clown or a happy clown in this charade?"

"A confused clown," he said.

"Then I think that you are very sad," she said matter-of-factly. "Confused clowns are the saddest clowns of all. They do not know which way to paint their lips."

"I perceive an expert on the subject."

"I travel with the circus," the woman agreed. "I see one every night in the mirror when I put on my makeup. They are the saddest of all, I tell you."

"I see. And which are you—a happy or sad clown?"

"I do not know just yet. The night is still young." She took a long pull on her cigarette. "Perhaps I too am confused."

"Perhaps."

"My lips—are they turned up or down?"

Rolf bent closer to inspect her mouth. "It is hard to say." He smiled at her. "Did you know that you have lovely lips?"

"And now flattery?"

"Truth."

She tapped her cigarette ash thoughtfully. "I used to have a lovely soul."

Rolf looked steadily into her eyes and saw a glint of something warm and human beneath the painted lashes, hiding, flirting with the light. "I think you still have," he said. "Yes, definitely."

She lowered her eyes embarrassedly.

"Is that a smile?" he asked, again inspecting her lips. "Yes, I can see it now. The corners of your mouth are definitely turning up. There they go!"

She giggled.

Just then three SS officers crossed the great room to the bar, where the bartender was busily filling orders. Rolf followed them with his eyes, then glanced back to where he and Margarete had first met by the Reich Marshal's train room.

Margarete touched the top of his hand. "What is it?"

"Pardon? Nothing," he said. "I was just thinking."

"I can see. Perhaps we could slip away," she suggested. "Find a happy place in town somewhere . . . just the two of us. Our two confused souls."

"I have no soul," Rolf said without emotion. "Besides, the war has put an end to happy places."

"You are breaking my heart."

"Truth is a harder master than either money or duty," he said.

An attendant walked past them carrying a trayful of drinks from the bar. Rolf stopped him. "Would you care for a glass of wine or schnapps?" he asked the woman.

"I'll have a white wine."

Rolf handed her a glass, and took a schnapps for himself. He put his hand lightly on her back, glanced over his shoulder at the three SS officers standing at the bar, then guided her across the room to where there were two Queen Anne chairs, side-by-side, off to the right of the string quartet. They sat down, and Rolf glanced beyond the woman's profile at the group of musicians. There were two violins, a viola, and a cello; the musicians, three men and a woman, were dressed very handsomely in formal attire as they played, looking very intently at their music.

Rolf crossed his legs and looked at Margarete. She was sitting with her ankles crossed and her legs folded to one side of the chair, watching the musicians, her foot tapping rhythmically as she smoked her cigarette. She crushed the butt in a crystal ashtray setting on the mahogany table between them. Immediately she retrieved another one from a convenient cigarette box.

"Are you nervous?" Rolf asked, lighting it.

She looked at him quickly. "Do I seem nervous?"

He raised his glass and smiled. "Here's to the two sad clowns."

She smiled back. "Not so sad now," she said. They sipped their drinks, continued smiling as their eyes met, then she looked away at the quartet.

Which woman are you now? he wondered, as Mozart's *Quartet in A Major* played in the background.

She must have felt his eyes on her, for she turned suddenly toward him and caught him in the act. He was looking at the delicate turn of her ankles, absorbed in thought, when she asked, "Do you like the music, Rolf?"

"Yes, very much," he said. He lighted his cigar and blew a thick cloud into the air.

"You see, *this* is a happy place, isn't it?"

He sipped his drink, feeling it warming through him as he looked over the glittery scene. He rolled the cigar in his mouth, puffing contemplatively.

She glanced away at the musicians. "They do play wonderfully, don't they?"

"Only the best for 'Our Hermann.'"

"The best . . . yes, of course," she said, leaning toward him confidently. She was the first woman again. The second was waiting downstage. "And *you* are the best, aren't you? The guest of honor."

"Trinket of honor," he corrected. "Trinket for the day, then I shall be forgotten on a shelf."

"Do we so quickly forget our heroes?"

Rolf chuckled as he sipped his schnapps.

Margarete looked at the Knight's Cross with Oak Leaves jiggling at his throat. "Have you really shot down two hundred planes, my hero? It seems fantastic."

The smile disappeared from his face for an instant, then reappeared as something else.

"Emmy told me that the Führer is going to award you the Schwertern. Is it true?" she pressed. "I think it is absolutely fantastic."

Rolf looked steadily at the quartet.

The music brightened, swelled, his mood lifting with it, then deepened with the somber notes of the cello.

She touched his hand. "There, I've gone and spoiled it, haven't I? I'm sorry, Rolf. Let's not talk about the war. Not here. Not in our happy place."

"Tell me about yourself, Margarete," he said, turning to her, not realizing the dangerousness of the question. *Who are you, really?* he did not ask. "Have you a family?"

"A family?" She shifted in her chair and looked down at her hands. A curl of smoke rose from her cigarette as she smoothed the meat of one thumb over the nail of the other. "I have a mother," she said.

"We all do," he smiled.

She returned his smile politely, smoked her cigarette, and thoughtfully folded it into the ashtray. "My mother is feeble and cannot work," she said, crushing the last of it. "I do what I can."

"What of your father?"

"My father died when I was a little girl," she said. "I had two older brothers, but they were both killed somewhere outside Moscow."

"Barbarossa?"

"Yes. The winter killed them," she said bitterly. She looked up at him. "Here I said I wouldn't talk about the war."

"It is all around us."

"Yes, isn't it?" The corners of her mouth turned up quickly, then fell as she looked over at the string quartet, seeing beyond it. "They had no warm clothes," she said distantly. "None of our soldiers had warm clothes. It was such a foolish waste."

"I would not say it too loudly."

"I would tell the Führer himself," she said.

"I'll bet you would." Rolf rolled the cigar ash in the ashtray. A whisp of smoke rose off the tip, then cut off as the coal suddenly died. He set the cigar down in the little groove. "Nothing else?"

"That's all," she said. "End of story. Now you know all there is to know about me."

"And this?"

"This is something I do to put a little bread on the table," she said. "I work for the library during the day."

"I was not judging," he said.

"It would not matter." A shiver went over her bare shoulders. She rubbed them, turned and smiled quickly at Rolf. "I am a daughter of the Reich, aren't I?"

Something cold went over Rolf too. "I am sorry, Margarete," he said. But the words sounded strangely hollow and unreal to his ear. "I am truly sorry," he said again.

The words were genuine, but he felt nothing for her, really, nothing of her pain. Only the coldness. *But why?* he wondered. *Why is there no feeling? Because she is not real,* he reasoned. *She is intangible. An abstraction. An Other Woman. Nothing personal.*

And then another line of reasoning struck a deeper chord. *Perhaps it is because you are cruel,* he thought. *Isn't that what Gretchen had said? Has all the kindness in you been killed by the war? By Hamburg? Is there nothing left of happiness but cruelty?*

"Rolf?"

"Yes, Margarete?"

She was looking steadily at him. A change had gone over her face, he saw, the sparkling light dimming in her eyes to a deep, almost forest green. She was someone else now; not the first woman, nor the second, but someone altogether new. The illusive something that had been hiding in the wings was now appearing center stage. A woman. Not an Other Woman, but one very personal. "I am tired of the game now," she said. "Please, call me Olga."

Looking into her eyes Rolf sensed a sudden premonition of danger prickle along his spine. "Olga?" he rasped.

"It was my grandmother's name," she said. "She was no battle maiden, but she was a lovely, lovely person." A tentative smile fluttered over her lips as she reached out, took his hand, and began rubbing each of his fingers thoughtfully.

Rolf looked quickly at his hand. It was as though she had touched him with an electric wire.

"You have beautiful hands for a man, did you know?" she said, admiring the length of his fingers that tapered finely, masculinely, to the clean, squared nails. "Like a pianist's. I think you can tell a lot about a man by his hands."

Rolf looked at her, a metamorphosis tearing at his face now. The heady scent of Olga's perfume drifted over his face, clouding over him, enveloping him, and he felt as though he were suffocating.

She looked at him, touching him, feeling his hands. "You *do* have a soul, you know?"

"I—I must excuse myself," he rasped, pulling away from her.

"Rolf?"

"Not now!" he shouted, almost choking. "Excuse me—please!" He started away, turned abruptly, forcing a grin into the taut mask of his features. He patted the air between them as though holding an explanation at bay.

Olga rose to her feet, smiling uncertainly. "Rolf? What is it, Rolf?" But Rolf waved her down, turned, and was gone.

Olga Strump stood looking after him, perplexed, the smile torn brutally from her face as she sat slowly down in her chair, a collection of feminine parts that described not a paid escort, neither a clown, but a lost and very lonely woman.

Beethoven's *Quartet in C-sharp Minor, Opus 131* followed Rolf across the room, pursuing him, it seemed. Accusing him. Condemning him. Stabbing him with heavenly strains of glory notes. He thought he might scream.

Rolf pushed into the rest room, locked the door behind him, and strode over to the sink. He tore his tie away from his throat while turning on the tap, then splashed cold water on his face several times. He paused, taking a cleansing breath as he held his hands against his face, allowing the water to drip off his face and down through his fingers.

He splashed himself again and again and glanced at himself in the mirror. Then he looked at himself steadily, stared unblinkingly at the predator behind the flat blade of the killer eyes. You were cruel to her, his eyes chided him. Have you too become a monster? Must you kill everything now that makes you feel human, that makes you feel like a man?

He turned off the tap and wiped his face with a towel. Again he stared coldly into the mirror.

This time he saw another self, saw the dark wretchedness of this barren Self-in-uppercase transcending the image in the mirror. What he saw was ugly and repulsive. Then he saw the sadness rising in his eyes, the pain and the duty and honor rising, and the love of something that was both dead and dying rising; each was a little dart of flame wavering on the cold, dead, black wick of his being.

"Is that you, Immortal Soul?" he said aloud. "Have you come to torment me? But I have no faith," he said. "You cannot trouble me if I have no faith. Faith is dead and God is dead and Nietzsche is dead. So you must find yourself another more suitable field to haunt." He did not say: *The field you see is nothing but acres of dead, black stubble, with faith mounting on brilliant flashing wings before it is gunned down.*

There was a knock at the door. Rolf started, and his knowledge of himself quickly careered away into the sheen of the mirror.

"I'll just be a minute," he said, folding the towel in its place. He retied his tie, straightened himself and combed his hair, then went to the door, unlocked, and opened it. It was one of the SS officers he'd seen by the bar.

"Good evening, Major," Rolf said, slightly taken aback.

"Good evening, Captain Schiller," the SS major smiled. "You are enjoying yourself this evening?"

"Yes, very," Rolf lied.

"Good, good," the SS major said. "It is important that those who are loyal to the Reich receive what they deserve." He smiled with just his eyes. "There is so much treachery about, wouldn't you agree?"

Rolf stared at him for a moment. *So they* were *eavesdropping,* he thought. The *sneaking*—it entered his mind to drag the man into the rest room and beat him to death. "Treachery, you say?" he asked the SS major. "That is your department, not mine, isn't it?" He nodded politely as he stepped past him, not looking back to catch the major's reaction.

Rounding the corner, Rolf took several deep breaths to clear his head. As he entered the great room the first thing he noticed was that the music had stopped; the second thing he noticed was that someone was yelling. Then he noticed that people were standing around in, what seemed to him, astonished huddles, everyone looking in the direction of the foyer. He followed their eyes and the sound of the yelling to a knot of officers gathered around the Reich Marshal, who was in an obvious rage. His head stood out as red as a turnip.

Everything was different, eerily changed, as though he had walked inadvertently into a stranger's apartment.

Rolf stepped forward warily. When he saw Olga crossing the room, striding toward him in long-legged shapeliness, looking very lovely in her white evening dress and heels and springing red mane of hair, a prickling of danger was already beginning to edge up his spine.

She had not changed. She was stunningly the same. He wanted her desperately in that moment—to hold her, kiss her, to ravage her, if need be. But something informed his mind that he should quickly turn and flee.

She came up to him and took hold of his arm with both hands. "Oh, Rolf, it is simply awful," she said. "Have you heard?"

Rolf looked at her, and when he saw it in her searching green eyes, eyes that laid him bare, the danger was already crouched at the base of his skull. "Heard what?" he heard himself ask through a gathering fog.

"The Americans have bombed Wilhelmshaven. It is just awful."

Rolf felt the blood drain from his face. He heard the words trail away, echoing, sounding nonsensical at first, then jumping back at him with an articulate shout. He felt suddenly weak in the knees. "What?"

"Wilhelmshaven," she repeated. "They've bombed Wilhelmshaven."

"Again?"

"Isn't that near your air base, Rolf?"

Rolf looked over at the Reich Marshal. He was gesticulating wildly as he raged at the generals, at the walls, at the generals, at the ceiling, at the generals. The generals were gaping down at the floor, like schoolboys receiving a good tongue-lashing from the headmaster, everyone impotent with fear. Looking at them, Rolf felt anger, contempt, then something darker yet rising inside him.

"Rolf, are you all right? Rolf?"

22 ★★★★

The Schiller house was shrouded in total darkness, save the yellow aureole of light spilling over the floor a few feet in front of the hearth. A thick quiet pervaded the darkness. The incessant ticks of the several clocks in the large Victorian house finding their way through the stillness of the hallways and rooms divided the quiet and the darkness into brackets of time. The pendulum of the grandfather clock swept out of shadow into the soft glow of light, the light flashing on the polished surface of the disc, then the disc sweeping away, and then back, flashing . . . flashing . . . flashing, like a brazen moon in an interminable orbit.

Rolf, wrapped in the mantle of darkness, sat slumped on the crushed velvet settee, brooding over the embers in the hearth with a flat-eyed stare. His elbow was draped over the armrest, his large, finely sculptured hand supporting the great weight of his head. The darkness continued to rise in him. It had been rising ever since he looked over and saw the generals cowering before the Reich Marshal. He tried to put up bulwarks against the darkness so the flood could be contained for a while. But the darkness was relentless.

The embers in the hearth stirred, cricked brittlely, but held.

The grandfather clock's chimes sounded once, a resolute and golden note, then sounded again. Had he been listening, he would have heard the soft padding of feet descending the stairs. The third step from the bottom creaked beneath the weight of the settled foot.

A moment later Gretchen peered around the library door. "Is that you, Rolf?" she whispered. She saw his form, the left side of his face angling forward and slightly toward her, with his shoulder and forearm darkly lit against the hearth to frame a triangle of reddish light. She smiled, happy to see him after missing him all day. "I heard you come in."

No response.

"Rolf?"

Silence.

She entered the room tentatively, her smile wavering as she padded over the carpeted floor in her bare feet. She saw the light flashing on his eyes. He was awake. "Rolf, are you all right?" she asked quietly. "You're sitting in darkness. Shall I turn on a light?"

He stirred, looking up at her as though rousing from a deep sleep. "Hello, Gretch. Didn't wake you, did I?"

She was relieved. "No. I couldn't sleep. I wanted to hear how it went today. I waited for you to come upstairs but you didn't—" She was suddenly frightened. "Rolf, what's wrong?" she asked, seeing his eyes in the light. She sat down behind him on the settee and lay her hand on his shoulder. "Has something happened?"

Rolf gazed back into the hearth. "They've bombed Wilhelmshaven."

Gretchen's hand rose slowly to her mouth.

"Viktor's been killed."

"Oh, Rolf," she gasped. The news hammered its way through her brain. "Oh, Rolf, no. Not Viktor."

Rolf said nothing.

"Are you certain?"

"He's dead, believe me."

She groaned inwardly. A cold shudder went through her, hollowing everything out that was left in her, leaving her numb, tired, and empty. Everything she had been looking forward to, waiting up for her brother and wanting to talk about all that had happened at Karinhall, was suddenly gone, as though someone had inadvertently opened the cage and the birds had gone winging in a rush.

She drew her legs up into her woolen nightgown against the cold and folded her arms around her legs. She did not know Viktor, except what she had read of him in Rolf's letters. Everything she was feeling now, or not feeling, was for her brother and because of him, and knowing that Viktor had been his closest friend.

"When did it happen?"

"This morning sometime," Rolf said, his voice flat and toneless. "I don't know . . . nine o'clock or something."

She shook her head sadly. "I'm so sorry, Rolf," she said, stroking the back of his head with her fingers.

They sat together in the silence and the darkness for a long while: he, gazing into the hearth at the tonguing spears of flame darting about the coals; and she, watching the nervous play of light on the floor.

"I suppose I should visit his parents," Rolf said. "Somebody's got to. The poor fool. I can't just send them a letter." He saw Viktor suddenly as he came into Werner's that night, wearing the American flight jacket and the cocky grin on his face.

"Do they live far from here?" Gretchen asked.

A tenuous smile curled over Rolf's lips. "Not too far," he said. "Only a few centimeters or so."

She looked at the back of his head, certain she had misunderstood him. She lay her head back on her knees as she felt a great sorrow welling up into her chest. Then she lay her head on her brother's shoulder.

The embers in the hearth cracked then fell in a crash of glowing cinders. There was a momentary burst of furious light. And the pendulum flashed . . . flashed . . . flashed, with the flashes growing imperceptibly dimmer in the dying light. The light from the moon crept into the room through the windows, giving everything a cool luminance, to reveal the silhouettes of Rolf and Gretchen sitting still and quiet on the settee.

The grandfather clock sounded the quarter note, as did the other clocks.

Rolf cursed. "It needn't have happened," he said bitterly.

She listened to his heavy heart beating.

"If we had generals leading us," he said, flushing with anger. "Men who were not afraid to—" He broke off abruptly, as though the direction his mind was taking him would lead to a room he was forbidden to enter.

Gretchen waited for him to finish his thought, but he left it hanging. The stairs in the hallway cricked suddenly, as though the house were settling. She looked over at the library doors and then back at Rolf and sighed.

Rolf stood up from the settee, stepped over, and leaned against the mantel. He gazed down into the hearth a long while. "I don't understand it," he said. "Without fighters we will not be able to stop the bombing. It is an obvious fact. I know that High Command sees it. General Galland even had the Reich Marshal convinced . . . got him to meet with the Führer."

Gretchen listened to him.

Rolf chortled incredulously. "But mention the subject now to the Reich Marshal and he goes into a tirade." He shook his head. "I don't understand it. It's . . . it's . . ."

He would not go into the room.

"If you could have seen their faces," he said, backing away but not too far from the room.

Gretchen watched him intently; in the ambient light she saw the ebb and flow of struggle over his features.

"Our mighty generals," Rolf said. "Like schoolboys cowering before a bully." He grunted contemptuously. "Cowards."

"What is it, Rolf?"

"Why can't he see it?"

"Who, Rolf?"

He began to pace back and forth in front of the hearth, his arms folded behind his back, thinking. "It seems . . . it seems . . . I don't know."

"What does, Rolf? Who can't see it?"

"For High Command to continue the way it is defies all sound strategic reasoning. And yet we do."

"Who can't see it, Rolf?"

Anger crept into his voice as he said, "We go hurrying to the cliff like a bunch of lemmings. There it is, plain to see: Danger. Destruction. And yet we step over the edge into the sea."

"Rolf, who can't see it?"

He looked at her quickly. "The Führer," he said. "Why can't the Führer see that we need more fighters?"

Gretchen watched him intently.

Rolf continued to pace. He stepped into the panel of light spilling through the library window, paused, and looked out upon the tree-lined curve of street that was lit only by the moon.

The street looked deserted, looking as he had remembered it from his earliest memories. A smile flickered over his lips. He had thought of it often as he lay in his bed at Jever, with the lights turned off and the utter quiet of the base closing around him. Lying there, he would remember the house, and the family, each of their faces. He'd think of the happy times they'd had boating on the Neuer See, or downhill skiing in the Bavarian Alps at Christmastime, and how everyone had hopes that everything was getting brighter and better in Germany. And then he would remember Katharina— lovely, beautiful, adoring Katharina. He would want her, and only her, as he lay on his bed thinking and staring at the dark ceiling, with an ache in his chest that he thought would crush him until she was in his arms again. And then the terrible knowing that he could never hold her again because of Hamburg.

Rolf groaned, pushing it all from his mind and, turning from the window, said plaintively, "If we do not put more fighters into the air, then Germany is lost. She is lost." Walking back to the hearth, the anger multiplying in his voice, he said, "It is simple mathematics. The Americans are building more bombers than we are fighters." He looked at Gretchen. "Do you know that they have a fighter now that can reach Berlin? Gretchen, do you realize what that means?"

Gretchen said nothing.

"Of course you do. Any idiot can see it plain as the nose on his face. But the Führer wants more bombers. Bombers! Why?" He cursed. "We do not need bombers, we need fighters!" He slammed the mantel with his palm. "I've got to do something."

"What can you do?"

"I don't know," he growled. "There's got to be something—someone. Someone in High Command who can convince the Führer that this is . . . that this is . . ."

He would not go into the room.

"Madness?"

Rolf looked at her quickly.

"Yes, madness," she repeated. "There is no reasoning with madness, Rolf."

He glared at her as though she had uttered a blasphemy. His shoulders hunched slightly, like a wolf at bay.

"Does it seem strange to you, Rolf?" she said. "How can you reason with something that has no soundness in it? You can't. The soundness has been eaten away by a cancer. There is only raging now."

Rolf seemed to stagger backward against the mantel.

She paused, waiting for him to speak. And then the sorrow that she had been harboring spilled over the breakwater. "Can't you see that none of this need have happened, Rolf," she said earnestly. "None of it. Not Poland, not France, not Britain, not Russia—" She broke off as tears welled in her eyes. "None of it, Rolf," she cried. "Not Hamburg, not Wilhelmshaven. It needn't have happened."

Rolf looked at her hard. And, looking at her, suddenly, all their words began to push through some crack in his mind: from their walks in the Tiergarten; from the ones at night, after supper, the two of them sitting up in her room; and from those in the little café that they both loved dearly, looking out through the linden trees onto the Charlottenburg Strasse. He now heard the truth of those words echoing back and sounding solid and resolute and, with the last note of the last syllable of the last word ringing off in his mind, he realized that he was standing square in the room he had not wanted to enter. He wasn't aware at what point he had stepped into the room, but he had stepped into it.

His head reeled a little. "Madness?"

"Rolf, can't you see it?" Gretchen said. She had seen the struggle building on his face, saw it peak, then smooth out with the release of his shoulders. "Tell me you can see it. You must. You said it yourself that we are like lemmings, stepping blindly over the edge. But not all of us are blind, Rolf. Not all of us have sold our souls for a shining bubble."

He was still looking at her hard, with the flat-bladed predator eyes. Then his expression became a contortion of pain, of grief, and, finally, of astonishment as something burst in his mind. "Yes," he said.

Again he walked over to the window and gazed out upon the street. There, along the moonlit curve of road that was once the entire length of his world, where he and his friends (all of them gone now) had played games of stickball and tag; where, during the long, hard, suffering years of Germany after the Great War, after the Versailles Treaty, after the mark was inflated to worthlessness, he had grown into a man. Grown up with the love of a country known only through songs drummed into him by his father, and with the knowledge of God dictated by his mother.

But neither love of country nor sound catechism could buy a loaf of bread.

And then there was Adolf Hitler, rising suddenly and brilliantly—the messiah—amid the ruin of German despair. In his train followed the orgiastic fervor of the Nuremburg rallies, where the ascending deities of the Reich, gleaming brightly as they stood proudly before the symbols of Teutonic power and supremacy, decried the long years of oppression with pounding fist and strident voice, promising that their light and glory would shine over the Fatherland for a thousand years.

And everyone—not everyone it seems—had gone after them with abandon, buoyed upon the swelling hysteria; the young men shouting with pulsing ardor, "Sieg Heil! Sieg Heil! Sieg Heil!" and the young women in desperate swoon, clutching their breasts, weeping openly, with their arms outstretched and their wet faces flashing in the lurid, chilling ambience of the night. Everywhere people were again singing "Deutschland über Alles" with passionate cry, in beer halls and in churches, the very old and the very young. No one looked to see the political purges, or the ethnic pogroms. No one saw that a cancer had gotten loose in their midst to consume not just the body but the very soul of the nation.

The moon shone brightly on Rolf's face as he stared out upon the street a while longer. "Yes, it is true, I'm afraid," he said, his face grave with a tragic foreknowledge. Then he cast off from the reverie with a sardonic chortle, running his hand through his hair as he looked back at his sister. "The shine's off the bubble, isn't it?"

తానే

On the other side of the library doors Ernst blinked into the darkness in stunned disbelief. His fifteen-year-old brain fought hard against the words that planed down against his mind with the force of a blitzkrieg. He knew about his sister, that she was a religious fanatic, that she was an enemy of the Reich. But he was not concerned about her. She would learn in time. After all, isn't that what his Youth leaders had told him? That they would teach her. And if she would not learn then they would send her off to a camp where her thinking would be retrained. It would be for her own good, he was convinced. She would learn. She would see the light.

But what of his brother? His brother was a hero of the Reich, a renowned fighter pilot, a bearer of the Eichenlaub, the sum of everything he had believed in and hoped for. How can one who has tasted glory fall so far from his lofty estate? He fought hard against the words but there was no prevailing against them; they came and they came and they continued to come, shouting that his beloved hero brother was a traitor.

A traitor.

An enemy of the Reich . . . of Adolf Hitler.

His mind was a whir of thoughts. His eyes suddenly suffused with tears as he imagined the devastation of his world. Then an angry tyranny rose in his chest and smashed through his weakness. He wiped his eyes with the back of his hand. His brows furrowed into a dark scowl. He would not do that again; he had clarity now. Pure light. He listened at the library door a while longer, heard nothing, then turned and began to creep back upstairs. The third step from the bottom cracked plaintively beneath his weight.

తానే

Gretchen looked quickly at the library doors and a jolt of fear shot through her. "Come, Rolf," she said, rising to her feet. "No more of this talk. It's time for bed." She took his arm. "In the morning you'll see things from a new perspective, you'll see."

"You go ahead," he said. "I want to think."

She looked at him.

219

"Quit mothering me, Gretchen. I need to be alone. I need to think. Now go to bed."

She looked in his eyes, then stepped forward and hugged him. "I will pray for you, Rolf."

"Pray for Germany, Gretchen."

"I will pray for you and for Germany," she smiled, kissing his cheek. She left Rolf standing alone in the library.

After a time he sat down in the settee and, in the silence and the darkness, with the pendulum marking the time, gazed into the blackness of the hearth. Soon Viktor's face rose like a flicker of flame among the dead coals. He saw him in Werner's tavern, laughing. And then another flame of him rose in Wilhelmshaven with his arm draped around a girl, the two of them singing. Then the flames spread and Rolf saw all of them off his left wing, the ghosts of his friends—his fellow warriors lining up on the squadron leader—ascending brightly in the pyre of Victory's torch. The opening lines from the Book of Ecclesiastes came to mind: "Vanity of vanities, saith the Preacher. All is vanity." Then thoughts that he had once held at bay came at him from every corner of the room, from the secret niches and keepers of shadows, and a tear went winging down his cheek for the vanity of it all.

෨∞ঔ

Outside, a black sedan pulled to the curb, about fifty yards up the street from the Schiller house. A man wearing a black leather coat emerged from the shadows of a tree and walked over to the curb. The rear door of the sedan opened and a smallish man, wearing the black uniform of an SS lieutenant, stepped out onto the sidewalk and greeted him. It was Lieutenant Klemmer.

Klemmer handed the man a container of coffee; they talked for a few moments, then both of them looked in the direction of the house. They talked a while longer, chuckled as the smaller man ran his hand along the back of the other, affectionately. Then Klemmer stepped back into the sedan. The car made a U-turn and sped away. The man wearing the black leather coat glanced at the Schiller house, then stepped back into the shadows and sipped his coffee.

23 ★★★★

*N*ovember 6, 1943. 1900 hours. Thursday. There was much to celebrate. The 52nd had gone over the one hundred mark the day before on a Ramrod to Münster, bringing down six German fighters to boost their tally to a hundred and one, and without the loss of a single American flier.

The music was provided by the Skyboys Dance Band, a big band in the Glenn Miller style comprised solely of airmen that were trucked over from the 94th Bomber Group. They set up on a makeshift stage at the far wall of the big T–2 hangar and had hung a large banner that read in big bold letters: Welcome to Dogpatch, USA! In smaller letters beneath it: Home of the 52nd Fighter Group and the First Annual Sadie Hawkins Day Dance . . . *Go get 'em, girls!*

Some American Red Cross nurses and USO helpers were brought up from London to help with the refreshments and to insure that none of the airmen were left withering on the walls. Some of the band and the women were dressed up like hillbillies. The men wore ragged shirts and patched overalls, and sported corncob pipes, while the women wore ragged skirts or shorts and tied-up blouses; all of them had bare feet, and a few had painted freckles on their faces. Three of the USO girls were fine singers, with tight harmonies like the Andrews Sisters, and helped the band with the vocal numbers. The dance got off to a roaring start.

The English girls who had come—there were scores of them from every neighboring village and hamlet—weren't quite sure what to make of everything. Everything was so big and loudly festive and none of them had ever seen anything like it. They thought the Americans wild, and the music wild and wonderful, but they were not sure about the girls asking the men to dance, and so they stood around in little clusters.

After a tight-harmonied rendition of "The Boogie Woogie Bugle Boy from Company B," the band played a slow number, and the floor crowded over with couples. Billy, a little flushed from his complicated footwork, went over to the refreshment tables that were set up along the left wall.

Billy asked one of the hillbilly USO girls jerking sodas if she could get him a beer. She flashed him a blacked-out, toothy grin and said, "Shore thing, handsome." She batted her eyelashes at him. "By the by, has you been spoken fer?"

"I don't know 'bout that," Billy grinned, going along with it. He held up a foot. "But my dogs is sure barkin'."

"Aw, shucks!"

Waiting for his beer, Billy tapped his foot to the music and watched the pan of happy faces gliding by: Sugar Suggs, Happy Molina, Bug Mallory, most of the boys. There was a little knot of English girls standing nearby, each one eating a bowl of ice cream.

He smiled at them and nodded his head. "Some swell shindig," he grinned. The girls paused momentarily, spoons in mouths, to look bewilderedly at him. "Some swell shindig," he repeated over the din. And the girls, glancing at one another with their eyes, giggled and resumed licking their spoonsful of ice cream.

The hillbilly girl handed him his beer and grinned toothily. "When them dogs a yorn is rested," she said, twirling a bright red pigtail with her index finger, "I'd be obliged if you'd give me a leetle holler, hear? It shore do git lonesum back here. Powerful lonesum." Wink, wink.

Billy winked back at her. "Sure thing, doll," he smiled.

He sipped his beer and watched the ebb and flow of couples dancing, the laughing faces. He looked over at the entry door next to the big hangar bay. A few stragglers trickled in and gaped about the place in awe. He smiled sagaciously at them as they filtered in to the great, moving mass.

The music swelled to a fever pitch, crashed like thunder in a can, then trailed off to a rumble of voices that moved over the undulating faces.

Joe Thompson pushed his way through the mill with his arm draped around an attractive English girl. "Hey, Montana!" he howled, swaggering over to him. "What were you doing out there earlier?"

Billy grinned at him.

"You ought to be locked up," Joe said.

"You don't like the way I jitterbug?"

"Is that what you were doing? It looked like you were breaking horses."

"Ain't this a rodeo?" Billy hooted. They both laughed. Billy smiled at the girl with Joe.

"What's your poison, beautiful?" Joe asked her.

"I'll have a cherry soda," the girl said, fanning herself and smiling at Billy.

"Cherry soda and a can of bellywash," Joe said to the blacked-out tooth soda queen. The drinks were served. The English girl sipped her soda thoughtfully as she looked around at the decorations and marveled at the American girls in costume.

Joe watched her, the corners of his hard mouth bent up; then he threw his head back and finished his beer with several long gulps. "Where're you from?" he asked her.

The girl looked at him with just her eyes, still sipping her soda. She let up on the straw and said, "Southwold." Then she put her lips on the straw and sipped delicately.

"Southwold? How about that?" Joe said. "Southwold. Don't you just love the names of their towns, Montana?"

"Sure," Billy said, nodding at the girl, who was now slurping the bottom of the glass.

The music picked up.

"Whaddya say, beautiful?" Joe growled. "Want to cut the rug some more?"

The English girl looked at him puzzled.

"Cut the rug," Joe grinned, taking her glass and handing it to Billy. "You know—dance! Trip the light fantastic!"

She nodded her head, smiled rather stupidly at him, and Joe whisked her out onto the floor.

Billy turned the soda glass in his hands as he watched them. Joe could certainly slow dance to make the girls weep, he thought. Smooth as hot buttered rum. Then he watched everyone dancing, the girls with their heads on the boys' shoulders, as everyone moved in slow shuffling circles to the music of "Moonlight Serenade."

Happy Molina was dancing with a Red Cross girl easily a foot taller than he was. Sugar Suggs and the rest of the boys were all out on the floor having a good time. It was a fine dance. Billy, smiling, looked across the hangar at the door.

"What do you think, sugah pie?" a woman's voice behind him purred. "Them feet a yorn still too tired to give a pore country girl a twirl?"

Billy turned around. The hillbilly soda queen was twirling one of her red pigtails and smiling at him with that big grin of hers.

He shrugged his shoulders. "Sure, why not?"

She took the soda glass from him and set it on the table. They danced one slow and one fast number, then, as they were walking back to the tables for refreshment, she, smiling and wiggling pertly, said, "You're too good lookin' to be alone on Sadie Hawkins." After this the hillbilly girl talked normal. She was from Brooklyn. "I've got a break coming up. What do you say we blow this place?"

"Sure, why not?" Billy pulled up suddenly and stared across the dance floor.

"Something wrong?" the girl asked.

Billy watched as Jane Worthing and her red-haired friend came in through the door of the hangar. She paused and, looking over the crowd, caught his eyes. "Well, whaddya know?" he said.

Suddenly the band and the crowd and the hillbilly girl fell away to a soundless tunnel of light with the English girl at the end of it. Billy could not take his eyes off her—a sail on the horizon to a man lost at sea. The men along the clearing were asking her to dance, he saw. But Jane kept shaking her head and coming straight for him, looking pretty and then stunning in a frilly sweater and light blue cotton print skirt that hit her calves.

Her hair was done up like Rita Hayworth's, and for a moment she looked like Rita Hayworth walking toward him. All the fellows turning and watching her as she passed must have thought so too. Somewhere along the way the redhead with her disappeared, and then it was only Jane Worthing coming straight on, coming gracefully, like a ship under full sail, the sails billowing majestically. And then she was standing before him, the tunnel gone, with only the light left shining in her hair.

Billy felt a lump in his throat. "You came," he said, clearing his throat.

"Yes."

"That's nice. Real nice."

"I won't be staying though," she added quickly. "My friend Julie needed a ride."

"Julie?"

"Yes, my friend," she said, making a vague gesture at the dance floor.

Billy followed her gesture, seeing no one in particular, as the words "That's too bad" staggered from his lips.

"I would like to apologize for how dreadful I was the other day," she said straight out.

He smiled at her. "You pack quite a wallop."

"I don't know what came over me," she said. "I feel simply awful about it."

"I deserved it."

"Yes, but I lost my temper. It was inexcuseable."

"No harm done," he said. "Like I said . . . I deserved it."

They looked at each other. Muted lights and shapes whirled in the background. A big grin spread over Billy's face, and he stuck out his hand. "This mean we can be friends now?"

She looked down at his hand and shook it lightly. Her fingers were cool, smooth—like porcelain, he thought. "Friends," she smiled.

They looked at each other for a moment longer, still smiling.

"You look nice," he said.

Jane demurred.

"Really, you look very nice."

"Thank you," she said. She looked over as a dead ringer of Daisy May jiggled by, and added, "I seem to be a bit overdressed."

"You look terrific," Billy said. The trio started singing "Rum and Coca Cola." He looked over at the band. "Would you like to dance?"

Jane looked out at the dance floor as Julie, twirling past them with a tall, lanky fellow, gave her a little finger wave. Jane gave her a little finger wave back. "No, thank you," she said.

"You're sure?"

She looked inquiringly at him. "Isn't this where the girls are supposed to ask the boys to dance?"

"Yeah. It seems a bit much for some of the English girls though," he grinned. "But if you're asking me to dance—" He took her hand.

She pulled it back. "No, really. I just came over to apologize. Really. Good night." She turned to leave.

"Wait a minute!" Billy said, getting around in front of her. "Wouldn't you like a soda or something? They make great sodas here. No? How about an ice cream? Do you like ice cream?"

She looked over at the table. "Ice cream? No, thank you. Really."

"Nothing?"

Jane started away, then she stopped and looked at him, catching the flash of dangerous blue in his eyes as he smiled beseechingly at her. She looked back at the table of refreshments. "Have they any coffee?"

"Coffee? Sure we got coffee." Billy went over to the big stainless steel coffeemaker, took a cup, and filled it with coffee. "How do you take it? Cream?"

"Yes, thanks."

"Sugar?"

"Oh, yes. Please."

"We've got loads of sugar," he said as he moved over to the condiment area. "How many lumps?"

"Two, please." Jane stirred the sugar into the coffee and took a sip. "It's delicious."

Billy watched her. "I didn't know Brits drank coffee," he said.

"Shows what you know of the Brits, doesn't it?" She smiled wryly, then took another sip.

Billy didn't know what to do with his hands, so he shoved them into his pockets. "Listen, if you don't want to dance, maybe we could just sit and talk. You don't want to stand around drinking coffee. There are some tables open."

She looked over at the round tables along the opposite wall, each one covered with a white tablecloth and a candle lamp in the center to give the place a cozy atmosphere.

"Just while you drink your coffee," Billy said.

"Really, I shouldn't."

The band was playing "In the Mood." Joe Thompson was gliding the English girl across the floor and looking like Fred Astaire. Julie Ellerby was dancing with the tall, lanky fellow, closer now, her eyes closed, and Happy Molina and the tall Red Cross nurse were keeping time to their own music in one of the corners. Both of them were holding each other; his cheek rested on her chest, and her chin rested on the top of his head as they stepped slowly from side to side, every so often making little quarter turns. Pete Skagway had a game of cards going behind the stage with several of the men from Special Services.

Billy and Jane sat at one of the small round tables, off to one side of the band, where the lights weren't so bright. She watched the couples dancing as she sipped her coffee.

"He went down somewhere in Egypt," she said, turning back to Billy. The candle made a soft glow on the table and on her face.

"In a Lancaster, you say?"

"Yes."

"No chutes?"

Jane shook her head. "It was overcast . . . thick as pea soup, they said. No one saw anything." She took a sip of coffee. "Bomber Command put them down as missing in action." She paused thoughtfully. "That was almost a year ago."

Billy watched her in the moody light. "It must be tough not knowing."

"One makes do," she said. "I burned a candle in my window every night for six months. Seems silly now." She sipped her coffee. "This is simply delicious." She smiled at him. "You're from Montana?"

"Yes," Billy grinned. "How long had you been married to him?"

"To Edmund?"

"Before he went off," he said. "You don't have to tell me if you don't want."

"It's all right." Jane watched the little spear of flame in the glass globe. "It was just three months. We had a lovely, lovely time." She smiled reflectively. She raised her eyes at him then smiled at her hands, twisting the wedding band around her finger. "Edmund so wanted to be married before he went off to war. Thought I might run off with some Tom, Dick, or Harry, I think. Eddie was a touch jealous." She laughed to herself. "Silly goose. I don't even know a Tom, Dick, or Harry."

Billy was mesmerized by the shadowy fingers brushing the candlelight into the soft hollows of her cheeks and across her brow.

She took a sip of coffee and cleared her throat. "Tell me about Montana," she said, her voice changing the mood.

"Montana? What's to tell? Rivers and mountains—sky bigger'n all Texas."

"Mountains?"

"The Rockies." He gestured with his hand. "Mountains so high they push through the sky and knock against the floor of heaven."

"It sounds so wild and unfettered."

"It's wild all right. Was he the pilot?"

"The pilot?"

"Your husband. Was he the pilot of the Lancaster?"

"Heavens, no," she laughed softly. "Edmund was terribly afraid of flying."

"I don't get it."

"Seems a bit ironic, doesn't it? He could have gone into the army."

"Why didn't he?"

"He thought he might be stationed at one of the local bases if he were in the air force. We could spend his leaves together. He really was frightened of flying."

"He sounds like a swell guy."

"He was."

Billy looked at her.

"Edmund is dead," she said. "I know it. I've known it for some time."

Billy looked down at the table.

"I should like to see the mountains," she said, brightening artificially. It was an attempt to clean the slate of gloomy conversation, Billy knew, and he let her clean it. "I've only seen them in books and magazines," she said, brightly moving on. "We don't have mountains in East Anglia. Everything is flat here in the fens. It was mostly underwater at one time, you know?"

"No, I didn't know."

"We can thank the Romans for putting us high and dry. Dug canals everywhere. Marvellous engineers, the Romans."

"They were some pretty tough soldiers too," Billy said.

"Tell me about your family," she urged.

He folded his hands around the cup and looked at her. "I'd rather talk about you."

Jane saw the dangerous flash of blue in his eyes and looked down at her hands.

"I have two brothers and a sister," he answered quickly. "Older brother named Ty—that's short for Tyler. And a runt brother named Trout."

She looked at him. "I beg your pardon? Trout? What an odd name for a boy."

"Short for Joseph Otto."

"I see," she smiled. "And your sister?"

"Jenny," he said. "She's got a little girl named Grace—I call her Little Bit. Cutest little bug you ever saw."

"You're a sweet," she said.

He glanced up at the band platform as the men stood up for a clarinet riff. Jane watched him as he told her about the ranch in Montana, watched his hands, the strong line of his jaw, saw the way his pale blue eyes lit up when his words took him away somewhere. She could not look at them for any length of time but only in furtive darts. "It all sounds so fascinating," she said. "Real Indians . . . the mountains . . . cattle ranching."

"I never thought of ranching as fascinating," he said. "Backbreaking— yes. I'll have to chew on fascinating a while." He sipped his coffee.

"And everyone lives on the ranch?"

"Sure, except Tyler and Kate. Kate's his wife. They're in Chicago. Ty's studying for the ministry."

"Really? The ministry?"

"At least one of us made good." He finished his coffee, and he was finished talking about himself. "This must be getting long in the tooth."

"No, it's not, really."

"There's not much more to tell," he said. "We've got a couple Labs. Twelve hundred or so head of stock. String of horses . . . some chickens and pigs."

"No one else?"

Billy looked at her. "You mean like a girl or something?"

"Or something."

He grunted. For some reason the first thought in his mind was not of Laura Miller but of Colette. But she was gone too, he thought. Gone for keeps. "No," he said. "No girls waiting under the apple tree for Billy Boy."

"You sound bitter."

"No reason to be," he said. "You play the hand you're dealt. You don't want to talk about this."

"Just making conversation," she said.

Billy looked across the table at her. Her eyes sparkled in the wavering candlelight, and the light and shadows played softly on her face. She was very pretty, the fresh-skinned kind of beauty that didn't need makeup to accent it. He felt a lump in his throat again. "You sure you don't want to dance?"

"No, thank you."

"Sure?"

"Positive."

He continued staring at her. "You're the prettiest girl in the place," he blurted. "I mean it."

She returned his gaze a moment before looking across the dance floor. He didn't know if he had offended her or if she had just gone off collecting her thoughts. She was a fragile one, he thought, brittle as a china doll.

"It's getting late," she said, coming back from wherever she'd been. "I really must be going." She stood up.

Billy held her chair. "I've done it again, haven't I?"

"You've been a dear," she said, not looking at him. She started to clear away the coffee cups.

"Hey, don't worry about that," he said, setting the cups back on the table. "Uncle Sam'll bus the dishes tonight." He shoved his hands in his pockets.

Jane looked around the dance floor. Things had thinned out a bit.

"What about your friend?" he asked. "Won't she need a ride?"

There was no sign of Julie. "She's a big girl," she said, glancing at him then looking away. "She knows her way home."

Billy walked Jane out to the car and opened the driver's door for her. Neither of them said anything as he watched the moon playing over her face, her eyes, her lips. "I had a swell time," he said.

She looked quickly at him. "Yes, it was lovely." She smiled, then slipped into the car.

He closed the door and looked through the open window. "May I see you sometime?" he asked. He saw a change go over her face. "I'm sorry," he apologized. "There I go again bein' clumsy."

She looked up at him. "It's the war that's clumsy," she said. "You're not so very clumsy at all."

It was more than she intended to say, Billy could see on her face. "You haven't seen me dance."

He watched her drive away in the Talbot, the taillights of the car moving away from him like tracers jiggling off into the dark after some unseen target. He felt a sudden hollowness spread through him.

He took a deep breath and looked up at the stars peeking through the cold, dark, scudding clouds. Then he glanced across the base at the moon showing through the trees of Tealbrook Wood. He looked back down the road Jane had taken, then found his bicycle.

Pedaling slowly away from the hangar, he could hear the song "Don't Sit under the Apple Tree" playing—suddenly louder, then quieter, as someone opened and closed the door—then it grew quieter, and quieter still until he heard only the grating of crickets and some frogs. It was silent then, the silence of night cloaking all around him, and all he heard was the lonely rattle of the bicycle chain.

The hut was quiet when Billy entered. He stood for a moment inside the door, in the silence that whined in his ears, allowing his eyes to adjust from the moonlight to the blackness of the hut, allowing his outside thoughts to adapt to their new surroundings. They came trailing in one at a time.

He did not turn on the light; that would have been too startling, too harsh a transition for his mood. No one was back from the dance yet, he saw now; it was early still, relatively speaking. He added some chunks of coal to the barely glowing bed in the stove. Then he kicked off his shoes and lay on his bed with his hands behind his head on the pillow. He stared at the curvature of the ceiling, and one by one the images of a thousand girls began to emerge from the shadows: Betty Grable, Greta Garbo, Marlene Dietrich . . . Rita Hayworth.

He was thinking of Jane Worthing but didn't quite know what to think or what to make of her. She was certainly pretty, he admitted, as pretty and fresh-skinned as they come. He liked the way she talked, the lilting rise and fall of her words—how she would lower her eyes when he'd ask her a question about herself. Everything about her was lovely. She was complex though, not like any girl he'd ever been with, and everything in his gut told him to leave her be. Men don't play with dolls, the rational side of him admonished, especially dolls made of porcelain. He would leave her be. But the hungry, male, lonely part of him gave him an argument. During the argument he lay, hands behind his head, fingers interlaced, staring up at the picture of Rita Hayworth.

The fire in the stove began to roar, gleaming through the vents.

Then, even though he was thinking of Jane, wanting to be with her and not wanting her, the face of the French girl rose to trouble him, like a spirit rising from the grave—beautiful raven-haired Colette, lovely, haunting, mysterious Colette, who had found that secret place in his heart, soul, or mind, that no woman had ever touched before. His pulse quickened.

"Leave me alone," he said.

"No," she whispered.

"Please."

But she would not leave him alone. He rolled over onto his side and blinked into the wall of darkness. In the living quiet and blackness of the Nissen hut, in the brutal loneliness that hollowed him out so that there was nothing left in him but the twisting pang of love hunger, he was strangely reminded of his forgotten vow to God. *Anything, God. You name it.*

A shudder went through him, and he groaned, "Won't you just leave me alone."

ॐ

Bathed in the soft glow of the little table lamp, Jane looked at herself in the wardrobe mirror. She studied the lines of her face, then, angling herself to catch a favorable light, glanced over her figure. She stood, gazing at herself for a long time, twisting her wedding band slowly round and round her third finger. She looked down at the picture of her husband on the nightstand. He was smiling up at her in his RAF uniform, his eyes locked in place and following her every action.

"He's really a nice boy," she said. "Not at all like the other Yanks. A bit rough around the edges, perhaps, but he's kind." Just then she saw the dangerous blue of his eyes flash through her mind. She shook her head.

"Oh, Edmund," she sighed, picking up the picture of her husband. "My dear, dear Edmund, whatever am I to do?" She could scarcely speak. "I'm so desperately lonely without you."

A tear fell from one of her eyes, and then the other, then both of them. She set the picture on the stand, then, surrounded by dolls and ribbons and the trappings of an adolescent girl, she lay down on the bed, her face buried into the pillow, and wept.

24 ★★★

Jane Worthing placed the shears at the base of the rose branch and snipped it off. She dropped the clipping in a little pile behind her. Then, scooting around sideways on her knees, she snipped another branch, and then another, pruning back the bush for winter until it looked naked and pathetic, like the image of herself in the wardrobe mirror. Standing up, she glanced down the narrow dirt and gravel road that wound up through the countryside to their house. The sky was mostly cloudy over the town, with patchy bits of blue showing here and there. Towering cumulonimbus clouds bullied the sea cliffs in the other direction.

Wearing a colorless pair of corduroy coveralls, one of her father's old billowing shirts, her brother's Wellington boots, and a drab red scarf tied over her hair, she hid her beauty well. She removed a gardening glove and shoved a wisp of hair back up under her scarf, then moved over to the next rosebush and continued working her way up the walk.

She looked up suddenly, a look of startled wonder on her face, as though someone had whispered behind her ear. She stared out over the bleak and barren countryside for several moments, lost in wide-eyed fantasy, her lower lip slightly agape and trembling. Then just as suddenly she frowned and shook it off.

She compressed her lips with grim determination and clipped another branch. She tossed the clipping carelessly to the side, then all at once, with everything changing on her face, she sat back onto her legs and again looked off into the distance at the low line of the horizon. Her shoulders eased resignedly as her body settled into wistful repose.

Over the past few days since the dance she had busied herself with distractions: digging out the beds, planting the winter flowers, working late at the bank, sundry odds and ends around the house that she'd been putting off. Still, no matter how she applied herself to industry, she couldn't escape the ambushing thoughts of Billy Hochreiter. He was so full of life, so unfettered, like a rush of wind up the sea cliffs that took her breath. Every thought of him—the way he moved, the way he laughed, the piercing look in his blue eyes that seemed to look right through her—caused her to stop whatever she was doing and look off in a wonder gaze. Because of it she had determined never to see him again.

"Oh, bother," she said, breaking free of her reverie. She looked down at the forgotten shears in her hand, worked them open and closed, then, summoning a battered resolve, finished her work. She collected the trimmings, carried them out back to be burned, then went upstairs to her room and cleaned up.

Anna brought her up a cup of tea and two cookies, each with a dollop of jam. "Thought you might like a little refreshment," she said. "You've been working so hard."

"Thank you," Jane said.

The plump woman smiled at her thoughtfully, glanced around the room, shook her head, then closed the door behind her.

Jane sat down at her small writing desk. She set the cup of tea and cookies on the right top corner of the desk and touched a cookie into place along the saucer. Then she pulled out her stationery from the top drawer, arranged her bottle of ink and pen, selected a piece of stationery, and smoothed her hand over the texture of the paper. It felt clean and secure-feeling. She took a bite of cookie, a sip of tea, then, angling the paper just so, pondered a choice of words and began to write.

Finishing the letter, Jane signed her name, added a postscript, then dabbed a blotter over the ink and folded it into an envelope. She set it on top of a small stack of letters piled neatly on the top left corner of the desk. A bit of sun fell through the window, splashing yellow warmth over the desk. She raised her face to it and smiled as she felt its rejuvenating rays over her skin. Looking down the road going along in front of the house, a movement caught her eyes; it was bright red, and she saw that it was Julie pedaling her bicycle. *Where's she been hiding herself?* she wondered.

She heard Anna at the front door, followed by a clatter of feet up the stairs, and moments later Julie burst into the room. "Jane, you'll never guess!"

Jane swung around in her chair. "Where have you been?"

Julie put her left hand up to her cheek, turned one way, and then the other. "Notice anything different about me?"

Jane eyed her hair, her dress, her shoes.

"No, silly," Julie said, twiddling the fingers on her cheek. "Look!" She came closer and held out her hand, poising it daintily in front of Jane's eyes. The light coming through the window charged the little chip of stone on her third finger with fire.

Jane took her hand. "Julie!"

Julie beamed. "It's a diamond!"

"It's beautiful," Jane said. "Where on earth . . . ?" She trailed off and looked up at her friend, puzzled. "Julie, what have you done?"

"I've gotten engaged!" Julie squealed, twirling with excitement. "Isn't it wonderful?"

Jane laughed, waving a deprecating hand. Then a look of disbelief swept over her face. "You're serious."

"I keep pinching myself to be sure I'm not dreaming." Julie chuckled. "Oh, Jane, I'm so excited I could just burst!"

Jane gaped at her. "You're really getting married?"

"I'm really getting married."

"But who, Julie? Who? I mean, this is absolutely—"

"Wonderful!" Julie said. "He's the most extraordinary man I've ever met!"

"But who? Who is?"

Julie put her hands to her face. "Why, *Thomas*, silly."

"Thomas?"

"The man I was dancing with the other night."

Jane frowned at her skeptically. "You were dancing with a tall American the other night."

Julie clasped her hands to her bosom. "Isn't he gorgeous!?"

Jane stared at her as though she had lost her senses.

Julie sat down on the edge of the bed, held out her left hand, and admired the ring. Then at once she got all dreamy-eyed. "Mrs. Thomas Huntington. It has such an American ring to it, don't you think, Jane?"

Jane wrinkled her nose. "Our history teacher was named Huntington, don't you remember? Attila the *Hun*-tington. Scourge of fourth form."

"Yes. Isn't it a lovely name?"

"Yes, lovely. So American." Jane looked at her soberly. "It's all so sudden, don't you think, dear?"

Julie chuckled. "It *is* a bit of a whirl, isn't it?"

"But Julie, he's an American. Have you given any consideration to that? He lives in America."

"Well, of course he lives in America, silly," Julie said. "He's an American, isn't he?"

"Then you would leave England?"

"I would live wherever my husband lives of course."

Jane pondered this for a moment. "Yes, yes, of course." She looked at her friend. "Julie. What do you really know about him? You've only known him—what—three days?"

"I know that I love him," Julie said seriously. "I know that he's kind, and witty—handsome, of course—and I know that he simply *adores* me."

"And his family?"

"There are no murderers or highwaymen in the lot, if that's what you're hinting at," Julie assured her. Then added seriously: "They're Methodists."

Jane scrunched her nose.

"Tom's told me all about them," Julie went on. "Said they're an upstanding family—pillars in the community—that have owned a textile mill in Beufort, South Carolina, since before the War between the States."

Jane blinked at her. "Where in the world is Beufort, South Carolina?"

"I'm not quite sure," Julie shrugged. "Somewhere in the South, I should think."

"That would figure."

Julie stood up and ran her fingers along the lace canopy over Jane's bed. "Soft ocean breezes rustling through palmetto leaves," she said. "Shrimp boats chugging up the sound, everyone talking with a Southern drawl and smiling all the time. It all sounds so lovely to hear Tom describe it."

She struck a theatrical pose against the bedpost. "I shall be a Southern belle, like Scarlett O'Hara, with garlands of magnolia blossoms draped all about me." She giggled. "Oh, Jane, we shall have the most wonderful—" She broke off. "Jane? Is something the matter?"

When Jane met her eyes, her own were glistening. "I, I don't quite know what to say," she said. A smile burst upon her face. "You're getting married! My best friend is getting married and going off to America!"

Julie looked at her expectantly.

"I couldn't be happier for you."

"Really? Oh, Jane, I do so want you to approve. Once you meet Tom I'm sure you'll know why I love him so."

Jane jumped to her feet. "Come here, you little fool," she laughed. "I shall miss you terribly." They hugged and cried and laughed, and for the longest time they talked of all the wonderful things girls talk about when they fall in love. Finally, the two of them went outside, hugged, and Julie pedaled away on her bicycle, waving back at her.

Jane stood in the middle of the road, watching her until she disappeared around a bend of trees. She waved one last time, then let her hand fall slowly, guiding it into the sheath of the other one.

She felt suddenly very much alone. The sky had changed color since she had last taken note of it; everything was darker now in the early, red dusk of the afternoon, the air bright and tart-smelling.

"Oy, Jane!"

Looking behind her, she saw her brother Robert walking up the road with a neighbor friend, both of them coming home from school in dark blue blazers and gray trousers, swinging their book satchels at one another. Robert's shirttail was hanging out of his trousers, and his cap was pushed back off a mop of hair. She shook her head, waved, and returned his greeting. Then she saw her father driving up behind the boys in the Talbot. She waved at him too, then went back into the house.

Upstairs in her room she shut the door behind her and stood with her back against the door. She stared into the room at nothing while gathering the quiet solitude around her shoulders like a shawl, thinking of Julie—of Mrs. Thomas Huntington, Southern belle—dancing and twirling on the clouds of folly. She tried to picture the tall American she had seen her with at the dance but couldn't. She just couldn't. Everything of the dance was a blur, whirled away in a wisp of thought smoke.

"Oh, Julie, what have you done?"

She went over to the desk and tidied up her stationery, putting everything away in the top desk drawer. She collected the neat little stack of letters and looked down at them. A thought occurred to her that she held in her hands the sum of her life, that everything of her world was folded neatly away and sealed in little envelopes, a tuppenny stamp on each one. Most of her friends had moved away, the war carrying them off to different parts of the country to be near their husbands. Only Julie was left, and now she was going off to America. To Beufort, South Carolina. It sounded so far away. So foreign. So remote.

"Oh, Julie."

She took a deep breath and sighed, wiped a tear from her eyes, and a shiver of terror pimpled over her arms. As she rubbed her arms her eyes went to the dolls peering dully at her from the shelves around her bed. Her eyes next moved to the multicolored ribbons tonguing over the ledge, to the knickknacks and trappings of a thirteen-year-old girl that crowded the walls and shelves, everything arranged neatly and kept tidily in its place. Her brows knit together into a scowl.

Going up into the attic, she rummaged around for some empty boxes, found three, then returned to her room and began to clear away the shelves: first the dolls, then the knickknacks, then the painting of the little girl leading the gaggle of ducks. She took the photograph of her winning the equestrian event off the wall, looked thoughtfully at it and smiled, frowned, then put it carefully into the box. She turned a scrutinizing eye on the lacy canopy over her bed and the matching curtains, as though seeing them for the first time. Her lips pursed in thought.

Everything went in a flurry of resolve: the canopy, the matching bedspread and pillow cases, the schoolgirl shoes and clothes in the wardrobe. The room was stripped bare, pruned back for winter. Only the lace curtains over the window and Edmund remained, the latter smiling perpetually at her and following her every action with lifeless, two-dimensional eyes.

As she removed the curtain rod from its brackets, she stopped suddenly and looked out the window with a look of bewilderment blooming on her face. She frowned, her lips compressing grimly as she fought hard against it. She tore the curtains off the rod, piled the untidy mess on top of the desk, and swore softly to herself. Everything gradually changed on her face, with the taut corners of her mouth loosening the steady resolve in her features. Something gave way deep inside her. Something surrendered.

Her body settled into the chair resignedly, her hands cradling the heavy weight of her chin as she gazed out upon the dark line of the horizon.

"Oh, bother."

25 ★★★

The Thunderbolts of Foxworth Blue Flight came in low from the east, wheeled into the wind, then touched down on the Halesbury airstrip, one after the other. The four planes rumbled down the strip, then taxied off toward the hangars, their big engines popping throatily. The crews rushed to each plane.

Killing the engine, Billy climbed out of his cockpit onto the wing, and immediately inspected the fuselage of his plane. He put his finger into a wicked-looking hole just behind the cockpit. There were several more holes perforating the fuselage and rudder, spreading across its length in a wavy line. He shook his head in amazement.

His crew chief—a thin, short, balding man in his early thirties—came over to the plane, and whistled up at the fuselage. "Looks like you got tagged pretty good, Lieutenant."

Billy looked down at the man and grinned. "You should see the other guy."

"One less Kraut to Sieg Heil?"

"I don't know about that," Billy said. "But you'd need a metal detector to find what's left of his kite."

"109?"

"FW–190."

The crew chief examined the holes. "Those twenty millimeters can sure chew up a good airplane."

"They can chew up a good pilot pretty good too."

"Yeah," the crew chief said with a wry grin. "But you guys don't cost the taxpayers no hundred-plus."

"Thanks. I'll remember that."

Joe Thompson came over to Billy's plane. "Way to go, Montana. That was some flying up there."

Billy climbed down off the wing.

"Thought he'd punched your meal ticket," Joe grinned. He looked at the fuselage and whistled. "Somebody upstairs must be looking out for your sorry hide. Another foot to the left and you'd be checking out a harp from Saint Peter."

"No harps for me just yet."

"That was sure some slick maneuver," Joe said. "He had you dead to rights."

"Yeah, but he's walking now, isn't he?"

"Goose-stepping, you mean," the crew chief put in.

The rest of the ground crew began turning the tail of the aircraft. Billy and Joe stepped out of their way and started toward their bicycles. "Can't wait to see the footage."

An image of the Focke-Wulf 190 shot through Billy's mind, twirling away from him, after the German had jumped out of the clouds with the burst of 20 mm cannon that tore through his aircraft. Billy had turned hard left rudder into a corkscrew when he saw the tracers rifling past his canopy as though they were caught with a fast-action camera. Then he heard the roar of the FW–190 overshooting him and cutting in front of Joe Thompson. Joe had fired a burst and drawn a wisp of white smoke from the 190's engine, but his guns jammed, and he was out of the chase. It was cat and mouse from then on between Billy and the German, with some fancy flying, until Billy got him in his sights and squeezed off three quick bursts. The 190 exploded and he watched the pilot fall free of the wreckage, tumbling, then the chute eventually opening.

"How will they mark it?" Billy asked.

"I just bloodied his nose," Joe said. "You came in with the knockout. I sure won't worry about you on my tail anymore."

"I like it when you worry about me," Billy grinned.

They watched as Yellow Flight made their landing approach. There were only three planes, Billy saw; Jim Cooly's was missing. The Thunderbolts looked big and clumsy again as they came in, flaps down. The noise of their engines was deafening.

"Anybody see Cooly go down?" Billy shouted over the throaty rumble.

"Don't know," Joe said. "We'll find out soon enough. Poor devil."

"Hope he made it." Billy remembered France for a moment. It all seemed like such a roll of the dice—sevens you live, snake-eyes you die. He felt a drop of rain on his head. He looked up at the sky, holding out his hand. "Looks like we're in for a gully-washer."

Joe scanned the heavy dark clouds. "Maybe we can catch up on some sack time."

"I'm for that."

They reached their bicycles, Pete Skagway and Warren Turlock joining them from their planes; then they all pedaled over to the debriefing hut, as White and Red Flights came in low over the trees.

࿔

As it turned out, Colonel Zeb Pilke had followed Jim Cooly to the deck, buzzed the area for German patrols, but didn't see any. The last he saw of Cooly he was running toward a farmhouse about a mile from where he had ditched his chute. The Maquis would pick him up if he was lucky. Wilfred Suggs wasn't so lucky. His fuel tank had been hit. Bug Mallory told him to ditch into the channel. Sugar said that he was going to try and make it back to England, said he was going to lean out the mixture, that he had enough gas, that he had done it before and had made it okay. But he crashed into the rocks along the coast. No one had seen a chute. Zeb said it was stupid. It was a needless death, and it took the shine off Billy's second victory.

Billy pedaled back to his hut, trying to picture Sugar Suggs's pretty-boy face. He remembered seeing him at breakfast, remembered loaning him five bucks for a stake in a card game the night before. Now he was dead. Ran out of gas. He should have ditched. It was stupid. It was so stupid. There was no roll of the dice in that one.

He went into the hut, got his things, went over to the latrine and showered. When he returned there were two letters on his bed. He picked them up and read the return addresses; one was from his brother, Tyler, in Chicago, and the other one was from Jane Worthing. He stared at the return address of the second one: Jane Worthing, Gull Roost Cottage, Southwold, Suffolk.

He tore it open and read it through quickly. He read it a second time, slower, sitting down gradually on the edge of his bed. He looked up from the letter.

࿔

At noon the following day, Billy pedaled up to a small two-story Tudor cottage about three miles outside of town. The letters were weathered, but he could just make out the name *Gull Roost* painted down the gatepost. *This must be the place,* he thought.

A boy's face appeared in the bay window.

Billy leaned his bike against the hedge and looked intently at the cottage now, feeling the significance of his visit rising in his chest with a flutter of butterflies no less violent than his preflight jitters.

He pushed through the gate and on up the walkway and, taking a deep breath, knocked on the front door. Moments later he was greeted by the boy in the window.

"I'm here to see Jane Worthing," Billy said.

The boy looked him over skeptically.

"This is the Bellamy house, ain't it?" Billy asked. "Gull Roost Cottage?"

"You the Yank?"

Billy grinned wolfishly. "I'm the Yank."

"I'll see if she's in," the boy said, then closed the door, leaving Billy standing on the stoop, a little perplexed, the grin sliding limply off his face, the butterflies flown. He turned around and looked at the hedgerows dividing the countryside into a green and brown checkerboard, looked up at the threatening sky, read the name *Bellamy* over the mail slot on the door, and waited.

He looked back at the front gate, still waiting. He looked down at the brass buttons on his overcoat, down at his feet, rocked back on his heels to examine his toes, rocked back and forth, holding a small bouquet of flowers behind his back, still waiting.

He was about to knock on the door a second time when he saw the boy's face again in the window, peering around the curtains with an impish grin. Billy nodded, forced a smile, and decided he didn't like the kid one bit. Then he heard a woman's angry voice, muffled, but drawing closer. Then the door opened and there was Jane. She looked a bit flustered, a bit out of breath, a wild, uncomposed smile forcing its way to her face.

"Please forgive my little twit brother," she said, collecting her breath. "Do come in, won't you?"

"Thanks."

There was a moment of uncertainty between them. Neither of them knew what to say, and it was awkward standing in the foyer, knowing they were on the brink of something, or nothing.

"Here—" he said. "These are for you." He handed her the flowers.

"Aren't you sweet," she said, touching a twist of hair into place at her temple. "Thank you."

"There's not much else in season," he apologized.

"They're lovely. Do come in."

Billy entered the house and took off his hat. He looked around, noticed the shotgun in the corner, the quaint English furnishings, the smell of pipe tobacco, and the something uniquely British that cannot be described without the aid of the senses. "Nice place."

"It's home."

Yes, it was home, Billy thought, again glancing over the furnishings. There was no other word for it than home. But it was she who made it home. Gull Roost Cottage was incomplete without Jane Worthing. She completed the picture. He felt the warm, secure, complete English hominess of the cottage and of Jane as he looked her over without seeming to.

She was wearing a brown woolen skirt and a cream-colored sweater over a white linen shirt with a Peter Pan collar. Her thick auburn hair was pinned up with barrettes, waving down the sides of her face and spilling down behind her shoulders. Her blue eyes were alive with emotion, darting wildly about his face, too wild to capture with his steady, unblinking gaze. He felt the cords in his throat thicken. He wanted to say something but couldn't, wanted to say that she was beautiful, more beautiful than Rita Hayworth could ever hope to look.

"You look terrific," he said.

"Thank you," she demurred. She looked down at his trousers.

He followed her eyes. "Oh, this!" He pulled the bicycle clip from his ankle and held it out to look at it. "Swell gadgets these."

She smiled at him. "They *are* useful, aren't they?"

He slipped the clip into his coat pocket.

There was a sudden ruckus in the hall, as though a large bovine creature were being goaded along a cattle chute. Billy looked beyond Jane as a thickly built man swung around the corner into the entryway, his eyes—like the boy's—blazing with mischief.

Seeing Billy, Mr. Bellamy threw his arms wide and boomed, "So this is the chap I've been hearing so much about!"

Jane turned bright red.

"Pleased to meet you, Mr. Bellamy," Billy said, shaking his hand, his mind assessing and recording this last bit of information.

"Martin. Call me Martin. Mr. Bellamy died ten years past, God rest his soul. Here, let me take your coat and hat."

Billy doffed his overcoat and handed it to the man.

"Robert! Where's Robert?" Mr. Bellamy thundered, looking up the stairs. "ROBERT!" The boy appeared from behind him. "Ah, there you are!" He took hold of the boy by the scruff of the neck. "Sneaking up on me, are you? Here—take this chap's coat and hat. There's a lad."

Robert hung the coat on a peg by the door and placed the hat over it.

"There's a bar of chocolate in the right pocket," Billy said to the boy. Robert fished around and found it.

"Ta, Yank!" he hooted as he went crashing into the dining room down the hall.

Mr. Bellamy turned to Billy. "It's a bit frightful outside, what?"

"You said it," Billy said. "It was coming down pretty hard this morning."

"I expect they'll ground you chaps 'til it tidies up a bit."

"Won't be for about a week."

Mr. Bellamy winked at his daughter. "Now there's a bit of luck, what?"

Jane glared at him.

Mr. Bellamy turned to Billy. "Come on in, lad; let me take a look at you in the light."

Jane grimaced. "Really, Dad."

"You're a fine-looking lad," Mr. Bellamy grinned appreciatively. "Isn't he a fine-looking lad, Jane?"

Jane looked down at the flowers.

Mr. Bellamy took Billy by the arm and led him toward the dining room. "Come meet the missus," he said. Then he howled, "Great heavens, Jane! Have you felt his arms?"

"Dad, really!"

Billy looked over his shoulder at Jane. She looked destroyed.

Mrs. Bellamy rose to her feet as they entered the room. She stood with much dignity, her angular face arched imperiously, as though she were about to make a royal pronouncement. She was certainly a handsome woman, Billy observed. Her silver hair was pulled up onto her head in an elegant roll, and she wore a gray dress with a white bodice that buttoned to her neck, with a Wedgwood cameo fastened to it. Billy got the feeling he should bow or something.

"Hello, ma'am," he smiled.

Mrs. Bellamy's eyes went quickly to her husband, a smile brittling on her face, then back to Billy. "Won't you please come in—William, is it?" she wondered. "Or is it just Billy?"

"Billy, ma'am." He chuckled. "Shoot! Only my ma and God call me William."

Robert looked up from his chocolate and laughed.

Mr. Bellamy roared.

A bit of color rose into Mrs. Bellamy's pale cheeks as she glanced sternly from her son to her husband. "Yes, I'm sure," she smiled uncertainly. "Jane says you're from Montana?"

"Yes, ma'am. My folks own a spread just south of Columbus. Run Herefords and Shorthorns. Run horses too." He barked out a laugh. "Shoot. My grandad used to run whiskey down from Canada until the Mounties got wind of him."

Mr. Bellamy roared.

"Isn't that nice," Mrs. Bellamy smiled, then, looking at her husband, said, "Shall we, Martin?"

Martin cleared his throat. They all sat down. Mr. Bellamy kicked Jane's foot under the table and winked. Jane shot him a scowl. Anna brought the rest of the lunch, eyeing Billy as she passed behind him. She winked furtively at Jane. Jane refused to acknowledge her or the rest of the winking.

It rained during the meal. After lunch, Jane and Billy went outside and walked to the front gate. The rain had let up and looked like it might hold for a while. Billy glanced back at the house and the boy was staring at him from the dining room window.

Jane smiled. "Robert thinks you're a—how did he put it? A swell Yank."

"He's swell by me too," Billy said. He waited until they were out of earshot. "I don't think your mother likes me though."

Jane raised her eyebrows. "She adores you."

"You think so? I don't think that comment about my grandad went over too well."

"We might have done without that," Jane admitted. "Dad, of course, thinks you're simply marvellous. He'll want to take you hunting, I suppose."

Billy perked. "Hunting?"

"Father loves his hunting. He'll want to impress you with his shooting. He's a wonderful wing shot."

"That'd be swell."

"You don't play golf, do you?"

"Never once."

"Pity."

They walked up the narrow paved road that was dotted with gorse and blackberry bushes spilling out here and there. Billy folded his arms behind his back. Jane's were folded behind her back as well. She was watching for puddles and swinging wide of them. Billy was looking up at the sky and around at the countryside. The clouds were low and gathered in a thick bank against the flat horizon. Thunder rumbled threateningly.

"This is swell country," he said. "I can't get over how green everything is."

Jane looked up at him. "What's that? Yes, isn't it?"

"We don't have that color in the States."

"That's one for the English, isn't it?" She smiled at him. "Tell me, how is your family? Have you heard from them?"

"Funny you should ask," he said. "I just got a letter from my brother yesterday."

"Really? From the minister?"

"His wife's expecting their second baby."

Jane looked at him. "Isn't that marvellous!" She looked off into the distance, musing. "So life goes on."

Billy looked at her.

"Oh. I was just thinking how flowers bloom in the most unlikely places—the war and all." She watched for puddles. "I suppose it's just God keeping the checks and balances."

"That's one way of looking at it."

She looked at him. "Is there another way?"

Billy shrugged.

"I can see that your brother has his work cut out for him," she said.

"We don't talk religion much."

"You're not an atheist, are you? Heaven forbid I should be walking next to an atheist with a storm threatening."

"I'm not an atheist," Billy insisted. "I believe in God. I just don't think God believes in me anymore."

"That sounds silly, God not believing in you. I say, you are lacking a bit in your catechism."

Billy looked off into the distance.

They didn't talk about it anymore. They continued on the narrow, pot-holed road past a few houses and hedgerows, and then past smaller cottages, arms folded behind their backs. About a mile up the road they turned left onto a footpath that wound away to the low bluffs overlooking the North Sea. Bits of wet grass and leaves stuck to Billy's trousers and shoes.

The sea was slate gray and cold looking, and there were whitecaps on the water. Small fishing trawlers worked along the coast with an orchestration of gulls floating and diving off their sterns. To the south they could just see the grayed and sloping promontory of Southwold, the lighthouse, and the small beach cabins nestled among the dunes that were closed up for the winter. There were a few men spread along the beach fishing.

"I'd like to try that sometime," Billy said.

"Really?"

"All I've ever done is trout fish."

"You'll have to try it sometime then, won't you?"

He looked at her. "Sure. Why not? Do you fish?"

"Sometimes." She looked out over the sea.

Billy took a breath of cleansing air. The wind, full of moisture and the smell of salt, came rushing up the cliffs and smacked him in the face. Below them was the shingly beach with the waves breaking against the rocks and sending up spumes of white foam and spray, with loud boomings and the hiss of water on the rocks. There were some gulls working the bluffs, and below, skittering after the foam, were curve-billed curlews and terns spiking the sand for small crabs.

Billy looked over at Jane. The wind was pulling her hair back away from her face, and the way it struck her face made it look as though she were gulping for breath. She drew her sweater over her shoulders and folded her arms in front of her.

"Thanks for inviting me over today," he said over the wind. "I've had a swell time."

She turned to him, and her hair lay flat against the wind, with some of the strands of hair whipping across her face. "It has been lovely, hasn't it?"

"I like your family."

She smiled at him, then looked quickly away at the sea.

"Jane?"

Jane gazed intently at the sea. "When I was a little girl I used to think the world dropped off just beyond the horizon."

"Jane?"

"I'd watch the fishing boats sail over the horizon and wonder if they would ever come back. Sounds silly, doesn't it?" She laughed to herself. "I could never wait long enough to find out."

"Jane?"

She looked at him suddenly, a look of fear and perplexity and something altogether woman pulling recklessly at her eyes through the strands of wildly blowing hair. "Please go slowly, William," she said, the wind ducking suddenly so that he could hear a whisper. "Please. I fear I shall lose my footing."

"I don't know what to make of this either," he said. "I'm kind of mixed up too."

She continued looking at him.

He could see the desperate look in her eyes, the fear and the hungering loneliness and the hope of rescue all mixed together, that were a reflection of his own soul. "You're beautiful, Jane," he said earnestly. He took her hand, put his arms around her, and pulled her close. He felt her shivering as she lay her head against his shoulder. They both looked out over the cliffs at the rushing tempest of the North Sea.

"Oh, Billy. This is ever so difficult for me."

"I'll hold you like a china doll," he said.

She looked up at him. "Will you?"

He smiled at her, wiped a wind-swept tear away from her cheek, and held her close. They stared out at the sea a long while.

26 ★★★

ovember 13, 1943. Headquarters Building, Office of General Olbricht, *Chief of the General Army.* Rolf was admitted into General Olbricht's office by an adjutant. In the spacious office the shades were drawn over two of the three windows, casting everything in shadows. A blade of afternoon sun lanced through the third window and cut the room in two, separating the shadows on either side. It took a moment for Rolf's eyes to adjust to the darkness, coming from the brightly lit anteroom of the adjutant.

General Olbricht was sitting behind his desk, writing. He looked up as Rolf entered his office and stood before the desk.

There was another man, a lieutenant colonel in the Army, standing next to the unshaded window that looked out upon the Unter den Linden. The blade of sun slashed across his upper torso and left arm, revealing a hand missing two fingers as it rested upon a bronze statue of a German eagle. Rolf saw the black patch covering his left eye. It made him think of Günther Specht, which led him to think of the rest of the men and the goings-on back in Jever; and, thinking of Viktor and of Wilhelmshaven, he felt the kick low in his stomach.

The lieutenant colonel glanced over his shoulder, then turned around to face him with his good eye.

Rolf snapped to attention and saluted with the Nazi salute.

The general glanced at the lieutenant colonel, then back at Rolf. "Heil Hitler," he snapped, his voice thin and seemingly projected from the front of his mouth. "At ease, Captain Schiller."

Rolf stood at ease, folded his arms behind his back, and looked down at the seated general. But he was not at ease. Wariness glinted in his eyes as though he had chanced upon a dangerous water hole in the last light of the day.

General Olbricht was balding and had a small, thin-lipped mouth that befit an accountant more than a military general. He had small, obsidian eyes that peered through round, steel-rimmed spectacles. They made him look very much like Heinrich Himmler.

Rolf distrusted him at once.

Lieutenant Colonel Klaus Phillip, also known as Count von Stauffenberg, the general's chief of staff, on the other hand, gave off a different air. A scion of German nobility, Rolf knew, the count was of a military genius that reached back to the days of Napoleon. He was operations officer with the 10th Panzer Division when the Wehrmacht drove the Americans out of the Kasserine Pass.

General Olbricht peered unblinkingly at Rolf. He reminded Rolf of a rather stodgy owl sitting on its perch, sizing up its next victim. The general twirled the fountain pen between his fingers, apparently receiving some tactile satisfaction as he smoothed his fingers over the thick barrel. He set the pen neatly to the side of his blotter. "I have heard that you are to be awarded the Schwertern in one week's time, Captain Schiller?"

"Yes, General Olbricht."

"Congratulations."

"Thank you, General."

General Olbricht added, "It is an honor for me to meet such a man of valor. It is not often that I meet a true patriot anymore."

Rolf considered his words. "I am only a Luftwaffe pilot doing his duty," he said.

"I see." The general looked at his chief of staff.

Count von Stauffenberg stepped away from the window and smiled, fixing his good eye on Rolf as he passed through the blade of light. He seemed quite personable, Rolf noted, and aside from his disfigurement, he was strikingly handsome.

"The crossed swords will look smart beneath the oak leaves," the count said, holding out his arms like a host greeting a dear guest.

Rolf saw that he was missing his right hand. He nodded respectfully. "Yes, Lieutenant Colonel."

"Come, relax, Captain," the count said brightly. "Enough of this military formality. Won't you sit down?"

"I'm fine standing, Lieutenant Colonel."

"Sit down. Please," the count insisted, gesturing with his partially mutilated left hand.

Rolf sat down in one of the two plush brown leather chairs situated before the desk. The count sat in the other. Rolf's eyes went quickly to the man's right arm.

"This?" the count said, glancing down at it. He chuckled. "A sacrifice to the Kasserine Pass."

"It was a great victory," Rolf said.

The count smiled. "Victory. The Americans have since made us pay dearly for such victories, haven't they?"

Rolf, not sure of his tone, adjusted his seating, glancing at his surroundings with just his eyes. The room was large, the floor carpeted in red, not at all ostentatious. A large Nazi flag filled the left wall behind the general's desk, a picture of Hitler hung on the wall facing him, and the statue of the eagle gleamed in the window. The eagle cast a shadow in the sharp wedge of light dividing the room, and it fell over the count's face.

General Olbricht, sitting just inside the shadows, nodded to his chief of staff.

"Would you like coffee, Captain?" the count asked Rolf.

"No, thank you."

"Some other refreshment? A schnapps, perhaps?"

"No, thank you."

"Cognac?"

"It is too early for me yet," Rolf answered respectfully.

"For me too," the count laughed. "I forget that you are a pilot in the Luftwaffe and not in the Wehrmacht."

The general laughed.

Rolf smiled uneasily and settled into his chair. He sensed a change in the room.

General Olbricht picked up his writing pen and, darting a quick look at the count, twirled it between his fingers and asked, "Why have you come to me, Captain?"

Rolf looked at both of the men, then settled on the general. He adjusted himself in his chair. "Helmut Schoenfield said that you were a reasonable man."

The general smiled, thin-lipped at him. "I have never been accused of being a reasonable man," he said to his handsome chief of staff. "That is one for my memoirs, don't you think?"

Count von Stauffenberg smiled, not taking his good eye off the fighter pilot. There was much smiling going on; still, Rolf sensed a current of danger eddying through the room.

The general turned to Rolf. "Ah, yes! The good but exaggerating Helmut Schoenfield." He set the pen down, his face flattening quickly into an expressionless, owl-like stare. "He is your sister's pastor, I believe?"

Rolf hesitated warily.

"You may speak freely, Captain," the count assured him. "The pastor is a friend of ours. He is a good man."

"I wouldn't know, Lieutenant Colonel. I have not met him."

"Did he not arrange this meeting?"

Rolf looked at the general. "Yes, sir. However I spoke with him only on the telephone."

"I see. What is it that I may do for you, Captain?"

Rolf shrugged his eyebrows. He looked at both men. "I do not know exactly, General."

The general barked a high-pitched laugh. "You do not know exactly? Come, come, my captain."

Rolf's gunmetal gray eyes flattened as he rose from his chair. "I see that I am wasting the general's time. With your permission?"

"Sit down, Captain," the general said evenly.

Rolf looked at the man.

"Sit down, Captain."

Count von Stauffenberg nodded at Rolf, gesturing with his left hand. "Please." Rolf sat down and stared at the penholder on the general's desk.

General Olbricht cleared his throat. "I have set aside time for this meeting, Captain," he said, leaning forward into the blade of light that sliced over his desk. "There is no need for theatrics."

"Theatrics?"

The count slapped his armrest. "Let us talk about your citation, Captain!" he said enthusiastically. "It fascinates me."

Rolf looked at him quizzically.

"Is it true that the Führer will personally present you the Schwertern?"

"Yes, Lieutenant Colonel," Rolf nodded. "It is to be a demonstration of goodwill. So the Reich Marshal informed me," he added. "A morale builder for the Luftwaffe."

"We all could use some morale building these days," the count smiled.

"I think our Uncle Hermann could use some building too," the general added, also smiling. "Not to his girth, mind you."

Rolf allowed a smile.

"What an honor this is for you," the general went on. "The Führer."

The smile left Rolf's face. "I do not shoot down enemy planes for honor, General—nor for the Führer," he added. "It is my duty."

"Yes, of course," Count von Stauffenberg interposed. "Your duty. A true patriot must fulfill his duty."

"To one's country."

"Yes," the count agreed. "We all live, or die, for the benefit of the Fatherland."

"Yes," Rolf agreed. He looked down at his hands and grinned. "It is better to live though, I think," he added, attempting some humor.

The count glanced quickly at the general. "Of course. It is better to live."

The general flipped a switch on his desk intercom. "Shultz?"

"Yes, General."

"Three coffees, please."

"Yes, General."

Rolf started to object, but the count touched his arm. "Tell me about your family, Captain," he grinned handsomely, putting Rolf more at ease. "I hear that your sister is most beautiful."

Rolf stared at him evenly.

The count laughed. To the general, he commented, "Just like a brother, eh?" He then addressed Rolf. "She is not married, I trust."

"No."

"Ah!"

"But she is Lutheran," Rolf grinned.

"I see. And I am Roman Catholic. Pity."

From there the conversation wheeled into Rolf's family history: his father's meritorious service during the First World War; his brother's involvement in the Hitler Youth; more about his sister's religious faith. It was all warm and bright in tone. And then the discussion turned to the person of Pastor Schoenfield, a man who, like Dietrich Bonhoeffer, believed Adolf Hitler to be the Antichrist, a worshiper of Satan, and one who must be eliminated for the salvation of the country.

Coffee was brought in by the adjutant. "Cream?" he asked. "No, thank you. Just black," Rolf replied. Each of the men sipped his coffee.

The banter continued through observations of the weather, a brief discussion of the opera and cinema, horses, the arts and literature, then back to religion.

"Are you a man of faith, Captain Schiller?" Count von Stauffenberg asked him.

"A man of faith?"

"Yes, do you believe in Jesus Christ?"

Rolf looked at him.

"It is a simple question, Captain," the count said. "There are no tricks in it. Do you believe in Jesus Christ?"

"Yes, of course," Rolf admitted. "As a man of history."

"Yes, he was certainly a man of history. But more, I think." The count looked up at the ceiling, thinking. "'Greater love hath no man than this, that a man lay down his life for his friends,'" he said. "I have often thought of that verse of Scripture."

Rolf took a sip of coffee, crossed his legs, and set the cup on the saucer. He set the saucer on his knee, noting how the light cast cruel shadows over the network of scars twisting out of the black patch over the count's left eye.

"It is a troubling verse," the count said.

Rolf eyed the man curiously.

"When a man throws himself on a grenade to save the lives of his fellow soldiers, you have it," the count said. "When a pilot draws the enemy planes after himself so that his fellow pilots might escape, there you have it also. There is true love."

Rolf thought about it for a moment.

The count raised his mutilated left hand into the blade of light, gesturing with one of the fingers. "Such an act is the greatest demonstration of love . . . of devotion . . . of valor. Germany needs such men, wouldn't you agree, Captain?"

Rolf felt suddenly uncomfortable. A chill prickled along his spine. There were the old words again, the dangerous words, the words that had raised an army of desperate men from the ashes of defeated Germany and marched them off to war.

"Such men are mostly dead," he said.

"Yes, but there are others," the count went on, his single eye bright with inspiration. "A remnant, if you will. A remnant of men who will insure that those who have died before them will not have given their lives in vain. Men who will save Germany from destruction."

Rolf sipped his coffee, watching the man closely.

The count again looked at the ceiling. "Faith. A man needs faith to do what he must to serve God and to serve his fellow man. To serve his country. Faith is the key."

"If one had faith," Rolf said flatly, taking another sip of coffee. He set his cup gently on the saucer.

"Ah! Faith *is* an elusive substance, isn't it?"

Rolf said nothing.

"I think you have more faith than you know," the count said, still looking at the ceiling. "But perhaps your faith has been hindered by a lack of guidance—by those who are not of the true fold of God."

"I have no faith," Rolf countered.

The count smiled at him. "Forgive me, Captain. Have I been preaching?"

Rolf shifted in his chair. "It is nothing." He finished his coffee.

General Olbricht, peering at him through his round spectacles while smiling benignly, gestured to his desk.

Rolf set the cup down on the corner. As though on cue, the adjutant knocked, entered the room, cleared away the empty cups and saucers with military efficiency, and left the room.

The discussion moved to the war, from the early victories and recent disasters, to the strength of the Allies, the American buildup in England, and the coming invasion. They agreed that the Allies most certainly would invade—Calais, most likely. They talked of the bombings of Germany, of Hamburg—in particular "the catastrophe" as it was called by High Command. Yes, we need more fighters, they agreed. Any fool can see we need more fighters. It is unfortunate that we will get only more bombers. Bombers and more bombers. Fighters that must double as bombers. Göring is a fool. But then, he was only acting on orders, I suppose. Still, Hamburg need not have happened. I am terribly sorry to hear of your fiancée. It is so tragic. Such a senseless waste.

"That is why I am here."

"Ah!"

"And how may we help?"

Rolf hesitated, gazing across the room at the German flag standing in the corner with dark, brooding eyes. "I do not know."

"Please speak freely, Captain. Please."

"Something must be done. Or . . . "

"Or what?"

Rolf turned his gaze on the count. "Or Germany is lost."

For a moment there was a thick silence in the room, the air growing imperceptibly darker as the words were allowed to age, were labeled, and stored neatly in the racks of thought.

The general gazed benignly at the squadron leader with his owl-like stare. "What are you saying, Captain?"

Rolf glanced quickly at him and smoothed his hand over the soft leather armrest. "Saying? I do not know that I am saying anything, Herr General."

The count shook his head philosophically. "Gentlemen, we are living in a time when wisdom must prevail."

The conversation turned seamlessly into the arena of politics. The count had not come right out and said it, but the inference was unmistakable: Politicians were to blame for Germany's troubles. They ran the war like bureaucrats and sapped the will of the field marshals and generals. There was also an occultic darkness pervading certain levels in the government, he said: men who would bring back the ancient Teutonic paganism and obliterate the remaining vestiges of Christianity. Because of these two factors Germany was heading for disaster.

"It is an affront to our Lord," the count insisted. "If we do nothing to intervene, what can we expect but judgment?"

Rolf listened quietly, remembering Gretchen's words. It seemed so chillingly clear; Germany was being led to the brink of doom by piping lunatics. "Intervene?"

The general and the count exchanged glances.

"When the body has a cancerous member, it needs to be excised, lest it kill the host," the count said cryptically. He went on to describe a group of idealists and Abwehr agents who were passionately anti-Nazi, known as the Kreisau Circle. He mentioned no names of course, and he kept the conversation teetering between the real and the hypothetical. However, the only real inferences that could be drawn were that there was a major plot brewing—had been for months—to assassinate Adolf Hitler, and that the conspiracy was far-reaching, pervading the highest ranks of the Luftwaffe, Wehrmacht, and military intelligence.

Rolf leaned back in his chair.

Their plan was simple in strategy, if not in tactical execution, the count continued: Someone wearing an overcoat loaded with explosives or carrying a briefcase loaded with explosives must get close enough to the Führer when they were detonated. Preposterous? Oh, but finding such men hasn't been so much the problem, Captain, as getting them through Hitler's tight security. Of course I'm serious. There have been several attempts already, each thwarted by some genius, or twisted fate, of the Führer's. He is a devil, that one. Getting someone close enough to him would not be an easy task. It sounds absurd, yes, but there seems to be no other way. One life for the many.

Rolf was stunned. *"Himmelfahrtskommando."*

"Yes, yes, the mission to heaven. The suicide mission."

"Why have you come to us?" General Olbricht asked him again.

Rolf was in a bit of a stupor.

"Captain?"

Rolf looked up at the general. "The bombing must be stopped," he said. "That is why I have come. The bombing must be stopped."

"Yes, and we need more fighters. We have already been over this ground. What do you propose we do? Have you an idea?"

"No . . . I don't know," Rolf said, struggling for words. The wedge of light, redder in hue now, swept over the room, and the shadow of the eagle played up the right side of his body. "Something—I—" He broke off. "Something."

There was a long silence. A long, eerie silence.

A tray of Schnapps was brought in by the adjutant, and in the reddish light the men toasted Germany, their families, their hopes for tomorrow. The conversation wheeled quickly back to Hamburg. Then on to Wilhelmshaven. Look what they are doing to Berlin. There are not many options left, if we are to save our beloved Fatherland. Do you agree? Germany needs men of action, men of faith. Without a vision the people perish.

Rolf looked at the count and felt a shudder go through him.

The count stood to his feet and put his left hand on Rolf's shoulder. Rolf stood out of protocol.

"I think we have talked enough for one day, Captain," the count said. "God will show you that faith grows in the least likely places."

"Never in a wasteland."

"Always in a wasteland," the count corrected him. "There is no soul too barren for the sweet water of God's grace." He smiled. His expression changed abruptly. "I hope we have given you food for thought."

Rolf nodded politely.

"Good. We shall meet again soon."

Rolf snapped to attention and started to salute in the Nazi manner but pulled his hand back. He saluted militarily. General Olbricht and Lieutenant Colonel, Count von Stauffenberg, returned his salute, both of them doing so militarily.

Once Rolf had left the room the general turned to his chief of staff and said, "He is a rare man."

"He is indeed."

"Do you trust him?"

"We have said nothing incriminating."

"The Kreisau Circle?"

The count shrugged. "What could he say?"

The general picked up his writing pen and looked down at it as he twirled it between his fingers. The red light was on his face now. "He will never go along with it."

Count von Stauffenberg walked over to the window and gazed down upon the street that was flowing with traffic and with pedestrians bustling along the walks, some of them crossing the street through the cars. The eagle was a burnished bronze color now, and the count, stroking his chin with the three fingers of his good hand, was in the shadows to the right of it. "On the contrary," he said, rousing from his thoughts. "I think we have found exactly the man."

27 ★★★

Rolf stepped outside, looked up at the sky, and breathed a cleansing sigh. A thin, red band of light spread over the western hills where the sun had bled away the last of its vigor, and the naked limbs of the trees along the Unter den Linden were sharp and dark against the bright turquoise gloaming.

He shrugged on his overcoat against the chill as he started down the steps of the building, the words of Count von Stauffenberg resonating in his mind. Neither of the men had stated it outright, but they couldn't have said it any clearer than if they had sent him a memo in triplicate: Dear sir, we were wondering if you might carry a load of explosives on your person during the award ceremony next week and be blown to pieces along with the Führer. One man's life sacrificed for the many. Thank you very much, Captain. Godspeed.

Rolf determined that there would not be a second meeting with General Olbricht and the handsome, disfigured count. They were mad.

He crossed the street, feeling frustrated and a bit despondent. The season had something to do with that though; autumn always meant the death of something. He thought of the look on Viktor's parents' faces as he told them of his death—the father's back stiffening with proud acceptance, the mother's shoulders sagging—the pride mingled with sorrow on their faces. He shut it from his mind. He was through with death. Death to death. To hell with death.

He hailed a taxi, climbed into the backseat, and told the driver to take him to the Tiergarten. The taxi swung out into the street. He settled comfortably into the seat, feeling the warm solitude of the cab closing around him, and immediately his mind began to flow back to the meeting, to the madness of it. A suicide mission. One for the many.

He sandbagged his mind against the meeting with pleasanter thoughts, shifted in his seat, and, gazing out upon the trees and the people walking, made a mental transition to what lay ahead. Yes. Life. Let there be life. Life is good. One for the one. A smile broke the corners of his mouth. He did not see the black Mercedes that slipped into traffic behind him.

The taxi pulled over next to the Column of Victory. Rolf paid the driver, went over to a park bench, sat down, and glanced at his wristwatch. Down the road from him, around a bend in the circle, a man wearing a black leather coat and holding a camera stepped out of the black sedan. He cast a furtive glance in Rolf's direction.

Rolf, agitated, stood up and paced around the circle. He could not shake it. Death. "It is the only way to save Germany. It is the greatest demonstration of love . . . of devotion . . . of valor. One man's life sacrificed for the many. Germany needs such men, wouldn't you agree, Captain? Why have you come, Captain?"

"Have we all become mad?" Rolf wondered out loud. Perfectly normal people doing that which is abnormal. Is that the only way to cope with it? Is that what happens when you are driven into a corner and given no way out? Or was it truly an act of the highest love?

A shudder of rage went through him.

He continued to pace around the Column of Victory. Every so often he glanced down at his wristwatch, then looked down the walkway leading to the circle. There were still a few painters catching the last of the light, racing the sun, he noticed abstractedly. But mostly there were sightseers huddled in small groups around the statuary, and lovers in pairs, set apart from the rest of the world. He watched a young couple pass in front of him, their arms wrapped around each other, oblivious to him, and smiled. Yes. One for the one. There was no best season for love; each was good. Love made it so.

The man in the black leather coat was clicking his camera at the various statues. Rolf glanced at him, not seeing him—just another sightseer. He looked once more at his watch. Where was she? And then:

"Rolf!" a woman's voice cried.

He looked up, thoughts of the earlier meeting suddenly vanishing in a rush of joy and happiness, and life was good again.

She was running toward him, the autumn-stripped trees framing her as she moved quickly over the sidewalk, waving happily, kicking up the leaves at her feet. She looked bright-faced and clean, and her red, wind-blown hair blazed in fingers of burnished light. She was wearing a long, red coat and matching felt hat, and black leather knee boots and gloves, looking pretty and awkward as women in long coats and boots look awkward when they run.

She looked radiant, Rolf thought. "There you are, Olga!"

"Hello, darling," she said, tossing her red mane on the wind. Her cheeks were flushed in the chill air, and her green eyes burned brightly and fiercely despite the beads of water at their corners. "I'm so sorry I'm late." They embraced, and he felt the smallness of her body in the thick coat. "Have you been waiting long?"

"Yes."

"I do hate being away from you," she said. "I've thought about you all day long, Liebchen."

"Good thoughts?"

"Bad thoughts. I cannot repeat them."

He looked at her, cupped his hand to the cool of her cheek, and gazed at her full red lips. "You are beautiful."

"Do you think so?"

"Very much. So very beautiful." He kissed her.

"Not here," she said, glancing around at the little groups of sightseers and couples.

"They do not see us."

"Yes, they do."

"Where then?"

"Do you love me?"

"I don't want to," he said.

She made a face. "But you *do* love me?"

"You know I do."

She smiled at him, looking intently at his mouth, his eyes, at the cut of his hair around his ears. "Come, darling, we shall be late for the start of the film."

"You should talk of being late."

"Do you forgive me?"

"I forgive you if you will let me kiss you again."

"You are a tyrant."

"Devotedly so," he said, then grinned. "Love brings the beast out in me."

"We shall have to go put you in the zoo."

Rolf gestured with his hand like a barker. "Come see the beast in his native environment. Please do not feed him; he has an appetite only for love." He growled at her and bit her hand.

They laughed. He put his arm around her, and they walked toward the street where there was a line of taxis waiting.

She tossed her hair to one side. "We shall have a lovely night, won't we?" she asked.

"The loveliest."

Olga had taken him completely by surprise at the Reich Marshal's dinner party. He had escorted her home that night, met her the next morning for breakfast, and, for the several days since, they had spent much of their time together. He had even brought her over to the house and introduced her to his family. She consumed his thoughts. She had climbed into the hole that was his chest and lit a flame on the cold, black wick of his being, helped him dig out of the depths of despair, until he felt like a man again instead of a machine.

"You smell wonderful," he said, looking at her, holding her close to him and feeling happy, truly happy.

"Do I?"

"Deliciously."

"Stop that, or we shall miss the cinema."

"Let us miss the cinema. I know a place."

She slapped his hand. "You and your place."

"It is our place," he corrected. "Our happy place."

"Yes it is. Oh, Rolf, you have made me so happy."

"Your happiness is my sworn duty," he said. "To protect and to cherish your happiness."

"Am I a duty then?"

"You are my only desire."

She stepped up onto her toes and kissed him.

"What of the others?" he grinned. "Are you not afraid we shall be seen?"

"Let them look," she said. "And let them find their own happiness."

"Come," he said.

They did not notice the man in the black leather coat when he turned as they passed him by, nor as he focused his telephoto lens to snap a picture of them. The man advanced the film and took another shot as they climbed into the taxi; then he turned and walked back to the black Mercedes.

28 ★★★

The office of Colonel Hans Rudel was located three blocks off the Unter den Linden, three floors up a dingy brownstone assigned to himself and his staff. There was not much of a view from his window—a wall of brick and brownstones crowding a narrow, treeless street choked with traffic— what he could see of it through the grime. But he was not interested in views outside his window; he was a man of singular interest.

He glanced through the open file on his desk, a tendril of smoke curling off his cigarette over his ashen complexion, as he pored over the black-and-white photographs. The photographs were laid out in three parallel rows, from left to right and top to bottom in a chronological sequence. The first two photos in the upper row showed Captain Rolf Schiller and his sister walking along the Neuer See. Moving slowly from left to right, he glanced at the photo of them observing a painter; a couple photos of them atop the Column of Victory; them in their library. Nothing incriminating. He paused at the one showing the girl in her bedroom, a night shot, grainy, the girl dressing. He picked it up, his thick-lidded eyes narrowing with interest, like a lizard eyeing a juicy cricket.

"He must have climbed a tree," he muttered, marvelling at how the photo might have been taken. "That Bricher could sneak up on the devil himself."

The middle row of photographs showed Rolf with Olga Strump, taken over a sequence of days following the night at the Reich Marshal's. Pretty legs. He studied the lower row of photographs taken the day before: Schiller and the woman eating breakfast in a café; Schiller and the woman walking through the zoo, arm in arm; the two of them laughing by the Neuer See, holding hands; he, pushing her on a swing; she, laughing; then the two of them kissing in a quiet nook in the park. More photos of them kissing.

The SS colonel shook his head and grunted. Love and war make strange bedfellows, he mused, smoking his cigarette. He studied the sequence of photos again. Such pretty legs. Nothing incriminating.

There was a knock on his door. He looked up as his adjutant admitted a smallish man wearing the dark winter issue of an SS officer.

"Ah, Klemmer."

The lieutenant stood smartly before his desk and thrust out his right arm. "Heil Hitler!"

"Heil Hitler!" the colonel returned. "Cigarette?" he said, offering the cigarette case.

"No, thank you, Colonel," Lieutenant Klemmer said, clicking his heels with a sharp bow.

"I have been studying your photographs," the colonel said, then dragged hard on his cigarette until his cheeks sank into his face. He blew a plume of smoke into the air and asked, "Well? You have news?"

The lieutenant opened his valise smartly and proferred a small bundle of photographs.

"More photographs?" Colonel Rudel coughed. He cleared his throat.

"Captain Schiller has just left General Olbricht's headquarters, Colonel."

"General Olbricht?"

"Yes. Lieutenant Colonel, Count von Stauffenberg is there also."

"And?"

"I find it interesting."

"It is nothing."

"Begging your pardon, Colonel, but why would General Olbricht entertain a captain in the Luftwaffe?"

"The award ceremony, of course." Colonel Rudel shrugged as he thumbed through the new photos. He paused at a particularly good one of Olga standing in profile. *She looks like a statue of a Greek goddess,* he thought to himself, smiling. That Bricher. "Schiller has good taste in women," he said.

Klemmer ignored the comment. "The award ceremony is being handled by the Reich Marshal's staff," he said.

The colonel sat for a moment, smoking, still admiring the photo of Olga. "You are certain the boy's information is accurate? We're talking about a hero of the Reich."

"The boy was correct about his sister, wasn't he, my colonel? They are in it together. I can smell it."

"We will need more tangible proof than what you can smell, Lieutenant Klemmer. We must have proof. Something unequivocal." He tossed the photo onto the stack of others. "I am swimming in photographs that prove only that Captain Schiller is a healthy pilot on furlough." He straightened the photographs and closed the file.

Klemmer looked at him.

"What do we know about General Olbricht?" Colonel Rudel asked.

"Very little so far, Colonel," Klemmer said. "He is an able commander, of course. Without blemish. Also, he has been meeting regularly with Lieutenant Colonel, Count von Stauffenberg."

"Another hero of the Reich," the colonel put in. "We have a conspiracy of heroes; is that what you are saying?"

"No, Colonel."

The colonel grunted, lit a cigarette off the one he was smoking, and spat out the bits of tobacco. "They are probably admiring their medals together."

"We have not yet been able to penetrate his staff," Klemmer said humorlessly. "But I know that one rat will lead us to another. They always do."

Colonel Rudel leaned back in his chair. "Let us examine what we have so far, Klemmer," he said. "Captain Schiller's sister is a religious fanatic. She writes her brother that the Gestapo have arrested Bonhoeffer and put him in prison. Nothing in the captain's letters, however, suggests that he cares a whit about religion, or politics, for that matter. You have an altercation with him in a tavern."

"He tried to kill me."

The colonel chuckled. "I suspect that if he tried to kill you, you would be dead, Lieutenant."

Klemmer did not see the humor in it. "There is the conversation overheard by their brother," he said. "They were talking treason."

"Hearsay from a fifteen-year-old boy."

"He referred to High Command as a collection of madmen."

The colonel laughed. "This is news?"

"Something should be done about it," Klemmer added, not at all seeing the jest in it.

Colonel Rudel looked at him.

"It was then we learned the name of Helmut Schoenfield," Klemmer said. "We have photos of this man visiting Bonhoeffer in Tegel. There is evidence that Schoenfield has been seen visiting General Olbricht and the illustrious count."

"Nothing incriminating there, Klemmer."

"No, sir. Not as yet. But I have someone on it."

"The boy?"

Klemmer smiled but said nothing.

"You have recruited him well, I am told," the colonel said with disgust.

"He is loyal to me, if that is what you mean," Klemmer said icily.

The colonel tapped an ash into a bronze ashtray. "Is Bricher still on Captain Schiller?"

"Yes. He followed him to a cinema downtown. The woman is with him."

"Good."

"Yes. We are processing the photos."

"More photographs."

"They will show you that he loves her," Klemmer said, a hint of triumph twisting the corners of his mouth. "They will show you that he is vulnerable."

"I would not underestimate this man, Klemmer. A man in love with a woman can be quite dangerous. Quite dangerous, indeed. You would not understand this, of course, Klemmer. But each to his own."

Klemmer took the insult with his usual smiling contempt and said, "Begging your pardon, Colonel, but you underestimate me."

The colonel looked at him and tapped his cigarette into the ashtray. "You're rather confident of yourself, Klemmer."

"I have reason to be, my colonel," Klemmer said. "I believe it is time to reveal a plan that I have been cooking, a plan that I believe will force Schiller's hand into the open. I did not want to inform you of it until I was certain that it would be successful."

"I'm listening."

"Our hero of the Reich is a man of appetite, my colonel. A man of passion. I have been following him, watching him closely. I think that now a little nudge will do the trick. A little heat and the insects will scurry out from their rocks." The lieutenant opened the file on the colonel's desk, picked up a photograph showing Rolf and Olga kissing in the park, and studied it. "I have given Bricher the go-ahead," he said. Then he added, "Provided it meets with your approval, of course."

"Tell me."

The lieutenant told him.

"The woman?"

"Yes, my colonel."

"She is a friend of Emmy Sonnemann's."

"She is a prostitute," Klemmer said acidly. "Who do you think arranged for her to be at Karinhall that night? It was not Emmy Sonnemann."

The colonel studied his face. "I see."

Klemmer smiled down at him.

"Your uncle?"

"Yes, Colonel. Major von Wuertzer went to school with Göring's wife. The Reich Marshal and my uncle frequently meet socially. They are quite good friends."

Colonel Rudel discerned the veiled threat. "I see that you are resourceful, Klemmer."

Klemmer clicked his heels. "Thank you, Colonel."

"I trust not too resourceful," the colonel said through a haze of cigarette smoke.

Klemmer looked at him.

Colonel Rudel picked up a photo of Olga and looked at it thoughtfully as he considered Klemmer's plan.

"It is a sound idea, my colonel," Klemmer said. "I have studied it from every angle."

"I'll bet you have." Colonel Rudel set the photo of Olga down gently on top of the others. "It must be handled delicately."

"Of course, my colonel."

"I do not wish to be embarrassed by this. I have given you a length of rope because of your uncle, Klemmer. Please see that you do not hang yourself with it."

"I will hang a traitor to the Reich," Klemmer said. "Several traitors, I think."

"And you think this will do it?"

"I know this man, Colonel. It will force his game into the open. I am certain of it."

"You are certain of many things, Klemmer."

"Begging your pardon, my colonel, but I was correct about Bonhoeffer. They are all in it together."

The colonel's face grew dark. "If there is a conspiracy here, Klemmer, I want it killed. I want this thing sewn up before the award ceremony next week. You must move quickly. Efficiently. But if this is a rabbit trail—"

"It is not, my colonel."

"I want proof, Klemmer. Tangible proof. I am swimming in photographs taken by a voyeur who loves his work. Remember, in the mind of the Führer,

Captain Rolf Schiller is still a hero of the Reich. Until proven otherwise he is still a hero to me as well."

"He is a traitor to the Reich, my colonel, and I will prove it."

"For your sake, Klemmer, I hope that you do."

"I would bet my life on it."

The colonel said nothing, but the look in his eyes said it clearly. "You are dismissed."

29 ★★★

Rolf and Olga came out of the film amid a stream of people, everyone milling through the opulent lobby of the old theater, talking about the film as they pulled on their coats and gloves. Some of the women were dabbing their eyes with handkerchiefs as the stream moved slowly, clogging at the double doors, and then at last spilling quickly out onto the wide, moonlit sidewalk. It was an American film with subtitles. Olga enjoyed the film very much; Rolf did not. He did not like having to read subtitles. He was not a quick reader, he said, and there were too many love scenes.

"I thought it very realistic," she said, dabbing her eyes with a handkerchief. "It was like us."

"Too many," Rolf grunted. "Five or six—all right—but there were too many. And everyone was smoking. I've never seen so much smoking. The film was on fire from so much smoking."

Olga slipped her arm into his. "It was from all of the love scenes," she smiled, pulling close to him. She looked up at the night sky and sighed. "It was a wonderful film."

"You cried through the whole thing."

"Yes, it was wonderfully tragic. They were so in love."

Rolf rolled his eyes.

All the streetlights were unlit. Everything was dark in the blackout except where the moon struck the sides of buildings and the limbs of trees, and where the slitted headlamps of cars played over the street. There was much traffic flowing both ways, and there were people hustling to and fro, going places. It was Friday night. A wind blew down the street and tossed leaves about. They walked down a narrow alley, the noise of the traffic growing muted behind them the farther they got away from the main street. The noise cut off as they turned a corner and went up a wider street and toward a small café that was nestled between two gray tenements. A small crowd of people loosely followed behind them.

"Where are you taking me?" Rolf asked.

"You'll see."

Inside the café the shades were drawn, and everything was dark and moody with candles wavering on the tables.

"Good evening, sir," Olga greeted the headwaiter.

"A table for two, please," Rolf said.

It was crowded and smoky, but Rolf tipped the man handsomely, and a table was found for them in the back along the wall. It was difficult getting through the tables without bumping them. Rolf helped Olga with her coat and gloves, then hung them and his overcoat on the wall peg behind their table.

He held her chair for her, then sat down and looked around him. Two women sat about an arm's length to his right. He smiled politely at one of them. Then he recognized a group of people from the cinema entering the café, standing, and looking over the crowd. There were no more tables available.

"Isn't this splendid?" Olga said. "It is my favorite place. I wanted you to see it." She had to lean forward to be heard over the noise.

"It is so intimate," he said.

She slapped his hand lightly. "Don't be stuffy. This is where the young people come."

"And they are all here, I see."

Their waiter was red-faced and out of breath as he stepped up to their table.

"Slow night, huh?" Rolf said.

The waiter fanned himself with a little towel. "Friday night." He caught his breath then recited the menu to them from memory.

Rolf looked at Olga. "Perhaps we should request subtitles."

She nudged him under the table with her toe.

The waiter finished his recitation and mopped his brow. "Perhaps the Maultaschen would be pleasant to start with?" he suggested.

Rolf was looking at Olga. She shook her head. "I'm not much for appetizers tonight, Peter. Perhaps the soup of the day?"

"Today we have a choice between potato or asparagus."

"I'll have the asparagus."

"It is delicious tonight," the waiter said. "And for the entrée?"

"I'll have the roast rabbit with fresh garlic and apricots, and," she thought for a moment, "a glass of Liebfraumilch to start things off."

The waiter kissed his fingertips. "An excellent choice, my Fraulein." He turned to Rolf.

Rolf looked at him with a straight face. "How is your Jägerschnitzel?"

"It is excellent, of course, Captain."

"You had Jägerschnitzel last night," Olga objected.

He looked at her. "Not here, I didn't. Besides, it's my favorite."

She frowned at him. "You must learn to try different things," she said. "Be bold . . . adventurous."

"I don't like to be adventurous when I eat," Rolf said. "I like to eat without worries."

"Might I suggest the Roulade?" the waiter offered. "It is superb tonight."

"Ah, the Roulade!" Olga agreed. "With the lovely dark mushroom sauce?"

"It is very tasty," the waiter nodded.

Rolf ordered the Roulade and a glass of Premiat Cabernet to go with it. He asked the waiter to bring him a glass of Weihenstephan Lager to start things off.

"My brave connoisseur," Olga smiled, once the waiter left.

Rolf grunted.

The waiter brought the drinks. While waiting for their food to arrive, the two of them looked into the other's eyes, smiling, then looked over the crowd and felt the energy in the place. It was quite lively with laughter and conversation and waiters going back and forth. The candle on their table wavered in the currents breezing through the room, then flickered wildly as people squeezed past their table.

Olga smiled at the festive atmosphere. She started when her eyes fixed upon the man sitting in the far corner of the room, wearing a black leather coat and smoking a cigarette. The man looked suddenly across the room at her, and when their eyes met a shadow crossed her face.

Rolf felt the change immediately. "Olga?"

She looked quickly at him. "Yes, my love?"

"Is something the matter?" Rolf looked over the crowd. He saw nothing but a noisy roomful of people.

"Nothing's the matter," she said, trying to recapture what had been lost. She watched Rolf looking over the crowd and lovingly observed the broken profile of his nose, the strong chin, and jawline. She started to say something, caught the words on her tongue, and touched his hand instead. Smoothing her hand over his and playing with his fingers she said, "I love your hands; did I tell you?"

"Every day. I am getting jealous of my hands."

"Your hands are nothing without your eyes," she smiled.

Rolf looked at her. She looked beautiful in the candlelight, and he felt his heart beating a solid, even cadence. He leaned across the table and kissed her.

"Rolf?"

"Yes, Liebchen?"

She looked away from him. "Nothing," she said, her eyes furtively probing the crowd. The man in the black leather coat was gone.

"Liebchen?"

"It's nothing," she said, looking back into his eyes. "Do you believe that love transforms a vile thing into a thing of beauty?"

"Ah, poetry. Let us talk poetry," he said. "Without subtitles."

"Do you believe that I love you?" she asked. She leaned forward and clutched his hands. "Truly love you?"

"Yes. Yes, Liebchen."

"Then it is true, Rolf. Don't you see?"

"I see that you are beautiful."

"Rolf, you must believe that I love you."

He smiled at her.

"There is much evil in the world," she said, "evil that would destroy the good in us. The good in you and me, my darling. I love you more than life itself. You must believe me."

He smiled at her. "You are being very dramatic," he said. "This is not a role that you are playing, is it? You are not Margarete now, or Madame M—"

"It is the truth, Rolf. You must believe me."

"I do, Liebchen. I do," he said, looking intently at her. "I like you this way. I think I will take you to the cinema more often."

She looked down at his hand and squeezed his fingers.

"Olga?"

She shook her head.

"What is it, Liebchen? You are crying."

She looked up at him. A tear leaked down her cheek. "I am so happy, Rolf," she said. "So very, very happy. I just don't want anything to ruin it."

"Ruin it? What kind of talk is this?" he said. "On second thought," he added, patting her hand. "I don't think I will take you to any more of these foreign films. They are much too sad and mysterious."

She smiled at him. "Yes. That is all it is," she said. She dabbed her eyes with her handkerchief. "I'm all right now. Really, Rolf. Let us have a wonderful time together."

"Good. Let's put all of this drama behind us."

"Yes, yes." She brightened suddenly. "To think, my darling, that you will shake the hand of the Führer in a few days. Aren't you nervous? I think I would faint."

"I will try to comport myself in a military manner," he said.

"I think it is wonderful. My hero. Aren't you thrilled?"

"I am thrilled to be holding your hand," he said. But something was missing, he sensed. Something had come between them again, and Rolf looked once more over the crowd. "Let us have no more talk of the Führer," he said with a military edge. "There is room at this table for only the two of us. Let the Führer find his own table; is that understood?"

She looked at him and smiled. "Yes, my love." And then their supper was served.

After they had eaten they walked back to the main road and caught an autobus that took them to the park. There they walked slowly along the Landwehr Canal, arm in arm, observing other couples in the shadows, smiling at them, then finally stopping in the middle of the Charlottenburg Bridge to kiss and watch the moon spangling the dark surface of the water below them. It was a beautiful full moon, and, with the blackout in the city, the stars shone over Berlin like they hadn't in years.

⟡

Rolf marched to the head of the column and stood at attention, his boots glistening in the morning light. There was a loud fanfare, and out of the corner of his eye he could see the Führer and his entourage moving toward him. Reich Marshal Göring was walking to his right, smiling and gesturing, and the others strode proudly behind the Führer.

Wearing his dress overcoat for the cold, Rolf felt the weight of the bombs pulling at him and hoped that the excess bulk would not give him away. The weight was suddenly unbearable, and a bead of sweat formed at his temple. It was the right thing to do, he assured himself. It was the only way. One life for the many. Better that one should die so others might live. Then the Führer was standing before him, smiling, taking the Schwertern from the Reich Marshal, the crossed swords glinting above the Knight's Cross, the two of them laughing and nodding their heads as the Reich Marshal regaled the Führer on the squadron leader's achievements. Olga, my dear, lovely Olga, save me. And then as the Führer reached out his hand to shake Rolf's there was a blinding flash.

"Olga!" Rolf gasped as he bolted upright.

He blinked into the darkness, waiting, thinking, his mind clearing, then feeling waves of relief pouring over him that it had only been a dream. The grandfather clock struck three times. The house was retired and quiet, and the faraway sounds of the clocks just reaching him reminded him that he was not sleeping. He wrung his hand over his face. It was wet with perspiration. Wiping his brow with a corner of the bedsheets, he lay back onto his pillow, thinking of Olga, of their lovely evening together, of her beautiful smile and lovely kisses, the smell of her hair and perfume. She was beautiful. He tried not to think of the other thing. One life for the many. It was madness. He closed his eyes and, in time, slept fitfully.

30 ★★★

here was a lace of frost on the windowpanes, and the sun came in through the window and edged over Rolf's face. He opened his eyes and blinked, remembering the dream. Then he remembered everything of the night before so clearly that he could touch it in his mind. He lay in the warmth and the waking sleep of his bed thinking of Olga.

Rolf was drawn downstairs by the smell of coffee, potato pancakes, and sizzling bratwurst. He stopped in the doorway of the kitchen and yawned. His mother and Gretchen were at the stove cooking; they were both in their robes and slippers. His father and Ernst were sitting at the table. Mr. Schiller was reading the morning newspaper and eating a bowl of hot oatmeal. Ernst was reading a magazine.

"Good morning," Rolf said, stepping into the kitchen. "Smells great. Am I ravenous!"

"Good morning, Rolf," said his mother. "Sleep well?"

Rolf made a so-so gesture.

Gretchen glanced at him and smiled. "If you would get home at a decent hour."

Rolf scratched his sides and yawned. "How do you know what time I got home?" he said. He raised an eyebrow. "Have you been spying on me?"

Gretchen hummed a tune as she flipped one of the potato pancakes. Rolf grunted. The sun streamed into the kitchen and made a warm pattern on the floor and wall.

Rolf sat down at the table, the sun hitting the left side of his face. "Hello, Father . . . Ernst," he greeted each groggily.

Ernst looked up at him, then went back to reading a magazine published for the Hitler Youth.

"Good morning, Rolf," Mr. Schiller said, looking at him over his spectacles as he turned a page of the newspaper. "I'll be finished with it in a minute."

"Take your time," Rolf said. "I'm in no hurry." He looked over at Ernst and watched him reading the Youth magazine.

Gretchen walked over to the table with his breakfast. She winked at him.

"Something wrong with your eye?" Rolf asked.

She walked away, smiling, then picked up the tune she had been humming.

"I'd have that eye looked at if I were you," Rolf said. Gretchen continued humming the tune. Rolf leaned across the table and read the back of the newspaper.

Ernst glanced at him with his eyes, then glanced over at the newspaper as Mr. Schiller turned the page.

"You're going too fast," Rolf objected.

Mr. Schiller peered around the paper and cleared his throat. "Would you like to read it, son? I would be happy to read the back."

"No, no, that's all right, Papa. I'll just wait until you've finished it."

"You're certain? I wouldn't want you to strain your eyes. Heaven forbid you should strain your eyes."

"All right, Papa, I can take a hint."

Mr. Schiller retired behind the newspaper.

Rolf cut a slice of bratwurst, spread mustard over it with the flat of his knife, and ate it. He ate some of the potato pancake and took a sip of coffee, chewing and then swallowing. He looked over at Ernst. "You are quiet this morning."

Ernst continued reading.

"It is these Youth rallies, keeping him out late hours," his mother said, coming over to the table and refilling Rolf's cup with coffee. "He has no time for sleep anymore."

Mr. Schiller grunted from behind the paper.

Ernst continued reading.

Rolf looked at him. "I am sorry about missing your rally," he said. "I'd forgotten all about it."

Ernst, still reading the magazine, said nothing.

"I will speak at your rally next week," Rolf said. "I promise. After the award ceremony. I'll wear the Schwertern. That should impress them."

Ernst looked up from his magazine. "The Schwertern? Oh, yes." He looked back at his magazine. "That will be nice, thank you."

Rolf looked at him. "I said I was sorry."

"It couldn't be helped, I'm sure," Ernst said, still reading his magazine.

You and your Youth rally can go bayonet yourselves, Rolf thought, still looking at him. He gave it up.

Gretchen sat down beside Rolf on his left and reached for a piece of toast. She spread jam over it. She looked at Rolf and leaned forward, smiling, as she bit into the thickly spread toast. Rolf could feel her eyes on him, and he cut another slice of bratwurst.

"Was it a good film?" she asked.

"No."

"That's it? No?"

"I thought I was in the library with all the reading I did," he said. "And there were too many love scenes." He made a face at her. "Everyone kissing all the time."

"Really? It sounds wonderful."

"Perhaps you and Olga should go see it," Rolf said. He grinned at her. "The two of you can blubber together. It's 'wonderfully tragic,' she says."

Ernst glanced at him.

Gretchen cut a wedge of potato pancake. "I wouldn't want to take away from your time together."

"The film will be showing after my furlough is over," Rolf said. "You can go then."

"Oh, let's not talk about it. I don't like to think about your leaving." She looked pensively at her plate, then broke into a smile. "I would like to get to know Olga better," she said. "She seems a wonderful girl. I shall like her, I think."

Rolf looked at her. "I hoped you'd be friends."

"I'm sure we will."

Rolf finished his potato pancake, took another sip of coffee, and glanced over at the paper. He leaned forward on his elbows to read the headline beneath a small photograph. A change went over his face. He laid his fork gently down on his plate, still reading the headline, then snatched the paper from his father.

Mr. Schiller threw his hands back. "What on earth!"

Rolf scanned through the article quickly, coughed, then staggered to his feet. He grabbed the back of his chair for support.

Gretchen looked up at him. His face had gone white. "Rolf? Is something the matter?"

He stared across the room at the cuckoo clock, his skin drained of blood. The newspaper fell from his hand onto the table.

"Say, what's going on here?" Mr. Schiller said. "Rolf?"

Mrs. Schiller was looking at him from the stove.

Ernst was watching him out of the corner of his eyes. He went back to reading his Youth magazine, the trace of a smile forming on his mouth.

"Rolf?" Gretchen said. "You look ill. What is it?"

Rolf walked away from the table, past his mother, and put his hand against the doorjamb. He paused, then he walked slowly down the hallway as though he were in a trance. His hand came up to steady himself against the wall.

"Rolf?" Gretchen ran after him and caught him as he was opening the front door. "Rolf, what is it? Tell me."

He looked at her as though she were a stranger, then he went outside and down the steps. There was a fine hoary frost on the grass, and the wintry wind came in through the door. Rolf was barefoot and wearing striped pajamas.

Gretchen's hand came to her mouth. She was suddenly very frightened. A groan sounded from the kitchen, drawing a wave of shivers over her. She turned, panicking, then she looked at Rolf who was now opening the gate and turning to the left onto the sidewalk. It looked strange seeing him walking down the street in his pajamas. "Dear God, please."

She ran back into the kitchen then drew up, slowing, seeing her parents at the table. Her mother was sitting back in a chair, her arms hanging limp at her sides. She was still holding the spatula in her right hand. Her father was standing up and bent over the table, his arms bracing his weight as he read the article. Gretchen approached them warily, everything in her tingling, numbing, preparing her.

"What is it, Papa?"

He looked up at her, shaking his head in disbelief. "It's . . . it's his girl. It's Olga," he said. "Someone's found her floating in the canal." He looked down at the picture of her. "She's been murdered."

Gretchen blanched. Her hands flew to her face. "Oh, please, God, no," she cried, refusing to believe it. "Please. Please no, God."

She looked down at the picture of Olga. It was an old picture; the hair was different, but it was Olga—there was no mistaking the eyes. Woman Found Floating in Landwehr Canal . . . the words blurred so that she couldn't read them. She looked down the hallway. The cuckoo clock sounded the quarter hour. "Oh, dear Rolf." She ran after him.

Ernst never looked up from reading his magazine.

31 ★★★

Gretchen ran through the gate and out onto the sidewalk after her brother, heading in the direction she had seen him going in his pajamas. She was still in her bathrobe and slippers, her right hand clasping the lapels of her robe. She expected to see Rolf just ahead on the sidewalk, but when she didn't she became frightened, really frightened.

Those people who were out in their front yards attending to morning duties looked at her queerly as she ran past them. They turned and stared. She angled her head, looking for Rolf, not seeing the people or caring what they might be thinking. And then she saw a middle-aged woman walking her schnauzer toward her. She ran up to the woman, took hold of her sleeve, and asked earnestly, "Have you seen my brother, Mrs. Stueben? You remember Rolf."

The schnauzer began to bark ferociously, its square body rigid and bucking off its front paws. The woman blinked at her, then looked down at her sleeve with a frown. "My dear!"

"He was just here," Gretchen cried. "You must have seen him!"

She let go of her sleeve, her mind beyond the woman and the still-yapping dog, and ran into the street. A car was speeding toward her. Gretchen was heedless of any danger, and the driver, suddenly seeing her, swerved to miss her with a squeal of brakes. The driver leaned out of his window and shook his fist at her, shouting a lungful of expletives. But Gretchen kept running, unaware of the driver, unaware of the people gaping at her from their lawns and windows, or of anything else except finding her brother.

She ran along the sidewalk, looking ahead, slowing to look down side yards and alleys, her hand clutched frantically at her bosom—looking behind her, then running ahead, then stopping, turning, craning her head, then desperately running ahead.

The houses on her side of the road opened into a large vacant field, grown-over and weedy with neglect, and she left the sidewalk and ran through the big chestnut trees lining the street. Rolf was standing in the middle of the field.

"Thank God," she said. She approached him cautiously, and spoke his name quietly as she touched his arm, "Rolf?"

He was staring across the street at the Tiergarten, the trees of the park stripped clean and standing gray against the brown of the grass, and the little clouds floating over them like boats on the Neuer See. The wind had died, but he was swaying slightly. Frost had soaked through the bottoms of his pajama legs where he had gone through some high grass, she noticed. The pajamas clung to his ankles, and she saw that there were pieces of grass stuck to his bare feet. His feet were red with cold.

She put her arm around his back. "Let's go home, Rolf."

He wouldn't move. She felt his back muscles tensing.

"Rolf?"

He wouldn't move.

"Please, Rolf."

He turned his head to her. But it wasn't Rolf's face looking at her; it was a frightening face, the features taut and dead-looking and all wrong.

"Come on, Rolf; let's go now," she said, stifling a shiver.

He looked off into the distance, his body still wavering. "She was a good swimmer," he said calmly. "She swam in competition when she was in school."

"I remember you telling me," she said, searching his eyes.

"They tied her hands behind her back," he said in that strange, calm-sounding voice.

"They?" Gretchen looked at him. "Do you know who did this?"

"They must have stood along the bank watching her."

"Who did this, Rolf?"

"Why would they kill her?"

"Who, Rolf? Who killed her?"

His hands trembled as he looked across the road. "I can just see her."

She took hold of his arm. "Let's go home. It's too cold to be out here in your pajamas."

They walked a little way, Rolf moving woodenly.

Rolf stopped abruptly. "Why, Gretchen? Why does God hate me?" His voice was suddenly low and choked with emotion. He glanced up at the sky.

"God does not hate you, Rolf."

"He hates me."

Gretchen said nothing.

His fists clenched. "I hate him," he said in a low, staggering voice.

"You're upset, Rolf."

"I hate him with everything in me."

Gretchen coaxed him to walk but he would not.

"Everyone I've ever touched, everyone I've ever loved, God has taken from me," Rolf said. He had turned around and was again looking across the field at the Tiergarten. "Why? What have I done to him?"

She looked at him. "This is not the work of God, Rolf," she said. "It is the work of evil." She touched his arm.

He reeled away from her. "Do not come near me, Gretchen, I am cursed." He had a wild look in his eyes.

"No, Rolf." She put her arm around him.

"Yes, I am. Cursed." He wiped his face with a hand.

She heard the wind gathering in his chest. "Let's go home, Rolf."

He looked up at the sky, his face drawn and lost in a swirl of chaos. "First Katharina, then Viktor, and now . . . Oh, God, why?" he cried. "Why do you hate me? What have I done to you? Tell me! What have I done?"

"Come, Rolf."

"Why must you take everything?" he shouted. He shook his fist at the sky. "Take me. Take me. Oh, God, why them and not me?" Tears streamed from his eyes. He covered his face with his hands. Then his shoulders hunched, and he began to weep.

Gretchen held him close to her. He turned his head into her shoulder and wept deep-chested and painfully. "Olga, my dearest love Olga," he cried. His shoulders began to heave. "Why, Gretchen, why will he not let me love?"

She looked heavenward. Her mind was racing with questions, or prayers, and she had no answers for him. She walked, holding Rolf by his arm, across the wet field, neither of them speaking, and the wind was in their faces.

32 ⋆⋆⋆

The planes were grounded until the storm front lifted off the European continent. A few more days, the meteorologist had said, and the cloud ceiling will have cleared over the target; even so, the skies were relatively clear over East Anglia. There were clouds and scattered showers, but the sun managed to get through from time to time, although it gave the earth little warmth.

In the meantime, the pilots of the 52nd lazed about in the day room of a large, community Nissen hut, playing cards and table tennis, reading books, magazines, and mail, writing letters, or catching up on sack time. Some of the men were given passes to London. Technical Sergeant Thomas Huntington and Julie Ellerby were married in the base chapel by the Chaplain, attended by a small gathering of friends and family, and were off honeymooning in parts south. Billy spent his days with Jane Worthing. There had been several of them.

❧❧

Jane, wrapped in a large bath towel with her hair piled up on her head, entered her room and went over to her desk. There were new curtains up around the window now, a blue floral print with a border of white lace. Looking out over the fields, she saw that the sun was up and peeking through a lace of clouds. Still there was no sign of them. Where are they? she wondered. The little electric clock on the desk showed that it was nearly eight-thirty, and they had promised to be back in time for breakfast. Anna was already clinking pots around down in the kitchen.

She crossed the room to her wardrobe and began to dress. The room, tidied of its adolescent trappings, was somewhat stark now, as though someone had just moved out of the place and she had just moved in, swept it clean, but had not yet time to furnish it. The shelves were bare; there were no pictures on the walls, except the one of Edmund, who was presently stationed on the bureau across the room, instead of on the night-stand by her bed. He was facing the door and smiling perpetually with a smile of devotion.

Pulling a woolen sweater over her head, Jane brushed out her hair, angling her head to one side, brushing and humming a little tune, then angling her head to the other side and brushing vigorously. She checked herself in the mirror, applied a bit of makeup, smiled at herself, then went back over to the window, looking out over the fields and frowning. Where are they? They had been gone hunting since before dawn.

Mr. Bellamy had taken to Billy as she knew he would, and Robert followed him everywhere, saying, "Ain't it swell?" or "Ain't it grand?" and was always asking him how he would say such and such in American. Anna thought he was the handsomest thing on two legs, and Mother seemed to be getting used to his dash and daring. She had changed her hairstyle to a more contemporary one, Jane had noticed, and was presently reading an old copy of Shelley's poems. It seemed the household had fallen into some current of anarchy.

"There you are," she said, seeing the three of them and the setters coming over the field. Billy, broad-shouldered, leanly muscled, and standing a good head taller than her father, with his strawberry blond hair tousled by the wind, was ranging over the ground with an easy confidence. She watched him for a while; it seemed as though he and the land shared a secret between them. He was a marvellous-looking man, she thought. Kind. Good-tempered. Generous.

Gazing thoughtfully at him, she smiled. She smiled a long while, and then the smile gave way to something else, gradually, like an eclipse, as she twirled her wedding band between her fingers. She pushed away from the window.

Breakfast consisted of a thick slice of ham, eggs cooked sunny-side up, boiled potatoes, thick slices of bread, orange marmalade, and coffee. It was eaten quickly amid a mannish conversation of game birds, bird dogs, and shotguns, and It's too bad you don't have elk in Britain. There ain't nothing like hunting elk in the Beartooths. I should like to hunt elk. There ain't nothing like it. The women were quite left out but listened politely and attentively as the men wolfed down their meals.

After they had eaten, Billy waited for Jane in the entryway while she went upstairs to gather a few things for their outing. The dogs were sitting patiently on either side of him. He scratched their heads. Mr. Bellamy came down the hall smoking his pipe and holding two leather rod cases, a wooden tackle box, a metal strainer, and an old tin bucket. He handed them to Billy.

"Would you like to come with us?" Billy asked.

"Come with you, did you say?" Mr. Bellamy drew on his pipe, considering it. "Well now, I don't know, lad. I don't really think Jane would go for it."

"Jane would most definitely not go for it," she said, coming down the stairs. "Besides, you had some errands to run in town, didn't you, Dad?"

"Errands? Oh, yes, of course—errands." He looked at Billy. "Terribly sorry, old sport. It appears I've forgotten some errands."

"Maybe next time," Billy said. He looked at Jane.

She was wearing a pair of brown woolen dungarees, a white wool pullover, and a long-billed cap over her hair, which was tied back in a ponytail. She went over to the door and began slipping into her brother's Wellingtons.

Billy watched her.

"Haven't you ever seen a girl in fishing togs before?" she asked.

He shook his head. "Can't say that I have. It's a sight for sore eyes, let me tell you."

Jane grunted. She began shoving her trouser legs into the rubber boots.

Billy looked at her. "You sure you want to do this?"

She stood up and made a pity face. "If you're tired from hunting . . ."

Mr. Bellamy laughed and walked away, trailing a stream of smoke.

"I'm not tired," he said. "I just thought you might want to do something else. Go into town, or something."

"I want to go fishing."

Billy and Jane climbed on their bicycles and rode east toward the coast; Billy carried the leather rod cases across his handlebars, and Jane stowed the bucket and tackle box in her wheel baskets.

The sky was a blend of colors, from the dramatic to the sublime. Big, dark, muscly thunderheads were bullying in the northeast, from which rain could be seen falling over the distant coast, and occasional petulant rumbling heard, muffled by the distance. To the west of these a rainbow arced away from dazzling white cumulonimbus clouds, then spilled into the sea amid showering lances of brilliant sunlight. Farther west, the skies moved from a wash of magenta to a bright azure blue, cloudless, save a tiny regatta of fluffy white tufts sailing through it. Billy had seen bold skies in Montana, but none like this.

The town of Southwold was a sleepy coastal village, built on a blunt promontory of land that elbowed into the North Sea, its squat lighthouse a beacon of light to weary seamen and an inspiration to poets and painters of seascapes. A line of Tudor cannons were pointed outward from Gun Hill, with their ancient cast iron muzzles aimed at a fleet of Dutch ghost ships. It was an idyllic, Edwardian village. The streets were lined with quaint shops, and the magnificent towered Church of St. Edmund dominated the skyline. And, as always, there was the muted roar of the sea and the screech of gulls in the background, as well as the smell of the sea.

Billy and Jane leaned their bikes against a whitewashed post. A white chain went through the post, draped heavily to another post, and on down the fence, each post spaced ten feet from the other, with brown weeds bristling up from their bases that were blowing in the wind off the sea.

Looking over the seascape, Billy took a deep breath of clean salt air. There were fortifications along the beach, he saw, some rolls of barbed wire and stakes, cement tetrahedra and iron jacks on the beach, and pill-boxes situated along the bluffs. The pier going out into the sea had been cut back from the deep water to prevent enemy ships from disembarking, and Jane told him that there were floating mines beneath the surface of the water.

A movement caught his eye and, turning, he saw a British soldier with an Enfield rifle slung on his right shoulder, walking deliberately toward them. His cheeks were ruddy and smooth, and he couldn't have been any older than eighteen. Jane waved at him. The soldier nodded, blushing it seemed, then he saw Billy's rank and saluted. Billy returned his salute, feeling a bit queer doing so in such a remote setting.

"Best watch your footing, miss—er, mum," the soldier corrected himself, noticing the band on her finger. He glanced quickly at Billy, then spoke with the diffidence of unpracticed authority. "The mines, you know?"

"Oh, we shall," Jane smiled. "Haven't moved any, have you?"

The soldier reeled with a boyish chuckle, his ruddy cheeks glowing. "I should say not." Then he started to turn, remembered to salute Billy, demonstrated a smart about-face with a stomp of his right boot, and marched off in the other direction.

"I think he's in love with you," Billy said.

"He's a dear, isn't he?"

Billy glanced down at the beach. "You sure it's okay to go down?"

"Oh, yes," Jane said. "It isn't likely we'll be invaded today. The Gerries've had their chance, haven't they?"

Billy looked southeast to the continent and reflected upon how close the Germans were really. "I suppose so. What about the mines?"

"You just stick close to me," she said. "I'll keep your feet out of harm's way."

"Oh, I will . . . I will."

Jane gathered her things. Billy carried the remainder of the gear down a flight of old wooden steps, the color leached out of them by the sun and salt, past rows of painted beach huts that were hunkered in the tall grass along the slope like nesting shorebirds, and then on to the pebbly beach.

Billy pulled the rods from their leather cases, each in three pieces, and jointed them. The rods were made of Tonkin cane; one was nine feet in length, and the other nine-foot-six inches. Jane took the shorter one.

Billy tried the action of his rod; it was stiff, and he felt something like a jolt of electricity crackling down the length of the rod and up into his arm. He felt the excitement he always did before a hunt or before fishing. He was eager to make his first cast. Quickly, he fastened an old brass Hardy reel to the handle, then threaded the heavy line through the holes and out through the tip.

"What do we use for bait?" he asked.

Jane smiled. "Here, you take the bucket, put a bit of water in it, and follow me."

Billy looked at the slate gray sea, at the rush of the waves and their foaming retreat, then he looked down at his feet. He was wearing his leather flight boots.

"Mind you, don't get your feet wet," she said, smiling.

Billy took off his boots and socks and rolled up his trousers past his knees, then he followed Jane dutifully as she waded out into the shore break. "Aiee! This is cold!" he cried. His legs and feet were quickly red and turning blue and numb with cold.

She laughed and skipped ahead of him, and he could see that she was suddenly happy and very carefree for an English girl.

The waves broke a ways out then came in a gentle surge of whitewater up the beach, splashing against the back of her rubber boots. As the water fell away from the shore in a rush of pebbles and sand and foam, she dug the metal strainer into the beach and brought up a scoop of sand. Several small crabs the size of a finger joint skittered about trying to burrow back into the small, wet mound of sand on the scoop, but she quickly had them in the bucket. The crabs shot sideways through the water and huddled in what corners they could find in the round bottom of the bucket.

"Bait!" she said. "Now you give it a go."

Billy looked at the strainer.

"This is mine," she said. "I've worked ever so hard growing my nails. But you can use your hands if you like."

"My hands?"

"Certainly. Just dig them into the beach and pull them up. You'll soon get the feel of it." She smiled. "It's really quite simple."

Billy looked inquiringly at the beach and then at his hands. He grunted. Piece of cake. He rolled up his sleeves and turned his back to the sea like Jane had done and, squatting with his hands poised like a second baseman, waited until the surf rushed up through his legs and hung in a scalloped reach of foam along the beach. Then he dug his hands into the roil of pebbles and sand and broken bits of shell as it all came rushing back down through his legs. He could feel the pull of the water against his legs, could feel the sand giving way through his fingers and, suddenly, the crabs wriggling through the wash as he pulled up a dripping handful of sand. Several crabs spilled through his fingers to the beach and quickly burrowed out of sight. He managed to snag a small one with the tips of his fingers, the crab scriggling free, then snagged it again with his other hand, back and forth like a hot potato.

"In the bucket!" Jane squealed.

Billy tossed the slop into the bucket, saw the crab winging clear of the lip. He dove after it like a defensive tackle but the crab was gone in a blink of time. Billy picked himself up off the wet beach and looked down at his sand-covered uniform.

Jane laughed. "My splendid bait catcher! You would make a marvelous rugby player."

Billy muttered something under his breath as he brushed himself off. He tried it again. And again. After several tries he acquired some sense of it and, between the two of them, they managed to collect enough crabs for the morning's fishing. Then Jane showed him how to rig his tackle, how to place the hook through the crab, and where to cast his line.

"Try to get it out beyond the first breaker there," she said, demonstrating with a two-handed cast. The tackle twirled in the air and, landing expertly behind the low roller, the line became taut in the pull of the undercurrent.

"Where'd you learn how to fish?" he asked.

She looked at him. "You mean, where did a British girl like me learn to fish?"

"Something like that."

"The British were fishing long before there were colonies."

"All right."

She turned and started away from him. "My father taught me when I was five."

"What else did your father teach you?"

"You'll just have to wait and see, won't you?" She smiled.

Billy watched her walking away from him down the beach, her rubber boots and fisherman clothes disguising her somewhat but not hiding anything.

The fishing was good along the coast, always had been, at all times of the day and in every season. When the fishing is good there is always the feeling that God is smiling upon the soul of the land and the people are happy and content.

Billy felt good. He glanced over at Jane from time to time, watching her fish with the offshore wind in her face. She was intense, all business. Occasionally she would look over at him while baiting her hook, the bill of her cap shading her eyes, and only the faintest curl of a smile showing as enigmatic as the Mona Lisa's. Then she would cast her line and continue fishing as though he wasn't there. He liked her form.

They fished for a couple of hours and caught several good-sized mackerel and cod, which were fierce fighters, and some smaller fish that they threw back, telling them each time to go find their older brothers. Then the wind picked up from the northeast, making it difficult to cast, and Jane said that was the end of it for now.

They collected their gear and walked back to one of the beach huts, cleaned the fish, and washed their hands in the cold water from a spigot between two of the huts. They sat down on the lee side of the hut, their backs against the wall, where the wind couldn't reach them, the sound of the surf was muted, and the sun reflected warmly off the slope in front of them.

Jane removed her Wellingtons. Her socks were discolored from moisture getting into the boots and they were pulled out at the toes. Brushing them free of sand, she pinched the toes back into place and let her feet air. She lay her head against the wall with her face angled up to the sun. The sun was unusually warm for late autumn, and it felt good and clean on her face and in her hair. She could feel the sun drying the saline moisture on her skin, drawing the skin tight against her cheekbones, and she could feel the thick torpor of the sun working through her limbs. Her mind drifted on the swelling lassitude.

"I do love coming here," she said, rolling her head to look into Billy's pale blue eyes. Then she took off her cap and, glancing at him, removed the ribbon from her ponytail and shook out her hair. She pushed her fingers through the thickness of it.

Billy watched her. He stripped a blade of shore grass, looked at her, stripped another blade, looked down at it, and then back at Jane. A mood change had gone over her, he saw, not with any clarity of what that meant, but he saw the change. Something moved in him too, and he was not quite sure what to do about it.

Jane turned her head and could just see a fishing boat moving out to sea; she watched it until the boat dropped over the horizon. She smiled, a faraway look in her eyes.

Billy studied the line of her nose and lips, the line of her chin and throat. She had skin as white and smooth as alabaster, like her mother's, with delicate shadows showing along the underside of her jaw and neck, and the sea had brought a healthy color up into her cheeks. He reached over and put his hand on hers; it was cool. She looked quickly at him.

"You're prettier'n a spring colt, you know?"

She looked down at her hands.

"You're really very pretty."

She looked up at him with her lovely blue eyes, and Billy felt a thickening in his throat.

She sat up abruptly, took hold of the paper sack, and peered inside. "Would you like some dinner?" she asked.

Billy reeled as though someone had burst a balloon behind his ear. "Dinner?"

"Yes, it's almost noon."

"You mean lunch?"

"We're in England, silly." She glanced at him with a quick smile. "Hungry?"

"Sure. I'm starving," he said. "What've you got?"

"Let's see. Cucumber sandwiches . . . a bit of cheese . . . two apples . . . a tin of sugar biscuits for dessert . . . two bottles of mineral water."

"Lunch," he muttered.

He watched her eat. She ate daintily, properly. Then she sliced an apple into wedges and placed a strip of cheese on one. She bit crisply into the wedge, the juice sluicing over her teeth and a bit of it dribbling out the corner of her mouth. She smiled embarrassedly. Then with a deft flick of her middle finger she wiped her chin and offered the apple to Billy. Her lips glistened in the sun. "Would you like some?"

He looked at her. "You bet." He leaned over and kissed her on the lips. She pulled back in a rush, her blue eyes blinking with alarm.

For a moment he thought she might slap him again. "I had to kiss you," he said. "Shoot, we've been together a week already."

He saw a shadow going over her face, like a window shade drawing up. He saw the face of a woman behind the shade crossing some invisible threshold, like the face of a bride, composed of fear, and apprehension, and knowledge, and desire, and the light of it going over her face in a slow-footed sweep of time. *Nuts*, he thought.

She leaned forward suddenly and kissed him, kissed him hard on the mouth, and threw her arms around his neck. "Hold me, please," she said. "Hold me, and promise you'll never let me go."

She lay her head against his chest, and, as he held her in his arms, Billy opened his eyes and could see the pebbly beach sloping behind her, as well as the rolls of barbed wire stretching along the coast—it seemed so incongruous. He could feel her heart beating against his like a trembling bird.

"Promise?" She looked at him intently. "Promise you will never leave me."

He said nothing.

"You won't go off and leave me alone to wonder?"

He felt as though he had inadvertently stepped over a "No Trespassing" sign onto a forbidden tract of ground and didn't quite know how to retrace his steps, or if he even wanted to. "Not if I can help it," he said.

"I couldn't bear it again," she said in earnest. "It's been horrid. Knowing and not knowing, being and not being. I feel like a ghost caught between two worlds."

"Do you believe in ghosts?"

"That's not the point, is it?" she said. "It's the dreadful loneliness."

Billy said nothing.

She looked intently at him. "You promise?"

"Scout's honor," he said, pledging three fingers. "I won't get my tail shot off and leave you to wonder."

"Oh, Billy, do be gentle."

They kissed, and as they embraced, the sun disappeared behind a small cloud, making everything shadowy and cool. In a moment the sun reappeared and everything was warm and bright again, with the sun slanting down behind the hut, so that there was a lovely little dome of quiet and warmth against the cold of the sea.

"Isn't this lovely?" she said.

"Sure is."

"I could stay here all day. Let's stay here all day; what do you think, Billy? The world can go fly a kite."

Forget the no trespassing ground. Billy felt as though he were suddenly moving out to sea in a small, rudderless, powerless boat and the shoreline was getting farther and farther away. "I ought to check in at the base," he said.

"Must you?"

"I must. Uncle Sam likes to keep a tight reign on his nephews."

"Beastly uncle."

"Yes," he said, loving the way she said beastly. And then all he could think to do was kiss her. He did, and she kissed him back.

Later, they gathered up their gear and cycled home. In the distance the clouds were gathering and brandishing their threat of rain and promise of continued grounding.

"Would you like to stay for supper?" she asked, once they had reached her front gate.

Billy looked down at his soiled clothes. "How about I freshen up a bit back at the base first?" he said. "Maybe we could go into town later. Have a bite to eat at the Guinea, or something."

She brightened. "Do let's. It sounds lovely."

"I'll pick you up around six, okay?"

She wrinkled her nose. "On your bicycle?"

"I'll pick you up in a chariot fit for a princess," he smiled. He made a pass at her, but she stepped away deftly and he nearly fell over his bike.

33 ★★★

It had rained heavily for two hours, then let up with a trailing of scattered showers that forced everyone to keep their umbrella—or "brolly"—close at hand. Night had come quickly, as it does in November, drawing with it a host of stars and small dark clouds over the British countryside, and the air was clean and brittle with cold. The roads were black and shiny in the aftermath of the rain.

At six o'clock sharp Billy pulled up in front of Jane's house and beeped the horn. The door opened, and Jane squealed with laughter. She stepped out onto the porch, pulling on her gray tweed overcoat and scarf.

"You're taking me to town in that?"

Billy stepped out of the jeep and made a sweep of his arm like a liveried servant. "Your royal chariot, m'lady," he grinned. "Compliments of the 8th Air Force."

Her hand came to her cheek.

"What's the matter; don't you like it?"

"Like it? I think it's splendid. How ever did you manage?"

"I have a fairy godmother in motor pool." He chuckled. "He said it'll turn into a pumpkin if I don't get it back to him by two."

"Don't you mean by twelve, darling?"

"The Yank version is two."

"Fancy that," she smiled.

Billy helped her into the passenger side and came around and got in himself; then the jeep—the top up against a light pattering of rain—sped down the road into Halesbury.

The Golden Guinea was crowded, mostly with locals, and buzzed with happy chatter. It was smoky and full of the close smell of working men, ale, musky wet clothes, and women's cheap perfume. At the far end of the dividing wall of the room were some tables of men playing cribbage and shove ha'penny. Others were gathered around the snooker table, and beyond the tables a man and boy were throwing a game of darts. People were sitting on the long wooden benches that ran around the outer walls, men with men, smoking pipes and cigarettes, and women with women. Both men and women held pints of dark ale in their hands, talking and watching the games and smoking. There were some RAF pilots in one of the booths, but Billy didn't recognize any of them.

The pilots looked over as Billy and Jane made their way to a booth along the center wall. He watched them, and they watched him. One of them nodded at Billy as he and Jane passed their table and raised his glass. "Oy, Yank!" he said. "You with the 52nd?"

Billy nodded. "That's right."

Jane took off her coat and laid it in the booth. Wearing a red, square-shouldered frock and matching pleated skirt, with the hemline of the skirt hitting just below the knees to show the shapeliness of her legs, she looked as though she had stepped out of Coco Chanel's salon in Paris.

Jane slid into the booth; Billy slid in across from her, and the waitress came over to the table. The waitress was a plump woman with red cheeks, bright blue eyes, and a snarl of reddish brown hair. She and Jane chatted a moment, and Billy glanced back at the RAF pilots. They had gone back to their conversation. He put his hands flat on the table, drummed a quick roll, and smiled up at the waitress as she took their orders.

A man with a white stubbly chin walked by and raised his pipe. "Good show, Yank!" he greeted. Billy nodded at him, and then they were alone.

Jane looked across the table at Billy. "It was wonderful today, wasn't it?"

"You bet." He drummed the table again.

Smiling, she took his hand and smoothed her fingers over his, feeling the masculine texture of his skin. Her eyes sparkled, seemed to suddenly come alive. She was at that stage in her love for Billy when just touching his hand was magical. Through her fingertips she could feel the first blush of the mystery to come later in love; she could feel all of the promise and hope, and the belief that love is good and eternal and true, without hypocrisy, and holding his hand was enough for the moment. Her face glowed in the secret knowledge of women.

Billy looked down at her hand and noticed for the first time that she wasn't wearing her wedding band. He lay his other hand over hers and held it. "You look terrific."

She smiled. "You make me feel terrific. I shall soon be talking like Robert."

"Don't, please," he said. "Say it in English."

"You make me feel simply wonderful. Or I could say marvellous or splendid. How's that, darling?"

"Terrific."

She rubbed his fingers. "Your hands are warm."

"Yours are cold."

"Cold hands, warm heart," she said, raising her face into a bit of light.

He looked her over as she turned her head, studied the straight line of her nose, the very British nose, and the lovely hollow of her cheeks, the swell of her lips. His eyes swept over her figure—what he could see of it showing over the tabletop. "I like your dress," he said. "Really, you look great."

She looked down at it. "Thank you."

An old man with a varicose face and an unruly nest of white hair sticking out of his rumpled tweed cap paused by their table and looked at Billy. The border collie with him sat down at his left heel. The old man smiled. His eyes were twinkling half-moon slits, and the way his chin rode up into his face suggested he had no teeth. Billy scratched the dog's muzzle. The man, still smiling, looked at Jane, and then at Billy. He gestured with his pint, chuckled, then he and the dog walked away.

Jane watched Billy. She rubbed a thumb over his forefinger. "You're quite an attraction," she said.

"For old men and dogs."

"Not just old men and dogs," she said. The way she looked at him made something give way inside him.

The waitress brought their drinks and a little while later brought out their food from the kitchen. Billy had ordered shepherd's pie and a pint of Bass ale. Jane ordered steak and kidney pie and a cup of tea. The plates were steaming, and Billy put his face into the vapors.

"Smells good," he said. Using his knife, he spread some shepherd's pie and peas onto the back of his fork tines, English style, and began to eat. He added a little salt to the potatoes.

Jane watched him eat. "Like it?"

"Didn't realize how hungry I was," he said.

"The food is wonderful here, don't you think?"

"You bet."

She took a bite of her meal, looked down at her plate, then cut into the crust of the meat pie with her fork. She looked at him. "Which do you prefer . . . American cooking or English?"

"I like 'em both, I guess. They're different." He smiled at her and took a sip of ale. "When in Rome, you know."

She smiled, sipped her tea. "I suppose you ate wonderfully on your ranch in Montana?"

"We sure did," he said. He took a couple of bites and eased into a current of thought. He took another sip of ale and smiled.

"We'd have folks over for the Fourth of July, or during roundup, and you talk about eating." He shook his head. "Pa'd have the fire pit going with a big old side of beef turning on the spit, and all the men would stand around talking cattle, or fishing, or politics—everyone just talking and havin' a good time."

As Billy reminisced, she watched his eyes, his lips—watched his fingers gently twirling his fork.

He grunted. "Ma'd cook up a mess of beans and coleslaw. And everywhere you looked—spread out over a half-a-dozen tables—were buckets of fresh corn on the cob, and potato salad, and watermelon. Food everywhere. A whole table full of pies and cookies."

"It sounds lovely. All those people over at your house."

Billy looked across the room as the waitress cleared away some empty plates. He smiled. "After dinner we'd shoot off a bunch of fireworks—shoot off some guns, too."

Her eyes widened. "Guns?"

"Quick-draw kind of stuff, you know? Like shootin' cans off a log." He laughed. "One year old Slick-draw Doob Wilkens shot himself in the leg—tore the back of his calf nearly in two."

Jane stared at him, but a strong current was moving in Billy.

"I remember the times when Big Bob Baker would get out his fiddle," he said, "and Pa and some of the men would get out their instruments, and we'd have ourselves a square dance! Everybody laughin' and stompin' . . . the girls all prettied up with their dresses twirlin' like maple spinners, clear into the night."

"It sounds wonderful."

"You bet it was," he said. "The summer twilights last forever in Montana, but eventually the moon would come out and get all spangly on the Stillwater—pretty as you please—and Jimbo and the hands would get to singin' their sad Crow songs in the bunkhouse . . . the cattle bawlin' in the distance. Everything was fine . . . real fine." He looked at her suddenly, then jabbed his fork into his potatoes. "Shoot. Listen to me going on like a broke record."

Jane smiled at him. "You miss it, don't you?"

"Miss it?" He looked down at his plate. "Yeah, I miss it."

"And your girl?"

He looked at her.

"You left that part out. Was she pretty?"

"Laura Miller?" He grunted. "I guess you could say she was pretty. Every boy in Stillwater County would've given his eyeteeth to dance with her."

"You were going to be married, I suppose, before she wrote you one of those awful letters? What are they called—Dear Johnnies, or something?"

"It doesn't matter." He looked at her plate. "Your food is getting cold."

They ate in silence for a few moments. Billy mopped up the rest of the gravy with a piece of bread and finished his beer.

Jane picked at her supper. "I'm happy she did though," she said. "Write you that letter, I mean. Does that sound wicked of me?"

"That's the way the cookie crumbles, as they say," Billy said. "All's fair in love and war. That's water under the bridge. No use crying over spilt milk." He looked at her. "I'm full of them. Want to hear another one?"

She patted his hand. "Did she hurt you terribly?"

"No, she didn't hurt me terribly," he said. "She never really was my girl, looking back on it now. I just happened to be the fella she was dancing with at the time." He grew silent. Rain drummed against the roof of the pub, making everything seem suddenly lonely and sad.

"I'm sorry for bringing it up," she said. "But I do so want to hear about your life. Everything."

"No, you don't. Not everything."

"Everything. The happy parts are lovely of course, but I want to hear the sad parts too."

Billy grunted reflectively. "It was a different time," he said quietly. "A different world."

She smoothed her hand over his. "Darling, I want to learn everything I can about your world."

Billy looked at her.

The door opened, and a man and woman entered the pub. Jane looked across the room and her eyes made contact with the man's. She smiled and waved. Billy looked over his shoulder and immediately his face drained of color.

Jane saw the change go over his face. "What is it?" she asked.

The man was in his mid-forties, with a thick head of graying hair, a high, intelligent brow, and bright blue eyes. He was well built and robust-looking. He wore a brown tweed coat and trousers, a dark brown fedora, and a burgundy-colored sweater. He shook out his umbrella and put it in a receptacle by the door. The woman was in her late-thirties. She had dark Latin eyes, was olive-skinned, and her dark brown hair was swept behind her head in rolls of curls. She wore a simple, though stylish, black suit and hat. She was very attractive.

Billy stared at her.

Jane touched his hand. "Are you all right, darling? You look as though you've seen a ghost."

The man and woman came over to their table. There were beads of water on their shoulders, and, as they came near their table, Billy could smell the rain and wet clothes on them.

"Hello, Jane," the man said, smiling down at her. "A bit nasty out there." Billy noticed he was wearing a white clerical collar.

Jane smiled at them. "Hello, Reverend Townsend . . . Angelique."

Angelique Townsend nodded and smiled. Billy looked up at her.

"May I introduce my friend William Hochreiter," Jane said.

Billy started to climb out of the booth.

"Don't trouble yourself, son," Reverend Townsend said. He shook Billy's hand firmly. "Pleased to make your acquaintance, William."

"Same here," Billy said. He looked at the woman. "Ma'am."

"Hello," she said. She studied him for a moment. "You're the American I've heard so much about, aren't you?" She spoke with a thick French accent.

Billy's head bobbled a little. He glanced at Jane, then back at the woman. "I dunno."

"It's all been very complimentary," the woman assured him.

"Jane's mother has told us so much about you," Reverend Townsend said. "Escaped from France, did you?"

"Yes."

"Angelique is from France."

Billy said nothing.

Angelique smiled embarrassedly at him. "I suppose my accent is rather difficult."

"Not a bit." Billy stared at her.

Reverend Townsend put his arm around his wife. "Angelique and I met when I was doing some studies in Paris, four years ago—before the war, you know. Isn't that right, dear?" He smiled at his wife. "Got her out before the Gerries came tromping in. Bit of a coup, don't you think?"

Angelique smiled. She looked at Jane. "Shall we see you in services tomorrow?"

"Yes, of course," Jane said. "Perhaps we can sit together?"

"I will look forward to it."

Reverend Townsend looked at Billy.

Billy, breaking free of Angelique's hold on him, looked at the reverend, then looked at Jane, then back at the reverend. "Me? No, no, I don't think so. You don't want me in your church."

"I think it would be splendid," he said. "Don't you, dear?"

Angelique smiled at Billy. Her eyes were wide-set and dark—big, knowing eyes that glistened in the light.

"No, really," Billy said, looking away from her. "You don't want me in your church."

"But of course we do," the reverend said. Then he grinned. "Not wanted by the constables for anything, are you?"

Billy smiled then flustered about for an answer. "You just don't want me in your church."

"Do come," Angelique said, touching his arm lightly. "After the service we shall talk of France." Billy saw a flicker of something in the darkness of her eyes. The woman quickly looked at Jane. "Perhaps we could have you both to tea afterward?"

"That would be lovely," Jane said.

"Will you come, then, William?" Angelique asked.

"I don't know if I'll be able to get away from the base," Billy said.

"Nonsense," Jane frowned. "You said yourself you probably wouldn't be flying for a couple of days yet."

Angelique smiled at him. "Do try," she said. She took hold of her husband's arm. "Shall we go and leave these two, young, love sweets alone, Malcolm?" They walked around to the other side of the room and sat down against the far wall.

Billy watched her through the glass separating the two rooms.

"I think I shall be jealous," Jane said.

A frown crossed his brow. "No need to be. She's old enough to be my aunt."

"A very beautiful aunt," she smiled.

Billy looked into his glass.

"What is it?" she asked.

"Huh? Nothing. Just thinking."

"Penny for your thoughts?"

"They aren't worth a penny."

"What's wrong, darling?"

"Nothing."

"Have I said something?" She touched his hand. "Is it Angelique? I was joking about my being jealous."

"She just reminded me of someone, that's all."

"Who?"

"Someone."

"Of Laura Miller?" She laughed. "I think I shall be jealous after all."

"No. Now, please, just let it drop."

"All right, Billy. I don't wish to quarrel." She retrieved her hand and put it in her lap.

The clamor of the pub closed in around them. Jane looked down at her plate and turned a bit of crust over with her fork. Billy stared at the corner of the table. It was suddenly very close and suffocating at the table.

Billy looked at her. "I'm sorry, Jane," he apologized. "I get a little goofy sometimes."

"It's all right," she said. "I shouldn't have gone on so."

"You didn't do anything." He set several bills and some change on the table, then took hold of her hand. "Let's go."

"Go? Where?"

"Anywhere. Let's just get out of here."

"Billy?"

"Someplace adventurous! Someplace where we can dance. I want to hold you and kiss you and be only with you. C'mon, let's get out of here."

"All right, Billy." She collected her things and slid out of the booth. As Billy helped her on with her coat, she glanced over the dividing wall and smiled at Angelique. Angelique smiled and waved. Reverend Townsend turned and waved also.

Billy did not look at them. He led Jane past the table of RAF pilots and out of the closeness of the pub into the black open space of the night.

They stood on the sidewalk while their eyes adjusted to the change of light. The street was empty. The rain had stopped. The air was brisk and clean-smelling and black, as the moon had not yet risen. Billy took a deep breath and blew out a frosty plume into the air, then he put his arm around Jane and led her toward the jeep. The stars were low and shining and showed the outlines of the buildings. They shone weakly on the empty wet street, on the puddles, and on the windows of the storefronts. There was only the faintest sound of the pub behind them now, and then there was only the hollow, clicking sound of their feet against the wet pavement.

34 ★★★

Angelique came toward Billy in the stillness of the night, padding silently in her bare feet like a nocturnal cat stalking its prey. She was wearing a black skirt and white blouse; her hair was wild and windblown—for there was a wind blowing—and there were bits of straw and sawdust in her hair. She was the most beautiful, terrifying woman he had ever seen. He backed away from her. But she came at him steadily, hungrily, backing him into some vague impression of a corner with a haunting look in her eyes, then, standing on her toes, she put her arms around his neck and kissed him lightly on the corner of his mouth.

"I will pray for you, Billy," she said. "May God go with you and my love . . . and my love," she kept repeating. "May God go with you and my love."

"No!" Billy shrieked, covering his ears with his hands. "Leave me alone! Leave me alone!" He pulled out his nickel-plated Colt, a gleam of light running along the length of the barrel as he leveled it at her breastbone, and pulled the trigger. He saw the solid impact of the bullet as it struck her chest and threw her backward like a hunch-shouldered doll. He watched as the awful crimson of the blood spread over the whiteness of her blouse.

She looked down at her breast, then looked up at him, a look of perplexity opening her features. "This will be for nothing if you do not live," she said. Then she twirled away from him, her arms outstretched as though she were nailed to a cross. And as she fell away, ever falling and twirling across a limitless reach of space, he saw that it was not Angelique at all but that it was really Colette whom he had shot; her cry echoed across the heavens, "My love . . . my love . . . my love . . ."

Billy woke with a start and blinked into the darkness. His heart drummed a frenzied beat. Perspective was lost against a lurid diffusion of light and dark, and for a moment everything was still as dreamlike and surreal as a Salvador Dali painting, complete with symbols and archetypes and nonsense that were in bizarre juxtaposition. It took him a moment to adjust to the fact that he was not holding Colette in his arms, that he had not killed her. That it was only a dream.

The moon was bright now and shone in through a window. Everything still possessed the dreamlike estrangement between fact and fantasy, between flesh and spirit. Gradually, the curvature of the ceiling lowered out of the darkness and everything in the room began to take shape: the two rows of beds, the wall lockers, the ghostly images of pinup girls on the walls. He took a deep, cleansing breath and felt the terror sheet away from him as he gained control of the slow, steady rhythms of his body.

Billy looked over at his nightstand and saw the silvery glint of the crucifix dangling from the lamp, the moon striking it fully, shining along its bloodless length, showing it twirling slowly in the currents that were eddying through the hut. He remembered now that he had been looking at it before he had gone off to sleep, thinking of Colette, praying for her, and resisting some inarticulate dread that was even now worming up through his chest. He thought he felt a haunting spirit in the room. "Are you there?" he whispered at the ceiling. "Are you really there? Or are you a figment of my imagination?"

Someone snored at the far end of the Nissen hut. Just then the door opened and a man entered the room. Billy turned his head and recognized at once that it was Joe Thompson. That he was drunk, or pretty close to it, was evident in his overcautious shuffling. Billy could smell the heavy scent of whiskey and a woman's perfume before the crash of wind that came in through the door behind Joe. He listened as Joe undressed and put away his clothes, heard the thump of a footlocker as he must have stubbed his toe against it, and then a curse. The snorer at the far end of the hut throttled down and everything was all right. The haunting spirit in the room was summarily dismissed by the familiar, and Billy closed his eyes and went to sleep thinking of his lovely evening with Jane.

ॐ✐

Billy sat alone at a table in the officer's mess. The mess was empty except for two airmen sitting in one corner. Their presence in a room normally bustling with activity only seemed to underscore the emptiness in the place. There was a messman behind the counter, polishing the metalware, and the skeleton crew of cooks who were on duty could be seen moving about through the galley doors. It was early yet. The morning rush had not yet occurred and likely wouldn't, since most of the men were still away on passes; many of those who weren't away were in their bunks paying the last tab of the piper for Saturday night.

The wind was blowing fair outside, and the trees in Tealbrook Wood rattled forlornly against a sky that was a seamless gray overcast. There were tatters of gauzy mist sifting through the trees, obscuring the horizon, and everything looked as dismal and mournful as most English mornings look in the morning after a good autumn downpour.

Billy stared down at his cold, half-eaten breakfast. His coffee, half-finished, was now as cold as his breakfast and black and murky as a spot of sin. He brooded over the cup, fingering the crucifix at his throat. He had elected to wear it this morning. But for Billy there was no magic in the thing; he did not think of it as a mystic talisman. He wore it to appease the nagging dread in his chest—a kind of penance to the dark memory of Colette. He did not hear the approach of footsteps to his table.

"It is not good for the soul, this heavy heart," a stranger's voice said.

Startled, Billy looked up and there standing before him was the little French cook, holding two steaming cups of coffee in his hands.

The little man smiled. "Your girl—she keeps you awake last night?"

"Something like that," Billy said, recovering.

"Ah, *l'amour! L'amour!*" the Frenchman smiled. "It is good to be young and in love, no?"

Billy let the crucifix fall back inside his open shirt.

The Frenchman's expression changed. "I did not mean to startle you," he said with a thick accent. He set a fresh cup of coffee down before Billy and moved the neglected one out of the way. "There is nothing more terrible on earth than cold coffee," he smiled.

"Thanks," Billy said.

The Frenchman watched him intently as he took a sip. "It is good, no?"

"The best."

The Frenchman smiled appreciatively but did not leave. He stood by the table looking down at Billy. "I did not know if you like it with the cream and sugar," he said, shrugging his shoulders mildly.

"No, it's perfect," Billy said. "I like it black." Then he noticed that the little man was holding another cup of coffee in his hands. He jerked his head toward the chair opposite him.

"It is not an imposition if I join you in—how do you Americans say—the coffee break?"

"Shoot, no. Have a seat."

"Merci." The Frenchman took the chair opposite Billy.

Billy had never seen the man up close before. Delicately built, he was wearing a starched white messman's jacket and trousers. His face was narrow and sharp. A narrow blade of a nose divided the face, beneath which the thin waxed mustaches curved up delicately at each tip. His hair was dark and slicked close to his scalp; his dark blue eyes were deep-set and intense and glistened with the cunning of a small carnivore.

His eyes twinkled as he looked down at Billy's half-eaten breakfast. "Perhaps the food is not so good this morning?"

Billy stabbed absently at a potato. "No, it's swell. I'm just not much hungry." He set the fork down. "I gotta tell you, though, the food is terrific here. Really."

The Frenchman bowed his head with a deprecating smile. *"Merci."*

"You take lessons or something?"

The Frenchman chuckled. "My papa was a chef," he said proudly. "And before him . . . his papa, and his papa before him. Who knows before? The Gréviers are always chefs, I think."

"Grévier?"

"Oui. Je m'appelle Maurice Grévier," the Frenchman bowed. "And you are Montana, *n'est-ce pas?* This is a name I have not heard before."

"Montana is a state," Billy said. "It's where I come from."

"Ah, *oui* . . . a state. A little like a *département* in France?"

"Something like that."

"Je comprend. I see." Maurice Grévier pulled thoughtfully at his mustache. His eyes were quick and sparkled intelligently; however, there was something behind them that set Billy on edge.

"The name's Billy," he said. "Billy Hochreiter." He leaned across the table and shook the Frenchman's hand.

"Ah, Billy. This is the nickname, as you say, for William, *n'est-ce pas?"*

"I guess so."

"In my country the name for William is *Guillaume."*

"Guillaume, huh?"

The little man seemed to study Billy's reaction. "Do you know the name Guillaume?"

"The name, sure."

"It is a quite common name in France, I admit." The Frenchman smiled pleasantly.

Billy took a sip of coffee then looked out the window at the starkness of the trees against the sky.

Maurice considered him for a moment then looked around the mess hall. The two airmen got up and left, and there was no one at the tables but Billy and himself. He looked back at Billy. "It is all right to sit down, I suppose, since we are lonely in here."

"Lonely? You mean *alone,* I think," Billy said.

Maurice laughed embarrassedly. "Ah, *oui,* that is what I mean. Alone . . . *oui.* These words are very much alike, I think. The English, it is a difficult language sometimes. To conjugate the verb is impossible." He chuckled, then looked thoughtfully at Billy. "You have no places to go?"

"Go?"

Maurice indicated the countryside with a gentle sweep of his hand.

"Right here suits me fine," Billy said. He set the coffee cup on the table and folded his hands around it. He looked at the Frenchman, smiled, then looked back out the window. He could hear the muffled throttle of a Thunderbolt. The engine revved and then quit, and the silence seemed heavier because of it.

"It is difficult being so long from home, no?" Maurice asked.

"It's not so bad."

"No? It is with me." He sighed. "There is much heaviness of heart being so far from my family."

"Sure," Billy said. He looked outside. "Some weather we been havin', huh?"

"*Oui,*" the Frenchman agreed politely. "It is no good for the flying?"

"Not especially." Billy glanced around at the empty, gray mess hall, then back out at the bleak autumn morning. He had nothing more to say. The room grew thick with quiet. One of the messmen called to another one, there was some rattling of pots, and then there was quiet.

The Frenchman sipped his coffee. He glanced at Billy over the rim of his cup, then lowered the cup delicately to the table, as though it were made of the finest bone china. His little finger was poised delicately off the handle. A change went over his face, a shade of cunning perhaps. He glanced over his shoulder, looked at Billy, then leaned forward slightly. "I have been wanting to speak with you, monsieur."

Billy glanced at him. "That right?"

"Oh, yes," Maurice said. "You are the pilot who is shot down over France?"

"Belgium."

"Ah. I was misinformed."

"I got out through France though," Billy said. And immediately his mind whipped him for saying it. He looked at his watch.

"I see," the Frenchman smiled. Seeing that Billy was about to leave, he put out his hand and touched his elbow. "I would like to hear of your travels in France," he said quickly. "You would not mind to spare a minute or two, would you?"

"Not much to tell."

"Still I would like to hear." He made a so-so gesture with his hand. "Here the news is, I'm afraid, not to be trusted."

Billy said nothing.

"It was very difficult for you in my country? The Boche, they are everywhere looking for you?"

"That was the feeling I got."

"You are so fortunate to escape quickly. I have heard the men talking." Maurice paused, then said, "Is it true that you get out by the aeroplane?"

"That's classified."

"Ah, *oui*. Classified. The top secret, *no?*"

Billy said nothing.

Maurice looked at him with quick darting glances. "I escape by the aeroplane," he said. "From Mâcon."

Billy's eyes flickered just perceptibly. "Mâcon, huh?" he said and shrugged his shoulders. "You were lucky."

"*Oui*. There was much luck, as you say. *Bonne chance*. The Boche, they are everywhere."

"You know it," Billy said without conviction. It seemed they had covered a circle of ground.

"I grew up in a little village in the Vosges," Maurice said. "But I leave there as a boy to find work as a chef. I go to Paris, but there is no work, so I go back home to work with my father." He chuckled.

Billy glanced once again at his watch. He still had a few minutes to kill before he had to go meet Jane, so he listened politely.

The Frenchman rambled on, seemingly aimless for a while, as he related one unrelated anecdote after another. Then his eyes grew suddenly misty in thought. "I stay for a while," he said, "but again I get the itchy feets, and I leave to find work in the big town. It is the pride of youth, I think. *J'ai en beaucoup de chance*. I am fortunate. Very fortunate. Before the war I am chef in the most respectable hotel in Vouziers. God is good, I think."

Billy looked at the little man. "What did you say?"

Maurice shrugged his eyebrows. "God is good?"

"No, before that."

"That I am a chef in Vouziers?"

"Yeah, that's it. That's a little town in the north of France, right?"

"*Oui* . . . Vouziers. It is a small village on the Meuse. You can see the Vosges in the distance. It is quite beautiful." His eyes sharpened. "Do you know Vouziers?"

"I've heard of it." Billy stared at the table and pondered a quick stream of thoughts. A strange prickling worked along his spine.

Maurice looked thoughtfully at him. "Have I said something to upset you, William?"

"No. Nothing. I was just thinking."

"You were wishing something to say," he said, then, smiling, added, "but the cat has eaten your tongue, perhaps?"

"No." Billy turned the coffee cup in his hands, staring into the blackness of the coffee.

"Ah, it is because you are not supposed to talk of your time in France, eh? *Oui?* That is it, I see. It is a wise policy."

Maurice sipped his coffee and looked out the window into the distance. There was a break in the clouds, and a thin shard of blue showed knifing through the overcast. He tapped lightly on the table with the palm of his hand, as though he were listening to a piece of music in his head. He lit a cigarette and smoked quietly, his foot marking time now as he continued to beat out his story.

Billy fidgeted anxiously in his seat but seemed unable to leave.

The two of them were a study in opposites: Billy, tall and well built, sat huddled over his coffee, his arms crooked guardedly over the table as though he were trying to keep something trapped between them, while the slighter Frenchman sat back in his chair with his legs crossed, his body open in the candor of a free spirit, his head tilted back, talking and blowing streams of smoke at the ceiling.

"My brother, Guillaume, he was the reckless one," the Frenchman said lyrically. "A tall one he is—good-looking. Not like Maurice." He chuckled. Paused. "I tell him to come with me—that it is no shame in leaving, but he would not. 'I will fight with the—'" He broke off suddenly, then grunted as he sat back in his chair. He blew a stream of smoke at the ceiling. "He is a fool, I think." He stubbed out his cigarette in an ashtray and brushed a few bits of tobacco off his trousers. From time to time he would glance shrewdly at Billy out of the corners of his eyes.

Billy was staring into his cup, holding whatever darkness there was at bay with his eyes. While one part of his mind listened abstractedly to the droning lilt of the Frenchman's voice, the other part wrestled with his feelings. They were all jangled inside him. How did he feel toward Jane? Did he love her? Yes. No. He had strong feelings for her, he knew; he cared for her deeply. But did he love her? He didn't know. How can you know? Really know? She is beautiful, but do I love her? Or is it just the terrible loneliness? Isn't that what she had said to him? The terrible loneliness?

And then, as always, thoughts of Colette would enter his mind; as always the image of her face—that perfect, haunting, omnipresent face—led him to ponder his forgotten vow to God. *Anything, God. You name it.* And, as always, his fingers would search for the silver cross, to fondle it tenderly as the hammer of guilt beat against his soul. Colette and his broken vow seemed inextricably linked. God seemed to be using her death as a measure to exact some kind of vengeance.

Billy hated him for it. How can you believe in such a God?

The Frenchman's voice droned in the background of his mind. Then, stealthily, like the stalking of a big cat, the words crept closer into Billy's consciousness and began to prick and needle. They were the words of a predator, and the hairs on the back of his neck began to bristle a warning.

"So I say to my brother, Guillaume, 'Marie is dead now, you must take care of your son. There is no shame in leaving. You must look out for the interests of Henri.'"

Billy looked at him suddenly. "Henri?"

"*Oui*, Henri." The Frenchman waited a moment, still watching Billy out of the corner of his eyes. "He is a good boy, Henri," he went on slowly. He chuckled. "Stubborn like his father, I think."

"Henri is your nephew?"

"*Oui. Qu Il est mon neveu.*"

Billy looked back into his cup. He stared into it for several moments, the strange prickling working all around his scalp. At last he said, "I met a man and a boy on their way to Vouziers."

"*Oui?*"

"That's all."

"This is how you know of Vouziers?"

"That's it."

Maurice looked at him intently. His sharp face angled to one side. "You were helped by this man and this boy, perhaps?"

Billy glanced at the man's face and, with a quick sweep of his eyes, made an appraisal of his features, his mouth, the hawkish blade of his nose, the deep-set blue of his eyes. He said nothing.

"You may speak freely, William," Maurice said, edging forward. "I see the look of distrust in your eyes. But I assure you, *mon ami*, that I am not of the Vichy."

"I can't tell you anything," Billy insisted.

"You may trust me."

"I could get court-martialed."

Maurice sighed. "Ah, *oui* . . . the war. We are living in such times when there is no trusting between men."

Billy glanced over his shoulder, then back at the man. They looked at each other inquiringly; each possessed a secret the other wanted to know. They both knew this. The air between them was bright and taut and brittle with distrust.

"It was just a farmer and his son going to market, is all," Billy said. "I saw lots of people in France. What are the chances that one of them was your brother?"

"I do not know," Maurice shrugged. "Perhaps none. But in the providence of God many strange things might happen. Who knows? That you are alive, that I am alive, that we are here together on the coffee break—is to God's credit, *n'est-ce pas?*"

Billy felt a pang in his conscience.

There was a sudden break in the Frenchman's expression. The previous look of cunning seemed to shatter as though it had been made of glass. An imploring look stood out of the broken shards. He seemed suddenly pathetic.

"You have met my brother Guillaume, William," he said. "I knew this in my heart when first I saw you come in to the mess hall. One of the airmen said to me, 'this is the one who has escaped from France.' It was then I heard a voice speaking in my heart, 'Maurice, this one—he has been with your brother Guillaume.' I do not know if this is God speaking to me, but I know that it is true."

Billy said nothing. It seemed clear to him that the little man was not Vichy, or a German spy, or a troublemaker of any kind. It seemed that he was exactly what he claimed to be—a Free Frenchman who at one time had been a chef in one of the finest hotels in Vouziers. A man whose path had, for reasons he could not begin to fathom, crossed his own.

"I will tell you something now," Maurice said, edging his secret closer into the light. "It is my trust of you that makes me say it." He paused, searching Billy's eyes. "I tell you that my brother Guillaume is with the Maquis. This is why he will not come with me. Tell me, William, was it not he and his boy Henri who helped you escape France? With the Maquis?"

"It's crazy."

"It is preposterous! But it is true. Did this man not have a—how do you say—a mark of the birth under his right eye? A little rosy star right here," he said pointing to his cheekbone.

Billy stared at him.

"Ah! This is not so crazy now, is it?" Maurice leaned forward in earnest. "You must tell me, William. Please, you must tell me if it is well with him. I have prayed for him every night in my prayers—for Henri too, and for the others. *Que sont-ils devenus?*"

"I can't talk about it."

Maurice searched Billy's eyes. Then a gleam of silver protruding from the V of Billy's shirt caught his eye. He reached across the table and took hold of the crucifix.

"What are you doing?" Billy objected.

Maurice gazed at the crucifix, turned it over, and read the inscription on the back: *"Affectueux, M. G."*

"It is true!" he said. "Do you not see the sentiment and the letters M and G? It is I, Maurice Grévier, who have put them there. This cross belongs to Colette, the daughter of Arnaud Dumortier."

Billy gaped at him dumbstruck.

"I give this to Colette when her mother is killed by the filthy Boche." He spat at the memory. "That you have this cross is proof you have been with my family."

"Your family?"

"*Oui.* Christina, the wife of Arnaud the woodcutter, was my sister."

"Then Colette—"

"Is my niece. And Jean-Claude and François are Christina's sons," Maurice explained. "Like Henri, they too are my nephews."

Billy turned his head and stared numbly at the table and cursed.

"Then it is true," Maurice said. "You have news of my brother Guillaume . . . of my family?" He took hold of Billy's hand. "Please, you must tell me, William," he begged. "I must know that it is well with them. *Que sont-ils devenus?*" he repeated.

Billy looked the little Frenchman square in the eyes. The secret in him was only darkness and sadness, he knew, but he could not withhold it any longer. "The Germans took your brother prisoner," he said. He told him of the long journey to Mâcon, the skirmish with the Germans, the betrayal of Pierre, the arrival of the plane, and the rest of it. "I do not know what has become of Henri, or Colette, or her brothers. Nothing good, I don't think. The place was lousy with Krauts."

Maurice listened intently, his eyes bright and fierce. Then, hearing the last of it, his eyes seemed to flicker, as a candle flickers before its tiny dart of flame is extinguished, then went suddenly void of expression. "I see," he said quietly. He sipped his coffee, then he looked out the window at the gloomy gray wall of overcast.

"I tried to make them come, but they wouldn't," Billy said. "There was nothing I could do."

"*Oui.* They are very brave, but they have the heads of bulls." Maurice chuckled without emotion. "I see that I am the lonely now."

Billy did not correct him.

"It is because I am a coward."

"No. You did right in coming here."

"So I can prepare the terrific meals for the American fliers? I think not."

"It's better than being dead."

"Is it?" Maurice took a final sip of coffee, then set his cup down delicately. He smiled at Billy and gently patted his hand. "I think that the coffee break is over." He started to rise.

Billy grabbed his wrist. "Wait!" He slipped the crucifix off his neck and put it in Maurice's hand. "Here. Colette would have wanted you to have this."

Maurice looked at the crudely carved figure of Christ then smiled at Billy. "*Les façons de Dieu sont mystère.*"

Billy looked at him puzzled.

"The ways of God are a mystery, *mon ami*," Maurice repeated. "But, no, this Colette has given to you." He poured the crucifix and chain back into Billy's palm, and closed his fingers around it. Without further word he cleared away the empty cups and dishes and walked back to the kitchen, very erect— holding his head up proudly, like a chef in a most respectable hotel.

Billy watched the little man take his familiar position behind the counter, watched him lift one of the metal covers along the counter to inspect the contents. The messman on duty stood to one side of the Frenchman and watched him like a spaniel.

Just then the door of the mess opened and three airmen entered, all of them laughing boisterously. They quickly strode over to the counter, stuck their noses over the trays and smelled what was for breakfast, then rubbed their hands together hungrily. Another man came in after them. It seemed the rush had begun. Billy looked down at the cross in his hand, shook his head, and swore.

As he exited the mess hall he saw Joe Thompson riding up on his bicycle.

"Hey, Montana!" he greeted. "You're all bright-eyed and bushy-tailed this morning."

Billy grunted.

"What's eatin' you?" Joe asked.

"Nothing."

"Okay, if that's the way you want to play it."

"That's the way I want to play it." Billy mounted his bicycle.

The big throaty roar of a Thunderbolt broke the quiet. Then another one revved its engine. And another one. The air was popping with the noise of several airplanes. The two fliers looked over toward the hangars.

"We have a briefing tomorrow," Joe said over the din. He leaned his bike against the corrugated wall of the mess hall. "Something big brewing."

"Yeah? What's up?"

"Something doing with the Brits is all I know."

"The Brits?"

"Don't ask me. Be in the briefing hut at 0700 tomorrow."

"Well, that's something," Billy said. "I'm getting sick of all this dead time."

Joe watched him pedal away, scratched his head, then went inside the mess hall. He brightened immediately. "Hey! What's cookin'!"

35 ★★★

Rolf looked carefully at the papers in his hands. His lips were drawn and pressed together, and his eyes moved slowly over each line. His hands were steady as he checked the spelling of each of the names, the destination and purpose for travel, the signature and seal of General Olbricht. He checked every detail again, very carefully.

"Are you satisfied, Captain Schiller?" Count von Stauffenberg asked, breaking a long silence. "Those papers will guarantee your family safe passage to Switzerland. No one will dare question the seal of the general."

Rolf finally looked up from the papers, his eyes cold and void of emotion. He looked from the count to the general. The general was sitting behind his desk, the large red Nazi flag behind him on the wall, and he wore a vague, benign smile, like an owl that has just caught a field mouse in its talons might smile from the shadows of its perch.

As at their first meeting, the room was in shadow except for the shaft of gray light streaming in through the half-opened drapes. Rolf, standing just outside the touch of light, looked back at the count. The count was standing by the corner of the general's desk, his right flank awash in the light. He was impeccably dressed in his Werhmacht field grade officer's uniform; his dark hair was combed neatly, and the black patch over his left eye gave him a roguish look.

"My life for the lives of each of my family," Rolf said, his voice sounding even and resolute.

"For the life of Germany," the count added.

Rolf grunted and looked back at the papers. "And you will provide the automobile?"

"Yes. A driver will pick up your family at seven o'clock, sharp. There must be no delays. They must be ready. One suitcase each."

"They will be ready." Rolf folded the papers and placed them inside the breast coat pocket of his uniform. "If the automobile is not there, the deal is off. Agreed?"

"Agreed."

In the room there was an air of consummation, of piety, of holy reverence; there was an unspoken knowledge between the three men that glowed in the half-light, between the worlds of darkness and light, of cruelty and mercy. The two superior officers glanced at one another with solemn expressions.

"Germany will long remember you, Captain Schiller," the count said. "The generations will bestow upon your memory a garland of praise."

Rolf was finished with words.

The count studied the lines of the squadron leader's face. Rolf was like so few men he had known—a guileless man. A man with convictions. A man without politics. He was a true warrior, he thought—a breed set apart from the flabby masses of smaller men; men who had no will of their own, no sense of what was good and what was not good; frightened men who moved along the well-oiled path like a rabble of pigs.

Looking at the squadron leader standing like a statue of bronze just to the side of the wedge of light, he felt the swell of pride rising in him. But pitching upon the surge came a sorrow. He wanted to put his arms around the man and kiss him on his noble warrior's brow.

Instead, he walked over to the window overlooking the Unter den Linden and, folding his maimed arms behind his back, he lowered his gaze upon the boulevard.

General Olbricht watched the count for several moments, then he turned his owlish head toward Rolf. "We must now discuss this matter of your girlfriend," he said.

Rolf stared flatly at him.

"Once again, if you please, tell us why you think this is the work of the Gestapo."

"Who else could it be, Herr General?"

The general shrugged his shoulders. "But why?" he asked. "What have the Gestapo against you? You are a hero of the Reich."

Rolf could think of only one reason; still, he said nothing. He was finished with words. The face of Olga appeared to him as a bright luminence in the gloom of that room. She was smiling at him from across the table in the little café, her beautiful face glowing in the soft aureole of candle-light, her long, slender fingers smoothing over his hands. A groan escaped his lips.

The count looked over at him. "Are you all right, Captain Schiller?" he asked.

"Yes."

"We do not need to discuss this matter further," he said.

"I am fine."

General Olbricht removed his steel-rimmed glasses, breathed on a lens, then wiped it clear with his handkerchief. He cleared his throat. "What do you know of this girl?" he asked. "You had been seeing her for less than two weeks." He polished the second lens, wrapped the wire ends carefully around each ear, and gazed at the squadron leader. "What do you really know of her? Of her past, I mean?"

Rolf considered this for a moment.

"She may have enemies that you know nothing of," the count offered. "Perhaps someone jealous of her recent affections toward you."

Rolf looked at him. It was possible, of course. He really knew very little about Olga, after all, except that she had breathed over the dead soil in his heart and brought forth a fiery hope, had nurtured a budding love. The pain of her loss once more tore at the inside of his chest like a caged animal. He felt like climbing a mountain and letting go his rage against the heavens. He merely shook his head.

The count put the stump of his right arm on the pate of the bronze eagle. "I am truly sorry for what has happened to her," he said sincerely. "It is a terrible loss."

"Yes, a terrible loss," the general agreed. "Still, we must use the utmost of precaution until the ceremony tomorrow evening. We may not have another opportunity like this one."

Rolf agreed that it would be best.

The count looked out the window, and something caught his good eye. "It would not be wise for us to meet here when we deliver to you the explosives," he said, following the course of a man in a black leather coat. The man disappeared around a corner.

Rolf said nothing. He waited patiently. He was thinking of only one thing now.

"We will contact you where it would be best to meet," the general said.

"Is there anything else, Herr General?"

General Olbricht looked at the squadron leader, picked up his pen, and began writing. "No, that is all for now."

The count stepped away from the window and put his left hand on Rolf's shoulder. "I will pray for you in church today, Captain Schiller."

Rolf looked at him with his flat stare. "I have told you that I have no faith."

The count smiled at him genially. "Ah, yes, so you have said. Still, I will pray that God will give you faith."

Rolf saluted the two men and left the office.

The general and the count looked at each other. The count shook his head and walked back to the window. He gazed down upon the Unter den Linden and felt the sadness rising in him. His shoulders stooped beneath the great weight.

Outside, the gray light of the morning smoothed out the contours of perspective, so that everything looked flat, uninteresting, gloomy, dead. The trees along the broad boulevard, now stripped of their leaves, afforded unobstructed vistas of the city. The trees held the city with a bony embrace.

Rolf walked along the sidewalk, looking straight ahead at some fixed point on the horizon, his eyes void of emotion, feeling nothing, nothing except the weight of the Luger on his hip. He had no feelings of remorse, or of fear; he was like a hollowed-out shell moving against the gray backdrop of the city, already dead. Dead like the city. He cared only for his family now—for Gretchen. Gretchen must survive. Everything else that he believed in had died. Hope was a dead thing, except that Gretchen must survive.

36 ★★★

Ernst opened the door to Gretchen's bedroom enough to see that no one was inside. He slipped quickly into the room, stuck his head back out the door, and glanced down the hall. He waited a moment until he was sure that no one had seen him enter the room, then closed the door quietly behind him. He looked at his wristwatch. It was 11:45 in the morning. His sister would be gone for at least two hours, he knew. She always used the excuse that she was going for some air in the park, but he knew where she was going. He and his friend Martin had followed her there the Sunday before.

He glanced over the room. A square of sun found its way through the window on the right and spread over the hardwood floor.

He moved quickly to the bureau directly ahead. On top of the bureau were two framed pictures. The first was a photo taken of the family on one of their visits to the Bavarian Alps. Father and Rolf were wearing lederhosen and Tyroler hats, and Mother and Gretchen were in pretty peasant dresses with their hair in braids. They were all smiling. Gretchen was holding a bouquet of wildflowers, and Rolf was holding baby Ernst, who seemed preoccupied with one of Rolf's ears.

Ernst grunted.

The second picture was a photo of Rolf standing in front of his Me–109 after his first victory. He wore a proud smile and looked rakish with a scarf around his neck and the wind in his hair. Ernst picked it up and gazed at it for several moments. He set it down, surrendered to momentary reflection, then opened the top drawer and carefully sifted through Gretchen's underwear. He frowned as he poked his fingers through several items, repulsed by the feminine silkiness of them. He felt in the back corners, then, pulling the drawer all the way out, felt beneath it, his fingers splayed as they swept over the coarse wood surface. He had learned this procedure in one of the Youth meetings and was pleased with himself to be using it. He found nothing.

Replacing the items, he made sure that everything was put back exactly how he had found it. As he slid the drawer forward it squeaked and he looked quickly at the door. He froze, listening for a moment. Then he shut the drawer and opened the one below it. There were a few blouses on one side and some work shirts on the other. That was all. Likewise, he felt beneath the drawer where an item could be concealed with tape, then made sure that everything was put back in the drawer neatly. Light, colorful sweaters were in the third drawer, and leggings and heavy sweaters for winter use were in the bottom one. But nothing else. Shutting the drawer, he stood up and looked across the room: first at the bed against the wall on the left, and then over at the writing desk beneath the window. He grunted.

He wore a smug expression. The pride of youth burned deeply in him, shone out through his eyes that glowed with a feverish triumph. He was doing his part for the Cause, for the Party, and he reveled in his private glory.

Walking as quietly as he could across the wood floor, he went over to the desk and glanced out the window that opened to the garden below. His mother was on her hands and knees digging out one of the beds with a trowel. She looked weak groveling in the dirt—old and weak—like his crippled father was old and weak. A curse rose in him, pushed through the stony soil of his heart and blossomed into a black flower of hate. He hated weakness. Weakness was like a cancer—yes, that was it, a cancer. It fed upon healthy tissue until only the cancer remained. There was no place for weakness in the new German order; it had to be disciplined or eliminated. He quickly inspected several items on top of the desk, checked through a row of books along the back.

Nothing.

Then he opened the drawer and snooped through the contents. He felt along the inside top of the desk and caught a splinter in his middle finger. He cursed, removed the splinter with his teeth, and spat it out on the floor.

He went over to the wardrobe, moved his hand along the top—nothing. He opened the doors and began to stab around through the dresses and coats. Nothing. He swiped at a dress, and it fell to the bottom of the wardrobe. He bent angrily to pick it up and threw it on its hanger. Turning, he looked hastily around the room. His right index finger tapped impatiently against his thigh. Where was it? She wasn't carrying it when she left. It had to be here. Where?

He went over to the bed, got down on his hands and knees, and looked beneath it, carefully pulling the covers back and shoving his hand between the mattress and the box springs. He slid his hand from one end to the other. Nothing. He stood to his feet and cursed.

A shock of brown hair fell across his brow, and he brushed it back with an angry rake of his hand. Then he went back to the desk, flipped quickly through each of the books before shoving them back into place. A pen rolled off the top and clattered to the floor. He ignored it. He checked behind the radiator. Nothing. His brow beaded with sweat, the fever of hatred glared through his eyes. He began talking aloud to himself as he yanked open the desk drawer and slapped his hand around inside. "Where'd you put it? Think you're clever, don't you? Don't you worry," he chortled. "I'll find it."

He hated his sister. She was weak, just like all the other religious fanatics of the Confessing Church were weak, serving a weak Christ. A weak Jew god. He hated her for what she was doing to Rolf, filling his mind with weak thoughts, corrupting him. He had heard her the other night, corrupting him with treasonous words. She was destroying a hero of the Reich. He'd find the proof. It was time for proof, for discipline. Cure the weakness or remove it from the body. It was a law of nature. It was the law of the New Order.

Ernst went once more around the room, rifling through the drawers, slamming them shut, leaving some partway open, each time cursing aloud. He spouted a diatribe of Party ideals under his breath—a denunciation of corrupters, of Christians, of Jews, of weakness. Thin Wagnerian strains of music whined stridently through his brain. His anger boiled over into a rage.

He clawed dresses off their hangers; he scattered books over the floor; he tore the covers off the bed. Nothing. He slammed his fist against the wall, growling obscenities. Then he plopped down on the edge of the bed, stewing in a black rage. He looked up at the corners of the ceiling, along the floor molding, back at the bureau and wardrobe. He pounded his thigh with his fist, beating out a martial cadence. Where is it? Where is it? Where is it? Something occurred to him, and he looked down at the pillow. As yet it was undisturbed. "No," he said, dismissing the thought. Still, he lifted the corner of the pillow, and a twisted smile curled over his mouth.

"Stupid girl," he muttered.

Ernst removed the diary and, chuckling, held it out before him. Quickly he tried the clasp, but it was locked. No matter. He found a hairpin on the bureau and, after a few tries, picked the lock. He smiled smugly. This too he had learned in one of the Youth meetings.

He sat down at the desk and flipped greedily through the pages, gloating over his found treasure. Turning to the front, he began to read carefully. The first few pages were filled with sentimental musings, some poems, verses of Scripture, and prayers—girl stuff. There were several pages devoted to some soldier home on leave that she hoped to convert to Christianity. He was a handsome man, according to her detailed description of him, charming and showed promise. Ernst thought he might retch. Then, according to the next few entries, matters didn't go so well. Ernst snickered. The soldier went back to the front a lost soul. There was a prayer for him, some more sentimental tripe. And then toward the middle of the diary his eyes narrowed. Suddenly he was rapt. He raced through the pages. This was it. This was everything he needed for proof. He chuckled throatily. What more would they need?

Suddenly a prickling of danger raced up his spine. He spun around and his face went wide with guilt. "Wh-what are you doing here?" he stammered.

Gretchen stood in the doorway aghast. "What am I doing here! What are *you* doing in here?"

Ernst looked down at his wristwatch in protest. "You're an hour early."

She gazed at her room, now in shambles, with disbelief. Clothes spilled out of the wardrobe, draped over the drawers of her bureau; books were strewn across the floor; sheets of peach-colored stationery curled up against the baseboard. "What have you done to my room?" she demanded.

The boy's ears were blazing red; his eyes darted quickly around the room like a criminal's. "I—lost something," he gasped. "I thought you might have it in here."

She saw him slip the diary behind his back, and a crimson line burned up her neck. She thrust out her hand. "Give me that. You have no business snooping in my things."

Ernst's face began to change. A sneer curled slowly along his upper lip like the twist of a snake. "I don't think so."

"Give it to me."

He chuckled. "I think I will just hold onto it for a while." The change in him was complete. He stood up and, with a recovered arrogance, flipped through the pages. "Very interesting reading, this. Very interesting. I am disappointed though." He clucked his tongue. "It is a pity that you could not hold dear Siegfried. 'His eyes are so blue,'" he read. "'Like brilliant sapphires in settings of chiseled bronze.'"

She snatched at the diary but Ernst put out his arm. Brother and sister were about the same height; however, he outweighed her by at least twenty pounds. He looked at her with contempt. "Are you so undesirable that you cannot attract a man? That is all right. You can always marry Christ."

Gretchen stood rigid, glaring at him. "You have no right."

"Oh, yes, I do, sister dear. I have every right."

"You have invaded my privacy."

"And it is a good thing too." He thumbed through the pages and stopped at a place he had marked. "Here's something interesting I wish for you to explain. 'We are a foolish people,'" he read. "'We have sacrificed our freedoms for the sake of economic prosperity, and now we have no faith. Our moral decline has overtaken us like a frog in a kettle.'" He turned to Gretchen. "What does this mean, Gretchen—a frog in a kettle?"

Gretchen glared at him. "Are you going to give me my diary?"

"Oh, but there's more," Ernst smiled. "Much more." He flipped a couple of pages. "Where was it? Ah, here it is! 'Martin Bormann has said that National Socialism and Christianity are irreconcilable. He is a fool. Whenever the state has been contrary to the cause of Christ, the state has crumbled. Consider Rome.'" Ernst shook his head and clucked his tongue. "This is treasonous, you know?"

Gretchen was so angry that tears spurted from her eyes. "Ernst, please. This is my private book."

"Not anymore it isn't." He chuckled triumphantly.

"Give her the book, Ernst," Rolf said.

Ernst looked quickly at the figure of his older brother framed in the doorway. His face was a dark scowl. "This is contraband. It belongs to the Reich."

Rolf stepped forward into the room. "Give her the book, Ernst."

"She has written treasonous words against the Reich," Ernst said, backing away. "She has called the Führer a madman."

"Give it to her, Ernst. I will not ask you again."

Ernst was backed against the wardrobe. "I won't, Rolf. Can't you see what she's doing to you? How she's corrupting you?"

Rolf stared at him. "As your superior officer I give you a direct order." He saw the vacillation in his brother's eyes.

"An order. Now you give orders," Ernst said, stiffening. "I cannot obey it, Rolf. She's vile. She's an enemy of the state. She has to be disciplined . . . for your sake."

Still Rolf stared at him. A dark red glow spread through his chest.

"Can't you see how she's drawing you in? She is making you weak," Ernst said, looking hatefully at his sister. "She should be shot as a filthy traitor."

A cold shock went through the air.

Gretchen's hand rose to her mouth.

Rolf's head oscillated unsteadily upon his neck. A crimson wash blurred his vision. He staggered forward, almost drunkenly, raised his arm, and struck the boy's face with the back of his hand as hard as he could. Ernst sprawled against the bed.

Gretchen covered her mouth with a gasp. She looked from one brother to the other and was suddenly very frightened.

Rolf stood over the boy, his fists doubled at his sides.

Ernst righted himself onto his elbow. He scowled at the looming figure of his brother, a trickle of blood leaking from his mouth. "You will pay for that . . . hero of the Reich. You're nothing but a traitor as well. I heard you talking the other night—you and her. You're both traitors. You think you're so clever. You're not so clever. You couldn't even protect that silly little tramp of yours."

"What did you say?" Rolf's voice was a low, hoarse growl.

Gretchen shook her head. "Ernst, don't."

"That's right," Ernst chortled. He saw that he had scored a hit. "Can't face the truth, can you? Maybe you didn't know she was a tramp . . . a favorite with the Wehrmacht, I'm told." He barked a laugh of contempt.

"Ernst," Gretchen begged.

"Where were you when she was begging for mercy, Hero of the Reich?" the boy spat venomously. "I can just see her now, can't you? 'Please . . . please . . . anything! Oh, anything, please!' What do you think she offered them to spare her worthless life?"

Rolf lunged at him. He put his long, strong fingers around Ernst's throat and began to choke the life out of him.

Ernst beat against him with his fists. His face began to turn red, then blue, as he gagged helplessly. His eyes bulged and watered. Then his arms fell limp.

"Rolf, don't!" Gretchen cried. She pulled frantically on his arm. "You're killing him! Rolf!"

A light flashed in Rolf's eyes and his hands flew off the boy's neck as though he had touched a hot iron.

Ernst coughed and sputtered, reeled onto his side, and clawed the covers over his face.

Rolf stood up with his hands wide. He looked at each of his hands and then down at his brother. But it was no longer his brother; his brother was dead, and this was something else. For a fleeting second he thought about drawing the pistol on his hip and putting a bullet through its head. He looked over at Gretchen. Her face was contorted by pain and confusion and pity. Immediately he forgot about the pistol. He put his arms around her and held her close.

Watching them with a single glaring eye that darted furtively over a fold in the covers, Ernst looked over at the diary now on the floor, then back at Rolf and Gretchen. They were still holding each other. He was patting her on the back. The fools. Seeing his chance, he bolted across the floor of the bedroom with a triumphant howl, snatched up the diary, and disappeared down the hallway.

Rolf and Gretchen spun around and listened as Ernst took the staircase two and three steps at a time. A moment later the front door banged shut, and a dreadful quiet rushed into the room.

"Rolf, was that really Ernst, our brother?" Gretchen asked wonderingly. "What has happened to him?"

"I don't know."

"I guess I've never seen it until now—truly seen it. I'm frightened, Rolf."

He said nothing.

"Rolf?"

He looked at her.

"Do you see the diary anywhere?" she said, panic quickly building in her voice. She glanced over the floor. "I think he's got my diary." And then she said, "He's got my diary." She looked at him, the horror of it registering on her face. "You don't really think that he would—"

"What was in it?"

She stared at him blankly. "I must warn Pastor Schoenfield."

Rolf appeared not to have heard her. He glanced around at the mess on the floor and picked up a discarded blouse. He handed it to her. "I want you to pack a suitcase."

"A suitcase?"

"We're leaving."

"I don't understand—"

"For Switzerland. Today. I've already made all of the necessary arrangements."

"Because of this?"

"I must get you and the family out of Germany."

She took hold of his arm. "Rolf, what is it? There's something else, isn't there? Something terrible."

"I don't have time to explain," he said. "Now, please, just pack a suitcase and don't argue with me."

"Rolf?"

"Please don't argue with me."

"All right," she said, searching his eyes. "But I must warn Pastor Schoenfield."

"He can take care of himself."

"No, Rolf!"

"I am not my brother's keeper," he said bitterly. "God is his keeper, remember? Let God take care of him."

Gretchen pulled away from him. "I'm not going anywhere until I've warned Pastor Schoenfield. Rolf, I have to." She began to cry. "They will come for him."

Rolf looked at her. She stood rigid, her fists clenched and straight at her sides, her jaw clamped grimly. Her eyes were red and tears streamed down her cheeks. Frowning and crying, she looked so fierce and pathetic at the same time that it was almost comical. He glanced down at his wristwatch. It was 1:00.

37 ★ ★ ★

Billy lay back on his elbows and gazed up at the great clouds trudging heavily across the sky with heavy burdens humped up on their backs. The Sunday afternoon sun shone brightly on the common that was green with autumn lushness, and people were out in number to enjoy the sudden and unexpected return of warm weather. "It's an Indian summer," he said to her.

"An Indian summer? How do you mean?"

"When you get a bit of warm weather in the fall," he said. "I don't know why, but we call it an Indian summer."

"We call it a St. Martin's," she said. "Don't ask me why either."

"St. Martin's, huh?" He looked out over the common.

People were walking along the pathways and sitting on blankets with baskets of food, some with big-wheeled prams parked next to them. Children romped across the broad, green lawns, chasing cloud shadows and one another. Everything looked lovely in the warming light of the early afternoon sun that fell in between the clouds. The war was far away, at least for the moment, and there was a faraway look in Billy's eyes.

His mind was broken into three large thought fragments. There were some smaller fragments that twirled in and out, glittering like pyrite in a stream, but these didn't matter for the time being. The first of the three larger fragments was occupied by the French girl. Colette was always there, her face frozen in a blink of time. *She's dead, Billy boy*, he told himself. *Let the dead bury the dead and quit being morbid.* But, strangely, he found himself thinking of her more and more, not less and less. And Angelique didn't help matters any either. A dead ringer for the dead, who rang up the ghost. *Let her go*, he thought.

The second fragment was larger and more prominent, simply because it had the advantage of proximity and flesh. Jane was sitting next to him. He could feel her sitting there; he could hear her breathing; he could smell the scent of her hair and perfume. He could turn and look at her at any time and see her, if he chose to. For now there were beautiful colors of reds and pinks and blues and flesh tones that changed mysteriously in the light, like a chameleon changes colors: now one thing, now another. If he chose to he could reach over and touch her, feel the softness of her skin, of her lips against his. Because he could, he chose not to. It was odd.

He would love her in time, he knew. She was a decent enough girl, more decent than he. What was not to love? Shoot. He'd be a jerk not to love her. A fairly lucky jerk up till now, he told himself. You've been lucky twice now, haven't you? Unlucky twice too. Unlucky with the first one—scratch that. That was really a bit of luck in disguise, wasn't it? Make that three times lucky. You found out about Laura before it was too late, and old Tom Baxter's got her now. Let that poor sucker deal with her.

Then you got lucky with Colette. That was the war. Both ways, lucky and unlucky. You got lucky with her because of the war, then the war took it back like an Indian giver. I wonder why they call them Indian givers? he asked himself. No Crow I ever knew ever took anything back. That's the government's job. Government givers is what they ought to call them. Bad luck on the Indians. This is getting complicated, Billy told himself, better stick to the Big Three.

You got unlucky with Colette, but you got lucky with Jane. Take it easy with Jane, he told himself. She's as fragile as a china doll and you don't want to break her. Break her and you're done for.

And then there was the third fragment. It was the third fragment that troubled him at the moment. There was no choosing or not choosing the third fragment.

"Yoo hoo," Jane said, nursing her fingers through his hair.

"Huh?" He swung his head at her. "What?"

She lifted her hand from his head, her hand hovering lightly off his ear. "I didn't mean to startle you, darling," she said, cupping the cool of her palm against his cheek. "You've gone off somewhere again."

He looked away, recovering, coming back from his thoughts now, looking now at the people and the greenness of the common, feeling the wind against his face. "I've been thinking," he said, as one of the Big Three edged back into his mind.

"Really?" She smiled playfully at him. "And what have you been thinking, my brilliant thinker of thoughts?"

"Nothing much."

"Really?" She polished an apple on her thigh and took a bite. She looked to see what held his gaze, saw nothing, then offered the apple to him. "Want some?"

"No thanks."

"How about a biscuit? Mum made us some lovely biscuits."

"No thanks."

She draped her arm around his neck and, coming up around the other side of his head with her middle fingers, stroked the hollow of his temple lovingly. "Care to let me in?"

"What's that?"

"Your thoughts."

"I'm sorry," he apologized. He was looking at her now and seeing her, only her. "I've just been thinking."

"We've already been over this ground," she said, her arm draped loosely around his neck.

"You're beautiful," he said.

"Thank you."

"Really. I mean it."

"I believe you. Really." She tickled her fingers through his hair. She bit into her apple and smiled lovingly at him.

He smiled back at her, the corners of his mouth jerking out quickly, then, not knowing what else to say, he looked away. Another length of silence fell between them. Jane looked up at the clouds, over at the woman rocking her pram. Billy stared across the common, seeing nothing now but the problem of the third fragment. He looked at her suddenly and asked, "Do you believe in God?"

She looked at him, somewhat amazed, then smiled. "It *was* a splendid sermon this morning, wasn't it?"

"Do you?"

She leaned close to him and whispered into his ear, "I thought you didn't like to talk religion." She bit his earlobe.

He shrugged his head away. "Do you?"

"You're serious." She placed the core of the apple beside her in the grass and wiped her hands on her napkin. "Of course I do," she said. "I have ever since I was a little girl." She watched some children playing a game of tag.

"I suppose everybody believes something about God when you get down to it—right or wrong. There are no atheists in the foxholes, as they say."

Billy looked away.

"Oh, I'm sure there are a few atheists about," she corrected herself. "Those who believe we come from monkeys and such. I never went in for that sort of thing though. Seems a bit far-fetched, don't you think? Monkeys," she clarified. "You know—*Origin of the Species* and all. I mean if we came from monkeys, where did the monkeys come from? It all gets back to first cause, doesn't it?"

Billy was looking across the common. "Do you think, if there's a God, he gives a hoot about any of this?" he asked. "What's he care about any of this for? Nothing but a bunch of bugs."

"We're not bugs," she said, "we're human beings."

"It depends on your perspective."

"And what is your perspective?" she asked.

"I think it's a big game somebody made up," he said. "Only it's no game. Roll a seven you go to heaven. Snake eyes you bought the farm, pal. Talk about a crap shoot."

"You're bitter."

He looked at her. "It stinks . . . all of it."

"Yes, all of it," she said. "Sin stinks. War stinks. Injustice stinks. That Christ died for sinners stinks. Why'd he do it? He didn't have to, you know?"

Billy said nothing.

"You fail to mention that God slapped the stink of the world on the back of his Son," she said.

"Let's not talk about it."

She tapped his hand. "You were the one who brought it up."

"You're right. Let's talk about something else."

Billy lay back on the grass in the lazy warmth, folded his hands behind his head, and gazed at the clouds scudding overhead. He closed his eyes and felt the cool cloud patterns move over his face.

Jane watched him, smiling, then she lay sideways on her elbow next to him, her elbow thrown above her head, and began sprinkling little bits of grass on his chest. She spread a circle over his chest then moved up to his face. Billy swatted the first piece away. When the second piece alighted on his nose he opened one eye and looked at her. She giggled. He grunted and closed his eye.

"You're sure you wouldn't like to have tea with Reverend Townsend and his wife?" she asked.

"I'm sure."

"Pity."

"Yes, pity," he said dreamily.

"It's because of Angelique, isn't it? You don't want to have tea because of Angelique."

He said nothing.

"She's very beautiful, I know. I saw you looking at her in church."

Billy sat up and brushed the grass off his shirt. "That's not it."

"What is it then?"

"Let's not go into it. Please," he added.

Jane looked up at him. "You said last night that she reminded you of someone. Was it someone you met in France?"

He folded his arms around his knees and peered down at the long spears of grass between his legs. He plucked one and tossed it on the breeze that was holding steady off the coast.

"What happened in France, Billy?"

"Nothing happened in France."

"Did you love her?" she asked and waited a moment. "Why won't you talk about it?"

He reached over and put his hand on hers. "Because you're here, that's why. Because you're here, and because you're alive, and because you look terrific in that dress. And because I want to kiss you." He rolled onto his side and kissed her lightly on the mouth.

She smiled at him.

"Besides," he said, rolling over onto his stomach now and propping himself up on his elbows. "Nothing had to have happened for me not to want to talk about it."

"You're right of course."

"Let's go."

"All right; if you like. But isn't it lovely here at the common?"

"Too many commoners."

She made a face at him. "Haven't we become the Royalist."

"Is that a royal We?"

"Thou. Thou art a scoundrel monarch," she said playfully. "It is the mark of a wise and noble king to condescend once in a while, to familiarize himself with his subjects."

"You're the only subject I want to get familiar with."

"Am I one of your subjects then?"

"My favorite. You were an elective course." He grinned at her. "An easy A."

She slapped his hand.

Jane put on her socks and shoes, then they gathered up their things and pedaled east, away from the village and into the countryside. Once they had gone about a mile or so, they turned off the main road and onto a dirt lane that was straight and tractor-rutted and crowded on either side by tall hedgerows. Everything was quiet in the lengthy stretch of hollow. The only sounds were the grate of their wheels over the ruts and the lazy clatter of bicycle chains. The air about them shone with a diffusion of light and shadow, giving the place an aspect of foreboding.

He felt a cold shiver go through him, starting from the base of his spine then washing up over his scalp, as though the finger of Death had reached out of the wall of the hedge and touched him. He looked over at Jane. She was staring straight ahead, smiling as she pedaled her bicycle.

The hedgerows fell away brightly and suddenly, opening acres and acres of turned-under farmland that was bordered with low, stone walls. The chilling wind was in their faces now, lashing their cheeks and hair and drawing water from their eyes. They rode for a while in silence, listening to the wind and to the rattle of their bicycle chains.

Just then Billy pulled up abruptly on his bike and looked off into the distance.

"What is it?" Jane asked him.

"Listen."

They stood, straddling their bikes, and craned their heads against the wind. The wind soughed through some elm trees on their left and over the fields, and they heard only the wind and the keening of blackbirds falling through the sky like dagger slashes. Then they both heard it.

Billy turned his head to the northwest, waited a moment, and pointed. "There!"

A line of dark specks jumped out from behind the clouds and into view, like a skein of geese, and flashed as the sun struck their burnished flanks. Billy and Jane shielded their eyes with their hands as the muffled throaty drone of aircraft climbed steadily on the wind.

"Can you tell what they are yet?" she asked.

"Bombers."

They continued watching as the planes grew, slanting larger and larger toward them, until they heard the solid roar of the heavy aircraft going by at ten thousand feet. The ground shook in terror, and they were overwhelmed with the seemingly omnipresent power of the bombers.

Billy tried to count the flights; there appeared to be at least three hundred aircraft heading east. "Something's up," he said. "Night raid. Gonna drop a load on some Kraut's head."

"Will you be a part of it?"

"Lancasters," he said, interrupting. "I can see the twin stabs."

"I see them. Yes, Lancasters."

They watched in silence as wave after wave of the British bombers slid high and proud against the sky as they made their way steadily, thunderingly for the coast and the continent beyond.

"Brave lads," she said, the bombers moving away now.

"Poor saps," Billy said. "I sure wouldn't want to be in their shoes. Sitting ducks in them buckets." He looked quickly at Jane. "I'm sorry—I—"

"It's all right, Billy. Really, love." She leaned over her bike and patted his hand. "I've buried my ghosts."

He looked at her. Then he said, "Have I told you yet today that you're beautiful?"

"Only twenty times."

"I must be slipping."

"Tell me again, or I shall be terribly hurt."

"You're beautiful, you're beautiful, you're beautiful—"

"You're insincere."

He moved his bike closer to hers and kissed her. "How's that for insincerity?"

"The definition is a bit foggy really," she smiled.

He kissed her again, hard on the mouth. An intense longing came over them, and they held each other, tightly, achingly, kissing and still kissing and holding until a fire caught, was good and caught now, and there was only one thing to do about it.

She pushed gently away. "Yes, well," she said, her eyes looking up at him then darting away, then looking steadily up at him. "Enough of this insincerity."

"Jane?"

"Yes?"

They stood astride their bikes, gazing into each other's eyes. There was a desperateness in her eyes, and there was a desperateness in his eyes, although it was not clear that they were the same desperateness.

And then she said, "Do you love me, Billy?"

Billy's head reeled as though he had been lashed. He blinked at her. "Love you? Shoot—"

She smiled at him. "That's all right," she said. "I'd rather you not lie. I can wait. Heaven knows I'm a good waiter."

"I don't want you to wait."

"You're a sweet."

He looked at the Lancasters over the coast—tiny black specks again. Then he looked back at her. "Anybody ever tell you you were a terrific gal?"

"No," she said. "Nor a swell gal or a keen gal either."

"Well, you are. You're a terrifically swell keen gal, and I think the world of you."

She smiled lightly at him. "We'd better be off."

"Another royal We?"

"A royal Us."

They pedaled away on the narrow dirt road and, after crossing several more fields, rolled over a cattle guard and turned back onto the main road out of town. The wind was in their faces again, and tart with the sea.

"Hello?" Jane said as her house curved into view. "What's he doing here?"

"The postman?" Billy grinned. "If I had to take a wild guess I'd say he was delivering mail."

"On Sunday?"

Mr. Bellamy was talking with the postman on the front porch, and when he saw Jane and Billy riding up to the house he waved at them.

The postman passed them as they came in through the gate. "Special delivery for you, Jane." He tipped his cap and climbed onto his bicycle. "Cheerio!"

"Special delivery?" She smiled at Billy. "Julie, I should think, writing what a splendid time she's been having."

Her father met them at the bottom of the porch stairs. He handed her an envelope that was long and official looking. She blinked down at it, still smiling. The letter carried all the immediate weight and puzzlement that unexpected correspondence from the government carries when you receive it.

"It's from Bomber Command, Jane."

"Bomber Command?" she repeated. Her smile fell away as she stared down at the stamps, at the government seal, and at the uppercase lettering that was always so cold and militarily impersonal. "What's it mean?"

"I don't know, dear. You'll have to open it."

She opened the envelope and, holding the letter away from her distrustfully, began to read carefully. Her lips moved silently over the words. She stopped abruptly and looked toward the coast, lowering the letter slowly to her side.

Billy and Mr. Bellamy exchanged looks.

"May I?" Mr. Bellamy took the letter.

"Edmund," she said in little more than a whisper. "It's Edmund."

Her father skimmed the letter quickly. He glanced up at Jane and then at Billy. "I say, this is a bit of news."

Billy watched him intently.

"They've located Edmund," he said. "By Jove, he's alive! Doing quite well it appears."

Billy stared at him, a smile contorting over his mouth. "Hey . . . how 'bout that. Edmund, huh?"

Reading enthusiastically, Mr. Bellamy chortled, "Seems the Gerries picked him up behind the Mareth Line. They have him in a POW camp in the south of Germany. Got him confused with some poor chap named Werthing. This *is* a bit of news, eh, what?"

He looked up at Jane, it seemed, with an eye to sweep her off her feet and twirl her around the yard. But seeing his daughter staring out over the empty acres of plowed fields, standing erect and unwavering against the fields as quiet and as inscrutable as the pillar of Lot's wife, he pulled up abruptly. He grunted once to clear his throat and then said with a cut of self-reproach, "Took their sweet time in getting it straight, didn't they, love?"

Jane continued looking toward the coast.

Billy was staring down at the ground now, running the toe of his shoe over a crack in the flags.

Mr. Bellamy looked at his daughter. "Are you all right, dear?" he asked, touching her lightly on the arm.

"Give us a moment, Dad," she said.

He looked at her for a moment, then at Billy. He scratched his head. "Rather clumsy business, war," he said. He stepped over and shook Billy's hand. "You're a fine lad," he added. "As fine a lad as ever I've known." He climbed the stairs quietly, folding the letter back into its envelope as he went into the house.

The wind picked up and knocked against the brittle silence. Big, brown, star-shaped leaves off the neighboring sycamore somersaulted across the road like a handful of furious children at play.

Billy looked up at Jane's back. She was still standing erect, with her shoulders back and her head lifted high on her neck, staring in the direction of the coast. Both of them knew that they would have to look one another in the eyes sooner or later.

"I'd best be going," he said.

Jane turned around in stages: first her face, tears leaking down her cheeks, then the rest of her came around. "Oh, Billy, please don't. Not just yet."

He just looked at her. She was never more beautiful than she was in that moment. Look at her, he said to himself. If you don't love her you're either a liar or a fool.

She took a step toward him and hesitated, and seeing it going over her face he knew that it was over. Like a great blue heron rising heavily off the misty solitude of the Stillwater then pumping gracefully to glide slowly away down river, it was gone.

She rushed over to him and sobbed, "Oh, Billy, I do care for you, so very deeply. Whatever am I going to do? Billy . . . Billy . . ."

He held her for a long while, looking off into the distance as another flight of Lancasters headed east toward the coast. Gonna be a big night, he thought.

He patted her back, and he could feel her crying, her shoulders heaving softly as she kept saying his name over and over, and telling him that she loved him. But he knew that everything between them was gone, that this was only the initial death throes of it, that it would die and wither away like everything else that dies. He felt nothing but a great, hollow emptiness inside. He would feel it later, he knew, laying on his bed and staring into the black solitude of the night. He'd feel it then all right. But right now he was through with it. Through with it and the rest of the Big Three.

He ran his hand through her hair and kissed her tenderly on her forehead. She looked up at him, her eyes red with crying, her nose wet. She looked lost and desperate as she searched his eyes.

With his thumbs he gently wiped the tears away from her cheeks, smiling down at her. "I wish you the best of happiness," he said. "You deserve it."

She looked at him, blinking through a wash of tears, the astonishment of loss playing over her face.

"I sure didn't figure this," he said, then chuckled. "I guess God's the biggest of all Indian givers, isn't he?"

"Billy—"

He walked out through the gate, mounted his bike, and, looking back at her once and seeing her standing at the bottom of the porch steps, holding her hands and looking small and lost and tragically beautiful, like when he had first seen her in the pub that night, he waved at her and smiled. Then he pedaled slowly away to the mourning rattle of the chain.

38 ★★★

We will be back no later than six," Rolf said to his parents as he and Gretchen exited the house. "The transportation will be here at seven o'clock sharp."

His parents stood in the doorway, gaping dumbfounded at him. Mr. Schiller was propped up on his crutches, and Mrs. Schiller was still wearing her gardening gloves. They had the horrible and confused look of two children who had just been told by their parents that they were illegitimate.

"Are you certain of all this, Rolf?" his mother asked him.

"Yes," he said sharply. "One suitcase each. Have everything packed and ready to go."

"It is awfully sudden," his mother said.

Mr. Schiller was at a loss for words, and seemed incapable of movement. "What of Ernst?"

"I don't know what to think of Ernst," Rolf said. "We'll be back no later than six o'clock," he reiterated. "Let's go, Gretch."

The two elder Schillers watched them turn away, looking like two terribly frightened children.

Rolf and Gretchen made their way down the porch steps and along the walk. Rolf opened the front gate for his sister and, doing so, noticed a large man in a black leather coat standing across the street and looking away just as their eyes met. The man patted his breast pockets and, retrieving a silver cigarette holder, lit a cigarette and blew a cloud of smoke into the air. He stood looking away and smoking his cigarette as though waiting for a bus.

As Rolf shut the gate a thought struck him. Odd. There was something vaguely familiar about the man, but he could not put his finger on it.

"What is it, Rolf?"

"Nothing."

"Do you really think Ernst would go to the Gestapo?" she asked him.

"I don't know," he said, still eyeing the man. He had seen him somewhere before, he was certain of it. But where? He took her arm and turned right, walking quickly up the street in the opposite direction. "Let's go."

"I can't believe it," she said, looking down at the sidewalk. "Not Ernst." Then seeing where Rolf was leading her, she pulled back on his arm. "This isn't the way," she protested.

"For now it is," Rolf said. He led her across the street, glancing quickly for traffic that was not there and catching the face of the man as he turned in their direction.

"There *is* something," Gretchen said, looking up at Rolf's face.

"There's nothing. Now, let's go."

She followed on his arm, glancing once behind them, seeing the man turning and walking after them slowly. The man looked away with a casual sweep of his head, slowed to examine the gates of a house as though to locate an address, and Gretchen thought nothing of him. It was just a man on the street looking for an address.

Where was it? Rolf was thinking. He thought hard, trying to place the face. But, like the annoying buzz of a mosquito, every time he thought he'd captured it, his hand was empty and he'd hear it on the opposite side of his head.

Rolf walked at a fair clip, trying not to appear evasive or even aware that the man in the black leather coat was probably following them. Sensing her brother's distraction, Gretchen looked up at him to read his face. She glanced over her shoulder after he did and saw nothing but the man keeping pace with them and looking at the gates of the houses.

They turned down a narrow residential street with big trees lining the walks. The man turned onto the street soon after them, smoking his cigarette and keeping about fifty yards behind.

"Rolf, that man—"

"I know. Don't look back. Just look straight ahead and keep walking."

"Who is he?"

"I don't know."

"Is he with the Gestapo?"

"Perhaps."

"Is it because of Ernst, do you think?"

"It's not likely. There hasn't been enough time for Ernst."

"I can't believe he would do it."

Rolf quickened his pace. The man in the black coat quickened his pace without appearing to do so.

"He's following us."

"Yes. And he's being rather clumsy at it." He had seen him before. But where?

Quickly his mind began sorting through the events of the past two weeks, as though going through a file cabinet. He opened and closed each of the files carefully, skimming through the details, events, and likely venues where he might have seen him, but nothing came to mind. He was looking too hard at it, he knew.

The sound of their footsteps struck echoingly against the cement sidewalk that went along the older section of the Berlin neighborhood. Big Victorian-style homes crowded the walk, and the neighborhood showed no evidence of the war. The slanting afternoon sun shone down through the big, leafless trees and made spindly shadow patterns at their feet. There was a brisk autumn chill in the air and the faint smell of coal smoke.

Rolf's mind was working. He had seen the man before; it was right there in front of him, or just to the side. He turned his head to his sister, as though in conversation, and doing so cast a backward eye on the man. And then he saw it. At first it was just the blurred shape of the man walking along the sidewalk, just a man-shape smoking a cigarette, nothing unusual, but seeing it out of the corner of his eye it grew upon him like a revelation.

"The Tiergarten!" he blurted.

Gretchen looked at him strangely. "Rolf?"

The day he was waiting for Olga in the park! He was the tourist at the Column of Victory, taking pictures of the statues! He remembered it because he thought it odd at the time that someone should be taking pictures of statues with a telephoto lens.

But that was not the only time he had seen him, he knew at once. There were other times.

He began to see it now, an imperceptible blur at first, a glimmer of light piercing the fog in his mind. Then it burst upon him in a series of recollections, one right after the other, with pristine clarity. An aberrant star— the repetition of a face—turning up in each of the constellations. He saw it now on more than one of his walks in the Tiergarten with Gretchen; in the museums and art galleries; in the foyer of the Opera House; at various places in the Zoological Gardens. It was never in the foreground, always in the background, a certain look, a casual glance, a practiced turning away as their eyes met. But he saw it now.

And then a shudder went through him. It was there at the park! The face—

The blood drained quickly from his head, leaving him cold with bitter awareness, then it all came in a hot wash of anger. He was in the park the night that Olga was murdered!

Rolf halted abruptly and stared at the man coming toward them. The man was looking off to the side and did not see that Rolf had stopped, and, by the time he did, had gone several yards. He pulled up suddenly. Recovering, he looked up at one of the houses, at the gate, fumbled for his cigarettes, all the while resembling a machine that had lost its timing belt. He remembered that he had a cigarette in his mouth, and the charade must have seemed suddenly ridiculous to him. He threw his cigarette to the ground and, turning deliberately, he stepped forward, reaching into his coat pocket for what had to be a gun.

Rolf turned and pulled Gretchen ahead.

As they rounded a curve in the road an alley opened on their left. Rolf glanced quickly over his shoulder, could not see the man for the curve, then pulled Gretchen into the alley and flattened against a brick wall. A wooden fence went along the opposite side. Trash cans lined the base of both walls behind the houses. Rolf flipped open the flap of his leather holster and pulled out his pistol.

Gretchen looked at it. "What are you going to do?"

"Quiet." His eyes had that flat, predator deadliness now as he pulled back evenly on the locking mechanism of the Luger. He waited, tensing, judging how long it should take for the man to reach the alley. Then he heard the footsteps.

The man came around the corner holding a Walther Parabellum pistol. He was looking straight ahead up the street, at where Rolf and Gretchen should have been, when Rolf stepped out, grabbed his left arm, and swung him hard against the wall. The force of the blow punched the wind out of the man and his pistol clattered to the ground.

Rolf cracked the man's head with the barrel of his Luger, stunning him, and then took hold of his coat lapels and pushed him up hard against the brick wall. He was a big man, half a head taller than Rolf, with a heavyweight's build. He had thick lips, a wide, pockmarked face that featured a flat, misshapen nose and a scar over the left eye. It took all of Rolf's effort, leaning into him, to support his weight against the wall.

A thin rivulet of blood trickled out of the man's short-cropped blond hairline and ran down the side of his face. His eyes rolled open and focused dully on Rolf.

The eyes were gray and void of fear, and Rolf could see the hate filling in behind the eyes. His breath was rancid-smelling from coffee and cigarettes; his hair was greasy and matted with blood now; he looked like a boxer past his prime.

"Who are you?" Rolf growled. "Never mind," he said quickly. "I will just see for myself." Pinning the man with his right forearm against the wall, with the muzzle of his Luger pressed up into the soft underbelly of the man's throat, he went through his pockets. He took his eyes off the man only to quickly inspect each item before discarding it. He found the silver cigarette holder, saw the initials H.B. engraved elaborately on the cover, then tossed it to the ground. The man's eyes went briefly to the cigarette holder then back to Rolf's face.

Rolf felt inside the man's breast coat pocket and retrieved a wallet, flipped it open and thumbed through his identity papers. "Sergeant Hans Bricher," he read. He looked at him. "Schutzstaffel." Rolf pocketed the wallet. "Well, Sergeant Bricher of the Schutzstaffel, what have you got to say for yourself? Just out for an afternoon stroll, are you?"

Bricher stared at him, showing neither fear nor emotion, only the professional hatred one fighter has for another before the bell. There is nothing personal. There is only the cold discipline of rage.

Rolf tapped the side of the man's cheek with the barrel of his gun. "Why are you following us?"

The sergeant said nothing.

Rolf tapped him again, harder, causing the man to wince involuntarily. "Who sent you?"

Bricher said nothing.

Rolf hit him twice with the muzzle, drawing a welt on his cheekbone just under the right eye. "Tell me or, so help me, I'll put a bullet through your thick skull."

"Rolf!"

Bricher's eyes shifted to Gretchen. Rolf slapped him with the back of his hand. "Look at me. Do not look at her. Tell me who sent you!"

The man stared at him.

Rolf could feel the thick pectoral muscles flexing through the leather coat and the controlled discipline of the man's breathing. He pushed the muzzle up into the throat. "You were in the park the other night, weren't you?" he demanded. "There was a girl—" He caught his anger. "There was a girl there with me."

A thin, mocking smile curled along the thick, sensual lips. "She was lovely."

"What did you say?" Rolf asked in a hoarse voice.

The man continued to smile at him.

Rage jumped into Rolf's chest, and he pistol-whipped the man across the face. The man fell back into the trash cans, clawing at them for balance as he fell hard to the ground. Rolf leveled the Luger at his chest.

Gretchen grabbed his arm. "Rolf, don't! Please!"

Rolf yanked his arm free of her and glared at the man.

Sergeant Hans Bricher looked up at him and chuckled. "You are a dead man, Captain." His voice was high and pinched-sounding, and it did not fit his pugilistic bulk.

Rolf aimed the pistol at his face, held the sight a touch beneath the bridge of his flattened nose. The tip of the barrel was quivering, he saw, as the rage in him shuddered out through his arm and into the man's face.

"You're built pretty good," Bricher said, smiling. "You look like you could handle yourself. Why don't you put the gun down, and we can see who is the better man. What do you say, Captain?"

"Shut up!" Rolf growled. "Just shut up!"

"Please, Rolf," Gretchen said from behind him. "Not this way."

"What other way?" he asked. "What other way is there to kill a cancer?" But he could not bring himself to murder. He stood glowering at the man, quivering with pent-up rage. He saw Olga's face through a blood-wash of rage, but he could not bring himself to murder. He lowered the gun with a curse, the murder cooling in his eyes, and looked down at the Luger in his hand. He did not see the man reaching surreptitiously for his ankle.

"Rolf!"

The afternoon quiet was shattered by the sudden discharge, and Rolf reeled, staggering backward, as the bullet struck the wall behind his head. He swung around, crouching, seeing the muzzle flashes from the man's pistol and hearing the sharp reports. The man was moving fast, he saw, scrambling to one side behind the trash cans, and Rolf saw his hand bucking with the muzzle flashes leaping out at him.

Rolf pointed his pistol and pulled the trigger. He was not aiming; he was only firing as fast as he could pull the trigger. He saw the bullets hitting wildly around the fast-moving bulk of the man, missing. He saw the hits spattering over the pavement and on the wall and into the trash cans, and not seeing others that he fired. Then he saw the man lurch up and forward, like a breaching whale, and he heard the clangor of the cans as he pitched into them. Then the echoing report of the shots coming back up the alley faded into a settling quiet. It had all happened in the span of five seconds. The man in the black leather coat lay still in a pool of his own blood.

From somewhere in the neighborhood the protesting sound of a barking dog cut into the awful quiet.

Rolf walked cautiously over to the man, feeling the taut constriction of nausea in his throat, and pointed the Luger at him. There were brass hulls scattered all over the alley. He looked and saw the empty breech of his Luger and the spent magazine; still he held the muzzle pointed at the man's head. The blond fighter was staring dully at him, the thick lips drawn in a sickly grimace. Rolf glanced over his body, and saw that bullets had struck the right calf and thigh; he saw the one through his shoulder and the last one in the head that had done the job. Just then he remembered Gretchen. He looked quickly back at her, and she was just picking herself up off the ground.

Stepping forward, she looked at the dead man and then at Rolf, and he could see that, physically, she was all right. Her face, however, was white with horror. "Are you all right?" she asked, her voice tremulous.

Rolf examined himself. There was a long tear along his right sleeve where a bullet had passed through, but he was not hit. Miraculously, it seemed, he was not hit. "I'm fine." His voice was flat and dead-sounding.

She put her arms around him and looked at the man in the black leather coat. "Is he dead?"

"He is dead."

"Who was he?"

"SS."

"Why? I don't—"

"He murdered Olga."

Gretchen looked down at the man again and her face went ashen gray.

Rolf holstered his pistol. He bent over the man, picked up his feet, and began dragging him. He was heavier than he realized he would be. The man's arms went out to his sides and acted like brakes, his head beat against the pavement, and it took all Rolf's effort to get him over to the wall. Once there he rolled the heavy bulk of the corpse behind the trash cans, the arms twisting around the torso. He laid some newspapers over the body and righted several cans to hide it.

He picked up the two pistols and thought, looking at the smaller automatic, how foolish he had been not to think that the man might have a backup. He was lucky on that one, he thought, then tossed the Mauser and the Walther into one of the cans and set the lid over it. He left the brass hulls and the other debris. The neighborhood dog was still barking.

"Let's get out of here," he said, glancing down at his wristwatch, and then at Gretchen. She was vomiting into one of the trash cans.

"Are you all right?"

"Oh, Rolf," she spat. "This is awful." She spat again and groaned.

He looked back at the dead man and saw the feet extending out from behind the cans, and the glint of light that he knew was the silver cigarette lighter. Forget it, he told himself. "We must go," he said. "Are you all right?"

"Yes," she said. "I think so."

"Brave girl," he said. He took her hand and led her along the alley to the end where it connected to a narrow residential street.

They went up the street, every so often glancing over their shoulders, until it dead-ended into the Tiergarten Strasse. On the corner next to the bus stop they hailed a taxi and made the driver turn north on Potsdamer Strasse, drive north through the park, then, exiting the park, turn west to follow a circuitous route, all the while watching out the rear window for cars. They were not being followed. Not that they could observe.

"You all right now?" he whispered.

"Yes, I'm fine. How are you?"

"Don't worry about me," Rolf said in a toneless voice.

"Rolf, that was horrible."

"Don't think about it."

"How can I not think about it?"

Rolf did not answer. He tried to let his feelings drain out of him. But he kept seeing the wide, pockmarked face with the flat nose and thick lips, and that wicked mocking smile: it was the last face that Olga ever saw on the earth. He looked out the window. She was gone, and the man who killed her was dead and lying in a heap of garbage. That was something, he thought. There was something in that. But there was more, wasn't there? he asked himself. The man was acting on orders. There was more to it than the dead man, and he could not let it all go out of him.

The driver looked at Rolf in the rearview mirror and asked for directions. Rolf told him to head south.

As they traveled through the districts of Südende and Lankwitz, Rolf looked out his window and observed the ravages of the past August's bombings. He watched without feeling as children played atop the pyramids of rubble and as people went woodenly about their business, seemingly unaware of—or unconcerned with—the backdrop of smashed and bombed-out hulls of buildings. His eyes were flat and half-lidded, like a reptile's, as the many evidences of ruin shuttered past his window. Then he felt an ache rising out of the emptiness in his chest, and it became a low, airless curse filtering out through his teeth.

"The fools," he kept saying to himself. "The fools. The stupid, cowardly fools."

Gretchen took his hand, startling him with her cool touch. He looked over at her and smiled. His sister was beautiful, he thought, seeing the deep yellow gold of the sun glowing in her straight-cut, silky mass of hair. He was proud of her, fiercely so. As proud and full of love for her as any brother could possibly be. She must live, he thought, pulling her close to him and looking out at the staggering brokenness of his homeland. Whatever else happens, she must live. At all costs she must get away from this wretched place and live.

A half hour later they arrived in the Gedächtniskirke district, and the driver let them out in a secluded part of the town. Rolf and Gretchen waited until the car was out of sight, then walked in the opposite direction.

Rolf looked up at the sky that was stacked high with red and black and yellow clouds with everything clashing in the violent roil of sunset. A flight of ducks was pumping furiously against the turbulence and holding a close V formation. Good pilots, he thought, watching them winging to the south. Holding it pretty tight—as tight as any of our fighters. No, tighter, he corrected himself. The Führer will no doubt want to fit you with bombs.

He chuckled sardonically. "Fly away while you may," he said aloud. "To Switzerland if you can."

Gretchen looked at him. "Pardon?"

"Nothing," he said. Then, following after Gretchen, he glanced once more over his shoulder.

39 ★★★

While Rolf and Gretchen were making their way through the poorer section of Gedächtniskirke, Billy was glaring down at the mystery meat the messman had dropped unceremoniously onto his plate.

Billy looked up at the messman, a little man with a scraggly moustache, then he glanced over his shoulder at the fat sergeant glaring at him from the kitchen door. He looked back at the messman. "Where's Maurice?"

"Beats me, sir," the messman replied. "Want some spuds?"

Billy looked disbelievingly at the milky swirl of goop in the metal tray. "Is that what those are?"

"Fresh out of the can, sir." Taking hold of a ladle from the metal container next to it, he lifted it and a beige-colored fluid dripped lumpily back into the soup. "Got some gravy too, sir."

Billy shook his head. "I'll pass."

Feeling a sudden pang of nausea twisting in his stomach, he went on to the coffeemaker. He filled a cup and, placing it onto his tray, crossed the mess hall to a table in one of the shadowy corners. He barely took notice of the sour faces staring down at their plates or of the low mutinous murmur that percolated throughout the room.

He sat down and sulked in silence for several minutes, occasionally stabbing at his dinner with his fork.

Joe Thompson plopped down in the chair across the table. "What gives with this slop?" he growled. "It smells like old sneakers. Maurice sick or something?"

Billy stared blankly at the wall.

"What happened to that little Free French fellow?" Joe wanted to know. "Couldn't get a word out of that snot-nosed messman." But he was met with a disinterested shrug from his wingman. "What's eatin' you? You look like you just lost a puppy."

Billy glanced quickly at him then looked away with a grunt.

Joe brightened. "Love troubles?"

Billy looked at him.

"Hey, it don't make no nevermind to me," Joe said. "If you don't want to talk about it, fine."

"They found her old man in a Kraut POW camp," Billy said. "That's it. Some bureaucratic snafu. He's alive, I'm dead. End of story."

"Tough break."

"It's tough breaks all around," Billy said without emotion. "I'm through with it." He lifted the mystery meat on his fork and looked at the backside of it. "It's all just a big crap shoot, Joe. Just when you think you got it all figured out, you roll snake eyes!" He looked up quickly. "Ain't life grand?" he laughed. "Pretty screwy, I gotta tell you."

Joe thought about it for a moment. "There's no way she can—you know?" He shrugged. "You know—maybe you can see the chaplain, or something? Aren't they supposed to work things out like that?"

"I'm through with it, Joe." Billy dropped the meat on the plate. "Wasn't meant to be, as they say."

"Who's they?"

Billy barked a laugh. "Shoot if I know anymore." He fished the round tin of Copenhagen out of his shirt pocket and tamped a pinch into his lip and sat quietly.

Joe was watching him with his blowtorch green eyes. "You've got it pretty bad, don't you, kid?"

"I don't know what I got."

"Why don't you just go over there and tell her that you're washed up without her? Tell her if she won't divorce that louse of a limey husband of hers you'll have the 52nd strafe the bratwurst out of that lousy Kraut camp he's in."

"Can't do it, Joe."

Joe looked at him and shrugged. "Suit yourself, pal. It's your guts." He cut a wedge off the mystery meat and began chewing laboriously. "Just don't go getting spooky on me, you hear me? We're up tomorrow." He made a face chewing. "Man, what is this? They shoot a horse or something?"

"You say it's with the Brits?"

"Near as I can tell. Zeb said something about the Brits."

"I saw a couple flocks of Lancasters heading east earlier. Must've been over three hundred."

"Well, something's up," Joe agreed. "Don't ask me how we figure in. Maybe a Ramrod. One thing's for sure, I can guarantee you we're gonna be in for a big hurrah." He swallowed hard, took a drink of coffee, and swore. "There're trying to kill us," he coughed. "This is the thanks we get for busting a hundred before Thanksgiving. The 4th got the new Mustangs. We beat 'em out three to one and they get the new kites."

Billy stared across the mess hall in silence while Joe sawed at his meat. "Hey, Joe, you got any religion to speak of?"

Joe stopped sawing and looked up at him.

"It's just a question."

"This 'cause of the girl?"

"Do you?"

Joe Thompson considered him for several moments. "I'm as religious as the next guy, I guess. I don't wear it on my sleeve, if that's what you mean."

"My folks are pretty religious," Billy said, looking out the window at the naked trees of Tealbrook Wood. "So is my brother."

"The minister?"

"Yeah, the minister. Old Tyler the perfect. I never took to it like he did though. I can't figure it. We grew up the same. Same Ma and Pa. Same house. Same church." Billy looked out the windows. "I tried. God knows I tried to live right—read the Bible from cover to cover one summer—but it didn't take. Something in me would always smash it down."

Joe eyed him curiously. "You taking to it now?"

Billy shot him a look. "Shoot." He loosed a lipful of tobacco juice onto his plate.

Joe shoved his tray across the table. "Well, you killed whatever appetite I had."

"You can thank me later. Want to go into town?"

"Trolling, or for eats?"

"You troll, I'll eat."

"It's a deal."

Just then Pete Skagway came over to the table with a kid that couldn't have been older than eighteen. Pete, wearing a cocky grin that was a challenge to the world, made the introductions. "Wheeler, meet Captain Thompson, Foxworth Blue leader. Joe, meet the new replacement, Jimmy Wheeler. You may now kiss the bride."

Joe shot the new kid a look. "You can't be Wheeler?" he asked. "Jim Cooly's replacement?"

The replacement possessed all of the knees-and-elbows awkwardness of a new kid on his first day in school. He shifted his weight to his other foot and hooked a thumb in his belt loop. "Yes, sir, I am," he said with an adenoidy voice. "Second Lieutenant Jimmy Wheeler, sir. Just got in this morning."

"Where you from, Second Lieutenant Jimmy Wheeler?" Joe asked the rookie.

"Schenectady, sir." The kid had bright red hair and the kind of freckled skin that goes with it, with acne on his forehead and smooth cheeks. He didn't look old enough to drive a car, let alone a P-47. "That's in New York, sir."

"Take it easy on the 'sir' business, okay?" Joe said. "You don't owe me any money. How old are you, anyway?"

"Twenty-one, sir," the kid said, scratching the side of his too-long nose.

"I don't believe it. You know how to fly a Jug?" Joe asked the kid.

"Yes, sir. Got my training at Kelly Field."

"That so?"

The kid blinked at him, smiling.

"Where'd you do gunnery?"

"Goxhill, sir. Second in my class."

"You don't say?" Something dark went over Joe Thompson's face. "You gonna shoot down a mess of Krauts for Uncle Sam, are you?"

"Just let me at them, sir."

"Sure. You keep telling yourself that when some Hun bounces you out of the sun and comes screaming up your tail with his 20 millimeters blazing."

The kid blinked at him, losing the smile. His mouth swung open.

"Take it easy, Joe," Billy said.

"I'll take it easy," Joe growled. He turned his green eyes on the rookie. "Let me tell you something, Schenectady, the Hun doesn't care spit where you came in your class. He only cares about protecting his homeland . . . his wife and kids. You hear me?"

"Yes, sir."

"With him it's personal."

"Yes, sir."

"He likes you," Pete said to the rookie. "He gives this inspirational talk to all the new guys. Ain't that so, Joe?"

Joe grunted. He shifted in his chair and looked up at Skagway. "You gonna show him the ropes, are you?"

"Why not?" Pete grinned at him.

Joe looked at the kid and then at Pete. He was himself again. "Try not to corrupt young Wheeler here all at once," he said. "I know how much pleasure it gives you to sign your name in a fresh blanket of snow."

Billy shook his head mildly and smiled.

Pete looked at him. "Something wrong, Hochreiter?"

Billy felt the sudden rise of heat into his ears. He looked at Pete who was still grinning. He said as calmly and without emotion as he could manage, "Beat it, Skagway."

Pete Skagway turned to the rookie. "See what I told you?"

Billy adjusted himself in his chair. "I said beat it."

"Shove off, Skagway," Joe Thompson said.

Pete chuckled and, still looking at Billy, said, "Come on, Wheeler."

Joe looked at Billy after they left.

"Don't say it," Billy said, pushing back from the table and standing up with his tray. "You coming?"

"Sure. Oh, sure," Joe said, and followed after him. "I can see we're going to have a lovely time tonight."

Billy shot a look over his shoulder. "It was your inspirational talk that did it."

"I *was* inspiring, wasn't I?"

"I thought the kid was going to lose his dinner, he was so inspired." They came up to the scullery window and Billy handed his tray through to the pair of rubber-gloved arms. "What got into you?"

Joe looked at him seriously. "Words don't mean nothing. When we go up tomorrow none of it means nothing. Killing Krauts is all that matters and getting your tail back home in one piece. What business does that kid have here anyway? Did you get a load of those pimples? There ought to be a law against those pimples in a war zone."

"You're getting inspirational again," Billy said.

Joe swore. "He got to me," he said. "This Jimmy Wheeler business ought to be home in Schenectady working on his Model A or something."

"Or something. You gonna stand there all night making speeches? I swear you look like you're collecting for the Salvation Army."

Joe looked down at his tray. "Funny man." He dumped everything through the scullery window, missing the pair of gloved hands, and the tray landed with a metallic clatter on the sideboard. The rubber-gloved hands made a lewd gesture after the two of them had gone.

Outside the mess hall they mounted their bicycles and pushed away from the wall. Billy glanced once, long and hard, at the sky.

Joe watched him. "You aren't gonna get all loopy on me tonight, are you?"

"Just checking the weather, you dope."

"That's you dope, *sir.*"

"Ah, go on."

As they pedaled slowly away, the sky, tinged with red and gold around the last of the twilight blues and greens, Billy wondered what Jane was doing at the moment. Writing a letter to her once-dead husband, no doubt. *Shoot,* he said to himself. *You gonna beat up the world tonight?*

He slung a stream of tobacco onto the pavement. He was through with it, he swore softly to himself. Through with all of it. He glanced once more at the sky over the coast.

40 ✯✯✯✯

At about the time Billy Hochreiter and Joe Thompson were ordering their third round of beers at a table in the Knight's Arms, both of them winking at the waitresses and tilting toward an evening of glorious abandon, Rolf and Gretchen were climbing the front stairs of a brick tenement apartment building.

Pastor Helmut Schoenfield was in his study, a wall of books going up to the ceiling behind him and covering two other walls in the small room that was cluttered with papers and journals. At the present he was poring over John Calvin's *Institutes of the Christian Religion.*

An elderly man, his skin shone with the white translucence typical of the scholar. Thick white hair pushed back off his brow in unruly waves to reveal an intelligent forehead, and the two deep creases between his eyebrows that came from years of glaring at his work gave him a perpetual scowl.

He looked up as his wife, Klara, showed Gretchen and Rolf into the room. A flush of impatience shot across his face. For just a moment, as his eyes adjusted to the distance, his gray eyes twinkled fiercely over the rim of his reading glasses. Then, seeing who it was, he smiled, the eyes cooled, and all of the lines on his face widened in friendly arcs—except for the creases between his brows that seemed bracketed around some deep and perplexing thought.

"It is Gretchen Schiller," Klara, a heavyset woman of the same vintage as her husband, said. She smiled maternally at the brother and sister, standing to one side of them with her hands folded beneath her ample bosom.

Pastor Schoenfield pushed away from his desk. "Of course it is!" he smiled. "Come here, Daughter! Come in! Come in!" He stood up and, walking with much dignity, came around to the front of his desk. He was a tall, brittle man with a slight stoop in his back; as he opened his long arms in greeting, the frayed cuffs of his faded tweed coat hit him high on his wrists.

He gave Gretchen a hug, then stood back and grinned at Rolf. "And who is this handsome young man with you?"

Rolf looked at him without emotion.

Gretchen took her brother's arm and led him forward. "I would like for you to meet my brother Rolf, Pastor Schoenfield."

The elderly man beamed. "So this is the famous brother of whom I've heard so much boasting!"

Rolf nodded politely, still without emotion.

"I can see the family resemblance," the pastor said. "Yes, I can see it in the eyes. Can you see it, Klara?"

Klara angled her head to one side and smiled beneficently at them, her eyes disappearing into mounds of healthy red cheeks.

"Yes, yes," the pastor nodded. "Such handsome children the Schillers are blessed with." He extended his hand to Rolf in greeting.

As Rolf shook his hand he noted the paperlike lids over eyes that were a dusty shade of blue. But as he looked into the guileless intensity of the old man's eyes something dark rose inside him, a kind of vague contempt perhaps, or fear.

"I am pleased to meet you at last," the pastor said. "I had pictured you differently. You know how it is when you hear someone over the telephone and you form an image of what he looks like?"

Rolf said nothing.

Gretchen smiled at her brother.

Schoenfield let it drop. "Your meeting went well with General Olbricht, I trust?"

"Yes."

"That is good," Schoenfield said. "He is a good man. A bit stodgy perhaps," he added with a smile. "Reminds one of an owl, don't you think?" He laughed. Rolf did not answer. "A decent man," Schoenfield said. "A very decent man. He was able to help you?"

Again, Rolf gave no answer.

The pastor did not press it. Then he noticed the torn shoulder in Rolf's coat. "Your sleeve. Klara—"

"It is nothing," Rolf said. He checked his wristwatch, made a mental calculation. *Ten minutes, no longer,* he told himself. He looked back at the pastor and said, "We can only stay a minute or two."

"Very well, son," Schoenfield said. Then a change went over his features that eclipsed everything of the greeting. "I am so sorry to hear about your Olga. There are no words for me to express my deepest sympathy."

"Thank you," Rolf nodded. He looked over at Gretchen, who was watching him closely.

"Gretchen told me that you both were very happy," the pastor said. "She said that it was—" He broke off. "It is a terrible tragedy."

"Yes," Rolf said without emotion. He folded his arms behind his back, stepped over to the bookcase that went up the wall beside the pastor's desk, and looked up at the rows of old volumes.

"I'm afraid you will find only theological books and commentaries. They are mostly dry, and full of dusty old men's bones." The elderly man smiled. "But they are a comfort to me."

Rolf looked to his right and nodded curtly to Gretchen.

Gretchen took her cue and glanced over at Klara. The heavyset woman was still smiling sweetly at her. Gretchen felt a sudden sadness rising in her chest.

The pastor saw the shade going over her face and because of it did not want to remain in the claustrophobic clutter of his study a moment longer. Brightening, he took Gretchen's arm and led her to the door, saying, "Come, Daughter, let us leave these fossil digs."

Rolf and Gretchen exchanged glances, and Rolf again checked his watch.

Schoenfield gestured to his wife. Klara went before them into the parlor and turned on the light switch.

Rolf quietly followed everyone into the parlor and, entering, glanced quickly at its Spartan furnishings. Several ladderback chairs went around the bare walls of the room. A few photographs lined the mantel, and on the wall above the mantel was Carl Bloch's painting of Christ being led bound through the courtyard of the High Priest.

As he gazed steadily at it, he saw in the glancing look of Christ toward Peter all of the kindness and the gentle majesty, and the pain, and the love that he bore him, even in the moment of Peter's denial. And he saw all of the remorse and shame that must have torn at the big fisherman as the cock crowed for the third time, and he saw all of the tears that would follow, and it was all there in the shadows and it was there in the reach of light around the Christ's face. The painting evoked a powerful feeling in Rolf.

Pastor Schoenfield was watching him. "It is my favorite painting," he said, stepping next to Rolf and looking at it with him. "I see myself in the scene, don't you?"

Rolf broke free from his thoughts and grunted. He looked down at his watch.

Gretchen turned to the pastor and said, "I'm afraid we've come with some rather distressing news."

The elderly man patted her hand. "Let us not hear of distressing news just yet," he frowned. "Klara, perhaps our guests would like some tea. Something to take the chill off the evening, perhaps."

Klara gathered herself with a hospitable smile.

"No, thank you," Gretchen insisted. "The news is quite pressing."

The pastor looked at her. "I trust your father is not ailing again?"

"He is always ailing," she smiled.

"Yes, of course," the pastor chuckled. Then looking thoughtfully at her, he said, "Please speak, Daughter."

As Gretchen began to relate the events of the morning, Rolf went over to the window that faced the street and pulled the curtain slightly to one side. He looked out onto the street and up and down the sidewalk three stories below them. There was no one in sight but a squirrel that was poised, tail perking, on the limb of one of the trees.

He watched as the last of the sun shone blazing on the windows of the tenement across the street, the street bare of traffic, and the buildings glowing with the first light of dusk. A face appeared in a window in one of the upper stories and looked down at the street. Rolf could just make out the features of a man, an old man, he thought. The face slid back into the gloom of the window, and Rolf let go of the curtains.

He looked down at his wristwatch; the ten minutes were spent. He glanced over at his sister.

"I fear I may have implicated you, Pastor," she concluded.

"I see." The elderly man was pulling on his lower lip and gazing at the floor. Klara was looking at him, her eyes wide and strained with the first shock of fear. She came over to him, and he put his arm around her big waist.

"We must go," Rolf said, again peering out the window. "It would not be wise for you to remain here."

The pastor looked at him. "You are not serious."

"I am gravely serious. I killed a man this afternoon. He was with the SS. There may be others."

"Dear God," Klara said.

"Where would we go?" Schoenfield asked.

"I don't know. But it is no longer safe for you here."

"Who would look after my flock?"

Rolf glared at him. "Perhaps you did not hear my sister correctly," he snapped. "If my brother has gone to the Gestapo with the diary, they will come and arrest you."

"Let them take me if they must," the pastor said. "What kind of shepherd would I be to desert my flock?"

"If you stay you will have no flock."

The elderly man smiled at him. A humorous light flickered in his eyes. "I think that the chains of Saint Paul would contradict your argument."

Rolf grunted. "They might just shoot you. Have you thought of that?"

"If Christ wills it, yes. But I will not desert the people whom God has placed in my charge."

"Then you are a fool."

"A bigger fool than I care to contemplate." The man smiled. "But the Lord has shown mercy to fools, hasn't he?"

Rolf could not believe his ears. He felt the dark glow of anger rising in his chest.

The pastor studied him now with sage eyes, eyes that had seen everything of the fall and the rise of Germany since the Great War. "You are not a man of faith, are you, young man?" he asked in a pastoral voice.

"I am a man of fate," Rolf said bitterly.

"Fate? What is fate? In all things God is Sovereign," the pastor said. He smiled gently. "It is God who raises men up, as he did Pharaoh, King of Egypt, that he might display his power through them."

"And the Führer?"

The pastor's expression darkened. "That wicked man," he said quietly. "Antichrist. God forgive my hatred of him." He looked intently at Rolf. "Yes, even the Führer. No man has authority but that which has been given him by God. It is God who elects men to rise, or to fall, to serve his good purpose."

"That sounds like fate to me."

"Fate is mindless. It is the philosophical excuse of man to keep himself from submitting to God. Fate cares nothing for a man's moral choices."

"We have a choice, then?"

"Oh, yes. Yes, indeed." The pastor smoothed his long brittle fingers over his words, as though sculpting them from the air. "A man is free to choose within his nature. He may choose to love or to hate; he is free to do an act of kindness or devilish cruelty. He may choose religion or rationalism, knowledge or ignorance. Always within his nature."

"His nature?"

"His mannishness. Man cannot choose the nature of God, for it is beyond his reach. It is God who reaches into the darkness of a man's soul. It is God who sets a man free to choose him."

Rolf grunted. He looked out the window and watched the squirrel scampering across the street. "And has God freed Germany to choose him?" he asked bitterly. "Or has he elected Germany to fall?"

"Who can know the mind of God?" the pastor said. "'But I know that in him 'mercy and truth are met together; that righteousness and peace have kissed each other.' God is both just and merciful."

Rolf looked at him darkly. "You speak of justice and mercy. What of those who died in the firestorm of Hamburg? Where is the justice in that? Where is the mercy in Olga's murder?"

Pastor Schoenfield shook his head gravely. "I do not pretend to know," he said. "It is truly difficult to understand." He looked at Rolf. "But I know that nothing will separate us from his love. He is Lord over the fires. The fires of Hamburg did not singe his garments; neither did the smell of smoke touch the souls of the righteous as the angels bore them into his arms."

"Ah!" Rolf waved him off and started to leave. "Let's go, Gretchen. He is as mad as the rest of them."

Schoenfield stepped in front of him and put up his hands. "Don't turn away from him, Rolf. I can see in your eyes that he has touched you."

"Get out of my way, old man."

"I am not in your way. It is your pride."

Rolf's body went rigid. He started to walk around the pastor but found that his feet would not move. Rolf looked hard at him. Suddenly he felt a change go through the room. It was as though the room had shifted abruptly to one side, opening a rift in the dimension of time and space, and through the rift came something bright and dangerous, something so pure and terrible and wholly Other that he was forced to take a step backward to steady himself.

Gretchen must have sensed it too. "Rolf, please," she said quietly. "Please, won't you let go this hatred of Christ?"

Rolf felt himself driven to the edge of a cliff where, teetering on the brink, he could almost feel the updraft rushing up his back. There was nothing he could do but charge forward into that dangerous Otherness that he felt certain would smash him, or step backward over the precipice into some black abyss. Neither choice was acceptable to him; both required a death. And then he was through with it.

He looked at his sister. "There is nothing left," he said in a voice that sounded strange and faraway.

Gretchen said, "It is the poor in spirit who possess the Kingdom of heaven, Rolf."

"But there is nothing. I have no faith."

The pastor stepped forward. "Faith is a gift of God," he said.

Rolf looked at him a long while. It made no sense—none of it. It was crazy. And then he could see it. Gradually the terror he had sensed in the room lifted, and he felt a peace settling over him. He chuckled, looked at Gretchen and said, "Perhaps God can speak German after all."

She smiled at him. "Fluently."

Just then a squeal of tires drew everyone's eyes to the window. Rolf rushed over to it and looked down at the street. Two black automobiles swung into the curb, the car doors opened, and several storm troopers rushed out onto the broken pavement.

"The SS," he said. He turned to the pastor. "Do you have a back exit?"

Pastor Schoenfield looked at him, confused. "The SS? They are here?" He hurried over to the window. The last of the soldiers could be seen hurrying into the building. "Oh, dear God."

Rolf grabbed his arm. "Quickly, man, is there another way out of this place?"

The pastor stiffened. "I'm not leaving."

Rolf glared at him. "You have no objection if I try to save my sister, do you?"

The pastor suddenly understood, then snapped with resolve. He looked quickly at Gretchen. "Hurry, Daughter!" he said, leading her out into the foyer and through the apartment door. He pointed left down the hall that was dark now except for a single lightbulb in the middle of the hall that cast a pale yellow aureole onto the floor. "There is a flight of stairs going down the back! Hurry and Godspeed!"

Rolf took Gretchen's hand. She pulled away from him. "I'm staying!" she cried.

"No, you're not!" he growled. He took her arm and pulled her behind him down the hall, through the light spill and beyond, into the shadows.

Gretchen was crying and looking back at the elderly couple standing in the doorway of their apartment. Klara's hands were over her face; she was praying feverishly.

"Rolf, no!" Gretchen cried, pulling at him.

"Don't force me to carry you!" Rolf shouted angrily.

"Hurry, Daughter!" the pastor said waving her on. "Hurry!"

The stairs descended in a spiral of three landings down the rear of the building, with a lightbulb dimly illuminating each of the landings. Arriving at the head of the stairs, Rolf cursed when he saw several storm troopers coming up the stairwell.

"The other way," Rolf said, and he pulled Gretchen back along the hallway. She was quiet now, just whimpering now and then, but she was no longer fighting him. As he led her past the elderly couple he saw the old woman's hands still covering her face, her wide, fearful eyes just showing over her fingertips and following their progress down the hall. She was praying still, and the pastor kept waving his hand, shooing them, it seemed, and calling, "Hurry! Hurry!" as if they had anything else in mind.

By the time they reached the front flight of stairs another group of soldiers were already crowding into the hall. Rolf opened the flap of his holster and grabbed his pistol, but the big sergeant in the lead leveled his machine gun at his chest, and growled, "Don't do it, Captain!"

It was then that Rolf remembered his pistol was empty. He looked at his sister, back at the big sergeant, then lowered the pistol back into its holster. He knew what he would do if he were alone, but he was not alone.

He took Gretchen's hand and backed down the hall with her, shielding her with his body, until they stopped in front of the Schoenfields. Rolf could still hear the elderly woman praying behind him, and he felt a tinge of disgust.

He stood watching as the storm troopers advanced steadily from both ends of the hall. The dim light illuminated the one group momentarily, giving them a ghoulish appearance, and then both groups of soldiers were gathered in a semicircle around the four of them with their machine pistols leveled at their chests. The big sergeant was in the front of the others and he stared at Rolf with military coldness.

A moment of calm descended upon the foursome, as it became clear that they were caught. Pastor Schoenfield stepped in front of the others. "What is the meaning of this?" he demanded of the sergeant. "There is no cause for this."

The big sergeant said nothing but looked at him with the brutish eyes of a soldier who did not know the meaning of mercy.

"You are under arrest," another voice said.

Rolf turned to see who it was but the black wall of storm troopers blocked his view. He could hear someone coming down the hallway, the martial tread of jackboots sounding hollowly over the wooden floor. The soldiers opened a gap in the circle, and Rolf saw that it was Lieutenant Klemmer of the SS.

"Well, well, such a pleasant surprise." Lieutenant Klemmer smiled, delicately removing his gloves. He clicked his heels and saluted. "Heil Hitler!"

Rolf did not return the salute. Looking at him, he remembered everything about the man that he despised: the proud SS uniform, the arrogant cant of the hat, the way his head turned with quick, birdlike movements that were so much like those of a toy. "You better have a good reason for this, Lieutenant," he growled.

Lieutenant Klemmer lowered his hand, his face darkening with a scowl. "Oh, I can assure you I do, Captain," he said. He indicated the pastor with his swagger stick. "I have come to arrest this man for conspiracy to commit treason against the Reich. What a tidy coincidence that you and your sister are here. It will save us a trip to your house, won't it?"

Rolf glared at him. "You are arresting us?"

"How very perceptive of you, Captain Schiller."

"On what charge?"

"For treason of course."

Rolf looked at the big sergeant who was staring at him without a hint of emotion. He looked back at the lieutenant. "You have proof of this?"

Lieutenant Klemmer smiled at him. "Now I do," he said. "Enough to hang you and the rest of your little pack of rats. Do not look so stunned, Captain. It has been a thrilling chase, but now you are caught." He chuckled. "'You cannot win them all,' as the Americans love to say."

Rolf said nothing.

Just then there was a small disturbance to his right and, turning, Rolf saw Ernst pushing his way in through the soldiers. Seeing his brother, he felt a stab of pain go through him.

Gretchen clutched Rolf's arm and stared incredulously at her younger brother. "Ernst," she said. "Why, Ernst? Why?"

If Ernst heard her he gave no indication of it. Instead he stood beside Lieutenant Klemmer and lifted his face proudly to the man, gazing at him with all of the love and devotion he had for the Reich glowing on his face and out through his eyes. He turned to Rolf, and a cruel smile twisted over his mouth.

Rolf knew that he was no longer looking at his brother; his brother was dead. Before him now was a monster, a devil in the guise of a fifteen-year-old boy, with blue eyes and short-cropped brown hair. In that moment everything seemed to drain out of his chest, and he felt nothing. "You're supposed to do it with a kiss," he said quietly.

Ernst glared at him with contempt.

41 ★★★

Lieutenant Klemmer was in no hurry to do anything now and was clearly enjoying himself. He slapped his gloves against his thigh and arched a brow as he looked each of the foursome over. At first his eyes swept over the group quickly then slowed down to single out each of the faces; he was taking time now to study each face as if he were admiring a prized animal he had captured. He reminded Rolf so much of a toy martinet that it would have been comical were it not for the storm troopers and their machine pistols leveled at their chests.

Rolf stood with his feet spread like a boxer's, his hands hanging loosely down at his sides as Klemmer's eyes settled on his. He was caught, and there was nothing he could do about it except to look for an opportunity to change the odds, which he knew would probably not come. He hated it. *Keep a clear head,* he told himself. *Do not hand them your sword just yet.* Still, he felt the sickness of defeat edging into his belly. It was the same feeling he'd succumbed to coming into the city on the train, seeing the city he'd grown up in bombed and smashed, only this was personal, and he hated it even more.

"I have been looking forward to this moment," Klemmer the martinet said, clearly enjoying himself. The boy Ernst was standing next to him, and every so often he would run his fingers through the boy's hair and comb the recalcitrant lock off his brow—it was disgusting to observe. "Yes, for some time," Klemmer said for added effect, stroking the boy's head affectionately.

Rolf stared at him in a calm that belied the animal tautness in his muscles, in his shoulders and legs, his long fingers flexing loosely, and his mind working fast as he considered each of his limited options. He had already counted the storm troopers—there were eight of them including the big sergeant—blocking both routes of escape, and they were each holding a 9mm machine pistol against his empty Luger.

"I must say that it has been a most interesting pursuit, Captain. Thrilling at times," said the martinet as he slapped his booted calf rhythmically with the swagger stick. Smiling, he made a detailed appraisal of the squadron leader. "You pilots have an expression for it, don't you? The love of combat. Yes, that is it." Then he said, "But now you are caught, and all the fun has gone out of it. Pity."

Rolf looked at him, but his mind was working over the men on either side of him, probing for weakness. *There is always a weakness, a blind spot*, he told himself. *A soft underbelly. Look for it, Rolf.*

Klemmer smiled at him as a cat, luxuriating over its catch, might smile at a mouse. He stepped over to Pastor Schoenfield, turned on his heels and slapped the swagger stick sharply against his calf. The pastor was standing very erect and with much dignity but the lieutenant did not see him. His mind was clearly on Rolf.

"Is that the way it is for you, Captain Schiller?" the lieutenant asked, looking at but not seeing the old man. "When you see the enemy plane twirling away from you in flames, does something go out of you? The *ecstasy* of the kill? You wish you could hold onto it like the very first time you killed; but each time it becomes more fleeting, doesn't it?"

Rolf's eyes were flat and expressionless.

"It is like love," Klemmer went on. "Once you have tasted the conquest you crave more, don't you? The first love is the purest, the most idealized. It is the love of youth. But, alas, she—if that is your preference," he added with a quick smile, "cannot satisfy in the end. No. So you must play the field like a bee, hoping with each flower to capture a little more honey. Just a little more honey. I am told you are quite the ladies' man, Captain."

Rolf tensed.

Klemmer continued looking at Pastor Schoenfield for several moments. The pastor stood quietly, his head raised not in pride but in the humility of true self-knowledge.

The lieutenant looked away at Rolf and said, "It might surprise you to know that I have some photographs of your little assignations, Captain. Some quite lovely ones actually." He was slapping his boot with the swagger stick. "Every step of the way I have been at your side. Not me personally, mind you," he admitted. "But I have been quite close to you in one form or another."

"One of your *forms* could stand tidying up," Rolf said with a flinty edge. Klemmer turned fully to him, breaking the rhythm of his stick.

"I did the best I could with him, but he was an ungainly brute," Rolf added and saw the effect of his words on the lieutenant's face.

"Hans . . ."

"He tried to kill me," Rolf said. "He was rather clumsy at it, for a professional. But then nosing around in sewers is really more your trick, isn't it, Klemmer?"

The lieutenant's expression narrowed petulantly. "You are a funny man, Captain Schiller. A real funny man." He looked sharply at the pastor, raised his swagger stick, and struck him across the face with such force that the old man's head swung out with the blow before he fell hard to the ground.

Klara threw her hands to her face with a shriek. Rolf lurched forward, but the storm troopers jerked their machine pistols at his chest. He looked down at the pastor, at the long, ugly red welt rising across his cheekbone. Gretchen and the old woman were at his side attending him now. Then he looked at Klemmer.

The lieutenant slapped his hand with the swagger stick. "What? Nothing funny to say, Captain Schiller?"

Rolf glared at him.

Klemmer barked a laugh of contempt. "No heroics? I'm disappointed. A hero of the Reich such as yourself."

Gretchen and the old woman helped the pastor to his feet. The welt was beading up now with blood, and a trickle of blood oozed down from the high point of the cheekbone. Using the tip of his swagger stick, the lieutenant angled the pastor's head to one side to examine the welt. "It will be a pleasure attending your execution," he said to Rolf. "Yours, and the rest of these filthy Jew lovers."

Ernst, who had been standing dutifully in the center of the semicircle, looked over at his sister and at the old couple, then looked at the lieutenant. A shade of bewilderment crossed his face. It seemed he wanted to say something.

"I'll have your head," Rolf growled.

"I sincerely doubt it." Klemmer turned sharply to the big sergeant. "Take his pistol. In case he changes his mind and tries something stupid."

The sergeant and one other soldier stepped forward, the one holding a gun on him while the sergeant went though his pockets with professional efficiency. He removed Rolf's pistol, patted his legs and crotch and, patting his chest, removed his wallet and the traveling papers and handed them to the lieutenant.

Rolf looked at the papers and felt sick to his stomach now, not for himself but for his family and for Gretchen and for everything else that could not happen now. He thought of the count, and the Kreisau Circle, the madness of the "suicide mission to heaven," and of everything else the papers implied, and the nausea spread up into his chest.

Rolf watched helplessly as Lieutenant Klemmer read through the papers very carefully. The thought of how foolish he was for getting caught went through his mind, and he hated himself for it.

"General Olbricht?" the lieutenant exclaimed. He put his hand to his face and laughed. "Here it is, right here! How marvellous! Isn't this just marvellous? It seems we have uncovered a whole nest of rats, Sergeant."

The big sergeant's expression did not change.

The lieutenant looked at Rolf, and the smile trailed off his face. "One rat has led us to another. Really a poor time of the year for Switzerland, don't you think? Unless, of course, you are going there for the winter sports. Are you one for the winter sports, Captain Schiller? Skiing? Tobogganing? Perhaps the luge?"

Rolf said nothing.

"I thought not. Besides, I do not see your name on the list of happy holiday-goers. Why is that?"

Gretchen looked at her brother. Rolf continued staring at Klemmer and said nothing.

"It is no matter," Klemmer said. He stepped forward and peered into Rolf's face. "You asked if we had proof? I should say we have proof." He folded the papers and put them into his breast pocket.

"Reich Marshal Göring will hear of this," Rolf said. The threat sounded hollow, he knew, like a lone voice in an empty gymnasium.

"I'm sure your report will make the most interesting reading for High Command," Klemmer said. "Though I'm sure not as interesting as this." He held out his hand to the big sergeant, and the sergeant put the diary into it.

Rolf looked at the diary. He glanced over at Ernst, and the boy, looking very much alone now, and confused, looked away.

Klemmer flipped through the pages. "Yes, this is all quite interesting."

"Rolf had nothing to do with that," Gretchen said, stepping forward. She thrust out her hand. "That diary belongs to me. It is my private property, and it was stolen from me. I would appreciate it if you would return it, thank you."

Klemmer flipped over a few pages in the diary. "I must commend you on your excellent writing, my sweet. It is really quite entertaining."

"Are you going to give it to me?" Gretchen demanded, still holding out her hand.

"Here is one—yes. Listen to this entry," Klemmer said, then he read: "'It is so wonderful to see the change in Rolf. He is falling in love, I just know it. These past several days he is like a new man. All of the anger in him seems to have taken winged flight.'"

"*Winged flight,*" he repeated. "I like that. Do you like that?" he asked the big sergeant. "It's quite poetic, don't you think? Quite appropriate for our Luftwaffe hero."

The big sergeant glanced at him briefly then looked back at Rolf, who was staring at the martinet with clenched fists. From then on he would not take his eyes off Rolf. He seemed to know something about Rolf that even Rolf did not yet know.

"Please," Gretchen said. "Will you please give it back to me?"

"There is more," Klemmer said. "However, I am afraid that it is very sad. This one is dated only one week ago. 'After Rolf returns to duty,'" he read, "'I think Olga and I shall be good friends. She is such a kind person.'"

The lieutenant looked at her with a pitiful shrug of his eyebrows. "Such a tragedy. So young. So beautiful. Cut down in the flower of youth. You might write something like that in your next entry," he suggested to her. "Better yet—" he brightened. "Cut down in the flower of love! What do you think, Captain?"

"Why did you do it?" Rolf said evenly. "She was nothing to you."

"Because she was no longer useful to me."

Rolf looked at him.

Klemmer laughed. "The great hero of the Reich. You still haven't put it together, have you? You are nothing but a lovesick fool. Do you think she was in love with you? She was in love with you because I told her to be in love with you."

Something in Rolf's eyes flickered imperceptibly.

"What are you talking about?" Gretchen demanded. "What have you got to do with it? Olga was in love with Rolf."

Klemmer was looking at Rolf. "Are you surprised that she was one of my operatives?" he said. "I handpicked her especially for you, Captain Schiller. That night at the Reich Marshal's? That was me."

Rolf's eyes were a flat-bladed coldness.

"You still don't believe me, do you?"

Gretchen turned to her brother. "What is he talking about, Rolf? What does he mean, handpicked?" But Rolf stared at the lieutenant and said nothing.

"All those walks through the park," the lieutenant said, slapping his hand with the swagger stick. "The private rendezvous, the trips to the museums, the secret lovemaking." He touched Rolf's chest with the stick. "And after she was finished with you she would report to me."

"What's going on, Rolf? Tell me. Rolf?"

"She never had much to say, I must admit," Klemmer went on. "Odds and ends, but nothing really of substance." He began putting on his gloves. "She proved to be rather tiring—a bit stupid, I think. Perhaps you won her over after all."

"So you killed her," Rolf said. The tone of his voice was as flat and as cold as his eyes.

Klemmer chuckled. "Do you think that I killed her? Is that what you think?" He laughed again. It all seemed very humorous to him. Had the SS lieutenant not been in love with the sound of his own voice, he would have known that the squadron leader meant to kill him. Rolf did not know the moment he had made up his mind to kill him, but the big sergeant knew and was waiting for him to make his move.

"I did not kill her," Klemmer went on. "I would not have soiled my hands on the little tramp. I left that business to Sergeant Bricher. Dear Hans was fond of that sort of thing."

The big sergeant's fingers flexed expectantly on his gun.

"I am told that she died quite heroically," Klemmer said. "Never uttered a word of protest." He handed the diary to the big sergeant who did not once take his eyes off Rolf. "Then again, perhaps she was enjoying herself. That is—"

Rolf sprang at him, took hold of his neck with both hands, and thrust him across the hall with all the power of his rage. The floor shook from the force of the lieutenant's body hitting the wall. The big sergeant was already moving. He swung and hit Rolf on the side of his head with the butt of his machine pistol.

Rolf bucked as a crash of light tore through his brain. Searing pain shot through a swirl of blackness that rendered him momentarily senseless. Still he clung to Klemmer's throat, driving his thumbs up into the soft hollow beneath his Adam's apple. The sergeant struck him a second time, jabbing the butt into the back of his head, and Rolf went down with a groan, clawing at Klemmer's coat and then at his trouser leg as he clung desperately to consciousness.

The lieutenant kicked away from him, his face red from the choking. "Shoot him!" he rasped. "Shoot him!"

The big sergeant looked at him.

"Dear God, no!" Gretchen shrieked.

"I said shoot him!" the lieutenant shrieked. Then, not waiting, he unholstered his own pistol, cocked it, and aimed it at Rolf's head.

"No!" Pastor Schoenfield cried. The old man stepped in front of Rolf as the crash of the pistol sounded, and the bullet, already rifling through the air, tore through his body. The old man jerked backward as if he had been struck in the chest with a sledgehammer.

A woman's scream cut through the shock waves of the three explosions. Immediately Klara was at her husband's side, her fingers trembling as she patted and smoothed his face and then his hand. Her eyes, certain and not certain, searched wildly for wounds across his body.

"Helmut?" She saw nothing at first and was confused. "It is me, Helmut." But when her eyes fixed upon the blood seeping through the nap of his sweater and the pool of blood spreading out from his side, she cried, "No, no, no! Oh, dear Lord, Helmut, no!"

Her husband rolled his head, his eyes looking for hers, then, finding them, blinked up at her and smiled. "Liebchen . . ."

"Yes, Helmut?" she said intimately. "It is me, your Liebchen." Something changed in the old man's eyes. "Helmut? Helmut? Please, Helmut, do not die. Dear Jesus, do not let my Helmut die!" Klara buried her face in his chest and wept bitterly.

Rolf rolled up onto his elbow and looked in disbelief at the pastor's face. He saw the look of kindness and peace in his eyes, the old, gray, sage eyes looking at him now, lovingly, seeing through him it seemed. Then the eyes fixed, glazed, and Rolf knew that he was dead. The old woman was weeping over him, her big body heaving pitifully. When Rolf realized what the pastor had done, a shudder of horror went through him.

He looked up at the SS lieutenant. "You monster."

Klemmer was looking down at the old man with a look of surprise. Then the surprise cleared from his eyes, and he was himself again. "How the mighty have fallen," he said, once more pointing the Luger at Rolf.

Ernst caught his arm as the pistol fired and the bullet tore harmlessly through the floor. "This is not what you said," he cried angrily. "You said you were just going to teach him a lesson! Get him to see how he was wrong!"

"Get away from me, you little pig," Klemmer growled.

The boy struggled with the gun, grabbed the man's wrist and twisted it. The second muffled explosion jerked his eyes wide open in astonishment. He jumped back to the wall, put his hand to his chest, and removing it, saw that it was covered with blood. "Mama," he gasped, staring at his hands. "I'm sorry, Mama. Rolf," he looked over at Rolf, "I didn't mean to, Rolf. I just . . ."

Then the boy's legs buckled, his back against the wall as he slid to the floor, slowly, staring at his brother Rolf until his knees finally were drawn up to his chest. The look of astonishment became his death face.

"God, have mercy!" Gretchen cried.

For several moments the hallway was deathly still. The soldiers looked on in amazement at the dead boy and at the old woman sobbing over her husband. Then they all heard a guttural chortling that had the effect on everyone's nerves of nails being dragged down a blackboard.

Rolf felt the skin crawl on his scalp as he turned and looked into the face of Lieutenant Klemmer, whose hiss of laughter twisted his mouth into a cruel slash. Klemmer was clearly mad. His eyes, mouth, and facial muscles contorted grotesquely as though several devils were wrestling for control of his features at the same time. Rolf felt as though he were looking into the face of the devil himself, a devil raising the muzzle of a pistol and centering the blade between his eyes.

The first bomb struck without warning. There had been warning, of course—air raid sirens were blaring in the distance, the 88s and 37s were popping rapidly—but in the terrible exchange in the hallway they had gone unheard and unheeded. The bomb, a two-thousand-pound high explosive, took out the front of the building with a terrific crash, sucking out the air with a concussion and fire blast that shook the building with such violence everyone in the hall was thrown to the floor. The second bomb struck a moment later and brought the ceiling and walls crashing down. Fire and smoke rose with the force of a blast furnace.

Several storm troopers lay dead beneath a shattered section of wall; others groped about in the rubble like blinded drunkards. Mrs. Schoenfield's legs extended from beneath a heavy pile of brick and plaster, where she had died next to her husband.

Rolf picked himself off the ground and blinked dazedly at the open night sky where the outer wall of the building had once been. The wind came in through the open wall and blew down the hallway, bringing with it the noise and smell of the night. It took a moment for his mind to clear, to make sense out of the seeming unreality. In the distance were flashes of light and the dull report of the bombs, like lightning and the retarded peals of thunder, and he could already see the flames rising over the city.

A curse formed then died on his lips. He looked around for Gretchen. Strangely, the electricity in the building was still on, and through the dust and beams fallen down from the upper story he could just see the pale glow coming from the single lightbulb down the hall. It was flickering now but still giving off light, and he could just see her sitting against the wall behind him, a jagged chunk of plaster covering her legs. "Gretchen!"

She looked up at him. "Rolf, help me!"

He rushed over to her and began clearing away the debris. "Are you all right? Are you hurt?"

"I'm fine, I think." Her legs were cut and bruised but did not appear to be broken. She stood up with his help, bracing herself against the wall, and immediately her right leg gave way. "My ankle. I must have twisted it, Rolf. It seems all right. Yes, I think so." She tried again, stepping gingerly forward. "Yes, I'm all right. Give me a moment."

Rolf knew that she was in shock. "You'll be fine," he said, helping her to walk. "There you go, you're doing it. There you go."

Fire was licking up the face of the building and throwing flames up past the blown-out wall, so that the light danced crazily on the walls and ceiling of the smashed hallway. Suddenly her expression came alive as she looked at the shambles and the strewn bodies. "Ernst!"

"He's dead, Gretch."

She saw the boy slumped over on his side, his body dusted with bits of plaster. She could not see his face. "Oh, Rolf—Ernst. And Pastor Schoenfield—"

"He's dead . . . his wife too." Rolf, his mind as keen now as a straight razor, pried a machine pistol from the dead fingers of a storm trooper. He could hear Gretchen crying behind him. He turned to her and said, "We've got to go, Gretch. We've got to go now."

"All right," she said, and Rolf knew that she was coming out of it. "All right, Rolf."

Just then one of the dazed storm troopers stood up and swung around with his gun. Rolf fired a quick burst at him, the burst throwing the man up and against the wall, then he turned and emptied the gun on others who were now climbing to their feet. As the roar of the automatic subsided, he fed another clip into the breech and released the bolt. There was no one moving now. It was quiet. Even the wind swept back through the hall and breezed away into the night and left everything a still and deathly quiet.

The sky was lit up with fires, and he could hear nothing but the dull pounding of the bombs that seemed miles away, then closer again with the shifting of the wind. Rolf got the feeling, looking out through the hole, that he was standing on the edge of the world and staring out over the fires of hell.

And then he heard a moan, a hoarse, guttural rasping of air through a human throat. He swung the muzzle of his gun toward the sound and stepped cautiously toward it.

The man lay with his head propped up on another man's legs, a dead man, he thought, though it was hard to see through the tangle of fallen beams and the section of torn lath and plaster. A thick supporting beam pressed down across the man's chest. His arms were extended up over the beam in a kind of two-handed Nazi salute. The man blinked at the ceiling, moaning as a trickle of blood oozed from his mouth and nostrils; seeing him, Rolf knew that he would be dead in minutes. It was Lieutenant Klemmer.

Rolf stepped carefully around the wreckage and the dead, glanced quickly at his brother, and then at the legs of the old woman. He looked over at Klemmer and saw that in order to retrieve the papers it was necessary for him to lift the beam clear of his chest. Setting the machine pistol to one side, he took one end of the beam and strained to lift it off the man's chest and lower it onto the floor.

Klemmer grimaced but made no sound, except to breathe, which he did in short, shallow gulps. Stooping next to him, Rolf could see that his chest was all caved in, looking like a cat run over by the wheel of an automobile. He could feel Klemmer's eyes following him as he felt in his breast pocket for the papers. The man struggled to say something but managed only a sharp, rasping noise. Rolf felt nothing for him now, neither hatred nor pity. He was a beaten enemy. But once he had removed the papers, he leaned up close to his face and, in a coarse whisper, said, "Heil Hitler."

The lieutenant just blinked up at him, taking in three sharp gulps of air. He gazed dully, then fixedly, at the play of fire patterns on the ceiling, his arms still extending upward from his crushed body.

Rolf went over and pried the diary from the big sergeant's dead hand. "Let's go, Gretchen," he said, taking her by the arm. He glanced once more up the hall; he could not see Ernst's body for the wreckage. Then he helped his sister walk down the hall, through the flickering pale light and on to the back stairs.

42 ★★★

O utside, the searchlights crisscrossed the night sky, probing for enemy bombers. Here and there were flashes of light as the high-explosive and incendiary bombs zeroed in on the marker flares, followed moments later by the thunderous reports. The horizon was a suffusion of glowing fingers reaching up into the sky and washing the low cloud cover a blood red. Everywhere there was the bedlam of people running and screaming and sirens blaring as the fires spread from building to building, and filling out the hellish ambience was the steady roar of aircraft.

Part of the bombed building had smashed one of the two black Mercedes, but the second one was untouched. Rolf helped his sister into the vehicle, then they sped away from the burning building, heading south toward the opposite end of town. However, the roads were choked with automobiles and trucks and horse-drawn carts, and they made only halting progress. Neither of them said a word. There was nothing to say.

Gretchen and Rolf watched intently as the twin blades of the headlights cut through the ruin of Gedächtniskirke. They were appalled at the seeming arbitrariness of the destruction that spilled its ruin across their route of escape, as though the gods of war took great sport in their caprice. Here a building was left intact, its contents and inhabitants unharmed, and there, just next to it, lay a building smashed into a heap of burning rubble—a crematorium and tomb piled into one. The Mercedes lurched forward as Rolf found an opening and turned off onto a side road.

Gretchen saw nothing of the devastation. Her mind was turned inward upon the dead strewn behind her in the shattered hallway—the pastor, his wife, Ernst. Poor Ernst. All of them gone. She saw nothing ahead of her but a swirl of shapes, black and firelit shapes; everything swept by her peripheral vision in an inarticulate blur. Out of the blur a face appeared, glaring, in the window. Glancing at it with unfeeling interest she saw that it was a woman, her face torn with grief, her mouth agape in a silent wail as she held in her arms the body of a small child. And then the image fell away into the inky obfuscation. Lost. She did not know if the child was dead. She did not think about it. She stared straight ahead at nothing.

Rolf's mind was focused on points ahead. Let the dead bury the dead. He kept glancing at his watch as he sped recklessly through the city, swerving wildly to avoid obstacles, backing up to career furiously away along an alternate route, racing the clock. The clock was their enemy now. It was like slaloming down the Zugspitze for time, only the obstacles were buildings now instead of flags, and the stakes were higher. Much higher. The car from General Olbricht's office would arrive promptly at seven o'clock to take on three, possibly four passengers. Three now, he thought. Three is better than none though. He glanced out his window as the sky flickered in the west. Moments later he heard the muffled report. The fools, he thought, gritting his teeth.

Ahead, a smoldering truck lay on its side blocking the road. Rolf cursed as he ground the car to a stop, jerked the transmission into reverse, and popped the clutch so that the wheels shuddered over the broken street. He cranked the steering wheel, and the car swung around and bucked up over a curb. Then he rammed the column shift downward into gear and floored the accelerator; the car bounced off the curb and squealed away in a cloud of smoke. After trying several possible detours he found a road that did not dead-end in a heap of rubble. He sped away down the lonely passage and glared once more at his watch, as though by an act of his will, he might intimidate the steady advance of time. It was 6:30. A nauseating feeling came over him as he calculated the time. He would be late.

An hour later they turned down their street, and Rolf saw the black sedan parked in front of the house. A jolt of hope went through him. The driver was putting suitcases into the trunk. Mr. and Mrs. Schiller were standing by the car, watching the fire glow in the distance showing over the rooftops.

Rolf swung the car over to the curb. The driver looked up from putting suitcases into the trunk and hurried over to him.

"I am sorry to have arrived so late, Captain Schiller," he said. "With the bombing the traffic is impossible."

Rolf nodded at him. "You are here. That is all that matters. Will you be able to find a route south?"

"I think so, Captain. The road to Zehlendorf is free," the driver assured him. "I should be able to find a road south from there."

"You must."

"There are reports of bombing in Ludwigshaven," the driver said, glancing reflectively to the southwest.

"Ludwigshaven?"

"Do not worry, Captain," the driver, who seemed very professional and knowledgeable, said. "I will find a road into Switzerland. The country will be clear, and everything will be all right with your family, I assure you."

"Is everything loaded in the trunk?"

"Yes, Captain."

Rolf handed him the papers. "You will have no trouble with these," he said.

The driver scanned quickly through the papers, then looked up at Rolf. "The boy will not be coming, sir?"

"No. There will only be the three."

Rolf went over to his parents. His mother was looking down the street, her body rigid and swaying slowly back and forth. Her face and eyes were taut with anxiety. "We cannot leave without Ernst, Rolf," she said.

Rolf steadied her shoulders and looked intently into her eyes. "Ernst will not be coming, Mama."

"What do you mean? Of course he is coming."

Rolf pulled her close to him. "He is dead, Mama."

She pushed away from him. "We will wait here until he arrives."

"Gretchen, help Mama," Rolf said. Gretchen went over and put her arms around her mother's shoulders.

"No."

"Yes, Mama," Gretchen said, guiding her to the curb. "It is true, I am afraid."

Rolf opened the rear door of the sedan, glanced quickly at his mother. "Gretchen will explain everything to you," he said, then kissed her cheek. "I am so sorry."

She blinked numbly at him.

Gretchen looked strangely at her brother as she helped her mother into the backseat of the car. "Here you go, Mama," she said. "You will be comfortable back here. It is very roomy."

Mrs. Schiller's eyes were wide open, their focus lost. "Gretchen?"

"I know, Mama. Here is your shawl." She wrapped the shawl around her mother's shoulders.

Rolf opened the front door for his father. "Papa, you sit in the front. There is plenty of room for your leg."

His father looked at him. "Ernst is dead?"

"Yes, Papa."

"How?"

Rolf felt a prickling go over his scalp. "You would be proud of him, Papa."

Mr. Schiller stared at him. "I see."

Rolf kissed him on the cheek, then he helped him into the front seat of the automobile. "You were with him?" his father asked.

"Yes, Papa. There is no time to explain now." Rolf put his crutches beside him on the seat. "You must go."

"You are not coming, son?"

"No, Papa. There will only be you, Mama, and Gretchen."

"What do you mean not coming?" Rolf turned his head; Gretchen was glaring at him. "Of course you are coming."

He went over to her, took her hands, and smiled down at her. Her cheeks were grimy from the dust and wreckage in the hall, and the moon just peeking over the rooftops caught the soft loveliness of her brown eyes. "I cannot come, Gretchen," he said. She started to speak, but he cut her off. "Please try to understand, Gretch."

"What is there to understand?" she asked. Panic edged into her features as she recognized the look in his eyes. "What are you going to do?"

Rolf just looked at her.

She glared at him. Then her voice rose. "Rolf, what are you going to do?"

"It does not concern you."

"Does not concern me?" She reeled away from him. "What are you saying, Rolf? My brother's life does not concern me?"

He took her arm, and she struck at him with the other. "No! If you're not going then neither am I."

"Yes, you are!" He held her close to him until she stopped flailing. "Do not do this, Gretchen. Please!"

She stopped abruptly, looked up, and, seeing the look in her brother's eyes, felt everything inside her crumbling. "I've already lost one brother today, Rolf. I don't want to lose another. I don't want to lose you."

Rolf smiled at her. "I love you, Gretchen. You will never lose that."

"Rolf?" Her lips trembled, then tears spurted from her eyes as she threw her arms around him. "Oh, Rolf," she cried. "Please, don't leave me. Please."

"What's this? Where is my brave girl?" He patted her back. "I need you to be strong for Mama and Papa."

"Who will be strong for me? Oh, Rolf, I can't bear it. I can't."

"Yes, you can," Rolf said. "You're the strongest person I know. You have a strength that no one can take away from you. Your faith."

"No, Rolf, I am weak," she cried. "I am weak." He held her until she was quiet. "I will pray for you, Rolf," she whimpered. She looked searchingly into his eyes. "I will pray for you."

"There's my girl." He kissed her forehead and then her cheek. "I love you, sweetheart," he said tenderly, then turned to the driver and said militarily, "Are you ready to leave?"

"Yes, my captain." The driver climbed into the automobile and started the motor.

Rolf helped his sister into the backseat and closed the door. She clung to the window, looking up at him desperately, her dirty face now smudged and streaked with tears. He watched as the car pulled away from the curb, swung around, then headed away down the street into the darkness. He waved at them. Gretchen and his mother looked out the rear window, their faces growing smaller and dimmer, until the car disappeared around the bend in the road.

He stood looking after them for a long time, feeling the layers of loneliness filling his chest, then spreading their weakness into every part of his body. He felt like sitting down on the curb and putting his head between his legs. Instead, he turned slowly and trudged up the walkway to the house, climbed the porch stairs, and stopped briefly on the stoop to massage the bridge of his nose.

He felt the tension in the muscles between his shoulder blades mount the back of his spine along either side of his skull. He kneaded his temples, put his hand on the doorknob, and went inside.

The house was quiet. Dark. Lonely. The life gone out of it. In the hall bathroom Rolf stirred a spoonful of aspirin powder into a glass of water and drank it down. He went through every room of the house, smoothing his hand over bureaus and chairs, running his fingertips over bedcovers and along the smooth countertop in the kitchen, releasing the Schiller smells and memories that over the years had been locked away in the fabrics and textures. At one point he lay the flat of his palm against the wall as though feeling for a pulse. The wall was cool. Still.

The old wood floor creaked beneath his tread as he crossed the foyer into the library. The pictures were gone from the piano and mantel, he noticed, the family Bible gone from the table next to Papa's chair; everything else was untouched, looking as though the family had just stepped out for an evening in town. He stood in the middle of the room and closed his eyes for several minutes, allowing the heavy silence to wash over him like waves of surf.

The pendulum of the grandfather clock dutifully kept time, the brazen moon gleaming rhythmically in the ambient light. In the cool quiet of the room he could feel the taut cords at the base of his head begin to unwind, the aspirin working, opening the constricted passages for the life-giving flow of blood to his brain, and clearing his mind for thought. He went over to the window and gazed out upon the empty street, the moon showing a desolate glow on the surface and in the bare-limbed trees along the walk.

He thought of his family, each one in turn. He thought of Ernst struggling with the gun and again felt the prickling go over his scalp. He could not shake the thought. Poor Ernst. He thought of what the elderly pastor had done for him and could not shake that one either—could not shake the idea that someone might give his life that he might live. Then he too, like the American Thunderbolt pilot hundreds of miles away, pondered the existence of God. Why, God? Why them and not me?

It seemed that love was a terrible risk.

The sound of the air raid sirens and the rapid pounding of the flak batteries pulled his thoughts outward. He looked out over the city and watched the searchlights slicing across the sky, probing it for the invisible bombers. Just then the horizon lit up in the south. He counted the seconds until the report, just like he would after a flicker of lightning, and he knew that they were bombing the factories in Mariendorf and Steglitz. Neukölln and Siemensstadt had gotten hammered earlier, he knew. He took a deep breath and blew it out hard. Ludwigshaven and Berlin in the same night, he thought. They have total domination of the skies. It is over. It is truly over.

His eyes narrowed with resolve. He went outside and closed the door gently behind him, locking it, then, closing the front gate, strode over to the black Mercedes. He looked one last time at the home in which he was born and grew up, then climbed into the car and drove away without looking back.

Inside the house, the heavy silence draped over each room and its furnishings like so many dustcovers. Suddenly the quiet was broken by the first chime of the grandfather clock. Joining it were the mantel clock, the cuckoo clock in the kitchen, and the wall clock in the hall, each striking eight times. Together they made a terrific row, for a time, and then fell silent.

43 ★★★

Rolf drove the black Mercedes into the air base at Staaken, northwest of Berlin, gave his name to the sentry, and explained that he was on important business for Reich Marshal Göring.

The sentry checked his log. "I am sorry, Captain Schiller, but I do not see your name."

Rolf frowned at him. "There must be a mistake. Isn't this the nineteenth?"

"Yes, sir."

"Then my name must be in the log. Now find it quickly, Corporal. I am in a considerable hurry."

"I am sorry, Captain. I have checked and rechecked, and your name does not show in the log. Wait one moment, sir, please, while I call ahead. I am sure that everything will be as you have said."

"As I have said?" Rolf nearly yelled. "Are you implying that I am lying, Corporal?"

"No, Captain. It is not what I meant."

"What is your name?"

The sentry clicked to attention. "Corporal Möller, sir. Please, sir, if you will allow me to call ahead. It won't take a moment." The sentry stepped quickly into the booth, turned his shoulder to Rolf, and began dialing the number of the sergeant of the guard.

Rolf tapped his fingers on the steering wheel, showing none of the bluff on his face, knowing that to break off the bluff would be to lose everything now, and he could not afford to lose everything just now.

He looked beyond the gate to the gray administration buildings on the left and on the right-hand sides of the road leading into camp. He looked beyond these to the several lines of hangars bracketing the taxi strip. There were FW–190s parked in front of the hangars, with ground crews working them over. Looking farther still, he could see the airstrip and the control tower with the wind sock fingering the wind in the first gray light of dawn. He looked back at the sentry, drumming his fingers impatiently, and waited, staring at him with a cold poker face and a pair of deuces.

"What is the delay, Corporal?" he demanded.

The corporal looked at him quickly, smiled politely, and said, "Just one moment, Captain. The sergeant of the guard is just coming." He turned his shoulder to Rolf and glared down at the phone, a bead of sweat crawling through the short-cropped hair at his temple.

The thickly-built sergeant of the guard, sitting at his desk, leafing through a girly magazine and pouring himself a cup of coffee from a thermos, let the phone ring two more times before picking up the receiver. "Staff Sergeant Hoffmann," he growled. His face immediately screwed into a frown. "Who . . . Möller? It is not time for your report."

He listened. "What's that? Captain Schiller?" He listened, frowning down at the magazine, not seeing it, then he glanced out his window at the main gate and saw the black Mercedes. He looked up at the wall clock. It read 0530. "It is 0530, Möller. Who has business for the Reich Marshal at this hour?"

He listened. "One moment."

The sentry at the main gate glanced at Rolf from the booth, nodded his head, and again smiled politely. "It will just be a moment, sir."

Rolf was staring ahead at the line of planes at the far end of the compound.

The sergeant of the guard ran the blunt end of a pencil down his log book. "I do not have his name," he spoke sharply into the receiver. "He is here on business for the Reich Marshal?" He listened. "Hold on," he growled. The staff sergeant picked up another phone and began dialing.

Rolf glared at the sentry who, standing rigidly in the booth with his shoulder turned to him, was alternatively glaring down at the telephone, and then back into the compound through the window. "What is the holdup, Corporal?" he demanded.

"Just one moment, please, Captain," the corporal said, glancing quickly at him. "It will just be a moment, I assure you." The corporal looked back through the window at the duty hut of the sergeant of the guard.

The phone next to the bed of the duty officer rang. A bare arm swung heavily out of the covers and fumbled with the receiver. "Lieutenant Köhler," the duty officer groaned. He listened . . . frowned. "Wait a moment."

He dug out an earplug, squinting at his wristwatch, and snapped, "Yes, yes. Proceed, Hoffmann." *Maybe this is a dream*, he thought. "Captain

Schiller, you say? I know a Captain Rolf Schiller. That is the one? Yes. He is to be decorated by the Führer this afternoon. What is he doing here?"

Lieutenant Köhler, a healthy-looking man in his mid-twenties, swung his legs out of bed and planted his feet on the floor. He glared across the room at the leg of a table, scratching the fine blond hairs on his chest. "He is on urgent business for the Reich Marshal! At this hour?" He rechecked his watch and cursed. "Why was I not informed? I am never informed. Tell Captain Schiller I wish to speak with him. Be civil, of course," he listened. "I do not care if he says he has urgent business, Sergeant!"

He slammed the receiver down, cursed, then grabbed his shirt off the bedside chair and went over to the window. He thrust his arms into the sleeves and, muttering to himself, could just see the main gate and the black Mercedes about fifty yards away.

"What is wrong, Liebchen?" a woman purred from the bed.

"Nothing. Go back to sleep."

The sentry listened as the sergeant of the guard relayed the duty officer's instructions. He replaced the receiver, swore silently to himself, then stepped down to Rolf's window. "Everything is in order, of course, Captain Schiller. However, Lieutenant Köhler wishes a word with you. It will only take a moment." The sentry pointed in the direction of the duty officer's quarters.

"I have no time for this!" Rolf snapped. "I have urgent business for the Reich Marshal!"

"I am sorry, Captain, but the lieutenant is quite insistent."

"I shall speak to his superior."

"Yes, Captain. That would be Major Reischer." The corporal let him pass with a sharp salute. Watching the car speed away, he blew out a breath of relief, thanking God that he was only a corporal. He lowered the gate then stepped back into the booth.

Rolf passed the sergeant of the guard's hut and the duty officer's quarters. He glanced at the corporal's white face through his rearview mirror, then swung the car over to the hangars on the far end of the base. The corporal followed him incredulously, then ducked quickly out of sight.

The telephone in the sergeant of the guard's hut rang. The burly staff sergeant looked up from the centerfold and cursed. Now what? He reached for the telephone. "Staff Sergeant Hoffmann." He stiffened immediately. "Yes, sir, Lieutenant. At once, Lieutenant!"

He slammed the receiver home, picked it up again, and began dialing.

Rolf pulled the Mercedes over to the hangar at the far end of the strip, where two mechanics were just closing a side panel on the engine cowling of a new FW–190D series fighter. They gave the man in the cockpit, a sergeant, the thumbs up, then looked over at Rolf as he climbed out of the driver's seat and strode over to them. They saluted.

Returning their salute, Rolf looked up at the sergeant and, raising his voice over the rumbling of the engine, asked, "What is the status of this aircraft, Sergeant?"

The sergeant looked down at him, bewildered. "The status?"

"Is the plane suitable for flight?" Rolf repeated, shouting.

"Yes, Captain," the sergeant said. "Of course. We have just gone through the preflight."

"Is it filled with petrol?"

"Yes, Captain."

"Good, then I will take it."

"I do not understand."

"You heard me."

The sergeant looked at Rolf, puzzled. "But this plane belongs to Lieutenant Bruner, Captain. I cannot allow you to take it without proper authorization."

"This is your proper authorization." Rolf pulled out a pistol he'd found in the glove box of the SS staff car and pointed it at the man's chest. "Please do not resist me, Sergeant. I would not like to shoot you."

The sergeant looked at the gun, glanced at the two crewmen, then looked steadily at Rolf. "I shall report this."

"Of course you will." Rolf gestured with the gun. "Now, if you will climb down out of there. Please. I am in a bit of a hurry."

The two crewmen were standing a little apart from Rolf, looking at him and at the pistol, then they looked at each other, perplexed. But the sergeant, climbing down from the aircraft, only looked at Rolf with the sullen, angry eyes of someone being robbed.

Rolf ordered the crewmen to remove the wheel blocks. Then the three of them, the sergeant and the two crewmen, waited until Rolf climbed into the cockpit and his back was to them before they turned and ran toward the hangar.

Inside the cockpit Rolf quickly familiarized himself with the controls. He had flown the FW–190B series in May of 1942, while on temporary duty along the Kammhuber Line in coastal France; still it did not take him long to readjust his thinking to the additional gauges and switches that reflected considerable advances. He went through a quick check of the flaps, rudder, and ailerons, then, throttling, he swung the plane toward the airstrip.

Just then a siren blared over the air base. Men scrambled from every quarter, some running for their planes, others running out of buildings and shielding their eyes against the sky for enemy bombers. Four motorcycles with sidecars and two Volkswagen 82 utility vehicles, each carrying four soldiers, roared out of the security compound and sped toward the flight line.

A strident voice cut into Rolf's headset, alternately demanding an explanation from him and commanding him to turn the aircraft around. Rolf switched off the radio and taxied the FW–190 into the wind, his mind calm, focused, his eyes trained on the gauges and on the bright orange wind sock. Then, seeing the security vehicles racing toward him on an intercepting course, he pulled back on the throttle, and the big Junkers Jumo 12 cylinders roared to life. The plane jumped forward, accelerating rapidly as it bounced over the tarmac. They were now in a race.

Rolf could see the security vehicles out of the corner of his eye as they swung onto the airstrip on a parallel course to his, the vehicles slightly ahead of the plane. The plane started gaining, passing the vehicles, and he saw the white faces glaring at him as he passed. And then he saw the little puffs of smoke from the machine pistols and felt the impact of the bullets along his rudder and fuselage. He waited until the tachometer showed 3,250 rpms before he pulled back on the stick and felt the tail lifting, responding to his touch, the plane lifting, climbing suddenly as the earth grudgingly relinquished its hold.

Looking out his cockpit he could see the two motorcycles and utility vehicles still racing along the airstrip, earthbound, going nowhere, small and falling away. He could still see the glaring white faces and the tiny puffs of smoke, but they were of little consequence to him now.

He pressed an electric button on his left to retract the undercarriage, then, wheeling the stick, banked the Focke-Wulf to the west. He adjusted the trim, seeing only the blue-gray of the dawning sky now and a light lacing of cirrus clouds high and delicate against the ceiling. The plane climbed steadily, effortlessly it seemed, then, leveling out, he saw only the hazy gray line of the horizon.

Looking over his shoulder to take one last look at his beloved city, Rolf saw the reaching light of the sun glinting off panes of unshattered windows, off the faces of buildings, with the sun bathing everything in a deep yellow-orange. He also saw the thick columns of smoke twisting up from the rubble of last night's bombing, looking as though the portals of hell had opened.

He turned and gazed steadily to the west. Sadness stirred in his breast, like a little wind over a bank of coals. It always happened this way at first. He did not enjoy the killing; he would be a monster if he did. He wasn't a monster, he knew. He hoped. However, he felt none of the little darts of flame in his chest, the love flames that purified the man in him. Those were extinguished now. All of them. He felt nothing for anything. And if that did not make him a monster, then what did it make him? Dead? Yes, dead, he told himself. Dead to the world and the world to him.

He glanced heavenward but could not bring himself to pray. He had no faith in prayer. Then his eyes narrowed into the flat blade of a predator, with the blade honed now by a single deadly thought.

44 ★★★

"What did you make of those eggs?" Happy groaned, nursing his stomach with his little brown fingers.

"Let's not talk about it," Billy said as they made their way up the center aisle of the briefing hut.

"I'll have nightmares about those eggs," Happy said. They stepped into a row of chairs and sat down next to Joe.

"You guys are gettin' soft," Joe said.

"Soft? Those eggs were like rubber," Happy insisted. He turned to Billy. "Did you see them bounce, amigo? I swear I saw that runt of a messman bounce one off the floor into the pan."

"I'd rather not talk about it," Billy said.

Happy glanced behind him. "Hey, don't look now, but here comes Turtle. Carumba, he looks worse than you do."

Warren Turlock shuffled up the center aisle, feeling his way from chair to chair with one hand, while holding his head with the other as though it were made of glass. His big, sad eyes held in them a vision of the end of the world.

"Hey, Turtle!" Happy boomed. "Where you been? We didn't see you at chow."

"Not so loud," Turlock growled, waving his hand to quiet him.

Happy chuckled.

Pete Skagway and the kid from Schenectady took seats behind them. The kid was sitting with the straight-backed, wide-eyed, hands-on-knees look of someone on his first day of school, and when Billy looked back at him the kid smiled and raised an index finger at him in greeting. He had the impossible apple-pie freshness of a Norman Rockwell cover, Billy thought. He certainly didn't look twenty-one.

"You with Yellow Flight?"

"Yes, sir."

"Who's with Yellow Flight?" Happy wanted to know. He jerked his head around and took one look at the rookie. "Ay, carumba." Then, narrowing his eyes, he looked him over carefully. "You Jim Cooly's replacement?"

The kid nodded his head, smiling.

"Jim Cooly the fighter pilot?"

The kid nodded, the smile locked into place.

Happy looked at Billy and crossed himself. "Our gooses are cooked."

"What's the matter, Hochreiter?" Skagway asked, watching Billy closely. "You're looking a little green around the gills."

Billy looked at him, then shook his head and again faced the front. He heard Skagway snickering behind him, then whispering something to the *Saturday Evening Post* cover.

"You want me to pop him one?" Happy asked Billy.

"Forget it."

"Did you get a load of Jailbait back there? We're cooked, you know?"

"You're cooked," Billy said. "He's in your flight."

"That's right. That's right," Happy chanted. "Ay, chihuahua, that's right."

The large briefing hut filled up quickly. There was an air of expectancy in the place, as there always was before a mission. Scuttlebutt winged freely about, none of it accurate, but all of it needed to take the edge off the mystery of the mission. Most of the men smoked and joked, but there were a few who were very quiet.

Billy was staring straight ahead and trying not to think about anything. But no sooner would he push all thoughts from his mind than the faces would return, one after the other: Jane first, and then Colette, and then that boy Henri and his father, the woodcutter, and the rest of the ghosts in France. All of their faces would come up and bob around in his head like a tub of apples. And then, as always, that stony knot of remorse, or guilt, or whatever it was that kept troubling him, would surface, wedge itself between the others, and grin at him like the face of Death.

Happy was right, he thought. This thinking business is no good. So he stared straight ahead and tried not to think of anything. Still, there was that tub of apples.

Happy looked over his shoulder, past the kid from Schenectady, at the door opening into the Nissen hut. "Uh-oh, here it comes."

Billy turned as Colonel Pilke, Lieutenant Colonel Mallory, the squadron leaders of the 62nd and the 63rd, and an entourage of staff officers entered and made their way along the side aisle. Someone shouted "Attention!" and everyone snapped to attention.

"As you were, men," Colonel Pilke said, arriving at the front of the briefing hut. The men took their seats, and there were a few moments of noisy settling.

"Let's settle down quickly, men," Colonel Pilke said.

"Ay, carumba!"

"What's the matter, Haps?" Billy asked. "You don't look so good."

"This doesn't feel so good, amigo," Happy moaned. "That Jailbait's got me thinking. I think I caught the spooks from you."

"Shut up, you boneheads," Joe growled.

Happy sank down in his chair and crossed himself.

"Smoke 'em if you got 'em, fellas," Zeb Pilke said.

Cigarettes were passed around, and plumes of smoke went up over the room.

"I'll get straight to it," Pilke said. He turned to his adjutant. "Lieutenant . . ." The adjutant stepped behind the colonel and pulled down a large map of northern Germany.

Colonel Pilke stepped over to the map with a pointer. "You may have already heard parts of this on the BBC this morning," he began. "Last night a small force of Lancasters and Mosquito bombers raided the flak batteries along the Frisian coast, here, here, and here." He indicated the islands on the map.

"As a diversionary tactic, three hundred and twenty-five Lancasters bombed the city of Ludwigshaven—here in the south, near the Swiss border. Kicked up quite a hornet's nest, we're told. However, the real pigeon was right here," he said, tapping the map of Germany north and central. "Berlin. The target areas were marked with flares by pathfinder Mosquitoes, followed by four hundred and forty-some-odd Lancasters. Of these, four hundred and two made it over the target and dropped sixteen hundred tons of high-explosive and incendiary bombs on Herr Hitler's head."

There were several low whistles.

Colonel Pilke grinned. "I'd say that was giving the Krauts a black eye, wouldn't you?"

The men laughed.

"The word out now is that Bomber Command is going to give it another shot on Monday," the group commander continued. "They were lucky last night, but on the twenty-second you can bet the Krauts will be expecting them. They'll throw everything but the kitchen sink at them—maybe even the sink too. That's where we come in."

"About time," Billy muttered. "I was beginning to think we were just going to get a history lesson."

"Yes, but you don't get shot at in history lessons," Happy whispered.

Billy looked at him, and the little guy really did look spooked.

"Bomber Command tells us that they caught a lot of heat from fighters, here around Calais; here at Antwerp and Rotterdam; and here around Bremen and Wilhelmshaven," Pilke said, pointing to the places on the map. "You boys have been itching for a fight; well, now you're going to get one. Our job over the next few days will be to attack German fighter bases, hit them hard, hit them often, knock them down for the count if we're able, to soften them up for the Brits on Monday. There are some mean boys along the coast, as you know. And I don't have to tell you about these fellas up here at Jever, do I?"

Colonel Pilke stood looking out over the men, smacking his hand with the pointer. "You can guess which base we're going to hit today," he said seriously. "It's going to be a scrapper. Any questions?"

"If we guess wrong, can we stay home?" someone asked. There were a few laughs.

"If we're gonna soften the Krauts up for the Brits, who's gonna soften them up for us?" someone else added. A few more laughs.

Pilke grinned at him. "If you wanted to fly milk runs, you should have joined a bomber group."

"No thanks."

"What about the other groups?" Turtle asked. "Are they going to be a part of this little soirée?"

"Yeah. What about the 4th and their new Mustangs? Are they going to get into this shindig?"

"Yes to the first question. Yes and no to the second," Colonel Pilke said, holding the pointer with both hands. "There will be several groups working this operation. Thunderbolts and Lightnings only, though. Forget the Mustangs. They're going to be used primarily for long-range escorts to Berlin after the first of the year. Maybe sooner. Any other questions?"

Happy raised his hand. "Will we be back in time for tea?" he asked, affecting his best British accent. "Or should I cancel my reservation at the Guinea?"

The group commander shook his head. "Somebody hit him."

Joe reached around Billy and winged Happy on the back of his head. "Hey!"

"All right," the group commander said. "If there are no further questions, then let's saddle up. Good hunting, men, and Godspeed. Don't forget to pick up your survival kits." He turned to Mallory and the other squadron leaders. "Okay, fellas, tend to your sheep."

The men were dismissed, briefed by their respective squadron leaders, then one-half hour later the three squadrons of the 52nd were up in the air, fifty planes strong, climbing, and approaching the coast.

Billy looked for Jane Worthing's house out the right side of his cockpit but could not see it for the fog. Then, through a gauzy haze he saw the light on the promontory of Southwold, the cannon of Gun Hill, and the tower of St. Edmund's, before the greens and grays of England fell quickly behind. He had a sinking feeling in his stomach and fought hard to keep from losing his breakfast.

৵⌒৲

An hour later Rolf turned his stolen FW–190 toward the airdrome at Jever, switched on his radio, and called ahead to identify himself. When he came in for a landing, coming in low into the wind, with the hydraulically controlled flaps and undercarriage working so smoothly and effortlessly that the wheels seemed to kiss the tarmac in a welcoming embrace, he taxied the plane over to his hangar. Group Commander Specht was standing in the bay waiting for him. He was smoking a cigarette.

Rolf hit the ignition switch, and the big radial engine of the 190 sputtered to a halt.

Captain Specht flicked his cigarette to the ground and walked over. "What have you done?" he asked in the sudden quiet. "The Gestapo have been here looking for you."

Rolf climbed down from the cockpit and said, "Good to see you too, Günther."

"This is no time for jokes, Rolf. They were here to arrest you. For treason," he added.

"Do you believe them?"

"It doesn't matter what I believe. They were here to arrest you. You can imagine my surprise." Specht lit another cigarette.

"What did you tell them?"

"I told them you were in Berlin on furlough . . . that the Führer was to decorate you this afternoon. I told them to look for you there. What else could I tell them?"

"What did they say?"

"They said you had flown the coop." He looked over at the FW–190 and grunted. "I also received word from Staaken this morning, from a very irate Major Reischer, that a certain squadron leader of mine, on special business for the Reich Marshal, stole one of his planes."

"It handles wonderfully, you know?" Rolf grinned. "Everything is so fully automatic. The plane practically flies itself. I think there will be no need for pilots before too long."

"They'll be back," the group commander said, ignoring him. He paused a moment, smoking his cigarette. "What did you do, Rolf? What *have* you done?"

Something went over the squadron leader's eyes. "What did *I* do? Berlin is in flames and you ask what did I do? I did nothing, Günther. That is the trouble, I did nothing."

Captain Specht, standing with his hands on his waist, looked down at the ground and shook his head. Flicking an ash, he looked up at Rolf. "I've got orders to detain you." He broke off and swore. "'Detain?' That's a good word. I've got orders to lock you up until the Gestapo can come and haul your tail out of here."

"Are you going to lock me up?"

"What can I do? I told you that little SS lieutenant was after your head, and here you've handed it to him on a silver platter."

"He is dead."

"Dead?" Specht looked at him. "Did you kill him?"

"No. But I tried to. He murdered someone very dear to me."

"Do not tell me—"

"It is no one you know, Günther," Rolf said quietly. "It is no longer important."

Captain Specht studied him, his face taking on a military blankness. "That he is dead is inconsequential. There were several men who came for you. The one in charge was a major."

"A major?"

"Yes. A Major von Wuertzer. You had words with him at the Reich Marshal's, apparently."

Rolf remembered the man as he left the rest room at Karinhall. He knew then that he had overstepped military etiquette. But he had never cared much for the strictures of military etiquette, especially when they involved a member of the SS. It was always the politics of war that jumped him out of the sun. Rolf grinned suddenly. "I suppose this shoots down my opportunity for a group command."

Specht threw his head back and laughed. "Your opportunity. What a kidder you are. If I didn't know better I would think that all of this was your idea to *keep* you from a group command." They both laughed. Then Captain Specht's smile faded.

"I am sorry about Viktor, Rolf. I know you were good friends."

Rolf looked away and grunted. "Yes, good friends," he said bitterly. "His chute did not open?"

"No." Captain Specht adjusted the patch over his left eye and smoked his cigarette. "I heard about your visit to his parents," he said, smoking and flicking the ash. "It was decent of you."

"There is nothing decent anymore, Günther. There is only the war. There is nothing decent in war, and there are no winners. There are only the dead and those who bury the dead."

"You are wrong. It was a decent thing you did. You are a decent man, Rolf, and I never believed for a moment that you were a traitor. A thief, yes," he grinned. "A traitor? Not for a moment."

The two fighter pilots looked at each other; both knew what was going through the other's mind.

Günther smoked the last of his cigarette, threw it to the ground, and stepped on it. "When this is over I would like to take my son hunting in the Black Forest," he said.

"Yes?"

Günther nodded his head. "My father took me hunting there when I was a boy, near the headwaters of the Danube," he said. "I was twelve, I think. There was no game, of course—game disappeared with the emperors." He smiled. "But still we had a good time. No king ever had as good a time." He looked off into the distance.

There were big, bouldery clouds stacked against the blue morning sky with the line of trees in sharp relief against the brilliant, sunstruck whiteness of the clouds. An invigorating chill in the air came in off the North Sea. "Karl should know what it is to go hunting with his father," he said, taking a deep breath of air. "Such are the times a boy should know and remember."

Rolf looked out over the airfield.

"I do not think we would find game there now," Günther said wistfully.

"It doesn't matter," Rolf said. "It is being with your son that matters."

"Of course," Günther agreed. "He is a good boy. It will be good to see him again." For several moments the two men stood looking at the clouds packed up over the trees, neither saying anything. Then Günther Specht looked at Rolf and said, "What am I going to do with you, my stubborn friend?"

"Let me do what I must do."

"Do?"

The air raid siren blared chillingly over the base. Both men looked up at the sky in the west. "Now what?" the group commander wondered.

"Let me go up, Günther," Rolf said.

Captain Specht looked at him. "You know I can't do that."

"I am not a traitor, Günther."

"I know it, but I can't let you go. They will arrest me if they find out I let you go."

"Tell them I held a gun to your head."

"You wouldn't."

A shade crossed Rolf's face as he reached for his pistol. He pulled it halfway out of the holster. Specht looked at the pistol, looked into the cold predator eyes, saw a flicker of light go through them, and then the tentative smile pulling at the corners of his mouth.

"This is foolishness," Rolf said. He shoved the pistol back into the holster. "You must let me go up, Günther," he said. "If our years of friendship mean anything to you, you must let me go up."

Both men watched as fliers began pouring out of the barracks, shrugging on their parachutes, and streaming toward the waiting lines of Messerschmitts.

"I have to go, Günther."

Specht looked intently into the eyes of the squadron leader. He could see everything changed on his face now: the gray flatness that had narrowed over the soft underbelly of his soul and the grim scar of a mouth that had once been a smile.

"You're not coming back, are you?" he said.

"I am not a traitor, Günther."

"You didn't answer my question."

Several engines fired up. Pilots climbed into their cockpits and went through a hurried series of checks. The air shook with the roar of their planes. "We do not have time for this, Günther. You must let me fly."

As Captain Specht looked at him, the air raid siren continued to blare over the air base at Jever.

45 ★★★

Had Second Lieutenant Jimmy Wheeler of Yellow Flight been looking ahead at the tail of his element leader he might have seen the metallic glint of light in the sun; as it was, he was looking down through a scattering of cumulus clouds at the coast of northern Germany. He had never seen Germany before, and he felt a certain thrill at seeing the coast and at everything the sight of it meant. He was wearing that same impossible, apple-pie expression of a Norman Rockwell painting, when he heard the cry of "Ay, chihuahua!" in his headset. "Bandits out of the sun!"

Looking up, his eyes wide and full of wonder and his mouth locked in a perpetual smile, his cockpit suddenly exploded into a million shards of glass and metal. He had made some terrible mistake, he knew. But his mind seemed incapable of focusing on it, focusing on anything, except that the words, "Bail out, Wheeler! Bail out!" penetrated some vague and oily impression of flames and heat blossoming over his body. He felt the movement of the plane through his body, the long clumsy bulk of the fuselage shuddering, beginning to roll, the wings tipping, and himself rolling with it and not able to keep from rolling. What followed, at last piercing through the shock in his brain, was the sudden knowledge that he would never see Schenectady again.

❧❧

The pilot of the Messerschmitt looked over his shoulder as the P–47 Thunderbolt, ensheathed in smoke and flames, slid over onto its back, then twirled away toward the earth trailing a thick auger of black smoke. Not seeing a chute, knowing that there would not be a chute, he pulled back on his control stick and chandelled toward the ceiling.

"They got the kid!" Happy yelled into his headset, watching the Thunderbolt spiraling down through the sky in flames. "They got the kid. The lousy Kraut got the kid."

"I see him!" Frank Johnson, his flight leader said. "109 at three o'clock high, beat-feeting it to the ceiling! Let's go!"

"I'm right behind you, amigo," Happy said, feeling a hot rage in his veins. He cursed every foulness in the universe, blasphemed every goodness, then, giving the big Pratt and Whitney full throttle, he pulled back on the stick, and the Jug roared away.

Billy had been scanning the sky very alertly, glancing down at the coast briefly as the four flights of the 61st Squadron, crossing the Zuider Zee, edged over into the Netherlands. He glanced down once again to make sure they were over Germany. He was a hunter now, everything in his mind honed and trained on the expansive theater of blue sky all around him. All of his instincts were tingling with the knowledge that they were in dangerous airspace.

Red Flight was ahead of them, and ahead of Red was Yellow Flight, and ahead of Yellow was Mallory and White Flight; each of the flights held a tight finger-four formation, at a cruising speed of 250 mph. The 62nd was below and ahead of them, and the 63rd was above and ahead of them. He had a good lay of the sky from his position, and when he had seen the Messerschmitt diving out of the sun to fall upon Yellow Flight, he shouted a warning into his mouthpiece. But Happy was a split-second before him and cut him off.

He watched helplessly as the 20mm shells tore through the canopy of the kid from Schenectady. Then he saw the flash of fire and smoke and the Thunderbolt rolling over on its side, looking like a wounded right whale, nosing down to begin its long spiraling descent to the earth. Breaking with Joe, everyone breaking away into pairs as the Messerschmitts of Jagdgeschwader 11 suddenly swarmed the sky like a pack of sharks drawn to the chum, Billy knew that the kid was dead, and that it was a lousy way to begin a battle.

❧⚬❧

The German pilot looked over his shoulder and watched the two Thunderbolts climbing up after him, one ahead of the other. They would not catch him, he knew. There was no catching a Messerschmitt in a climb. Then his eyes narrowed with a thought.

Glancing down at the black and white photograph on the instrument panel, he bent the stick to the left, working his pedals at the same moment, suddenly feeling the Gs pulling against his face and his chest and groin, then feeling the G forces shifting across his body to finally lift off with a leaping tickle in his stomach. He rolled the stick forward, and the plane responded with a sharp banking turn, nosing down, leveling, then throttling the engine as the Messerschmitt surged forward into a dive.

"What's he doing!" Happy wondered, the rage in him aborted in his throat.

"Looks like he's coming back," Frank Johnson said.

"Coming back? He's not supposed to do that. He's supposed to run away from us."

"I've got news for you, amigo," Frank said. "Looks to me like he wants to play chicken."

"Carumba! Is he crazy? That's all we need today are loco Krauts."

The Messerschmitt floated in and out of Frank Johnson's sight reticle and, as the enemy plane edged into his line of sight, he fired a burst. His eyes were widely intent as he watched the tracers bending and missing under the wings. He let off on the trigger and paused, sighting.

The 109 grew larger in the sky every second, both planes on a collision course. Watching the bulk of the 109 fall back through the reticle, filling it, he squeezed off another burst and watched the tracers just skimming over the wings.

He fired again and, missing, cursed. As he was about to squeeze off another burst, he saw the papery flashes of light over the 109's cowling, ducked instinctively, and immediately felt the bullets tearing through his wings and fuselage.

"Break! Break!" he cried, hitting hard right rudder. He swung hard to the right, and Happy veered hard to the left the instant before the Messerschmitt barreled down through their prop wash.

Happy screamed. "He is crazy! He's trying to kill himself!"

He jerked his head over his shoulder and the blood rushed from his face. "Did you see his plane? It's the one with the checkered cowling. *Katharina!* I saw it, amigo, it was *Katharina!* The crazy Kraut." He blew a short, shrill whistle, then turning his Jug toward Frank Johnson's Jug he saw a thin line of white smoke streaming from the engine.

"I'm hit," Frank said. "He got my fuel line, I think. Can you see anything?"

Happy came up under his left flank, so that his cockpit lined up below and just behind the cowling. "That loco Kraut tagged you pretty good. You're losing fuel fast. Looks like he chewed your flaps up pretty good too."

"They seem okay," Frank Johnson said, working the stick so that his wings waved up and down. "I'm heading back to the barn."

"Want me to ride shotgun? I'd be happy to escort you back to the barn!"

"No. I'll be all right as long as I don't run out of gas. My controls seem to be working fine."

"I'll escort you back as far as the Zuider Zee," Happy said. He looked around him. "I think maybe that loco Kraut will want to finish you off."

"He's long gone," Frank said. "Now, get out of here."

"Suit yourself," Happy said. *"Vaya con Dios, amigo."*

He watched as Frank Johnson's Thunderbolt headed west, dropping to 10,000 feet, trailing a thin line of white smoke. "I'll buy you a beer at the Guinea tonight."

"Sure," Frank's voice crackled back, and then he was gone.

Happy looked below him for the Messerschmitt, but it was nowhere in sight. It had vanished as quickly as it had appeared. He shook his head. "This doesn't feel so good," he said to himself. "Crazy Krauts trying to kill themselves." Pursuing the Messerschmitt they had swung wide of the main body of action, so he turned his plane back toward the east. "I'm here, amigos," he said into his mike. "Anybody need an assist from a lucky Puerto Rican?"

૭ન૭

In the photograph Rolf was holding a girl in his arms. Her arms were wrapped around his neck and she was laughing, her head thrown back and her legs scissoring playfully, and he was grinning broadly and happily at the person taking the picture. He remembered what happened immediately after the photograph, how they had stolen away to the harbor, walking arm in arm along one of the piers, past the sights and smells of the fishermen fishing off the pier, and looking out over the water as a big tanker came down the Schilling Roads.

He remembered watching the stevedores unloading the cargo from its hold, and how he had caught her gazing up at him with that certain smile of hers that always took the wind from him—how that longing loveliness in her big blue eyes had made everything in his throat thicken. She had pulled him into the lee of a pile and kissed him.

"Will the war continue for very much longer, Rolfie?" she had asked him, leaning lovingly against his chest.

"I hope not."

She had paused, thinking, smoothing a hand thoughtfully over the buttons of his uniform. "I cannot bear the thought of being apart from you."

"Nor I from you."

"I am nothing apart from you," she had said. "I am incomplete. It is frightening how incomplete I am without you holding me."

"Do not be frightened. It is the same with me. I am half a man without you." He grinned at her. "And twice the man when I am with you."

"Your arithmetic is faulty," she smiled. She stepped up onto her toes and, running her fingers over his cheek and around his ear to the back of his head, kissed him. Then a shade of something crossed over her face.

"What is it, Liebchen? Is something the matter?"

"I am afraid of losing you," she said, looking up into his slate gray eyes that were warmly and tenderly gazing at her. "Sometimes I see you—"

"Yes?"

"Nothing."

"What were you going to say?"

"It is nothing. Truly."

"Truly? Katharina, you must tell me truly. We must not hold secrets from each other."

She let out a deep sigh. Then fondling the button of his breast pocket, she said, "Sometimes I see you dead in your airplane."

"Yes?"

"Your plane has crashed," she continued morosely. "There are many bullet holes across the side of your plane, and I see you sitting there with your arm draped over the side, with flames all around you. You are all alone in your plane, calling out for someone to help you, but there is no one." She looked up at him. "There is only the smoke and the flames, and a vast empty field."

"Your imagination is quite vivid," he said. "Are my eyes open or closed in this apocalypse of yours? Did I look like this? Or like this? Perhaps my head was twisted back this way with my tongue sticking out."

"This is no matter for joking," she said, slapping his arm. "Or for these ridiculous faces of yours." She looked at him intently. "Oh, Rolfie, the thought of you in such a way destroys me."

He smiled at her. "Do not think of such things, Liebchen. I shall not let them touch me." He chuckled. "I am invincible. I shall not let them touch me, or us."

The dark mood broke on her face. She stroked the underside of his jaw then again lay her cheek against his breast. "Is this a good war, Rolfie?" she asked. "I hear of wars that are good wars, and wars that are not good. Is this a good war?"

"I do not think that there are any good wars," he told her. "There are necessary wars, of course. But there are never any good ones."

"Is this a necessary war then?"

And now he had paused to think, to look out over the harbor and reflect upon the enormity of the question that he had asked himself so many times, and as yet had failed to answer with any satisfaction.

"I do not know," he said. He held her close to him with his left arm, with his right he supported the back of her head, and with his fingers he stroked the fine texture of her hair. "I do not involve myself with the politics of war. I am a soldier. It is enough for me to follow orders and to do my job as best I can."

"Blindly?"

"Sometimes blindly. Always with the conviction that I am a German officer and that I am fighting for the love and preservation of the Fatherland."

"We will win, won't we?"

"Such a question," he laughed. "Look what we have accomplished in so short a time. Of course we will win, Liebchen. Never doubt it." He kissed the top of her head.

She was silent for several moments. "I do hope we will win soon," she said quietly, "so that we may be together always. I hate the thought of us being apart, of you flying in the air with enemy fighters shooting at you. I hate it. And necessary or not I hate this war because of it."

He felt her crying through his chest. "These are strong politics, these words of hate," he said, smiling and smelling the sea in her hair. "And your tears have made your politics invincible."

"Will my tears make the politics of you and me invincible? Will they keep you from the burning plane? Would that I had something to make us invincible."

Rolf, holding her close to him as he looked out over the harbor at the gulls swooping behind a fishing trawler, said nothing.

Katharina said, "I wonder if those men you shoot down from the sky have women who will weep for them, women who have had visions of their lovers in burning planes?"

"I do not think of it," he said. "I think only of my duty to the Fatherland and that I do it efficiently and with honor."

She did not hear him. "That there may be those such as us holding each other even now as we—"

"Do not speak of it," he snapped. "There are only enemy planes that come to destroy our homes and cities with their endless bombs. Think of this, Liebchen. The other is foolishness."

She looked up at him and a tear trickled down her cheek.

"I am a brute sometimes," he said, pressing his lips together. "Truly a brute. Please forgive me, my dearest one."

"The thought of you burns in my heart," she said. "And I think I shall be consumed with it. Sometimes I think it is unholy what love I have for you, Rolfie. It burns so in my breast."

"It is a holy fire," he said. "It burns also in me."

"Does it, my love? Does it burn in you?"

"Yes, Liebchen. It burns so in me. It is the fire of true love."

"Will it not consume us? Will there be nothing left of us after the fire?"

He looked at her, smiling. There is only one true love in a man's life, he had thought, holding her and feeling their hearts beating in unison. If he is lucky. He wasn't certain about this, but he reasoned that there is only so much of a man that may die upon the holy altar, and die he must certainly do if it is true love. The rest of it—duty or desire or need—must be placed upon the altar, and what is left after the fire (if there is anything left) is the purest, most holy love—the selfless love. It is the selfless love that matters truly.

"We shall be as gold," he had told her, kissing the tears off her cheeks. "We shall be as gold refined in God's holy fire. It shall be the purest, most eternal love."

"Oh, Rolfie, I am frightened."

"Do not be frightened, Liebchen. I am not in this burning plane of yours. I am here beside you." He held her face in both of his hands and said, "Let us put away this talk of burning planes, and this business of enemy lovers. Let us talk only of you and me and the week we have left together." He kissed her and, guiding her along the pier past the fishermen and the stevedores, said, "Come, my sweet. I know a quiet place."

Rolf saw it all now, and he felt the sudden shock and pain of it again, his eyes filling with an immense sadness as he remembered how he had wanted to die when he was told about the bombing and the results of the firestorm in Hamburg. That night he had gone up and charged into a flight of Lancasters, heading into them, nose-in, destroying two of them with his rockets and crippling a third. He attacked again and again, defying the enemy gunners, half-crazed, like a madman, until he was out of ammunition. And then a dark thought had entered his mind, a strange and terrible thought that he had never before contemplated. It was a sin, he knew, what he knew of sin. But as luck, or Fate, or Providence, would have it, his plane ran out of fuel, and he was forced to land in a newly plowed field. As always, he had walked away from his plane unharmed.

Rolf looked away from the photograph with a cold, hollow numbness spreading through his chest that quenched all the warmth and the heat that had burned in him from the memories. He searched the sky for enemy aircraft—Fat Autos, hopefully, but he saw nothing of bombers. He had plenty of fuel though. With his plane equipped now with a belly tank, there was plenty of fuel this time. A glint of light caught his eyes and, turning, he saw two Thunderbolts on the tail of a lone Messerschmitt below him at two o'clock, and his eyes narrowed again into the flat, predator blade of deadliness.

46 ★★★

Warren Turlock's eyes were wide and intent on the Messerschmitt. The BF–109 was in a slow, downward-banking turn to the left, about three hundred yards ahead of him. Turtle was moving faster and, as he rotated his stick to the eleven o'clock position, edging just inside the 109's circle, the enemy fighter began gradually falling back into his sight reticle.

"Let him have it!" Pete Skagway, his wingman, howled into his headset.

Turtle lay his finger gently over the trigger and squeezed off a two second probing burst of his eight wing guns. He saw hits all over the tail and fuselage of the enemy fighter. Tightening his turn, banking gently and leading the yellow nose of the Messerschmitt, he squeezed off another burst, saw the bending, rifling tracers reaching, touching, and the engine of the 109 suddenly burst into flames. He let off on the trigger, watched as the cockpit slid open, releasing a puff of smoke, and saw a man climb out of the burning plane.

The man, small against the plane and sky, glanced down at the wing and then he looked back at Turtle, his face a featureless, white spot through the black smoke that was billowing all around him. Turtle was looking at him now with his sad poet's eyes, thinking for a moment how strange it seemed for a man to be climbing out of such a thing in the air, and he watched as the man fell clear of the plane.

"That's it!" Skagway crowed, not watching their tail, nor the sky above them, nor anything but the German pilot tumbling down through the empty sky. "That's got him. The lousy Kraut."

A loud *pop* drew his attention back to Turtle's Thunderbolt. A dazed expression crossed his face when he saw the left wing of the plane fluttering away from the fuselage. Not connecting a cause to the effect, he continued to gape stupidly as the huge, ungainly bulk of the Thunderbolt fell twirling like a maple seed, round and round, trailing an auger of black and white smoke.

"T-Turtle?" he stuttered.

There was no response.

Then, suddenly connecting the dots very clearly, he jerked his head over his left shoulder. His eyes went wide and a curse clipped through his teeth when he saw the shark-shaped, yellow-nosed Messerschmitt bearing down on him like a hawk on a ground squirrel.

Immediately Skagway jerked his control stick to the right and rolled his Jug into a dive, and the Messerschmitt loosed a burst of its 13mm wing guns.

Pete felt the hits all over his tail. "Foxworth Blue! Foxworth Blue!" he yelled into his mike. "I need an assist!"

"That you, Skagway?" Joe Thompson's voice crackled in his headset.

"Who else would it be! Give me a hand, Joe, there's a Kraut chewing up my tail!"

"I can't see you. Where's Foxworth Blue leader?"

"Turtle's down!"

"I still can't see you!"

"I'm right here!" Pete shouted angrily. "Somebody get this Kraut off my tail!" He felt the sudden impact of the bullets tearing through his fuselage and jerked a look over his shoulder. "Somebody get him off me!"

❧❦

Billy had looked up instinctively at the sound of Skagway's distress cry, but he saw nothing of his plane. There were BF–109s and P–47s buzzing everywhere, he saw, like a sky full of angry hornets. But he had no idea which one of them, if any, was Skagway. There was a frenzy of chatter in his headset, pilots calling out to each other, lining up on enemy targets, high, low, and at various points of the clock. Cutting through the chatter came Skagway's thin pleading voice. "Somebody . . . somebody . . . get him off me!"

Billy looked around for any sign of Turtle's plane—a dark oily smear swiped across the sky, a column of smoke on the ground to mark it—but he saw nothing. A Messerschmitt was going down in the distance.

"You see him, Montana?" Joe Thompson asked him.

"Negative."

"See a chute?"

"Not a thing."

"Tough break."

"What about Skagway?"

"He's on his own, poor devil. Wait a second . . . here we go! 109 at twelve o'clock low, all by his lonesome. Do you copy?"

Billy looked below him and saw the lone Messerschmitt at around 15,000 feet. "Roger that." Tough break is right, he thought. Poor devil.

Joe nosed his plane down after the enemy plane. Billy followed after him, the two of them in a fast-banking turn to the right, then leveling out to line up, one after the other, on the tail of the unsuspecting BF-109. Just then a movement on his left caught Billy's eye and, looking up, he saw the sun flashing off two planes in the distance, a Thunderbolt, he saw, with a Messerschmitt in hot pursuit. The planes were slicing down through the sky in the steep attitude of shooting stars. Pete's voice was screaming into his headset.

"Somebody help me! Somebody! Dear God, somebody help me!"

"It's Skagway, Joe. You okay here?"

Thompson glanced quickly, saw the planes. "Sure thing," he said. "I'll join you as soon as I send this Hun to Valhalla."

Billy looked around him and saw no bogies on their tail. Then he turned his plane on an intercepting course with the diving Thunderbolt and Messerschmitt.

❧❦

"Oh, my God, I am heartly sorry for having offended thee!" Pete chanted furiously, jerking his head back and forth over his shoulder to see the nearness of the Messerschmitt. Tears streamed down his face as he alternately cursed and cried out to God, "Help me, God; I am heartly sorry! Curse. Hail Mary, Mother of God. Curse. Somebody get this dirty, lousy Kraut off my tail!"

Seeing the ground rushing up at him he pulled back on his stick, his teeth clamped shut against the weight of the G forces, and the Jug began to pull heavily out of the dive. The Thunderbolt was pulling over seventeen thousand pounds—the weight of four large automobiles—against the heavy downward pull of gravity. It fell through the sky, its massive frame and wings shuddering, then leveling to sweep fifteen hundred feet above the deck. Skagway used the accrued speed of the dive and the big Pratt and Whitney's 2,300 horses of power to slingshot his plane back into a fast climb.

"Don't do it," Billy muttered, seeing everything from a distance and reading it as clearly as though reading a textbook. "Don't do it." The German pilot had anticipated Pete's move, he saw, for the Messerschmitt had begun pulling out of the dive seconds before and, because it was a lighter plane, was able to close the gap it had lost in the dive to line up perhaps three hundred yards behind the Thunderbolt.

"Hold on, Skag," he shouted into his mike. "I'm right behind you."

"That you, Hochreiter? Hot dog!" Pete cried, breathless relief chuckling in his voice. "Hot dog! Shoot him! Shoot him!"

Billy was five hundred yards away now, on a higher plane, dropping quickly to the level of the Messerschmitt. He squeezed off a deflecting burst, knowing that it was an impossible shot. He was ahead and high, he saw, and he swore quietly through his teeth. The German pilot looked in his direction and even at that distance Billy could read the unaffected intensity in his tiny white face. It was as though he were approaching an intersection where a train was passing, and there on the train saw the face of a man glance up from his newspaper at him with a calm, momentarily distracted expression, seeing him and not seeing him, then look back at his reading.

"Shoot him, Hochreiter! What are you waiting for? Shoot him!" Pete cursed. "Shoot him! Now! Now!"

Billy lined up for a second shot. He was lower, closer, but it was still an improbable shot. He lay his finger over the trigger, judging the angle and the lead, but could not get a bead on him; the Messerschmitt was moving all around his sight reticle. Then, as his plane drew down closer to the intersection where the three planes would converge, he noticed the checkered pattern behind the cowling of the Messerschmitt. Everything inside him went suddenly cold for a moment.

It's him! he thought. The coldness spread through his limbs and collected in the pit of his stomach.

He took aim, forcing thoughts of the German from his mind, then squeezed off a long burst. The elevation was still high, he saw, but the windage was right. So, dropping his nose he began centering the gray, moving shape in his sights, knowing he had him now—waiting, centering. Now! He squeezed the trigger.

Nothing happened.

What? He squeezed the trigger again. Nothing. Squeezed again. Nothing. Again. He cursed. The blood drained from his head as he realized his guns were jammed.

He watched helplessly as the German pilot drew to within two hundred yards of Skagway's tail. The Messerschmitt held there for what seemed an eternity before loosing a rolling spatter of 20mm machine gun fire. He saw what appeared to be three long, wicked tongues of fire lancing out from the cowling and wing guns. The rifling hot tracers froze in his mind for a fraction of a second as they stitched a white pattern across the sky.

Billy saw the hits all over Skagway's plane, and he heard the cry, "I'm hit! I'm hit! Hochreiter—" a split-second before the canopy shattered. He felt the shudder of the plane as surely as if it were happening to him all over again. Then he saw the right wing tip sharply up and the Jug, skewering down, fell plummeting to the earth, the long, round belly rolling slowly, with smoke boiling out of the cowling and spreading a dark diagonal slash against the sky.

"Pull up, Skag! Pull up!" Billy shouted.

The Thunderbolt came screwing in at a steep attitude and smacked hard against the ground, throwing up a cloud of earth and smoke. Then it lifted up to skip along the surface like a stone thrown over a pond, everything moving as though in a dream, it seemed, as the belly of the plane again smacked heavily, bounced, then dug in, nose-first, bent-propped, to settle in a wash of dust with its tail pointing into the air.

Sweeping low overhead, so low he could see the shape of Pete Skagway slumped forward in the battered cockpit—either dead or unconscious, he couldn't tell—Billy saw the curdling black smoke and flames rising from the smashed cowling the instant before the plane exploded in an orange, flowery ball of fire and smoke. A jolt went through him.

"Skagway's bought it!" he called weakly into his mike.

Watching the mushrooming rise of the smoke and the flames against the loneliness of the field—behind him now, farther away now, farther still now—he felt a sickening kick in his stomach. Suddenly everything that had been between them, the schoolboy rivalry that was certainly one-sided, and the sneering, mocking, churlish antics and looks, was gone. It all seemed so silly and such a waste of time, he thought, looking back now at the black plume bending to the wind. He felt the sickness of remorse compacting around the stony knot in his belly; he could feel it poking up through the apples in the tub to bob leeringly at him. A curse filtered through his teeth.

As he was looking back and feeling lousy he suddenly felt the stick in his hand, the feeling of the stick reminding him that he had gone away somewhere in his mind, and he looked ahead in a mild panic. He realized that he had made a mistake, and he knew, feeling the sick, fear-accompanying knowledge of it, that there was little time to correct it. He looked over his left shoulder and saw that the Messerschmitt was gone.

A myriad voices were suddenly screaming obscenities at him. Pull up, you fool! Gain altitude. Now! Now! He started to jerk back on the stick, but through the voices another voice shouted, No! Dive! Dive!

So he drove his stick forward, hitting full throttle and hard left rudder, and his plane screwed toward the deck. Immediately, rolling with the plane, he saw the white hot tracers rifling over his canopy, through the air space where he would have been had he pulled back into a climb, and he knew that the move had saved his life.

Billy looked over his shoulder and saw the Messerschmitt with the checkered cowling tipping after him.

47 ★★★

The German pilot matched Billy move for move, anticipating each of his evasive maneuvers, each time closing the gap between them. Racing four hundred feet above the deck at 350 mph, Billy zigzagged back and forth and banked wildly in the turns, hoping to lose him, but the Messerschmitt closed quickly to within five hundred yards. That's okay, he thought. I'll lose him. I can still lose him. I'll gain some altitude and lose him.

Far ahead of him Billy saw that there was a town. He had no idea the name of it, only that they were flying south and that the town had risen suddenly on a low hill. There was an avenue of trees leading to it, and there were trees clumped around low hills beyond the town, and beyond the hills was a river that had to be the Ems. He turned toward the town, hoping that the German would not fire at him for fear of hitting his countrymen. That's cheating, he thought. Or cowardice. Not cowardice. What kind of thinking is this? he asked himself. You getting screwy?

Looking over his shoulder, he saw that the Messerschmitt had closed to within four hundred yards. That's all right, he thought. I can still lose him. I can still out-fly the lousy Kraut. Come on, baby. Come on.

The throttle was opened wide and the ground flew beneath him at a dizzying pace. He could see cattle and other livestock in the fields, looking like little stuffed toys. A truck rumbled along a dirt road, a cloud of dust lifting behind it and spreading off to one side, and he could see the white of the driver's face clearly as he leaned out of the cab to look up at him. More fields flashed by, then a farmhouse with a narrow road leading to it, and a thought entered his mind to just set his plane down and have it out with the German. Man to man. A duel with pistols at twenty paces. His Colt against the German's Luger, or Mauser, or whatever pistol he used.

I've still got the Colt, he thought. My Colt isn't jammed. He looked over his shoulder. This is crazy. That kind of thinking will get you killed. That is the thinking of a cornered animal. Don't lose your nerve here, Hochreiter. Panic is a luxury that you cannot afford.

Still, he had to gain some altitude. Like cornered bears need to climb trees. But bears are not Thunderbolts, he reasoned. Bears don't weigh eight tons, either. Turning his plane, he pulled back slightly on the stick, so that the Jug began a slow, steady climb. He swung away from the town in a wide, flat-climbing circle to the north, back over the river, and he noticed a barge loaded with grain chugging slowly upstream. It looked like one of those "Come and visit France" advertisements in magazines before the war. The two fighters roared over the barge, one, and then the other, and the bargeman looked out the pilothouse and shielded his eyes to watch them fly away.

The German stayed with Billy, cut steadily inside his circle and gained on him, like he had gained on Skagway. Billy tightened his circle, hoping to gain some distance and altitude in which to fly as the two enemy planes climbed up through the sky. He wagged his head looking for a friendly plane. But there weren't any planes in sight, friend or foe, just an endless expanse of blue with cumulus clouds sailing continuously over the earth. He sent out several distress calls but there was no response. He could hear the distant garbled chatter in his headset, though. It seemed a million miles away.

At five thousand feet now, they were still climbing in a wide upward spiral, the two planes in a deadly game of cat and mouse. Billy was the mouse. A mouse with eight jammed wing guns. That business with pistols back there was nuts, he thought. He couldn't hit the broad side of a barn with a pistol at ten paces, let alone hit someone who was probably a crack shot. That German was a crack shot with a Messerschmitt, he knew, if those ranks of kills on his rudder were any indication.

They were clearly in a circle now, and Billy looked across the circle and could see the German, just a featureless head now, but he could see the sun glint off the goggles as the Messerschmitt swung into the east. To break out of the circle now would be suicide, he knew. Got to get higher, he told himself. At a higher altitude the Thunderbolt's big radial and supercharger would become a factor and the balance of power would take a dramatic turn. Just a little higher and he would be able to break free. He could outfly him at a higher altitude, he told himself. Shoot, who are you trying to kid? This guy is the devil on fire.

The two fighters continued round and round, climbing higher and higher like two minute hawks wheeling on a warm thermal. They were at 10,000 feet now. To anyone observing from the ground, the planes were tiny specks against the enormous sky full of clouds, with the sun flashing on their flanks and wings, the sound of their engines a dull and lofty drone.

The German closed to within three hundred yards. It should come pretty soon now, he thought. He knew he was in range now. Shoot, he'd been in range for a hundred yards or more. Still, the German had not fired once since the pursuit had begun. He's been saving his ammunition, he told himself. He's not only a killer, but he's a frugal killer. Did you see the number of kills on his rudder? He had not remembered that many kills, and then he thought of Pete and Turtle and cursed. Half of Blue Flight shot to pieces. Now him. He had welshed on his vow to God, and now God had come to collect. God was no respecter of welshers. He saw the irony in it, of course, how God was using the same debt collector. He saw the humor in it. Still, it was lousy, a big, lousy deal. Beads of sweat mounted on his brow as the Messerschmitt closed to within two hundred fifty yards.

☙◌❧

Rolf saw the face of the American jerk back at him, look away, then jerk quickly back again. He had seen that look before in how many faces now, fear showing in the fast, jerking movements of the featureless heads. How many faces, God? How many faces had looked back at him with the same pleading expression the moment before death? Two hundred plus now, wasn't it? He felt nothing but coldness for the face. Coldness and contempt. The face and the plane were one, and contemptible, and he would kill the plane. Just another plane. Kill it.

He pivoted the control column to the left and worked the rudder and ailerons adroitly to cut away even more of the American's circle. He had him now, he knew, watching the big Thunderbolt falling back into his deflective sights. He would take him. Now he would take him. His eyes flattened into a predator blade as his index finger edged over the trigger. He felt nothing of anything, except cold hatred, and certainly no warming thoughts of family, or country, or duty. Only hatred filled his eyes as they narrowed with a single thought—squeeze the trigger. Kill the plane. Kill the American.

The wind was blowing steadily from the east, and in the west there was a banking wall of brilliantly white cumulonimbus clouds, rolled up into the big, bouldery, piled-up shape of some enormous charioted goddess—the Goddess of Victory, dazzlingly bright and awe-inspiring as she drove the Teutonic winds ever westward, ever conquering, ever making war against puny mortals.

But Rolf saw nothing of the goddess. Instead, he suddenly saw an image of himself careering wildly down a snowy slope on a toboggan with his brother Ernst shrieking on his back. He saw the rain spattering against the panes in the library and his father sitting in his easy chair before the hearth, his good leg propped up on the ottoman as he read the newspaper and grumbled about politics. And he saw his mother bending over the stove in the kitchen, wagging a spoon at him to wash his hands before supper. He felt the warm and secure environment of home and the easy laughter beating against the stony shell of his chest.

A smile etched across his lips and froze, frozen like his finger poised over the trigger was frozen. Then he saw Gretchen, beautiful Gretchen, standing atop the Column of Victory, looking up at him with her big brown eyes, and a tear rolling down her cheek as she said, "I will pray for you, Rolf."

The smile shattered as his finger twitched over the trigger. The dynamic in his mind shifted radically. Then, looking at the Thunderbolt, now two hundred yards ahead of his guns, he saw beyond it to the image of his sister. "But I have no faith," he argued.

"I will have faith for both of us," Gretchen told him. "I will have faith for our home and for Germany."

"It is not enough," he said to her image. "I cannot believe it."

"Cannot, or will not?"

He did not know. And then he felt the tremor. Turning into the east the sun struck his face, forcing him to squint from the sudden Messianic glare of light, and something gave way deep in his belly. It was as though an earthquake had suddenly, violently broken apart the hardened crust of the earth, unearthing its smoldering core, then leaving strewn over the shattered surfaces the jutting shards of an ideal, of a course of life. Of duty.

"But what of duty?" he asked, the sun circling around now to his back and the glare off his face. "What of duty?"

He saw his sister in the library now. She was sitting on the crushed velvet settee, and he was pacing before the mantel, and she was saying, "How can you reason with something that has no soundness in it, Rolf? You can't. The soundness has been eaten away by a cancer. There is only raging now." Raging and madness. A self-destructive raging.

He was suddenly in the room again. The forbidden room. There is something greater than duty, he saw in the room. There is faith. Yes, faith. There is the duty of faith. One must fight for what is right, die if need be, but one must know the right, first, and defend it. There is the duty. To God, to family, and to country. In that order. Always in that order. The order will determine the duty.

"But I have no faith, Gretchen," he said. "I have wanted to believe," he said numbly. His eyes blinked heavily, dully, an obdurate veil closing back over his thinking. "God knows how I have prayed for faith."

It is a gift, he heard resonating through the fuselage of the plane.

"But I am filled with darkness," he replied. "Only darkness and hate now. God, forgive me for what I must do."

The Thunderbolt suddenly came into focus, the plane close enough now that he could see the detail of the tail section, could see the slight adjusting movement of the flaps, the identification numbers on the rudder, and then the rivets, seeing everything now. He lifted his finger off the trigger, and moved his left hand to the throttle lever. His eyes narrowed with resolve.

Do not do it.

"I must. There is nothing left."

There is faith.

"There is only the suicide mission to heaven."

There is your soul.

Circling east, the sunlight slicing across his face so that he was forced to squint, he saw it again. Suddenly. Unveiled. With terrifying clarity. He saw the tragic, haunting face of Christ looking at him from the wall of Helmut Schoenfield's parlor, seeing all of the pain and rejection in his eyes, seeing all of the love and kindness and gentle majesty that were more than he could bear.

Rolf stared ahead at the tail of the Thunderbolt, his eyes glistening with tears. "Have I truly a soul, God?" he asked quietly.

He listened intently to the whine of the plane. It was all or nothing at all, he knew, seeing it clearly now. The suicide mission to heaven. In death there is triumph. Death to hate, to lust, to self-will, to the terrible duties of the flesh. Death to the legacy of Adam. Put it to death, man, all of it. Kill it. Kill.

His hand trembled over the throttle. "Forgive me, God," he said. "Forgive me." His eyes narrowed again with resolve. With his lips compressed into a grim smile, he pulled back sharply on the throttle lever and the Messerschmitt surged forward.

そﾟ◌ﾟ◌

Billy turned his head but could not see the Messerschmitt. A jolt of terror shot through him. He could almost feel the enemy finger settling over the trigger. He could certainly feel the prickling sensation of knowing there were crosshairs on the back of his head. He ducked instinctively, his heart racing, the terror stabbing the backside of his rib cage with little knives of fear.

"Oh, God," he prayed weakly, hunching down lower into his seat, bracing himself now for the hammering of bullets. "Oh, God. God."

He waited for it, feeling it. Nothing. Raising his head, he looked around. Nothing. Craning his head, he looked out both sides of his cockpit, up, back. Nothing. His heart raced faster. Nothing. Where'd he go?

And then a movement, low and left, caught the tail of his eye. Looking quickly, he saw the vague shape of a yellow cone, the shimmering light on the wheel behind the cone that was the propeller, the blunt gray shape of the checkered cowling nosing up, close, closer, very close now, and his heart slowed to pump thickly and heavily in his throat.

For a split-second he did not know what it was. It was not supposed to be there. Then he watched with amazement as the deadly shark shape drew alongside him, rising up steadily from behind his left flank, rolling sleekly, showing the dead gray underbelly with the belly tank like a sucker fish, showing the wing now, the wing leveling, cockpit showing now with the man shape, the head turning, looking at him, then everything smoothing out until the wingtips of both fighters were no more than twenty feet apart.

It was the Messerschmitt, Billy saw now, though still not comprehending it. It was the Messerschmitt, alongside him. Flying parallel. Not behind him. A thought occurred to him to hit full brake flaps and split-ess to the deck. But he could not feel his arm. His arm was dead. The control stick felt frozen in place.

The pilots flew side-by-side, looking across the flat-bladed length of their wings at one another. Billy saw the face of the pilot clearly. He recognized him fully now, it was the same face, all right: the same ranks of kills on the rudder, the same *Katharina* painted behind the exhaust ports, the same checkerboard pattern behind the same yellow nose. There was a different cast in the eyes though. There was something different in the eyes.

&ᴗ&

Rolf felt a great sadness rising in him now, a heaviness of pity. Rising through the sadness and the pity came a flicker of hope, a little tongue of flame darting up from the cold, broken deadness of his soul for everything he held dear in the world and beyond. As he looked over at the American pilot he raised his right hand in salute.

Billy returned his salute automatically, then, conscious that only moments before the man had been trying to kill him, he lowered his hand. He stared warily into the eyes of the German pilot.

Rolf was looking up at the sky now, through the regatta of cumulus clouds under full sail. "Yes," he said. "Yes." Then he looked down at his fuel gauge and made a quick mental calculation. It is enough, he reckoned. Just enough with the added belly tank. Rocking his control stick, the wings of the Messerschmitt waved, then the plane banked away toward the south, the sun flashing on its wings as it sped ever southward—toward Switzerland—to a greater and more lasting duty.

Billy watched the enemy fighter grow small against the southern sky, and he blew out a long, low whistle. It was then that he realized he could feel his heart beating, could feel the slow, steady pumping of it against his rib cage, and the echoing pulse in his temples. He was conscious of the stick in his hand now, could feel the hardness and vibration of the seat beneath him, and hear again the ear-numbing roar of the engine.

What was that all about? he wondered. It made no earthly sense at all. Not a lick.

The Messerschmitt was a tiny speck now, a tiny dart of light moving away from him, until it became nothing more than a glint of light narrowing to a brilliant point and holding over the horizon, holding, flaring brighter, and then suddenly gone.

Billy shook his head in wonder. Then suddenly, violently, a fiery thought lanced through the cockpit into his chest. It was a thought more terrible and frightening than any that the Messerschmitt had given him, and certainly more deadly. "Yes," he said contritely, remembering everything now with terrible clarity. He squirmed in his seat. "Yes, Lord," he shuddered. "I won't forget. Never."

The Thunderbolt climbed steadily to 20,000 feet, passing through a diaphanous lace of cirrus clouds into a bright blue expanse of sky.

"Foxworth Blue leader to any lost sheep out there," Joe Thompson's voice crackled in his headset. "Lost sheep, do you copy?"

"Lost sheep here," Billy said.

"That you, Montana?"

"Roger that."

"Where've you been? You been out joyriding again?"

Billy smiled. "Something like that." Shaking his head, he pulled back on the stick, and the big Thunderbolt swung away to the north, climbing like a rocket.

48 ★★★

The following days brought several more forays against German Luftwaffe bases. Then on Monday the 13th of December, 1,462 USAAF Flying Fortresses and Liberators, with the aid of the new long-range P–51 Mustangs fitted with belly tanks, dropped well over three thousand tons of high-explosive and incendiary bombs on the cities of Bremen, Hamburg, and Kiel, causing crippling damage to the German war machine. The ratio of American-to-German victories was eight-to-one, and spirits were ebullient. On the evening of December 20, while escorting bombers to launch sites along the coast of France, Second Lieutenant William "Billy" Hochreiter scored his fifth victory against an FW–190 over the Pas de Calais and became an ace.

It was late morning on the 21st, the sky was gray and wet with the dismal threat of snow, and Billy, Joe, and Happy struck off across the countryside on their bicycles, heading for the Golden Guinea, to avoid eating lunch in the mess hall. The air was cold and the chilling wet wind off the coast brought the blood to their faces, and nipped at their ears and throats. There were a few locals out and about, but mostly people were snuggled in their homes before their hearths. The smell of coal smoke hung about in the air.

Billy looked over the bleak countryside, the trees dark and spindly against the soggy fields and sky. "That's something about Turtle," he said, turning to Joe. "He ought to do okay, don't you think?"

"He's probably happier now that he doesn't have to worry about getting his tail shot off," Joe said.

"He'll find something to worry about, I expect. Probably drive the Krauts nuts."

"They may send him back to us."

They heard a moan and both looked back at Happy, who was lagging behind them.

Being thin-blooded, Happy looked the picture of misery with his head hunched down into his collar, his shoulders up, and his dark eyes downcast and fixed on the patch of road immediately in front of his wheel. Great shivers shuddered through him frequently, and he looked like he was afraid to move for fear of breaking.

Joe winked at Billy. "I sure do love the winter, don't you, Montana?" he grinned. "Reminds me of home . . . sledding . . . ice-skating . . . curling up in front of the fire, drinking hot buttered rum with your girl. Everything real cozy and Christmasy."

"It's the best," Billy agreed, taking in an exaggerated breath of air. "Can't you just feel Christmas in the air, Haps?"

Happy was sullen. They rode down a low hill, past a break of trees. A frigid wind keening over the ground struck them sideways, pushing their bikes across the road. Happy's teeth began chattering.

"Just think, Billy," Joe said, "we get to ride back in this."

"It'll be colder by the time we go back," Billy corrected. "Much colder."

"By then I won't be feeling anything, you can bet," Happy growled. The wind whistled and another shiver rippled over him. His teeth were chattering fiercely. "W-whose id-dea . . . was this . . . anyway?"

"Yours," Billy said. "You wanted to celebrate your knocking out that Me–110, don't you remember?"

"For the fourth week in a row," Joe added.

Happy muttered something under his breath.

"We could be in the warm mess hall right now," Billy said, "enjoying the gourmet cuisine of mystery meat and liquid potatoes."

"Don't forget the lima beans," Joe put in.

"Oh, you bet—the lima beans," Billy said. "Taste like chalk."

"Paste," Joe corrected. He looked back at Happy. "It was your idea. Remember that, you sawed-off Puerto Rican."

Happy said something in Spanish. Joe and Billy chuckled.

The town was just ahead. Billy looked up as a train whistle receded into the distance. The whistle had a bittersweet wail to it, like all trains. People going. People coming. Change. A shiver went through him now. Then, as they turned onto the main street, the row of shops suddenly cutting off the wind, he saw Jane Worthing down the street by the red mailbox, bent over her bicycle fiddling with her seat satchel.

"You fellas go ahead," he said to Joe and Happy. "I'll join you in a few minutes."

"S-sure thing, amigo," Happy mumbled. He never even looked to see what had caught Billy's attention.

Joe looked at Jane, then at Billy, and shook his head. He pedaled away slowly, singing, "We are poor little lambs who have lost our way. Baa, baa, baa."

"Get outta here."

☙❦☙

Jane, retrieving a small bundle of letters from her satchel, looked up as Billy pulled his bike next to hers. She was wearing a tweed overcoat, a plaid scarf around her neck, and a woolen stocking cap pulled so low over her forehead that her blue eyes were featured prominently and seemed larger than normal. Her rabbit-lined gloves were set on top of the bicycle seat.

"Billy," she said.

He saw the flush of color going over her already rosy-from-the-cold cheeks. "Hello, Jane."

"William," she repeated, taking a step backward.

Billy watched her and it seemed to him that she had stepped behind a partition, changed out of her dungarees, then come out in formal attire. "How have you been?" he asked her.

"Fine. Just fine."

"I haven't seen you in the Guinea, or anywhere."

"I don't get out much these days," she smiled. She looked at him briefly then looked up at the sky. "The weather's been frightful, you know."

"Yeah." He looked up at the sky too. "Looks like it might snow."

"Could do."

"How's your family?" he asked, talking to her now as though they were in the lobby of a very expensive hotel.

"They're fine."

"And Robert?"

"Robert?" She smiled. "He speaks of you frequently. You've made rather an impression on him. Wants to join the Americans, it seems, and fly Thunderbolts."

"Not Spits?"

"Heavens, no. He's quite determined. Mum says you've ruined him."

"How *is* your mother?"

"Mum?" Jane laughed. "She's a dear. Nothing changes with Mum. The sun rises and sets on her British constancy."

Billy smiled. Jane smiled. They looked at each other longer now that all the obligatory preliminaries were out of the way. They were still standing in the lobby of the hotel, waiting, it seemed, for different people to show up.

"How are you, William? You look well."

"So do you."

She made a face. "For an Eskimo, you mean?"

Billy laughed. "It sure gets cold here."

"Not like in your Montana?"

"Shoot, no. We don't have cold like this. This is wet cold. It goes right through you."

"It does, doesn't it?"

He looked at her, glanced away, then looked back at her.

"Are you taking care of yourself?" she asked.

"What's to take care of?"

"Listen to you." She wagged a finger at him playfully. "I remember a certain young man and his bait bucket."

"I've signed off on crabs. I catch my fish in the pubs now."

"As well you should. You were a sight."

"Pitiful."

They both laughed, the laughter coming from the back of their throats. The laughter died away. Jane was still smiling. She looked down at the small bundle in her hands. Her fingers were red with cold, he saw.

"Mailing some letters?"

"Yes." She smiled quickly. "They're my little lifeboats, actually. I send them out, then a few weeks pass and back they come with little bits of news."

"And in between?"

"I write more letters."

He could see her standing by the lighthouse on the point, alone, the wind in her face, looking out to sea for the return of one of her little boats, and with it a bit of news or salvage from the sea.

"Any news from your friend Julie?"

"Why, yes. Thoughtful of you to ask," she said. "She and Thomas are in America now. He's been reassigned, you know?"

He shook his head. "No, I didn't know."

"She wants me to come visit." She laughed. "Imagine that . . . me visit America. Silly goose."

He smiled at her. "Any news from your husband?"

She looked at him quickly. "Edmund? Yes, actually. His letters come regularly now."

"Everything okay?"

"Okay?"

"I mean—"

"Oh, yes. As well as can be expected, I suppose. He complains about the food of course." She smiled quickly at him, her eyes wide, darting about as though fleeing capture. She put the letters into the mail slot.

"Jane—"

"Don't say it, Billy. I couldn't bear it."

"I thought that maybe—"

"Don't say it. Please."

"Do you love him?"

A flash of anger went over her face. "Yes, I love him," she said. "I love him dearly." He could see it mounting her brow, the tears glistening in her eyes as the anger mounted and then abated, and then she only looked helpless. "You promised to be gentle, Billy."

"I'm sorry, Jane, I didn't mean to—"

"I lay on my bed at night looking at Edmund's picture smiling at me, thinking of him in that horrible prison camp, cold and miserable, wondering what has become of his world. I pray to God to help me love him as I should, to be a good wife and a strength for him. But no sooner do I finish my prayers than I start thinking of you, of tossing cares to the wind and running off with you to your beautiful mountains, to your wild and unfettered way of life, with your cattle and horses and people shooting six-guns, and—oh, Billy, it's been dreadful," she cried. "Simply dreadful. I haven't been able to eat or sleep, it's been tearing so at my heart."

"I know."

She looked at him abruptly. "Do you? I wonder." She wiped her eyes and chuckled bitterly. "No, this is my own private war. A jolly good war I'll have, you know. Neither side winning." She grunted. "I wish I'd never gone into the Guinea that night. I wish it was me rotting in that prison camp instead of Edmund."

Billy started to say something.

She stepped back from him, stood erect, and straightened her shoulders. "This is best then."

"It's a lousy deal," he said.

"Yes. It's a lousy deal, as you say." She blinked at him, her lower lip trembling with cold and emotion. "I hate it. I hate all of it. It all seems such a cruel joke."

They looked at one another. It was time to go.

"Take care of yourself, now, William," she said. "I don't want to hear of you getting into any more fights with our boys."

"Nevermore."

"Quoth the Raven," she added, smiling, but the humor was gone out of it. "Promise?"

"Scout's honor."

They looked at each other and smiled, wanting to hold on to something, then glanced down at their respective views of the town. There was a gray loneliness spreading over the empty streets, the little English shops and teahouses were shut against it and the fingering wet cold. They both felt it.

He looked up at the sky. "Yep. It sure looks like it's gonna snow," he said, then winced inwardly for having said it twice now.

"Rather. I'll say," she said. "Any minute now, I should think." She took a deep breath and looked down at her wristwatch. "Well, then. I guess I should be going, shouldn't I? Mum will want help with dinner."

"Dinner? You mean lunch, don't you?"

She frowned at him.

He smiled, said nothing.

"Well then—" Jane reached out her hand and Billy shook it. It was all gone now, he knew, feeling the coldness and the smallness of her fingers, and the awkward touch of skin. They were no longer in the lobby of the hotel. They were now standing on the fantail of two passing ships, not passing during the night, as the saying goes, but passing in the broad light of day, looking over the swelling reach of water at the other, gazing, waiting, and now the ships were moving away and crossing into the other's wake.

"Jane?"

"You'd best go."

"I wish you every happiness in life."

"Thank you, William," she said, turning quickly from his eyes as she stepped into her bicycle. "That is very kind of you to say."

"I mean it."

She smiled, nodded her head, then, glancing back at him, said, "Good-bye, Billy."

"Good-bye, Jane."

Billy, standing in the street holding his bicycle, waved, then watched her pedal away. He stood there waiting out of politeness, or of something else, in case she might look back and wave a final time. She did not look back. She continued pedaling away from him until she rounded a bend in the street and then she was gone.

He looked at the postbox, thought for a moment of the letters she had written—the little lifeboats—wondering if one of them was addressed to her husband. What a stupid thing to think, he told himself.

He looked down the street toward the Golden Guinea and saw that it had started to snow there. He looked up at the sky, squinting into the brightness of the overcast, and it began snowing where he was now.

"Well, that settles that, Billy boy," he said to himself. He took a deep breath of the cold, biting air and blew out a cloud.

He walked his bike along the curb through the falling snow, looking down at the pavement, then stopped abruptly and looked back up the street. A breath of wind, a lingering scent of perfume, a shadow of something moving on the air caused him to look suddenly after Jane. A voice, perhaps. A whisper. But she was gone. There was only the gray bleakness of the town, the shops on either side crowding the street, with everything quiet now in the falling snow. Everything a muffled deadness. And then a chill went through him, starting from the base of his spine, then working up his back and prickling over his scalp.

"William?" a woman's voice called.

"What's that?" He spun around, startled, and he saw Angelique, the Reverend Townsend's wife, standing alone on the pavement ten feet behind him with the snow falling all around her, looking like she was in one of those Christmas scenes in a bottle. She was wearing a black woolen cape and leather boots, with the hood of the cape pulled onto her head so that her eyes were just hidden in the shadows, and the red of her lips showed beneath the shadows of the hood. Snow fell and lightly dusted her hood and shoulders.

"Hello, William," she said, her English sounding beautifully French as if every word was kissed. She was smiling at him with her gloved hands folded in front of her, her head tilted down, and her eyes looking out at him from the shadows of the hood.

He stood staring at her, his mouth slightly agape as his mind became suddenly very confused. "Angelique?" he said.

"Je m' excuse?" She looked at him, puzzled. Then after a mild shrug of her shoulders, said, "We saw you walk by."

"We?" Billy's eyes moved to the window of the tea shop beside her, saw the dark face with the little mustache looking out at them from one of the tables inside. It was not the Reverend Townsend. His eyes moved quickly back to the girl, to her eyes, to the mass of raven-colored hair spilling out of the hood framing the fine line of her jaw, to her eyes, to the haunting, unnaturally colored eyes, and a thought struggled through his mind.

"My uncle," she said, reading his expression. "Maurice."

"Maurice?"

"You have met my Uncle Maurice, no?"

His bicycle fell to the ground with a clatter that he did not hear. It was not Angelique, he saw now.

"It can't be you."

"Pardon?"

"Colette?"

"*Oui,*" she said, again puzzled. "It is me." She looked down at his feet and smiled. "Your bicycle has fallen."

He stood looking at her as though she were a ghost. "You're here."

"*Oui.* I am here. I—we," she gestured to the tea shop, "have just arrived on the train from London. Uncle Maurice thought we might have something to warm us before going to his flat."

Not hearing her, he took a step forward and stopped, dumbfounded. The town fell away in a rush, the streets, the shops, the bitter cold. Everything gone. "You're alive," he heard himself say, the words sounding as though coming from a great distance. It was both a question and a statement. Certainly a revelation.

She glanced down at herself, then, breaking into a smile, looked back at Billy. "*Oui,* I am alive." She moved a step closer. "Would you like to touch my hand?"

He felt blood swell suddenly in his throat. "I, I saw you fall on the field that night," he said, his voice thick, still not believing that she was not some illusion of his mind. "That night of the battle . . ."

She put her finger to her lips and shook her head. "There is much to tell you, William, but not now. Not here." The snow was falling heavier now, giving her all the more the appearance of a ghostly apparition.

"*Il fait froid.* It is cold," she said, and the look in her eyes caused a movement to go through the length of his body and up into his throat so that he coughed.

"Yes, yes, it is cold," he said with difficulty.

He stepped toward her, still uncertain that she was real, doubting, yet believing that she was truly a miracle.

"It is good to see you, William," she said. "You are looking well."

"Yes. And you . . ." He could not say it.

They moved together, and his arms were around her now, awed at feeling the soundness of her shoulders beneath the cold, woolen texture of the cape. "It is really you."

"*Oui*, it is me, William. God has heard every one of my prayers, and we are at last together."

"Yes," he said, smelling the cold in her hair, tightening his arms around her, and feeling a spring of life bubbling up then rushing through him. She had been dead. He had been dead. Now they were alive. Here. Now. "Yes, we are."

"I have prayed—so hard have I prayed for this moment, and now it is here. Like a dream. It is too wonderful, is it not?" she said, holding him tightly.

"Yes." He could hardly breathe. "Yes," he said, feeling the tears in his eyes. "You are a miracle."

"*Oui*, a miracle. That is what we are."

Any awkwardness between them was gone. It was as though they had always been together, the two of them one, having always been one and now the two halves of time and space that had separated them rushed together and everything made sense to him now.

She looked up at him, and the hood fell back from her head, so that he could finally see the bright, ruddy freshness of the weather on her cheeks. Her eyes were no longer haunting but beautifully robin's-egg turquoise and sparkling in the light. Snowflakes lighted in her hair and in the sweeping black lashes of her eyes as they searched his. And when he looked at the full, red poutiness of her lips, he tried to speak, but the words got caught in the swollen thickness of his throat.

49 ★★★

They were sitting on a sofa before the small coal fire in a tiny flat on the outskirts of town, near the base. There was a stuffed chair on either side of the hearth facing each other, and a wrought iron fender going around the hearth. A coal scuttle and fire tools stood in front of the fender. The room was dark, the curtains closed, and the light from the well-banked fire made shadows of their heads and shoulders against the flower print of the wallpaper. They were holding hands. Uncle Maurice was in the adjoining kitchen rattling pots and pans.

Colette was wearing a burgundy pullover and a black woolen skirt. Her thick, raven-colored hair was brushed away from her face and lay wavily on her shoulders and down her back. Her legs were curled up onto the sofa, and she was sitting on her feet. "And so you see I was not shot," she was saying, the firelight playing over her face. "I must have tripped and fallen. That is all. My mind was not on the battle; it was on the airplane, knowing that you were inside and getting safely away."

He was looking intently at her.

"I was so happy," she said, a quick smile breaking on her face, "and yet so sad when the sound of the airplane was no more and I knew that you were gone forever. Looking up I must have fallen, though I do not remember it. Everything was moving so fast. All around me men were running and shouting, stopping to shoot at the Boche, then running. I was running and crying—crying with happiness for you, and also with the sadness of knowing I would never see you again."

She looked at him quickly, smiled, then glanced down at their hands.

Gazing at her, Billy was in another world from the one in which he had awakened in the morning—the one of the cold showers, the lousy breakfast in the mess hall, riding into town with Joe and Happy, and Jane. All that world seemed illusory now, while this world—looking at the girl by the fire, holding her hand, listening to the French-accented words singing off her tongue—was the only true world. The only world that mattered now.

"How did you escape?" he asked, again seeing the horror of the battle through the window of the plane. "The Germans had broken out onto the field."

"*Oui.* The Boche were everywhere," she said. "Coming quickly and shooting. Papa took my brothers and some men and fell back along the trees. As the Boche followed after us, moving quickly over the field, Papa and the men shot at them from the flanks. The Boche were forced to halt and fight Papa, setting up that awful gun of theirs, while Major Dubois and the rest of us escaped into the hills."

As she looked into the fire, Billy could see the pain on her face. He wished they could just sit in the dark before the fire and forget everything about the war, holding each other, and moving along in the miracle of their being together. But it had to come out, he knew. All of it had to come out to get it behind them; still, he wished this part were over. He had many questions to ask her, and he did not want to ask them for fear of the answers.

"We waited for Papa in a place of rendezvous," Colette said, the tone in her voice moving the story now to a different level. "In this place there were many large rocks from which we could see anyone coming; the moon was out, showing the ground clearly as it sloped up to the rocks where Major Dubois and his men were positioned with their guns. It was a good place to fight if need be, the major said, and it had been prearranged with those of his men who had stayed behind with Papa.

"We waited in the rocks, listening to the distant sound of the battle, hearing the terrible voice of that big machine gun, knowing that Papa and the others were fighting so that we might escape." She broke off, reflecting. "They seemed so far away," she said dreamily. "So very far away. Then suddenly there was silence. There were a few shots in the silence, and then there was silence continually, and we knew that the battle was over.

"We waited," she said quietly. "It was terrible waiting. Major Dubois was looking very concerned at the field below the rocks, as were his men, and I was praying very hard. When I saw Jean-Claude and François returning with some of the men I began to cry with happiness. Then I saw that Papa was not with them, and all of the happiness was gone. Jean-Claude told us how valiantly he had fought, how he had charged the big machine gun that was causing such destruction, and how, even though many bullets had struck him, he still went forward, killing the Boche, more bullets striking him, until he threw a hand bomb on the big gun."

Her story stalled. The coals shifted in the hearth and crackled and sparked. "I am sorry," Billy said.

She smiled and squeezed his hand.

He knew that she did not wish to talk further; still he had to know more. He waited a moment, then asked, "How did you escape to England?"

"*L'avion,*" she said, forgetting that she was talking in French. "*Nous avons voyagé dans un avion au moteur puissant et aux ailes surévevées—*" She caught herself and smiled. "We flew in a plane with a wing on top and a big motor," she repeated. "I do not know how it is called."

"Sounds like a Westland Lysander," Billy said.

"*Oui,* that is it. I remember the name now. That is what we flew."

"We?"

"Yes. Jean-Claude and me. Jean-Claude sent word to Uncle Maurice as soon as we arrived in Tangmere, and Uncle Maurice came at once."

"That explains it," Billy muttered to himself.

"*Pardon?*"

"It is nothing. It was a selfish thought concerning my stomach." He smiled at her. "Where is Jean-Claude now?"

"He is now in London with General de Gaulle, working with the FFI."

He looked at her. "And Henri?" he asked tentatively. He had been waiting for mention of him, but she hadn't said a thing. He already knew the answer and did not want to hear it spoken. "Is he all right?"

"Henri is with Major Dubois."

"Really?"

"*Oui.* He is with the Maquis, and he is well. They have all moved into the hills to fight the Boche."

"That's something," Billy said, feeling a weight lift off his chest. "Good, good."

"He is a good boy."

"Yes. And what of your other brother? François."

She looked back into the fire. "The Boche caught François not long after the night of the battle," she said very quietly. "Poor François. They put him against a wall and shot him."

"No."

She was looking into the fire.

"I'm sorry," he said, feeling the jolt go through him, and then the dumbfounding heaviness descending again.

She nodded and smiled. "Let us talk no more of the war, William. Not tonight." She looked small and suddenly very foreign and out of place in an English flat. He wanted to kiss her, just then, kiss her to make everything right, and to kiss away the war and the pain and to see her smile. They were both looking into the fire now and listening to the roar of the flames.

Just then a square of light opened into the room, and Uncle Maurice came out of the kitchen holding a tray. "Come, you two love doves," he smiled, crossing the room to the table beneath the window. "Let us put away this sadness and come eat. Colette?"

"*Oui?*"

"*Peux-tu m´aider à porter ces plats sur la table?*"

"*Oui, Oncle Maurice.*" The girl leaped to her feet and Billy watched her walk into the kitchen. She walked on the balls of her feet, he noticed, now that she had taken off her boots. He loved watching her move. She had the very quiet and silky movements of a cat. He smiled, feeling the shift in mood.

The door was open and showed the small, lighted kitchen, the stacks of canned goods in the cupboards, their colorful labels facing outward. He watched her take a towel in each hand and lift a steaming casserole dish off the tiny stove. Seeing her in the kitchen, here, now, he felt everything moving strangely in him. It was like he was in a happy dream that he wanted to hold on to before waking, but knew that thinking of the dream meant he was already wakening, and that he would soon lose it.

She came out of the kitchen with the steaming dish, glancing at him with a smile that made him forget the sadness of her story, and think, instead, what it would be like to kiss her. That would be the test to see whether it were a dream or not. Yes, that would do it. He could smell the fragrance of the cooking following her to the table, and, getting to his feet, he asked Maurice, who was leaning over the table lighting candles, "Anything I can do?"

"*No, no, no,*" the little Frenchman said. "You come and sit here. *Permettez-moi,*" he said, pulling out a chair for him like a waiter in an expensive restaurant.

"It smells delicious," Billy said, putting his nose over everything. "I had forgotten what real food smelled like."

"It is not much," Maurice said, twisting the end of his mustache. "But I think you might find it a little tastier than the food in the mess hall tonight."

"You said it." Billy noticed there were only two places set. Two glasses and a small carafe of wine. He looked up at Maurice.

Maurice was standing beside the table with a towel draped over his arm. *"Une table pour deux, Monsieur,"* he said with a slight bow. "This night is for you and for my beautiful niece."

"You're going?" Billy asked him.

"Oui. I must go out for a little while," he said. He seated Colette across from Billy, then poured the wine. "I will not be gone too long." He went over to the radio and tuned to a station with some music playing. *"Bon,"* he smiled to himself. *"Bon."*

Billy glanced at Colette then looked back at Maurice. The Frenchman was wrapping a scarf around his neck, then he put on a heavy overcoat and, turning to the two of them, kissed his fingertips. *"Bon appétit,"* he smiled. He closed the door behind him, and Billy and Colette were alone.

The fire in the hearth was glowing wonderfully. Benny Goodman was playing something up-tempo on the radio. Colette was sitting across the table from him, the candlelight lighting her hair softly and showing the lovely hollows of her cheeks and the hungering loneliness in her eyes. She was looking down at her plate and smiling, then glancing shyly at him, as she had when she first smiled at him in France. He was looking back at her, steadily, and she looked quickly down at her plate.

"You're beautiful," he said, wanting nothing but to kiss her.

She blushed. *"Merci."* She looked up at him with just her eyes. "And you are handsome."

"Me? Naw!"

"Oui," she said, looking at him fully now. "I think you are very handsome."

"You think so?"

She nodded, smiling, then biting the meat daintily on the tines of her fork, said, "Oh, yes."

They looked at each other, a thought flew between them, and they both looked down at their plates. There was a pause during which they concentrated on their eating.

"This is delicious," he said, picking through the sautéed mushrooms.

"Uncle Maurice is a very good chef," she agreed.

"The best."

She looked at him and then down at his plate. "You are not eating very well."

"What's that? I'm not so hungry all of a sudden."

"No?"

"No."

The song changed on the radio, and with it the mood.

"I am not so very hungry either," she said. She took a sip of wine.

"Want to dance?" he asked her.

"Dance?"

"Sure. Let's dance," Billy said. "Work up an appetite." He took her by the hand.

"No, no, no," she protested. "Please, no, William. There was little opportunity for dancing in the mountains."

"Come on," he said. "You'll do fine."

"William, please. No, William."

"Moonlight Serenade" was playing on the radio, sounding like maple syrup smoothing through the air. Billy took her hand and held her close to him, the two of them turning slowly, hardly moving at all; he, leading; she, in her bare feet with her head laying on his shoulder as the heavy rhythm of the music filled the small living room of the flat. "You dance terrific," he said.

She looked up at him and frowned.

"Really," he insisted. "You're a natural."

"It is all right, then, to step on your feet?"

"I hardly notice. You have a light touch," he said, smiling down at her and wanting desperately to kiss her. "You're a natural, I tell you."

"*Bon*," she said, smiling. Then she looked suddenly at his shirt, feeling between the buttons with her fingers.

"What is it?" he asked. He looked down at himself. "I spill something on me?"

"You are wearing *le croix*."

"The what? Oh, the crucifix. Yes," he said. He had forgotten that he was wearing it. "All the time," he said. Then, smiling, he added, "Always next to my heart."

"You have a good heart," she said, smoothing her hand over his chest. "I can hear it beating. It is a good and strong heart."

"Sometimes. Lately there's been some renovation going on in there."

"Renovation? I do not know this word. Is this a bad or good word?"

"Painful," he said.

She looked at him concerned. "You have a pain in the heart?"

"Deeper than that," he said. "Much deeper. It seems I have a soul that needs tending."

"*Oui?* Ah," she said, understanding now, laying her face against his chest. They danced, the music sweeping them, and after a time she said, "God is good, no?"

"Yes." As he looked down into her eyes, he was again struck by the miracle. "Yes, he is good." And then: "I love you, Colette."

"Truly?"

"Yes, truly. I love you more than I ever thought it possible to love." She looked up at him and he kissed her. Her lips were full, tasting of the wine and, kissing her, they became suddenly very wet and salty. He stopped dancing and looked at her wet cheeks. "You're crying," he said. "I'm sorry, I shouldn't have—"

"No, no, William, it is all right," she smiled, laughing and crying at the same time. "It is for happiness that I cry. Your kissing was lovely." She held him tightly and swayed with the music. "I am so happy, *my love.* So very, very happy. God is good."

"Yes," he said, holding her close to him. "Yes, he is."

Michael R. Joens is the owner of Stillwater Productions, an animation company that produces cartoons and commercial spots for television. His previous work includes producing the animation for the McGee and Me and Adventures in Odyssey series for Focus on the Family. He and his wife, Cathy, and their three children live in Santa Clarita, California.